Readings in Russian Civilization

Readings

VOLUME I

RUSSIA BEFORE PETER THE GREAT, 900–1700

in Russian Civilization

EDITED, WITH INTRODUCTORY NOTES, BY

THOMAS RIHA

SECOND EDITION, REVISED

THE UNIVERSITY OF CHICAGO PRESS

CHICAGO AND LONDON

ISBN:0-226-71852-2 (clothbound); 0-226-71853-0 (paperbound)
Library of Congress Catalog Card Number: 69-14825

THE UNIVERSITY OF CHICAGO PRESS, CHICAGO 60637
The University of Chicago Press, Ltd., London

CONTENTS VOLUME I

*Items added in 2d edition.

Contents

CONTENTS   VOLUME II

*Items added in 2d edition.

CONTENTS   VOLUME III

*Items added in 2d edition.

viii

PREFACE TO THE SECOND EDITION

This new and enlarged version of *Readings in Russian Civilization* is the result of fairly extensive revisions. There are now 72 instead of 64 items; 20 of the selections are new. The first volume has undergone the least change with 3 new items, of which 2 appear in English for the first time. In the second volume there are 6 new items; all of them appear in English for the first time. The third volume has undergone the greatest revision, with 11 new items, of which 6 are newly translated from the Russian. It is the editor's hope that items left out in the new edition will not be sorely missed, and that the new selections will turn out to be useful and illuminating. The aim, throughout, has been to cover areas of knowledge and periods which had been neglected in the first edition, and to include topics which are important in the study of the Russian past and present.

The bibliographical headnotes have been enlarged, with the result that there are now approximately twice as many entries as in the old edition. New citations include not only works which have appeared since 1963, but also older books and articles which have come to the editor's attention.

The editor would like to thank several persons who have contributed to the improvement of the text. Some sixty professors answered a questionnaire sent out by the University of Chicago Press and suggested changes or improvements in the *Readings*. Most of these suggestions have been heeded, and the editor is grateful for this generous cooperation by his colleagues. Professor Josef Anderle should be singled out, since he offered particularly detailed comments and had been most helpful in the preparation of the first edition as well. Professors Richard Wortman and Richard Hellie suggested new documents and, in the case of Mr. Hellie, translated them as well. Howard Goldfinger, Sylvia Fain, and Walter Gleason helped with the translations.

Once again I should like to dedicate this new version of my work to my students at the University of Chicago and at the University of Colorado. They have made this enterprise not only a duty but also a pleasure.

BOULDER, COLORADO
JUNE, 1968

THOMAS RIHA

PREFACE TO THE FIRST EDITION

In selecting the readings for these volumes, I was guided by several considerations. The selection, first of all, was to be important for the period of Russian history under consideration. Second, it was to lend itself fairly easily to class analysis—if possible, by the discussion method. This meant that polemics were preferable to descriptions, though I could not, and indeed did not wish to, manage without the latter. The selection was to stimulate curiosity to the point where the reader would wish to pursue the subject further.

All things being equal, I tended to lean toward primary sources. Thus, of the final sixty-four items, forty-six, or 70 per cent, are of this nature. Nevertheless, this remains a book of readings, not a collection of documents. I did not want snips and pieces, no matter how important; each essay is intended to be of sufficient length to develop a point of view or an argument reasonably and sensitively. I wanted my selections to be readable; there is not all that much good writing in this often turgid field, and I made a deliberate attempt to hunt for those authors who took pride in their language and exposition.

At certain crucial points I made a deliberate effort to bring a Soviet point of view into play. This I found to be not only healthy for argument's sake but sometimes quite enlightening in its own right. I carried this principle into the bibliographies as well. These were intended to provide a few guideposts to those who might wish to investigate an individual problem. Paperback editions were indicated because they might lead to the building of small private libraries. One could, these days, build quite a respectable collection of paperbacks on Russia.

I tried to give each period of Russian history its due. The order of selections will be found to be approximately chronological, though in a few places items are grouped topically for the sake of convenience. Each volume concludes with a general assessment of the period where more than one point of view is presented. It was my hope that Russian civilization would thus be given certain stages and a definable shape. If the general contours turn out to be approximately accurate, my aim will have been achieved.

ACKNOWLEDGMENTS

My thanks are due, to begin with, to the College at the University of Chicago, which conceived of the Russian civilization course and gave it elbow room to develop. Donald Meiklejohn, Warner Wick, and Alan Simpson were sympathetic initiators and tolerant supervisors. For a colleague they provided Meyer Isenberg, whose warm participation was essential to the first years of the enterprise and who always reminded me of the aims of general education. Chicago's Russian specialists —Michael Cherniavsky, Leopold Haimson, Arcadius Kahan, and Hugh McLean— gave their time to make improvements in the selections. Richard Hellie, Jean Laves, and Marianna Tax Choldin acted as able assistants. Elizabeth Ireland and Wells Chamberlin first suggested publication. Michael Petrovich inspected the volumes and made valuable suggestions. Ruth Jensen piloted the manuscript through its many stages over three years and proved to be the ideal secretary. Last, but most important, my students at the University of Chicago supplied the curiosity and enthusiasm which is their valued hallmark. To them these three volumes are dedicated.

THOMAS RIHA

CHICAGO

1

THE RUSSIAN PRIMARY CHRONICLE

EXCERPTS

This chronicle (also known as "The Tale of Bygone Years" or the "Laurentian Chronicle") is the earliest native written source for Russian history. It is probably a combination of several texts and covers the period 852–1120. Compiled in the twelfth century, it is not a contemporary account but relates events which took place more than two centuries earlier. It contains heavy borrowings from Byzantine Greek sources which served as models to the Russian monks who wrote the chronicles. While some of its content is legendary, it remains the only written source for many events in the earliest Russian past. Its heavily religious bias is understandable in view of the authorship. Our excerpts are taken from the English translation of the late Harvard scholar Samuel H. Cross (1930), as revised in 1953.

For a close analysis of the Primary Chronicle as a historical source see Vasilii Kliuchevsky, *A History of Russia*, Vol. I, lectures 5 and 6; N. K. Chadwick's *The Beginnings of Russian History: An Enquiry into Sources*; and two works of Henryk Paszkiewicz, *The Origin of Russia* and *The Making of the Russian Nation*. Three works devoted to the Kievan period utilize the Chronicle: George Vernadsky's *Kievan Russia*, and the Soviet studies by Boris Grekov, *Kiev Rus*, and Boris Rybakov, *Early Centuries of Russian History* (richly illustrated). A Soviet work on Russian cities including Kiev is Mikhail Tikhomirov's *The Towns of Ancient Rus*.

Regarding the Russian expeditions against Constantinople see Alexander Vasiliev's *The Russian Attack on Constantinople in 860*, and his "The Second Russian Attack on Constantinople," *Dumbarton Oaks Papers*, No. 6 (1951), pp. 161–225.

On the origins of Russian Christianity see Ihor Sevcenko, "The Christianization of Rus," *Polish Review*, 1961; Nicholas Zernov's "Vladimir and the Origin of the Russian Church," *Slavonic and East European Review*, XXVIII, 123–38, 425–38; Dmitry Obolensky's, "The Heritage of Cyril and Methodius in Russia," *Dumbarton Oaks Papers*, No. 19 (1965), pp. 45–67; and George Fedotov's *The Russian Religious Mind* (paperback). A Soviet view is in Mikhail Tikhomirov's "The Origin of Christianity in Russia," *History*, XLIV (October, 1959), 199–211.

The Primary Chronicle as literature is analyzed by Dmitri Cizevskij, *A History of Russian Literature*, and by the Soviet scholar Nikolai Gudzy, *A History of Early Russian Literature*.

From Samuel H. Cross and Olgerd P. Sherbowitz-Wetzor (eds. and trans.), *The Russian Primary Chronicle* (Laurentian Text; Cambridge, Mass.: The Mediaeval Academy, 1953), pp. 64–68, 78–80, 82–84, 95–98, 110–13, 116–17. Reprinted by permission of the Mediaeval Academy of America. Footnotes by the editor.

A.D. 904–907. Leaving Igor' in Kiev, Oleg attacked the Greeks.[1] He took with him a multitude of Varangians, Slavs, Chuds, Krivichians, Merians, Polyanians, Severians, Derevlians, Radimichians, Croats, Dulebians, and Tivercians, who are pagans. All these tribes are known as Great Scythia by the Greeks. With this entire force, Oleg sallied forth by horse and by ship, and the number of his vessels was two thousand. He arrived before Tsar'grad, but the Greeks fortified the strait and closed up the city. Oleg disembarked upon the shore, and ordered his soldiery to beach the ships. They waged war around the city, and accomplished much slaughter of the Greeks. They also destroyed many palaces and burned the churches. Of the prisoners they captured, some they beheaded, some they tortured, some they shot, and still others they cast into the sea. The Russes inflicted many other woes upon the Greeks after the usual manner of soldiers. Oleg commanded his warriors to make wheels which they attached to the ships, and when the wind was favorable, they spread the sails and bore down upon the city from the open country. When the Greeks beheld this, they were afraid, and sending messengers to Oleg, they implored him not to destroy the city and offered to submit to such tribute as he should desire. Thus Oleg halted his troops. The Greeks then brought out to him food and wine, but he would not accept it, for it was mixed with poison. Then the Greeks were terrified, and exclaimed, "This is not Oleg, but St. Demetrius, whom God has sent upon us." So Oleg demanded that they pay tribute for his two thousand ships

at the rate of twelve *grivnÿ* per man, with forty men reckoned to a ship.

The Greeks assented to these terms and prayed for peace lest Oleg should conquer the land of Greece. Retiring thus a short distance from the city, Oleg concluded a peace with the Greek Emperors Leo and Alexander, and sent into the city to them Karl, Farulf, Vermund, Hrollaf, and Steinvith, with instructions to receive the tribute. The Greeks promised to satisfy their requirements. Oleg demanded that they should give to the troops on the two thousand ships twelve *grivnÿ* per bench, and pay in addition the sums required for the various Russian cities: first Kiev, then Chernigov, Pereyaslavl', Polotsk, Rostov, Lyubech, and the other towns. In these cities lived great princes subject to Oleg.

[*The Russes proposed the following terms:*] "The Russes who come hither shall receive as much grain as they require. Whosoever come as merchants shall receive supplies for six months, including bread, wine, meat, fish, and fruit. Baths shall be prepared for them in any volume they require. When the Russes return homeward, they shall receive from your Emperor food, anchors, cordage, and sails and whatever else is needed for the journey."

The Greeks accepted these stipulations, and the Emperors and all the courtiers declared:

"If Russes come hither without merchandise, they shall receive no provisions. Your prince shall personally lay injunction upon such Russes as journey hither that they shall do no violence in the towns and throughout our territory. Such Russes as arrive here shall dwell in the St. Mamas quarter. Our government will send officers to record their names, and they shall then receive their monthly allowance, first the natives of Kiev, then those from Chernigov, Pereyaslavl', and the other cities. They shall not enter the city save through one gate, unarmed

[1] The Byzantine Empire is meant by "Greeks." "Tsar'grad" (or "Emperor's City") refers to its capital, Constantinople.—Ed.
While the description of the Russian raid on the imperial city contains legendary details, it is based on actual events. The text of the treaty given here is authentic.—Ed.

and fifty at a time, escorted by an agent of the Emperor. They may conduct business according to their requirements without payment of taxes."

Thus the Emperors Leo and Alexander made peace with Oleg, and after agreeing upon the tribute and mutually binding themselves by oath, they kissed the cross, and invited Oleg and his men to swear an oath likewise. According to the religion of the Russes, the latter swore by their weapons and by their god Perun, as well as by Volos, the god of cattle, and thus confirmed the treaty
. . . .

A.D. 912. Oleg dispatched his vassals to make peace and to draw up a treaty between the Greeks and the Russes. His envoys thus made declaration:

"This is the copy of the treaty concluded under the Emperors Leo and Alexander. We of the Rus' nation: Karl, Ingjald, Farulf, Vermund, Hrollaf, Gunnar, Harold, Karni, Frithleif, Hroarr, Angantyr, Throand, Leithulf, Fast, and Steinvith,[2] are sent by Oleg, Great Prince of Rus', and by all the serene and great princes and the great boyars under his sway, unto you, Leo and Alexander and Constantine, great Autocrats ·in God, Emperors of the Greeks, for the maintenance and proclamation of the long-standing amity which joins Greeks and Russes, in accordance with the desires of our Great Princes and at their command, and in behalf of all those Russes who are subject to the hand of our Prince.

"Our serenity, above all desirous, through God's help, of maintaining and proclaiming such amicable relations as now exist between Christians and Russians, has often deemed it proper to publish and confirm this amity not merely in words but also in writing and

[2] The Scandinavian names are evidence of the fact that most members of the Russian Prince's retinue during this period were non-Russian in origin.—Ed.

under a firm oath sworn upon our weapons according to our religion and our law. As we previously agreed in the name of God's peace and amity, the articles of this convention are as follows:

. . . "Whatsoever Russ kills a Christian, or whatsoever Christian kills a Russ, shall die, since he has committed murder. If any man flee after committing a murder, in the case that he is well-to-do, the nearest relatives of the victim shall receive a legal portion of the culprit's property, while the wife of the murderer shall receive a like amount which is legally due her. But if the defendant is poor and has escaped, he shall be under distress until he returns, when he shall be executed.

"If any man strike another with a sword or assault him with any other sort of weapon, he shall, according to Russian law, pay five pounds of silver for such blow or assault. If the defendant is poor, he shall pay as much as he is able, and be deprived even of the very clothes he wears, and he shall also declare upon oath that he has no one to aid him. Thereafter the case against him shall be discontinued.

. . . "If any person, whether Greek or Russ, employs abusive treatment or violence against another and appropriates by force some articles of his property, he shall repay three times its value.

. . . "From this time forth, if a prisoner of either nation is in durance either of the Russes or of the Greeks, and then sold into another country, any Russ or Greek who happens to be in that locality shall purchase the prisoner and return the person thus purchased to his own native country. The purchaser shall be indemnified for the amount thus expended, or else the value of the prisoner's daily labor shall be reckoned toward the purchase money. If any Russ be taken prisoner by the Greeks, he shall likewise be sent back to his native land,

and his purchase price shall be repaid, as has been stipulated, according to his value.

"Whenever you find it necessary to declare war, or when you are conducting a campaign, providing any Russes desirous of honoring your Emperor come at any time and wish to remain in his service, they shall be permitted in this respect to act according to their desire.

"If a Russian prisoner from any region is sold among the Christians, or if any Christian prisoner is sold among the Russes, he shall be ransomed for twenty bezants and returned to his native land.

"In case a Russian slave is stolen or escapes or is sold under compulsion, and if a Russ institutes a claim to this effect which is substantiated, the slave shall be returned to Rus'. If a merchant loses a slave and institutes a complaint, he shall search for this slave until he is found, but if any person refuses to allow him to make this search, the local officer shall forfeit his right of perquisition. . . ."

A.D. 945. In this year, Igor's retinue said to him, "The servants of Sveinald are adorned with weapons and fine raiment, but we are naked. Go forth with us, oh Prince, after tribute, that both you and we may profit thereby." Igor' heeded their words, and he attacked Dereva in search of tribute. He sought to increase the previous tribute and collected it by violence from the people with the assistance of his followers.[3] After thus gathering the tribute, he returned to his city. On his homeward way, he said to his followers, after some reflection, "Go forward with the tribute. I shall turn back, and rejoin you later." He dismissed his retainers on their journey homeward, but being desirous of still greater booty he returned on his tracks with a few of his followers.

The Derevlians heard that he was again approaching, and consulted with Mal, their prince, saying, "If a wolf come among the sheep, he will take away the whole flock one by one, unless he be killed. If we do not thus kill him now, he will destroy us all." They then sent forward to Igor' inquiring why he had returned, since he had collected all the tribute. But Igor' did not heed them, and the Derevlians came forth from the city of Iskorosten' and slew Igor' and his company, for the number of the latter was few. So Igor' was buried, and his tomb is near the city of Iskorosten' in Dereva even to this day.

But Olga was in Kiev with her son, the boy Svyatoslav. His tutor was Asmund, and the troop commander was Sveinald, the father of Mstikha. The Derevlians then said, "See, we have killed the Prince of Rus'. Let us take his wife Olga for our Prince Mal, and then we shall obtain possession of Svyatoslav, and work our will upon him." So they sent their best men, twenty in number, to Olga by boat, and they arrived below Borichev in their boat. At that time, the water flowed below the heights of Kiev, and the inhabitants did not live in the valley, but upon the heights. The city of Kiev was on the present site of the residence of Gordyata and Nicephorus, and the prince's palace was in the city where the residence of Vratislav and Chudin now stands, while the hunting grounds were outside the city. Without the city stood another palace, where the palace of the Cantors is now situated, behind the Church of the Holy Virgin upon the heights. This was a palace with a stone hall.

Olga was informed that the Derevlians had arrived, and summoned them to her presence with a gracious welcome. When the Derevlians had thus announced their

---

[3] Dereva, the territory of the Derevlians, a pagan people living northwest of Kiev. Igor succeeded Oleg on the Kievan throne; Olga was his wife.—Ed.

arrival, Olga replied with an inquiry as to the reason of their coming. The Derevlians then announced that their tribe had sent them to report that they had slain her husband, because he was like a wolf, crafty and ravening, but that their princes, who had thus preserved the land of Dereva, were good, and that Olga should come and marry their Prince Mal. For the name of the Prince of Dereva was Mal.

Olga made this reply, "Your proposal is pleasing to me; indeed, my husband cannot rise again from the dead. But I desire to honor you tomorrow in the presence of my people. Return now to your boat, and remain there with an aspect of arrogance. I shall send for you on the morrow, and you shall say, 'We will not ride on horses nor go on foot; carry us in our boat.' And you shall be carried in your boat." Thus she dismissed them to their vessel.

Now Olga gave command that a large deep ditch should be dug in the castle with the hall, outside the city. Thus, on the morrow, Olga, as she sat in the hall, sent for the strangers, and her messengers approached them and said, "Olga summons you to great honor." But they replied, "We will not ride on horseback nor in wagons, nor go on foot; carry us in our boats." The people of Kiev then lamented, "Slavery is our lot. Our Prince is killed, and our Princess intends to marry their Prince." So they carried the Derevlians in their boat. The latter sat on the cross-benches in great robes, puffed up with pride. They thus were borne into the court before Olga, and when the men had brought the Derevlians in, they dropped them into the trench along with the boat. Olga bent over and inquired whether they found the honor to their taste. They answered that it was worse than the death of Igor'. She then commanded that they should be buried alive, and they were

thus buried.

Olga then sent messages to the Derevlians to the effect that, if they really required her presence, they should send after her their distinguished men, so that she might go to their Prince with due honor, for otherwise her people in Kiev would not let her go. When the Derevlians heard this message, they gathered together the best men who governed the land of Dereva, and sent them to her. When the Derevlians arrived, Olga commanded that a bath should be made ready, and invited them to appear before her after they had bathed. The bathhouse was then heated, and the Derevlians entered in to bathe. Olga's men closed up the bathhouse behind them, and she gave orders to set it on fire from the doors, so that the Derevlians were all burned to death.

Olga then sent to the Derevlians the following message, "I am now coming to you, so prepare great quantities of mead in the city where you killed my husband, that I may weep over his grave and hold a funeral feast for him." When they heard these words, they gathered great quantities of honey and brewed mead. Taking a small escort, Olga made the journey with ease, and upon her arrival at Igor's tomb, she wept for her husband. She bade her followers pile up a great mound and when they piled it up, she also gave command that a funeral feast should be held. Thereupon the Derevlians sat down to drink, and Olga bade her followers wait upon them.

The Derevlians inquired of Olga where the retinue was which they had sent to meet her. She replied that they were following with her husband's bodyguard. When the Derevlians were drunk, she bade her followers fall upon them, and went about herself egging on her retinue to the massacre of the Derevlians. So they cut down five thousand of them; but Olga returned to Kiev and prepared an army to attack the survivors.[4]

. . . A.D. 948–955. Olga went to Greece, and arrived at Tsar'grad. The reigning Emperor was named Constantine, son of Leo. Olga came before him, and when he saw that she was very fair of countenance and wise as well, the Emperor wondered at her intellect. He conversed with her and remarked that she was worthy to reign with him in his city. When Olga heard his words, she replied that she was still a pagan, and that if he desired to baptize her, he should perform this function himself; otherwise, she was unwilling to accept baptism. The Emperor, with the assistance of the Patriarch, accordingly baptized her. . . .

After her baptism, the Emperor summoned Olga and made known to her that he wished her to become his wife. But she replied, "How can you marry me, after yourself baptizing me and calling me your daughter? For among Christians that is unlawful, as you yourself must know." Then the Emperor said, "Olga, you have outwitted me." He gave her many gifts of gold, silver, silks, and various vases, and dismissed her, still calling her his daughter.[5]

. . . Thus Olga arrived in Kiev, and the Greek Emperor sent a message to her saying, "Inasmuch as I bestowed many gifts upon you, you promised me that on your return to Rus' you would send me many presents of slaves, wax, and furs, and despatch soldiery to aid me." Olga made answer to the envoys that if the Emperor would spend as long

a time with her in the Pochayna as she had remained on the Bosporus, she would grant his request. With these words, she dismissed the envoys.

Now Olga dwelt with her son Svyatoslav, and she urged him to be baptized, but he would not listen to her suggestion, though when any man wished to be baptized, he was not hindered, but only mocked. For to the infidels, the Christian faith is foolishness. They do not comprehend it, because they walk in darkness and do not see the glory of God. Their hearts are hardened, and they can neither hear with their ears nor see with their eyes. For Solomon has said, "The deeds of the unrighteous are far from wisdom. Inasmuch as I have called you, and ye heard me not, I sharpened my words, and ye understood not. But ye have set at nought all my counsel, and would have none of my reproach. For they have hated knowledge, and the fear of Jehovah they have not chosen. They would have none of my counsel, but despised all my reproof" (*Prov.*, i, 24–31).

Olga remarked oftentimes, "My son, I have learned to know God, and am glad for it. If you know him, you too will rejoice." But he did not heed her exhortation, answering, "How shall I alone accept another faith? My followers will laugh at that." But his mother replied, "If you are converted, all your subjects will perforce follow your example." Svyatoslav did not heed his mother, but followed heathen usages, for he did not know that whoever does not obey his mother shall come to distress. For it is written, "Whosoever heedeth not his father or his mother shall suffer death" (*Exod.*, xxi, 17). But he was incensed at his mother for this reason. As Solomon has said, "He that correcteth the unrighteous getteth to himself reviling, and he that reproveth a wicked man getteth himself a blot. Rebuke not the evil, lest he hate thee"

---

[4] Needless to say, the account of Olga's triple revenge is legendary.—Ed.

[5] Olga's reception in Constantinople is related by the Emperor Constantine Porphyrogenitus himself. There is, however, no evidence that he baptized her, or desired to marry her. All we know is that she became a Christian about this time.—Ed.

(*Prov.*, ix, 7–8). For rebuke addressed to evildoers provokes offence. . . .

A.D. 983. Vladimir marched on the Yatvingians, conquered them, and seized their territory.[6] He returned to Kiev, and together with his people made sacrifice to the idols. The elders and the boyars then proposed that they should cast lots for a youth and a maiden, and sacrifice to the gods whomsoever the lot should fall upon. . . .

For at this time the Russes were ignorant pagans. The devil rejoiced thereat, for he did not know that his ruin was approaching. He was so eager to destroy the Christian people, yet he was expelled by the true cross even from these very lands. The accursed one thought to himself, "This is my habitation, a land where the apostles have not taught nor the prophets prophesied." He knew not that the Prophet had said, "I will call those my people who are not my people" (*Hosea*, ii, 23). Likewise it is written of the Apostles, "Their message has gone out into all the earth and their words to the end of the world" (*Ps.*, xix, 5). Though the Apostles have not been there in person, their teachings resound like trumpets in the churches throughout the world. Through their instruction we overcome the hostile adversary, and trample him under our feet. For likewise did the Holy Fathers trample upon him, and they have received the heavenly crown in company with the holy martyrs and the just. . . .

Vladimir was visited by Bulgars of Mohammedan faith, who said, "Though you are a wise and prudent prince, you have no religion. Adopt our faith, and revere Mahomet." Vladimir inquired what was the nature of their religion. They replied that they believed in God, and that Mahomet instructed them to

[6] Vladimir (978–1015) was the Grand Prince of Kiev. Later he became known as St. Vladimir since he established Christianity as the official religion of Russia (989).—Ed.

practice circumcision, to eat no pork, to drink no wine, and, after death, promised them complete fulfillment of their carnal desires. "Mahomet," they asserted, "will give each man seventy fair women. He may choose one fair one, and upon that woman will Mahomet confer the charms of them all, and she shall be his wife. Mahomet promises that one may then satisfy every desire, but whoever is poor in this world will be no different in the next." They also spoke other false things which out of modesty may not be written down. Vladimir listened to them for he was fond of women and indulgence, regarding which he heard with pleasure. But circumcision and abstinence from pork and wine were disagreeable to him. "Drinking," said he, "is the joy of the Russes. We cannot exist without that pleasure."

Then came the Germans, asserting that they were come as emissaries of the Pope. They added, "Thus says the Pope: 'Your country is like our country, but your faith is not as ours. For our faith is the light. We worship God, who has made heaven and earth, the stars, the moon, and every creature, while your gods are only wood.'" Vladimir inquired what their teaching was. They replied, "Fasting according to one's strength. But whatever one eats or drinks is all to the glory of God, as our teacher Paul has said." Then Vladimir answered, "Depart hence; our fathers accepted no such principle."

The Jewish Khazars heard of these missions, and came themselves saying, "We have learned that Bulgars and Christians came hither to instruct you in their faiths. The Christians believe in him whom we crucified, but we believe in the one God of Abraham, Isaac, and Jacob." Then Vladimir inquired what their religion was. They replied that its tenets included circumcision, not eating pork or hare, and observing the Sabbath. The Prince then asked where their native land was, and they replied that it was in Jerusalem. When Vladimir inquired where that was, they made answer, "God was angry at our forefathers, and scattered us among the gentiles on account of our sins. Our land was then given to the Christians." The Prince then demanded, "How can you hope to teach others while you yourselves are cast out and scattered abroad by the hand of God? If God loved you and your faith, you would not be thus dispersed in foreign lands. Do you expect us to accept that fate also?" . . .

A.D. 987. Vladimir summoned together his boyars and the city-elders, and said to them, "Behold, the Bulgars came before me urging me to accept their religion. Then came the Germans and praised their own faith; and after them came the Jews. Finally the Greeks appeared, criticizing all other faiths but commending their own, and they spoke at length, telling the history of the whole world from its beginning. Their words were artful, and it was wondrous to listen and pleasant to hear them. They preach the existence of another world. 'Whoever adopts our religion and then dies shall arise and live forever. But whosoever embraces another faith, shall be consumed with fire in the next world.' What is your opinion on this subject, and what do you answer?" The boyars and the elders replied, "You know, oh Prince, that no man condemns his own possessions, but praises them instead. If you desire to make certain, you have servants at your disposal. Send them to inquire about the ritual of each and how he worships God."

Their counsel pleased the prince and all the people, so that they chose good and wise men to the number of ten, and directed them to go first among the Bulgars and inspect their faith. The emissaries went their way, and when they arrived at their destination they beheld the disgraceful actions of the Bulgars

and their worship in the mosque; then they returned to their country. Vladimir then instructed them to go likewise among the Germans, and examine their faith, and finally to visit the Greeks. They thus went into Germany, and after viewing the German ceremonial, they proceeded to Tsar'grad, where they had appeared before the Emperor. He inquired on what mission they had come, and they reported to him all that had occurred. When the Emperor heard their words, he rejoiced, and did them great honor on that very day.

On the morrow, the Emperor sent a message to the Patriarch to inform him that a Russian delegation had arrived to examine the Greek faith, and directed him to prepare the church and the clergy and to array himself in his sacerdotal robes, so that the Russes might behold the glory of the God of the Greeks. When the Patriarch received these commands, he bade the clergy assemble, and they performed the customary rites. They burned incense, and the choirs sang hymns. The Emperor accompanied the Russes to the church, and placed them in a wide space, calling their attention to the beauty of the edifice, the chanting, and the pontifical services and the ministry of the deacons, while he explained to them the worship of his God. The Russes were astonished, and in their wonder praised the Greek ceremonial. Then the Emperors Basil and Constantine invited the envoys to their presence, and said, "Go hence to your native country," and dismissed them with valuable presents and great honor.

Thus they returned to their own country, and the Prince called together his boyars and the elders. Vladimir then announced the return of the envoys who had been sent out, and suggested that their report be heard. He thus commanded them to speak out before his retinue. The envoys reported, "When we journeyed among the Bulgars, we beheld how they worship in their temple, called a mosque, while they stand ungirt. The Bulgar bows, sits down, looks hither and thither like one possessed, and there is no happiness among them, but instead only sorrow and a dreadful stench. Their religion is not good. Then we went among the Germans, and saw them performing many ceremonies in their temples; but we beheld no glory there. Then we went to Greece, and the Greeks led us to the edifices where they worship their God, and we knew not whether we were in heaven or on earth. For on earth there is no such splendor or such beauty, and we are at a loss how to describe it. We only know that God dwells there among men, and their service is fairer than the ceremonies of other nations. For we cannot forget that beauty. Every man, after tasting something sweet, is afterward unwilling to accept that which is bitter, and therefore we cannot dwell longer here." Then the boyars spoke and said, "If the Greek faith were evil, it would not have been adopted by your grandmother Olga who was wiser than all other men." Vladimir then inquired where they should all accept baptism, and they replied that the decision rested with him.

After a year passed Vladimir proceeded with an armed force against Kherson, a Greek city, and the people of Kherson barricaded themselves therein.[7] Vladimir halted at the farther side of the city beside the harbor, a bowshot from the town, and the inhabitants resisted energetically while Vladimir besieged the town. Eventually, however, they became exhausted, and Vladimir warned them that if they did not surrender, he would remain on the spot for three years. When they failed to heed this threat, Vladimir marshalled his troops and ordered the construction of

an earthwork in the direction of the city. While this work was under construction, the inhabitants dug a tunnel under the city-wall, stole the heaped-up earth, and carried it into the city, where they piled it up in the center of the town. But the soldiers kept on building, and Vladimir persisted. Then a man of Kherson, Anastasius by name, shot into the Russ camp an arrow on which he had written, "There are springs behind you to the east, from which water flows in pipes. Dig down and cut them off." When Vladimir received this information, he raised his eyes to heaven and vowed that if this hope was realized, he would be baptized. He gave orders straightway to dig down above the pipes, and the water-supply was thus cut off. The inhabitants were accordingly overcome by thirst, and surrendered.

Vladimir and his retinue entered the city, and he sent messages to the Emperors Basil and Constantine, saying "Behold, I have captured your glorious city. I have also heard that you have an unwedded sister. Unless you give her to me to wife, I shall deal with your own city as I have with Kherson." When the Emperors heard this message they were troubled, and replied, "It is not meet for Christians to give in marriage to pagans. If you are baptized, you shall have her to wife, inherit the kingdom of God, and be our companion in the faith. Unless you do so, however, we cannot give you our sister in marriage." When Vladimir learned their response, he directed the envoys of the Emperors to report to the latter that he was willing to accept baptism, having already given some study to their religion, and that the Greek faith and ritual, as described by the emissaries sent to examine it, had pleased him well. When the Emperors heard this report, they rejoiced, and persuaded their sister Anna to consent to the match. They then requested Vladimir to submit to baptism before they should send their

---

[7] Kherson was located on the Crimean Coast, very near the modern port of Sevastopol. It belonged to the Byzantine Empire.—Ed.

sister to him, but Vladimir desired that the Princess should herself bring priests to baptize him. The Emperors complied with his request, and sent forth their sister, accompanied by some dignitaries and priests. Anna, however, departed with reluctance. "It is as if I were setting out into captivity," she lamented; "better were it for me to die at home." But her brothers protested, "Through your agency God turns the land of Rus' to repentance, and you will relieve Greece from the danger of grievous war. Do you see how much harm the Russes have already brought upon the Greeks? If you do not set out, they may bring on us the same misfortunes." It was thus that they overcame her hesitation only with great difficulty. The Princess embarked upon a ship, and after tearfully embracing her kinfolk, she set forth across the sea and arrived at Kherson. The natives came forth to greet her, and conducted her into the city, where they settled her in the palace.

By divine agency, Vladimir was suffering at that moment from a disease of the eyes, and could see nothing, being in great distress. The Princess declared to him that if he desired to be relieved of this disease, he should be baptized with all speed, otherwise it could not be cured. When Vladimir heard her message, he said, "If this proves true, then of a surety is the God of the Christians great," and gave order that he should be baptized. The Bishop of Kherson, together with the Princess's priests, after announcing the tidings, baptized Vladimir, and as the Bishop laid his hand upon him, he straightway received his sight. Upon experiencing this miraculous cure, Vladimir glorified God, saying, "I have now perceived the one true God." When his followers beheld this miracle, many of them were also baptized.

Vladimir was baptized in the Church of St. Basil, which stands at Kherson

upon a square in the center of the city, where the Khersonians trade. The palace of Vladimir stands beside this church to this day, and the palace of the Princess is behind the altar. After his baptism, Vladimir took the Princess in marriage. . . .

Hereupon Vladimir took the Princess and Anastasius and the priests of Kherson, together with the relics of St. Clement and of Phoebus his disciple, and selected also sacred vessels and images for the service. In Kherson he thus founded a church on the mound which had been heaped up in the midst of the city with the earth removed from his embankment; this church is standing at the present day. Vladimir also found and appropriated two bronze statues and four bronze horses, which now stand behind the Church of the Holy Virgin, and which the ignorant think are made of marble. As a wedding present for the Princess, he gave Kherson over to the Greeks again, and then departed for Kiev. . . .

Thereafter Vladimir sent heralds throughout the whole city to proclaim that if any inhabitants, rich or poor, did not betake himself to the river, he would risk the Prince's displeasure. When the people heard these words, they wept for joy, and exclaimed in their enthusiasm, "If this were not good, the Prince and his boyars would not have accepted it." On the morrow, the Prince went forth to the Dnieper with the priests of the Princess and those from Kherson, and a countless multitude assembled. They all went into the water: some stood up to their necks, others to their breasts, and the younger near the bank, some of them holding children in their arms, while the adults waded farther out. The priests stood by and offered prayers. There was joy in heaven and upon earth to behold so many souls saved. But the devil groaned, lamenting, "Woe is me! how am I driven out hence! For I thought to have my dwelling-place here, since the apostolic teachings do not abide in this land. Nor did this people know God, but I rejoiced in the service they rendered unto me. But now I am vanquished by the ignorant, not by apostles and martyrs, and my reign in these regions is at an end."

When the people were baptized, they returned each to his own abode. Vladimir, rejoicing that he and his subjects now knew God himself, looked up to heaven and said, "Oh God, who has created heaven and earth, look down, I beseech thee, on this thy new people, and grant them, oh Lord, to know thee as the true God, even as the other Christian nations have known thee. Confirm in them the true and inalterable faith, and aid me, oh Lord, against the hostile adversary, so that, hoping in thee and in thy might, I may overcome his malice." Having spoken thus, he ordained that wooden churches should be built and established where pagan idols had previously stood. He thus founded the Church of St. Basil on the hill where the idol of Perun and the other images had been set, and where the Prince and the people had offered their sacrifices. He began to found churches and to assign priests throughout the cities, and to invite the people to accept baptism in all the cities and towns.

He took the children of the best families, and sent them for instruction in book-learning. The mothers of these children wept bitterly over them, for they were not yet strong in faith, but mourned as for the dead. When these children were assigned for study, there was fulfilled in the land of Rus' the prophecy which says, "In those days, the deaf shall hear words of Scripture, and the voice of the stammerers shall be made plain" (*Is.*, xxix, 18).

2

MEDIEVAL RUSSIAN LAWS

SELECTIONS

"Any Englishman," wrote the late British scholar B. H. Sumner, "who reads the *Russkaia Pravda* feels that, in many respects, he is moving in more or less the same world as that of the laws of the Wessex kings." A comparison of medieval Russian laws with those of the West would doubtless be enlightening but has not been undertaken so far. Professor Vernadsky's work which we are using here remains the most thorough study of Russian law before the Muscovite period available in English.

We have already met with some legislation in the excerpts from the Primary Chronicle reprinted above; the Chronicle ought to be studied for additional material on early Russian law. Excerpts from the Novgorod Charter reproduced here should be studied in relation to the selections devoted to the life of that city.

A review of Professor Vernadsky's work is available in Vladimir Gsovski's "Medieval Russian Laws," *American Slavic and East European Review*, VI, 152–58. A close analysis of the *Russkaia Pravda* is available in the first volume of Vasily Kliuchevsky's *A History of Russia*, as well as in *Kiev Rus* by the Soviet scholar Boris Grekov. The following works draw on the *Russkaia Pravda*: George Vernadsky's *Kievan Russia*, Jerome Blum's *Lord and Peasant in Russia* (paperback), and Boris Rybakov's *The Early Centuries of Russian History*.

INTRODUCTION

In the reign of Iaroslav the Wise (1015–54), the first Russian code of laws was compiled. Known as *Pravda Russkaia*, The Russian Law or Lex Russica, and Iaroslav's *Pravda*, this brief document is based upon the customary law and contains chiefly norms of penal law. There is a striking resemblance between some of its clauses and some of the provisions of King Alfred's Wessex laws. Iaroslav's Lex Russica played in the de-velopment of Russian laws a role comparable to that of the Lex Salica in Frankish law. Some twenty years after Iaroslav's death his sons brought about a number of additional ordinances tending chiefly to reinforce the princely authority. That collection is known as the *Pravda* of Iaroslav's sons. In it, considerable attention was paid to the better protection of princely servitors and estates, as a result of which the document, by its purpose, may be compared to

From George Vernadsky (trans.), *Medieval Russian Laws* (New York: Columbia University Press, 1947), pp. 4–25, 35, 48–50, 54, 83, 84, 86–87, 93–95. Footnotes have been omitted, and the glossary has been abbreviated. Reprinted by permission of the publisher.

some *Capitularia* of the Frankish kings, especially the *Capitulare de Villis*. Taken together, Iaroslav's *Pravda* and the *Pravda* of his sons are known as the Short Version of the *Pravda*. In the course of the twelfth century the whole code was considerably enlarged and revised. Thus, the so-called Expanded Version of the *Pravda* came into being; this served as an intermediary link between the rude and primitive code of Iaroslav and the much more elaborate "charters" of the city-republics of Pskov and Novgorod of the fourteenth and fifteenth centuries.

Lex Russica is not, however, the only monument of princely legislation in the pre-Mongolian period of Russian history. Separate charters, statutes, and ordinances were issued by princes on various occasions. Of these, only those issued for the benefit of the church, or of bishops and monasteries, have been preserved, in full or in part. Perhaps the most important among the documents of this kind is the Church Statute of Vladimir the Saint which may be called the cornerstone of church organization in medieval Russia. As will be shown later, certain groups of the population were subject to the ecclesiastical courts exclusively; therefore, statutes issued by church authorities should not be neglected in any general study of Russian legal history. It is noteworthy that one such statute, the so-called "Metropolitan's Justice" (*Pravosudie Mitropolichie*), but recently discovered, presents interesting parallels to some clauses of the *Pravda Russkaia*.

For the understanding of the general background of Russian jurisprudence in the Kievan period, intimate ties between the Russian and Byzantine law should not be overlooked. Manuals of Byzantine law, especially the *Ecloga* of the eighth century and the *Prochiron* of the ninth, became known in Russia soon after her conversion to Christianity and

eventually were translated into Slavic. A Bulgarian compilation of the Byzantine laws, known as the *Zakon Sudnyi Liudem* ("Court Law for the People"), the original version of which appeared not later than the tenth century, was extremely popular in Russia and, characteristically enough, in some collections of Russian law of the twelfth and early thirteenth centuries it was amalgamated with the *Pravda*. While no direct influence of the German law can be ascertained in the documents of the eleventh and early twelfth centuries, by the close of the twelfth century, the German expansion in the Baltic, and, eventually, the organization of the Hanseatic League resulted in a lively commercial intercourse between the German Baltic and the north Russian cities. Commercial treaties concluded between the two groups in the course of the thirteenth and fourteenth centuries played an important role in the development of some institutions of northwestern Russian law, as for example the judicial duel, which is first mentioned in the treaty of 1229 between the city of Smolensk and some of the German cities.

The role of those Russian-German treaties in Russian legal history may to a certain extent be likened to that of the Russian-Byzantine treaties of the tenth century. However, there was an important difference between the influence on Russian jurisprudence of the Byzantine law and that of the German. The Byzantine law—which was an historical extension of the Roman law—affected the very foundations of Russian juridical thought, creating the atmosphere in which Russian law developed in the Middle Ages. From the German law, on the contrary, only certain specific norms or institutions were borrowed in the laws of Novgorod and Pskov, the feudal spirit of the *Sachsenspiegel* (1220–30) being entirely alien to Russian jurisprudence of the period.

Incidentally, even the German municipal law of the Middle Ages, the *Weichbild*, which, in the form of the so-called Magdeburg law, extended to Poland, Lithuania, the Ukraine, and White Russia in the course of the thirteenth, fourteenth, and fifteenth centuries, is of much narrower scope than the law of the northwestern Russian cities of the, same period. While the Magdeburg law tended to assure immunity and special privileges to certain cities and to the merchant and artisan guilds within those cities, the north Russian law of the fourteenth and fifteenth centuries covered the status of the people at large.

The two outstanding juridical monuments of the period are the Charter of the City of Pskov (1397–1467) and the Charter of the City of Novgorod (1471); of the latter, unfortunately, we possess but a fragment. Another remarkable document of the same period is the Charter of Dvina Land, which was issued by the Grand Duke of Moscow in 1397. Here the ascendancy of Moscow is already felt, although the Charter itself represents a confirmation of the old usages rather than a declaration of the new monarchical principles. As the Moscow rulers extended their authority over more and more territories, charters similar to that of Dvina Land had to be issued from time to time in order to confirm the autonomy of a newly acquired province or to grant special privileges to the population of certain towns or village communes. Copies of a number of these charters, dated in the late fifteenth and early sixteenth centuries, have been preserved in local archives. The most important of them is the Beloozero Charter of 1488.

By the close of the fifteenth century most of central Russia was controlled by the Grand Duke of Moscow, and in 1497 a new Code of Laws effective in all of the territories subject to Moscow was issued. This Code was simultaneously a digest of the earlier laws and the first formulation of the basic principles of the new monarchical regime that was built upon both Mongol and Byzantine foundations. Thus, the Code of 1497 brings to a close a fruitful period of Russian legal history and inaugurates a new and markedly different era—that of Muscovite law.

Of all the various Russian codes, charters, and statutes issued prior to 1497 we have selected for translation in this volume the four most outstanding. They are the Russian Law (in both the Short and the Expanded Version), and the charters of the city of Pskov, of Novgorod, and of Dvina Land. Taken together they illuminate the main trends in Russian legal history of the pre-Muscovite epoch. But more than that, they contain much material illustrating the general historical background of medieval Russia. No student of Russian history can afford to neglect the valuable evidence on old Russia's social and economic life that is to be found in many of these legal clauses. Thus, for example, the *Pravda* of Iaroslav's sons contains precious data on the administration of princely domains in the eleventh century as well as on the groups of population subject to the authority of the prince. The Statute of Vladimir Monomach—which is a part of the Expanded Version of the *Pravda*—uncovers the deep social gulf between the propertied classes and labor in Kievan Russia of the twelfth century. The charters of Pskov and Novgorod reflect the turbulent life of the north Russian democratic cities, their political strife, their powerful merchant class, their concern for securing fair protection to labor, and their basic concept of justice and equality for all before the law.

It is the attitude of both the Expanded Version of the *Pravda* and the north Russian city charters toward loans for interest which may be considered one of the most striking features of the medieval Russian law as compared with the Western law of the period. In the Roman Catholic countries of medieval Europe, under the influence of the church, any interest on loans was considered "usury." In Roman law, of course, "usury" (*usurae*) was simply the word for "interest" in the modern sense ("premium paid for the use of money," according to Webster). It goes without saying that the Greek Orthodox Church forbade the practice of "usury" in exactly the same words as did the Roman Catholic Church. Nevertheless, interest on loans was legalized both in the Byzantine and the Russian jurisprudence. The failure of the Eastern Church in this matter, as contrasted with the partial success of the Western Church, is to be explained by the difference in economic background of the East and the West.

With all due reservations, one cannot but characterize the economic regime of the early Middle Ages in the West as that of a "natural economy" based on agriculture. On the other hand, "money economy" was one of the essential features of Byzantium. As to Kievan Russia, its economic growth and blossoming was chiefly the result of an extensive commerce with both Byzantium and the Orient. A number of Russian historians now argue that agriculture must have been much more highly developed in Kievan Russia than had hitherto been supposed. Even granted that this was the case, the outstanding role of commerce in medieval Russia cannot be denied. Not only was there then in Russia a strong merchant class, but the princes themselves invested heavily in both overland and oversea commercial transactions. Loans at interest constituted an important corollary of such transactions. There was no alternative to legalizing them. This situation is duly reflected in the Russian law of the period.

II

While there is a great difference between the component parts of the Russian Law (*Pravda Russkaia*) of the eleventh and twelfth centuries, as well as between the Russian Law as a whole and the charters of Novgorod and Pskov, all these codes are based upon the same principles of court procedure. It would seem proper therefore to give here a brief outline of the characteristic features of the medieval Russian courts and court procedure. Such an outline might also be helpful for a better understanding of the single clauses in each code.

As has been already mentioned, the people, the princes, and the church were the three main factors in the development of Russian legislation. The influence of these three factors may be felt— to a different degree in regard to each— both in the organization of the courts and in the court procedure. In the oldest part of the Russian Law—Iaroslav's *Pravda*—we find a cooperation between the courts of the prince and the institutions of the people. In the *Pravda* of Iaroslav's sons, as well as in the Expanded Version of the *Pravda*, the princely court is obviously the dominant institution. By contrast, in the Novgorod and the Pskov charters we find a combination of the princely courts and the people's courts, together with the church courts. In Novgorod, there is a division of competence in judicial matters between the prince and the city authorities. The prince and his officials conduct most of the criminal cases. Of the city authorities, the mayor (*posadnik*) is in charge of litigation about land and the chiliarch (*tysiatsky*) is responsible chiefly for litigation concerning commercial transactions. Similarly in Pskov, the princely and city authorities cooperated in legal matters.

Everywhere in medieval Russia, all citizens were subject to the church courts in ecclesiastical matters, including marriage and divorce; church people—not only the clergy but every kind of attendant, as well as peasants and laborers on church estates—were subject to the bishop's court in all litigation. Cases involving laymen and churchmen were tried jointly by lay and church authorities. In court procedures, the optional steps permitted to both of the litigants played a very important role. The role of the judge was limited to supervising the contest and equalizing the means and chances of the litigants. There were very few instances, if any, of participation by the state in a trial in the capacity of a claimant, or of any inquisitorial system of procedure.

Prior to the hearing of the case, the state authorities did not interfere in the negotiations between the contestants. Only after they had agreed among themselves about the subject matter of their litigation, as well as about the time of their appearance before the court, did they ask the judge to approve their agreement. The judge had then to issue a "term-writ," which was to be properly signed and sealed. Not until this had been done, could the matter be formally accepted by the court; thereafter there was no further opportunity for a free agreement between the litigants. Prior to the issue of the term-writ the attitude of the state authorities was passive. The local community or guild was of greater assistance to a plaintiff who had difficulty in establishing the identity of the defendant. For example, a man who had lost something, or from whom something had been stolen, could make an announcement of his loss in the market place of his town. If the article was not surrendered within three days, anyone found holding it after the expiration of

this period was considered the thief—that is, the defendant in the case. If, before the end of three days, the owner found his property in another man's possession or in another town, the possessor could reject the accusation of theft by stating that he had bought it from a third party, in a bona fide transaction. He was, however, to assist the owner in establishing the identity of the seller. This was done by means of the so-called *svod* ("confrontment"), an important feature of medieval Russian pre-court procedure. This institution was similar to *Schub* in Germanic law; in Anglo-Saxon it was known as *team*. It appears to have been much more highly developed in Russian law than in Germanic, however, and was more generally applied in Russia than in the countries of Romano-Germanic Europe.

The modes of proof at the disposal of the contestants at the court trial were threefold: witnesses; appeal to God's judgment; and, in civil litigations, deeds, notes, and other documents.

1. According to the Russian Law, there were two kinds of witnesses: the eyewitness (*vidok*), and the witness proper (*poslukh*). Later texts deal with the second classification only. The role of the *poslukh* was much more important than that of a witness in modern procedure. He was an active factor throughout the proceedings. For example, according to the Pskov charter, in certain cases a *poslukh* was required to accompany one of the contestants in a duel. According to the laws of Novgorod and Pskov, only one *poslukh* was recognized by the court in each lawsuit.

2. There were several means whereby people in the Middle Ages—not only in Russia—believed God's will could be revealed to them. The habitual approach to God in the court procedure was to have one of the contestants, or the witness, take the oath (in old Russian,

rota). In Novgorod and Pskov, the oath was accompanied by kissing the cross. Another method of appealing to God's judgment was through the ordeals—by water or by iron. The oath as well as the ordeals were known not only to the Russian but to the German law as well. Moreover, in some cases the German law also recommended the judicial duel (*Zweikampf*). This institution is not mentioned in the *Pravda Russkaia*. It constituted, however, an important feature of the Novgorod and Pskov laws and presumably was borrowed from the German law. A judicial duel did not necessarily end in the death of either contestant; when one of them was knocked to the ground, he was recognized as the loser.

3. Deeds and other documents were valid only when certified by public authorities. In Pskov, copies of all such documents had to be filed with the office of the archives at the Holy Trinity Cathedral.

A few words may be added concerning old Russian penal law. In the *Pravda Russkaia* the transition from blood revenge to punishment of the criminal by the state has been recorded. State punishment, in the period of the *Pravda*, consisted in the prince's imposing a "composition" (money fine) on the criminal. It is noteworthy that the *Pravda* does not impose any capital punishment, and recommends corporal punishment only once and in regard to slaves only. On the other hand, both in the Dvina charter and in the Novgorod and Pskov laws we find several clauses recommending capital punishment for certain crimes. As to corporal punishment, the Dvina charter recommends the branding of thieves, while the Pskov charter prescribes stocks for a rioter in the court hall (this was not so much a punishment, however, as a preventive measure). Presumably, the introduction of capital punishment into the Russian

legislation was the result of the influence of the German law on one hand (in western Russia), and of the Mongol law on the other (in eastern Russia).

III

Let us now examine one by one the four legal monuments selected for publication in this volume, starting with the oldest—the *Pravda Russkaia*—which may be called the cornerstone of medieval Russian jurisprudence. . . .

The Short Version consists of two parts: Iaroslav's *Pravda*, and the *Pravda* of Iaroslav's sons. It is known that, according to the chronicles, Iaroslav granted important charters to the city of Novgorod in 1016 and in 1019. After the death of Prince Vladimir (1015), there followed a protracted strife between his sons, in which Iaroslav finally overpowered his opponents and occupied the throne of Kiev. The loyalty of the Novgorodians to him was one of the important factors in his victory, and it is natural that they expected some reward in the form of certain political and civil guarantees. It is in answer to these claims that Iaroslav must have issued the charters mentioned in the chronicles. Whether any of those charters was identical with Iaroslav's *Pravda* is not known. In any case his *Pravda* must be connected with his Novgorod charters in one way or another. And, indeed, Section 1 of his *Pravda* guarantees equal consideration to Kievan Russians and to Novgorodian Slavs by making the man of each group worth the normal wergeld of 40 *grivna*.

However, the core of Iaroslav's *Pravda* must be much older than the beginning of the eleventh century. It is apparent that Iaroslav codified old customary laws, adding a few ordinances of his own. The Russian Customary Law (*Zakon Russkii*) is mentioned in the Russo-Byzantine treaty of 945. The customs themselves must have originated long before that time.

The *Pravda* of Iaroslav's sons was the fruit of the sons' legislation and was intended to supplement their father's code. The new laws were eventually codified and the new code was approved at a meeting of the three princes and their councilors, held, presumably, at Vyshgorod in 1072. It is obvious that the chief objective of the three brothers was to enforce the authority of the prince by prescribing the payment of a double "bloodwite" for the murder of their high officials and by protecting the servitors on their domains by a system of fines. The *Pravda* of Iaroslav's sons is thus not a general code of laws but rather a collection of princely ordinances issued with a specific aim. The compilation and the promulgation of these ordinances must have been caused, at least to a certain extent, by the growing opposition to the princely authority both in the city of Kiev and in some country districts. And, indeed, serious riots had occurred in Kiev in 1068. As a result, the eldest of Iaroslav's sons, Iziaslav, Prince of Kiev, was forced to relinquish his throne, if only for a brief period. By issuing their *Pravda*, the princes apparently intended to reinforce their authority so as to avoid the possibility of any repetition of the events of 1068.

Let us now turn to the Expanded Version. It may be divided into three parts: (1) the revised *Pravda* of Iaroslav's sons; (2) the Statute of Vladimir Monomach; and (3) other enactments.

The revision of the *Pravda* of Iaroslav's sons consisted in a certain systematization of content as well as in the addition of some new materials. Thus, for example, the handicraftsman and woman were inserted in the list of people protected by princely legislation. The section on the master of the stables may enable us better to understand the methods of the editorial work of the compilers of the *Pravda*. Sometime between 1054 and 1072 Prince Iziaslav of Kiev imposed a double bloodwite, to the amount of 80 *grivna*, on the murderer of his master of the stables at Dorogobuzh. In the text of the *Pravda* of 1072 we find a general enactment concerning the double bloodwite for the murder of the master of the stables accompanied by a reference to Iziaslav's ordinance of Dorogobuzh. In the revised *Pravda* of Iaroslav's sons that reference to a specific case has been omitted.

The promulgation of the Statute of Vladimir Monomach (Prince of Kiev, 1113–25) in the very beginning of his reign was the result of dramatic events which followed closely the death of Vladimir's predecessor of the Kievan throne. A serious political and social crisis had been in the making long before that. While the three princes—sons of Iaroslav—attempted to curb the popular opposition by issuing, in 1072, special ordinances for the better protection of princely servitors, the situation apparently required a more constructive legislation. Both the middle-class burghers and the owners of medium-sized landed estates suffered from the high rate of interest on loans contracted by them. Laborers and artisans were in an even worse position since they were threatened with virtual enslavement in the case of inability to meet their financial obligations. The explosion came in 1113 when popular riots reached the force of a social revolution in the city of Kiev. Houses of wealthy boyars and merchants were plundered, and popular resentment turned its fury upon the moneylenders, Jews among the others.

Considerable wisdom and quick action were required on the part of the ruler. Vladimir Monomach—then Prince of Pereiaslav—was the only man to whom the various social classes could turn for guidance, and he was invited to assume the throne of Kiev. Vladimir accepted on condition that there be no opposition to any measures, however drastic, that he might consider necessary. He convoked at once a special Council of State to approve his "new deal" program. This program, as expressed in Vladimir's Statute, consisted in limiting the abuses of short-term loans, limiting the interest on long-term loans, and in issuing special enactments to prevent enslavement of indentured laborers and other lower-class workers caught in the financial web of landlords and moneylenders.

Even after the addition to the Russian Law of such an important piece of legislation as Vladimir's Statute, that Law still contained many lacunae. The original *Pravda* dealt chiefly with the court procedure and penal law. In the revised *Pravda* of Iaroslav's sons a few clauses concerning commercial law were inserted, but other aspects of civil law remained as yet outside the legislator's attention. Further additions to the code were therefore necessary. These additional enactments constitute the third part of the Expanded Version. One group of clauses deals with the family and the inheritance law. Another covers the juridical nature of slavery. In this latter group an attempt is made to put certain limits on the spread of slavery by establishing a number of specific requirements to be observed in the process of enslavement.

The insertion of these additional enactments rounded out the contents of the *Pravda*. Simultaneously, the code must have been revised once more *in toto*. The completion of the Expanded Version as a whole may be referred to the second half of the twelfth century; some scholars are even ready to accept the beginning of the thirteenth century as the date of the final revision. In my opinion, however, there are some reasons to connect the completion of the Expanded

Version with the reign of Rostislav, originally Prince of Smolensk and later Prince of Kiev (1160–68). It is noteworthy that the treaty between Smolensk and the German cities, concluded in 1229, contains several clauses borrowed from the Expanded Version of the *Pravda*. Presumably the latter was the base of Smolensk laws, and if so, it might have been familiarized there by Rostislav.

IV

It is to the princely power, as we have seen, that the initiative belonged in the process of the codification of the Russian Law. In contrast, in the Novgorod and Pskov charters of the fourteenth and fifteenth centuries the prince plays a subordinate role. It is the people themselves who, through the city assembly (*veche*), make and approve the law.

The great city of Novgorod was a rival to Kiev from the early ages of Russian history. Situated on the riverway "from the Varangians to the Greeks," Kiev commanded the exit of commercial caravans from Russia southward in the direction of Constantinople. During the age of the Hanseatic League, Novgorod, which stood at the entrance from the Baltic to inner Russia, was the seat of one of the overseas "factories" of the German merchants. From the time of the establishment of the Teutonic Knights in Prussia and the Livonian Order in Latvia direct overland contact between Novgorod and Pskov on one hand and the Germans on the other likewise became possible. That contact was not always friendly; years of peaceful commercial relations interchanged with periods of war. Alexander Nevsky's famous victory over German crusaders (1242) was but one of the episodes in the protracted Russo-German struggle.

Novgorod had two faces. It was a city democracy, and it was also the capital of a huge colonial empire controlling vast territories northward to the White Sea and Arctic Ocean and eastward to the Urals. Within this area Novgorod was "the city" (*gorod*), other towns, even such important ones as Pskov, being known merely as "boroughs" (*prigorod*, literally, "by-town"). The supreme authority was vested in the city assembly (*veche*), in which theoretically all Novgorod citizens could take part, but actually only a few of the borough inhabitants could be present, especially when the *veche* met on short notice to handle some emergency business. According to the old customs, a unanimous vote was required to make any *veche* decision valid. As a result, when a considerable group of citizens objected to a bill and did not want to withdraw their objections, force was applied by the majority group. Therefore the *veche* meetings were usually lively and often unruly. In case of a deadlock, both parties might appeal to the spiritual head of the Novgorodian democracy—the *vladyka* (archbishop). Thus, the church was able to play a considerable part in the political life of Novgorod. To the Novgorodians, the Cathedral of St. Sophia, built in the eleventh century, symbolized their city, in any case spiritually. From the political angle, they spoke of their city-state, as "Lord (*Gospodin*) Novgorod the Great" or "Sovereign (*Gosudar'*) Novgorod the Great."

The leading officers of the Novgorod administration—the mayor (*posadnik*) and the chiliarch (*tysiatsky*)—were elected by the direct vote of the city assembly. Usually but not necessarily, they were chosen from among the members of wealthy boyar and merchant families. The retired mayors and chiliarchs, together with other prominent boyars, formed the so-called *Gospoda* (House of Lords), which discussed city affairs prior to the meetings of the *veche*. This added an aristocratic touch to the Novgorodian constitution. The monar-chical element was represented by the prince, who must be acceptable to the people of Novgorod and who, on assuming his duties, had to take oath not to violate the city's customs. In most cases the prince was also asked to sign a formal contract in which the limits of his authority were clearly defined. In addition to the copies of those contracts, records of the decisions of the *veche* were kept in the city archives.

It was not until the fifteenth century, however, that the Novgorod law was codified, at least in part. By that time the international position of Novgorod had become precarious, since the city was threatened by two rapidly growing states—the Grand Duchy of Moscow on the southeast and the Grandy Duchy of Lithuania on the southwest. For some time Novgorod was able to play the two rivals against one another by entering into agreements with each of them in turn. In any such agreement the rights and prerogatives of the city had to be made perfectly clear, hence the necessity for the codification of the Novgorodian law. In 1456, the Moscow Grand Duke Vasili II approved a "charter" of Novgorod laws and customs. In 1470 the city signed a treaty with Kazimir IV, king of Poland and grand duke of Lithuania, in which that potentate was recognized as the prince of Novgorod, but his authority was curbed by a number of specific provisions. The treaty proved to be an ephemeral one, however, since in the next year war broke out between Novgorod and Moscow. Receiving no support from Kazimir, Novgorodian troops were outmaneuvered and defeated by Grand Duke Ivan III's skillful generals, and the proud city had to sue for peace. Ivan III was a master politician and believed in expanding his authority by gradual moves. He agreed for the time being to guarantee Novgorod's privileges in exchange for recognition as her "Lord."

It was under such circumstances that the Novgorod "charter" of 1471 came into being. Two copies are extant, both incomplete. Even though the charter has been preserved in part only, it constitutes an important piece of medieval Russian legislation and presents an interesting parallel to the Charter of the City of Pskov, of which we possess the full text.

V

Pskov, like Novgorod, was one of Russia's oldest cities. And like Novgorod's, her prosperity was based chiefly upon the Baltic trade. Until the middle of the fourteenth century Pskov was not an independent city-state but merely a "borough" of Novgorod. The Pskovians were entitled to take part in the meetings of the Novgorod *veche,* and thus were connected with the partisan strife in that city. Their voice was, however, not strong enough to affect the decisions of the *veche* to an extent sufficient to compel consideration of the specific interests of Pskov commerce. On many occasions the Pskovians complained that Novgorod was selfishly disregarding their city's needs. Eventually, a movement arose in Pskov to bring to an end the subordination to Novgorod. By the middle of the fourteenth century the movement had succeeded. According to the treaty of 1347, the Novgorodians granted independence to Pskov, recognizing it as a "younger brother." After that time the Pskovians themselves referred to their city as "Lord Pskov." The provisions of the treaty were confirmed in 1397.

As an independent city-state, Pskov had her own princes with whom agreements similar to those in Novgorod were concluded. In church affairs she remained subject to the authority of the archbishop of Novgorod, who was represented in Pskov by a lieutenant. The Pskov church enjoyed, however, a considerable degree of autonomy, the clergy being organized in several "cathedral districts." The main sanctuary of the city was the Holy Trinity Cathedral, which enjoyed as much local prestige as did the rival Novgorod Cathedral of St. Sophia.

Like Novgorod, Pskov had to pay much attention to her relations with neighboring states and to the preservation of political equilibrium among them. For a long time the Pskovians were successful in keeping the balance between Novgorod, Moscow, and Lithuania.

The city charter was approved by the assembly after the assertion of Pskov liberties in the treaty with Novgorod of 1397. The charter was expanded and revised by 1467. A fragment of the Pskov charter, from Article 109 to the end, was found by the "historiographer" N. M. Karamzin and published by him in the notes to Volume V of his great work, *Istoriia Gosudarstva Rossiiskogo* (1816). Later a complete copy was discovered in the private archives of Count Vorontsov by Professor Murzakevich, who published it in 1847.

VI

We now turn to the Charter of Dvina Land. Dvina Land was the name for the territory in the basin of the Northern Dvina River centering around the towns of Vologda and Ustiug. This remote northern country was at the junction of two important commercial ways, one leading from Novgorod eastward to the Urals, and the other northward from Moscow to the White Sea. The country was abundant in forests and rich in fur-bearing animals. Even in the fourteenth century hunting was so profitable an occupation that people paid their taxes in furs. However, commerce and agriculture also played an important role in the Land's economy.

Dvina Land was a Novgorod Dominion from at least the eleventh century. By the fourteenth century, however, the boyars and wealthy merchants of the region, although Novgorod citizens, were dissatisfied with the policies of the Novgorod *veche*. In their opinion, Novgorod treated their Land as a colony, demanding excessive taxes and neglecting local interests. They therefore turned to the grand dukes of Moscow for protection, in the hope of striking a better bargain with them. In 1397, when an uprising against the Novgorodian rule occurred in Dvina Land, Muscovite troops seized the opportunity to enter the territory. Anxious to secure the loyalty of the Dvina people, Grand Duke Vasili I of Moscow issued a special charter to guarantee the autonomy of local courts and administration.

The Muscovite intervention proved to be premature and in the next year the Novgorodian authority was re-established in Dvina Land. Vasili's charter, although of short duration, presents an interesting legal document. The text of the Dvina charter was first published by N. M. Karamzin in 1818.

VII

... The *Pravda* is not a systematic code in our sense; it consists mostly of casual juridical notes and comments rather than of comprehensive definitions. It has a logic of its own, which we must discover. The compilers of the document addressed themselves not so much to the general public as to the judges and court officials. It was assumed that the latter were thoroughly familiar with the whole body of the customary law and needed only some supplementary information concerning new ordinances. As a result, there are logical lacunae in almost every clause of the document. What has not been said is often as important for our understanding of the text as what is said. Obviously, for rightly interpreting the text we must

somehow make up the deficit in wording in order to obtain a more or less adequate idea of what the compiler meant. The best way to fill in the gaps—logical or literary—is by analogy with similar clauses in other parts of the same code or in other contemporary sources. If this is not possible, one has chiefly to rely upon a minute analysis of the economic and social conditions by which the clause in question may have been conditioned; understanding these may help to clarify the interpretation. Unfortunately our knowledge of Kievan economics is still far from adequate and such an approach cannot always promise success.

The present translator has tried to do all this preliminary work; accordingly, each clause is translated without bothering the reader with the process of argumentation. In some cases, however, it seemed indispensable to supply at least part of the phrase implied but not expressed in the text. This supplementary material is enclosed in brackets.

The treatment of specific juridical and social terms presented another problem by itself. There still exists no consensus of opinion among scholars about some of them. The easiest method would have been not to translate such terms but merely to transliterate them, in each case explaining the connotation in the notes. This would, however, result in a text littered with Russian terms in italics and would also mean shifting the responsibility from the translator to the reader. Therefore, the opposite method has been adopted, that of translating each Russian term into the closest possible equivalent in modern English and, for the original term, referring the reader to the notes. Thus, the reader will find in the text only English terms, such as, for example, "bailiff" and "peasant"; he will have to look in the notes, if he is eager to know the original Russian terms (in the present example *ognishchanin* and *smerd*, respectively). The only exception to the rule is the term *izgoi* which I have left untranslated in the text, explaining it in the notes. This was necessary because the connotation of the term as used in the *Pravda* must have been entirely different from the usual one, and, although I have an explanation for it, I did not consider it proper to impose my conjecture on the reader.

Furthermore, for obvious reasons, the names of the Russian monetary units could not be rendered into English. Nor would it be expedient to explain the value of each unit in the notes separately, since the reader needs first of all some general information on medieval Russian money and monetary system, without which the value of a specific unit could not be understood. Therefore, it seems proper to insert herewith a brief note on Russian money in the period of the *Pravda* as well as in that of the Pskov and Novgorod charters.

Since furs constituted in the early periods an important item of Russian commerce—as they were to do in Siberia in the sixteenth and the seventeenth centuries—it was but natural that furs may have played, at least in some periods and in some districts, the role of currency. However, Russian commerce with Byzantium and the East also brought to Russia gold and silver in considerable amounts, and while, in the Kievan period, the common Russian word for "money" was *kuny* (marten skins), the Russian monetary system— or rather systems, since there were several of them—was based on metal rather than on fur.

The basic monetary unit, in the Kievan period, was the *grivna*. There were three kinds of *grivna*: gold, silver, and *kuna*. It is not always easy to determine which kind is meant in a given article of the Russian Law. The gold *grivna* presumably corresponded to one-half a

troy pound of gold. The silver *grivna* must have equaled approximately one troy pound of silver. The gold *grivna* was seldom used. The silver *grivna* was a standard unit in all commercial transactions and particularly in foreign trade.

In the payments of taxes and fines of smaller amount, as well as in other every-day specie transactions, the reckoning was in *grivna* or *kuna*. Fractions of this were known as *nogata* and *rezana*. There were 20 *nogata* and 50 *rezana* in one *grivna* of *kuna*. The lowest unit was known as *veksha* (literally, squirrel) or *veveritsa;* in Smolensk, one *nogata* was equal to 24 *veksha*. Somewhat later, the term *kuna* in the specific sense of a fraction of *grivna* was introduced. There is no consensus of scholarly opinion about the exact value of one *kuna* in relation to one *grivna* of *kuna*. According to Prozorovsky, there were 50 *kuna* in a *grivna*, which would mean that one *kuna* was equal to one *rezana*. However, according to Mrochek-Drozdovsky, there must have been 25 *kuna* in one *grivna* of *kuna*, making one *kuna* equal to two *rezana*. As to the relation between the silver *grivna* and the *grivna* of *kuna*, it is known that in Smolensk one silver *grivna* was considered equal to four *grivna* of *kuna*. It may be mentioned furthermore that in chronicles as well as in some other sources, one more term for money occurs: *bela*. It is hard to say whether this was a general word for a silver coin, or a term denoting a specific monetary unit.

While both the silver *grivna* and the *grivna* of *kuna* were still in use in Novgorod and Pskov as late as the fourteenth and fifteenth centuries, a new monetary unit, called "ruble," gradually assumed predominance. The word "ruble" (*rubl'*) is usually considered a derivation from the Russian verb *rubiti* ("to cut"); ruble is supposed to have originated from cutting a *grivna* into four pieces. In my opinion, however, *rubl'* is the Russian spelling of *rūpya*, which, in Sanskrit, means "silver." A Novgorodian ruble corresponded originally to a silver *grivna*. In the fifteenth century the ruble amounted to only one-half of a silver *grivna*. The Novgorodian ruble of the fifteenth century was equal to 216 *denga*. In Pskov they counted 220 *denga* to the ruble; in Moscow, 100 *denga*. *Denga* is a term borrowed from the Mongolian language.

And now, let the documents speak for themselves. . . .

THE ORDINANCES OF IARO-SLAV, SON OF VLADIMIR

ARTICLE 1. If a man kills a man [the following relatives of the murdered man may avenge him]: the brother is to avenge his brother, or the father [his son], or the son [his father]; or the son of the brother, or the son of the sister [their respective uncle]. If there is no avenger the wergeld is set to the amount of 80 *grivna* in case [the murdered man] was a prince's councilor or a prince's steward; if he was a [Kievan] Russian—a palace guard, a merchant, or a boyar's steward, or a sheriff —or if he was an *izgoi*, or a [Novgorodian] Slav, [the wergeld is] 40 *grivna*.

ARTICLE 2. And after Iaroslav his sons: Iziaslav, Sviatoslav, and Vsevolod, and their councilors: Kosniachko, Pereneg, and Nikifor met in a conference and canceled the [custom] of blood revenge, and [instead ordered] composition of [the crime] by money. And as to anything else, all that Iaroslav had decreed, his sons confirmed accordingly. . . .

On Beards

ARTICLE 67. If anyone tears [another's] beard, and [the offended either comes to the court] with the sign of it,

or produces men [as witnesses], [the offender pays] a 12 *grivna* fine; but if there is a claim and no men [to support it], there is no fine.

On Teeth

ARTICLE 68. If they knock out anyone's tooth, and blood is visible in his mouth, or men [as witnesses] are produced, 12 *grivna* fine, and 1 *grivna* [damages] for the tooth.

[On Theft of Game]

ARTICLE 69. If anyone steals a beaver, 12 *grivna*.

ARTICLE 70. If there are traces on the ground or any evidence of hunting, or a net, the guild must search for the poacher or pay the fine.

If Anyone Obliterates the Sign on a Beehive [or Any Other Marker]

ARTICLE 71. If anyone obliterates the sign on a beehive, 12 *grivna*. . . .

On Hunting Nets

ARTICLE 80. If anyone cuts a rope in the hunting net, 3 *grivna* fine, and to the owner 1 *grivna* of *kuna* [damages] for the rope.

ARTICLE 81. If anyone steals from a hunting net a hawk or a falcon, 3 *grivna* fine, and to the owner, 1 *grivna;* and for a dove, 9 *kuna;* for a fowl, 9 *kuna;* for a duck, 30 *kuna;* for a goose, 30 *kuna;* for a swan, 30 *kuna;* and for a crane, 30 *kuna.*

[On Stealing Hay]

ARTICLE 82. And for [stealing] hay or lumber, 9 *kuna* [fine], and to the owner according to the number of cartloads stolen, 2 *nogata* for a cartload.

On the Threshing Court

ARTICLE 83. If anyone sets fire to a threshing court, he is to be banished and his house confiscated; first, the damages are paid, and the prince takes care of the rest. The same for setting fire to anyone's homestead.

ARTICLE 84. And whoever vilely maims or slaughters [another's] horse or cattle [shall pay] 12 *grivna* fine, and, for the damages, amends to the owner.

ARTICLE 85. In all the above litigations the trial is with freemen as witnesses. If the witness is a slave, he is not to take [a direct] part in the trial; but if the plaintiff so desires, he seizes [the defendant] and says as follows: "I am seizing thee on the ground of this [man's] words, but it is I who seize thee, and not the slave." And he takes him [the defendant] to the ordeal. If he [the plaintiff] succeeds in proving his guilt, he takes back from him [the defendant] his own; if he does not succeed in accusing him, he pays him 1 *grivna* [amends] for the pain inflicted, since he seized him on the ground of a slave's words. . . .

On Slavery

ARTICLE 110. Full slavery is of three kinds: [first] if anyone buys [a man] willing [to sell himself into slavery], for not less than half a *grivna,* and produces witnesses and pays [the fee of] 1 *nogata* in the presence of the slave himself. And the second kind of slavery is this: if anyone marries a female slave without special agreement [with her lord]; if he marries her with a special agreement, what he agreed to, stands. And this is the third kind of slavery: if anyone becomes [another's] steward or housekeeper without a special agreement; if there has been an agreement, what has been agreed upon, stands.

ARTICLE 111. And the recipient of a [money] grant is not a slave. And one cannot make a man one's slave because [he received] a grant-in-aid in grain, or [failed to furnish] additional grain

[when repaying the grant]; if he fails to complete the term of work [for the grant], he has to return the grant; if he completes the term, he stands cleared. . . .

THE CHARTER OF THE CITY OF NOVGOROD

[PREAMBLE]. Having referred the matter to the Lords—the Grand Dukes—Grand Duke Ivan Vasilievich, of all Russia, and his son, Grand Duke Ivan Ivanovich, for their approval, and having received the blessing of the Archbishop-elect of Novgorod the Great and Pskov, Hieromonk Theophilus, we, the mayors of Novgorod, and the chiliarchs of Novgorod, and the boyars, and the middle-class burghers, and the merchants, and the lower-class burghers, all the five city districts, the whole Sovereign Novgorod the Great, at the city assembly in the Iaroslav Square, have completed and confirmed the following:

ARTICLE 1. The Archbishop-elect of Novgorod the Great and Pskov, Hieromonk Theophilus, in his court—the ecclesiastical court—shall conduct trials in accordance with the rules of the holy fathers—the Nomocanon; and he shall give equal justice to every litigant, be he a boyar, or a middle-class burgher, or a lower-class burgher.

ARTICLE 2. And the mayor in his court shall conduct trials jointly with the Grand Duke's lieutenants, according to the old customs; and without the concurrency of the Grand Duke's lieutenants the mayor may not conclude any lawsuit.

ARTICLE 3. And the Grand Duke's lieutenants and justices have authority to re-examine causes in appeal proceedings, according to the old customs.

ARTICLE 4. And the chiliarch conducts trials in his court. And all of them must conduct trials justly according to their oath.

ARTICLE 5. And each contestant may elect two assessors to sit in the court. And once the assessor is chosen by the contestant, he must continue to deal with him. But the authority of the mayor, and the chiliarch, and the archbishop's lieutenant, and their judges, in the conduct of the trials, must not be interfered with.

ARTICLE 6. And the litigant must not bring along with him his partisans for intimidating the other litigant, or the mayor, or the chiliarch, or the archbishop's lieutenant, or other judges, or the members of the Court of Re-examination. And whoever brings his partisans for intimidating the mayor, or the chiliarch, or the archbishop's lieutenant, or other judges, or the members of the Court of Re-examination, or the other litigant, be it at the trial, or at the re-examination of the case, or on the duel field, stands guilty, and the Grand Dukes and Novgorod the Great fine the culprit for bringing his partisans to the amount, as follows: the boyar, 50 rubles; the middle-class burgher, 20 rubles; the lower-class burgher, 10 rubles; and besides he pays damages to the other litigant.

ARTICLE 7. And if anyone wants to sue for a landed estate—for a farm homestead, or two of them, or more, or less— he may not, prior to the court proceedings, come to the land or send his men there [in an attempt to seize it by force], but must refer the matter to the court. And if he wins the suit, he receives from the judge a copy of the court decision assigning the land to him and entitling him to collect damages from the defendant. And the judge may not claim any taxes [but only the customary court fees]. . . .

ARTICLE 14. Anyone commencing a lawsuit [after the promulgation of this charter] must kiss the cross once, [promising to obey the law]; and if he comes to the court hall without having kissed the cross, he must kiss it and only then is allowed to sue; and if the defendant has not yet kissed the cross after the promulgation of this charter, he likewise must kiss the cross and only then may sue; and if either litigant refuses to kiss the cross he loses his case.

ARTICLE 15. And if a litigant refuses to kiss the cross under the pretext that he is represented by an attorney, he has to kiss the cross once just the same, and only then his attorney may conduct the suit; and if he keeps refusing to kiss the cross, he loses his case.

ARTICLE 16. And if the widow, either of an upper-class man, or of a middle-class burgher, is a defendant in a suit, and she has a son, that son may kiss the cross on behalf of both himself and his mother, once; and if the son refuses to kiss the cross on behalf of his mother, the mother has to kiss the cross in her home in the presence of the plaintiff and of the Novgorod constables.

ARTICLE 17. And in litigations about land the boyar, the middle-class burgher, or the merchant, shall kiss the cross in behalf of himself and his wife.

ARTICLE 18. And if they sue a boyar, or a middle-class burgher, or a merchant for his land or for his wife's land, he may, after having kissed the cross, defend himself, or he may send his attorney in behalf of himself and his wife.

ARTICLE 19. And in litigations about boats the attorney and the witness must kiss the cross.

ARTICLE 20. And the same members of the Court of Re-examination who accept a case shall conduct it to the conclusion.

ARTICLE 21. And when the assessors state the case, the judge orders his secretary to write down his statement, and the assessors seal the copy.

ARTICLE 22. And it is not permissible to produce a witness against [an already recognized] witness. And neither [an alien, such as] a Pskov citizen, nor a full slave may serve as witness [in regular cases]. But a slave may be a witness against another slave.

ARTICLE 23. And if the litigants refer to a witness, the allowance for travel expenses of the officials [sent for the witness] must be paid in advance: to the sergeant, up to 100 *versts,* according to old custom; to the constable, or the archbishop's squire, or the herald, or the informer, four *grivna* up to 100 *versts.* And if a litigant refers to a witness whose residence is more than 100 *versts* distant, and the other litigant agrees to refer to the same witness, the latter is summoned. But if the other litigant refuses to pay his share for summoning a witness from a distance over 100 *versts,* he may produce his own witness. And the term for summoning a witness from a distance not over 100 *versts* is three weeks. And it is the loser of the suit who finally covers the expenses for the summoning of a witness, but the amount is paid in advance to the sergeant. . . .

GLOSSARY

BELA, silver coin; fur, presumably ermine.

BLOODWITE, *vira,* a fine payable to the prince for the murder.

BOT, *golovnichestvo,* amends payable to the relatives of the murdered man.

CHELIADIN, a member of the lord's household; a slave.

CHERNYE LIUDI, literally "black men," men of lower classes.

DACHA, grant.

DENGA, a term borrowed from the Mongolian: a monetary unit. In modern Russian the plural form, *dengi,* is still used to denote "money."

DIKAIA VIRA, "dark" bloodwite, that is, bloodwite paid by the members of the guild collectively, especially when the murderer is unknown.

DOKLAD, in Novgorod, Court of Reexamination; proceedings by which a case was referred to the higher court by the judge of the lower court.

DVORIANIN, a princely servitor of lower grade; in modern Russian, a nobleman.

GOLOVA, head, *see* WERGELD.

GOLOVNICHESTVO, *see* BOT.

GOSPODA, in Pskov, the Supreme Court; in Novgorod, the House of Lords.

GRIVNA, monetary unit.

GUILD, *see* VERV'.

IZGOI, in the twelfth century, a freedman. However, as used in the Short Version of the Russian Law, the term must have had a different connotation.

IZORNIK, tenant farmer.

KHOLOP, slave.

KLIUCHNIK, a home steward; in Novgorodian administration, sealer.

KNIAZH MUZH, literally, the prince's man; a princely official, a boyar.

KONETS, in Novgorod, a city district.

KONIUKH STARY, steward of grooms; master of stables.

KOSTKI, a tax on merchandise.

KUNA, marten fur; a monetary unit. (See Introduction, Section VII.)

LIUDIN, a man; a member of the guild; a commoner.

LIUDSKAIA VIRA, literally, "men's bloodwite"; bloodwite paid by the members of the guild collectively (see DIKAIA VIRA).

MIR, community; township.

MOLODCHI CHELOVEK, literally, "younger man," a lower-class burgher.

MUZH, a man; a man of noble birth, a knight.

MYT, custom duties.

NAMESTNIK, lieutenant.

NOGATA, monetary unit.

OGNISHCHANIN, a man belonging to the prince's hearth; princely servitor; bailiff.

OGNISHCHE, hearth.

OGORODNIK, gardener, vegetable gardener.

PERESUD, in Novgorod, Court of Appeals; appeals procedure.

POKRUTA, in Pskov, subsidy in money or seeds granted by the owner of the land to the tenant farmer.

POLE, literally, field; duel field, hence, judicial duel.

POSADNIK, mayor.

POSLUKH, witness.

PRIGOROD, borough, literally, "by-town."

PRISTAV, constable.

REZANA, monetary unit.

RIADOVICH, contract laborer.

ROLIA, plow land.

ROTA, oath as part of the court procedure.

SAMOSUD, taking the law in one's own hands; settling with the criminal in a private way.

SHABR, a co-owner; a member of a cooperative corporation.

SHESTNIK, infantry soldier; a sergeant.

SLUGA, literally, servitor; in late Middle Ages, a princely councilor of second class, lower than a boyar.

SMERD, peasant.

SOBOR, cathedral; in Pskov, also an ecclesiastical district.

SOFIAN, literally, St. Sophia's man, that is, one connected with the cathedral of St. Sophia in Novgorod; a squire in the service of the Archbishop of Novgorod.

SOTNIK, hundreder.

STAROSTA, elder, alderman.

SVOD, "confrontment," examination; procedure for identifying a thief.

TAMGA, a term borrowed from the Mongolian: internal customs duty.

TIUN, a steward; a justice.

TIUN OGNISHCHNY, bailiff, see OGNISHCHANIN.

TYSIATSKY, chiliarch; commander of the "thousand," that is, of the city militia. In the Novgorod court system, the chiliarch was in charge of the conduct of litigations about commercial transactions.

ULITSA, street; in Novgorod, an association of neighbors living in the same street, a guild.

VDACH, the recipient of a grant (*dacha*).

VECHE, people's assembly; city assembly.

VEKSHA, literally, a squirrel; a monetary unit.

VERST, VERSTA, measure of length, equal to 0.6 miles.

VERV', guild; an association of neighbors in a country district.

VEVERITSA, see VEKSHA.

VIDOK, eyewitness.

VIRA, see BLOODWITE.

VIRNIK, collector of bloodwite payments.

VOLOST', a country district.

VOLOSTEL, bailiff.

WERGELD: GOLOVA, ZA GOLOVU, literally, "head"; the value of the head, that is, the value set on a man's life. It is according to that value that the normal amount of the *bot* as well as that of the bloodwite was computed.

ZAKUP, indentured laborer. *Roleinyi Zakup*, agricultural laborer; see ROLIA.

ZHIT'I LIUDI, in Novgorod, middle-class burghers.

3

THE CHRONICLE OF NOVGOROD

EXCERPTS

No medieval Russian town is as well known to us as is Novgorod. This is due, primarily, to the vast archeological excavations undertaken there in the 1930's, and again in the 1950's. A large number of excellent studies on every aspect of Novgorod life is available in Russian. The literature in English is still rather scanty, but we are fortunate in having a translation of the Novgorod annals. These illustrate many facets of the life of this medieval center of more than a quarter-million population. The chronicle speaks rather plainly and records the joys as well as the woes of the republic's life. The entry for the year 1471 is of course of Moscow authorship.

For documents on Novgorod see George Vernadsky's *Medieval Russian Laws* and Basil Dmytryshyn's *Medieval Russia*. Two general works which treat of Novgorod are Vasily Kliuchevsky's *A History of Russia*, Vol. I, and George Vernadsky's *Russia at the Dawn of the Modern Age*. Novgorod's geographic expansion is described in Robert Kerner's *The Urge to the Sea* and in Raymond Beazley's "The Russian Expansion towards Asia and the Arctic to 1500," *American Historical Review*, Vol. XIII. The life of the Novgorod church is described in George Fedotov's *The Russian Religious Mind*, Vol. II. Novgorod's foreign relations are analyzed in J. F. I. Fennell, *Ivan the Great of Moscow*, and in his article, "The Campaign of King Magnus against Novgorod in 1348," *Jahrbücher für Geschichte Osteuropas*, March, 1966. Sergei Eisenstein's film *Alexander Nevsky*, dealing with one of the city's heroes, can be obtained from Brandon Films (offices in New York, Chicago, and San Francisco). See also two new articles: Jel Raba, "Novgorod in the 15th Century," *Canadian Slavic Studies*, Fall, 1967, and his "The Fate of the Novgorodian Republic," *Slavonic and East European Review*, July, 1967.

GENERAL INTRODUCTION   *By* ROBERT MITCHELL AND NEVILL FORBES

1. THE REPUBLIC OF NOVGOROD

. . . From the beginning of the Crusading Age to the fall of the Byzantine Empire Novgorod is unique among Russian cities, not only for its population, its commerce, and its citizen army (assuring it almost complete freedom from external domination even in the Mongol Age), but also as controlling an empire, or sphere of influence, extending over the far North from Lapland to the Urals and the Ob. The modern provinces of

From Robert Mitchell and Nevill Forbes (eds.), *The Chronicle of Novgorod (1016–1471)* (London: Royal Historical Society, 1914), pp. vii–xxviii, 1–2, 11, 14, 21–22, 50, 64, 83–84, 86–87, 96–97, 141, 169–70, 186–88, 208–9, 211, 213, 216. Reprinted by permission of the Royal Historical Society.

Novgorod, Olonets, and Archangel, with portions of Vologda, Perm, and Tobolsk, represent this empire. . . .

As in the Middle Ages, the *Side* or *Quarter of St. Sophia* still lies on the left of the Volkhov, the *Commercial Side* on the right. The eleventh-century Cathedral of the Holy Wisdom, "Saint Sophia," is still one of the historical monuments of Russia, while the walls of the Kremlin of Novgorod show how slender was the fourteenth-century Russian skill in fortification. . . .

Novgorod, in the days of its power, is in name an elective Principality, in fact something like a democratic Republic. The *Veche,* or General Assembly of the citizens, is the ultimate and irresistible authority, though its ordinary activities are of course limited by other forces, ecclesiastical, commercial, aristocratic, and princely.

(i) The power of these Electoral Princes rests mainly on their own personality, and their capacity of maintaining popularity and organizing support. In modern language, Novgorod is largely governed by the party system. While the Prince can command a majority, or at least avoid open defeat, he is secure, except against surprise: as soon as his party is the weaker, the result is inevitable. In the language of the Chronicle, they "show him the way out."

From the earliest times the citizens are noted for their "free spirit." At the beginning of Russian history we have their traditional revolt against the very Rurik they had just called in to found the new Slav-Scandinavian people of Rus—"Our Land is great, but there is no Order or Justice in it; come and . . . rule over us." A century later, Svyatoslav proposes to govern Novgorod by ordinary officials, but the city insists on a son of the Grand Prince. "We know how to find another Prince." The menace is heeded (964–72).

Yaroslav the Lawgiver (1016–54),

one of the real statesmen of Russian history, fully recognizes the power and value of Novgorod. Above all his other favours, tradition singles out the Charters or Privileges granted by him to the city—a Russian parallel to the "Good Laws of Edward the Confessor," or the German Town Charters of Charles the Great.

As the old Russian Federation, under the Grand Princes of Kiev, falls to pieces in the twelfth century, Novgorod republicanism develops. The sovereignty is treated as purely elective, and deposition becomes well-nigh parallel to election. A prince installed one year may be "shown out" the next. . . .

There is another side to the picture. In the changeful line of Novgorod princes we meet sometimes with men who rule. Yaroslav the Lawgiver, in the eleventh century, is such a sovereign; Alexander Nevsky, in the thirteenth, is another. From 1240, when he gains his "eponymous" triumph upon the Neva, till his death in 1263, Alexander dominates Novgorod. He even makes the Republic diplomatic. After the intoxicating victories of the Neva over the Swedes (1240), and of Lake Chudskoe over the German Knights (1242), it was hard to submit to the Mongol taxgatherer (as in 1259). But Alexander realizes that to defy the Horde is to complete the desolation of Russia. The hero of Novgorod at last persuades her of the humiliating truth. He rides out with the Mongol emissaries, whom he had guarded day and night from mob violence, and under his protection "the accursed ones" go "through the streets, writing down the houses of the Christians." To save the Russian remnant, Alexander journeys repeatedly to the Western Tartar army (or *Golden Horde*) upon the Volga—once at least to the Great Khan in Mongolia (1246–50). Death overtakes him on his way home from the Golden Horde in 1263. The news reaches Novgorod as the Eucharist is finishing; turning to the people, Archbishop Cyril tells the disaster—"The sun of the Russian land has set, my children." "Grant, Merciful Lord," exclaims the Chronicler, "that he may see Thy Face in the age to come, for he has laboured for Novgorod, and for the whole Russian land."

Yet even this hero of the North, fresh from the victory of the Neva, has for a time to leave Novgorod, "with his mother and his wife . . . having quarrelled" with the citizens. Better thoughts come with reflection. At the beginning of the next year Alexander is recalled (1241). . . .

(ii) The crisis of 1471, ended by the victory of Moscow, brings into relief the second person in the temporal polity of the Republic—in "the accursed" *Posadnitsa* Martha, wife of the *Posadnik,* Governor, or Burgomaster Simon Boretsky. This remarkable woman, a Russian parallel to Elizabeth of England, Catherine de Médicis, and the rest of the brilliant female offspring of the Classical Renaissance, almost succeeds in detaching Novgorod from Russia and the Eastern Church, and is therefore not greatly flattered by the Chronicle of the city, in a last section thoroughly pervaded by Muscovite influence. The hatred of her opponents shows the influence which one *Posadnik* at least is able to exercise. But usually the *Posadniks,* like the princes, are creatures of the popular will. They are set up and cast down almost as frequently, and their fate is harder. Deposed princes are "shown the road," but deposed or unpopular governors are often killed. Thus in 1134, 1146, 1156, 1161, 1171, 1172, 1175, 1189, 1205, 1219, we hear, within one century only, of *Posadniks* expelled or restored; in 1167 and 1209 of *Posadniks* executed or proscribed. . . .

Strong governors perhaps appear more often than strong princes. And such governors play a leading part in home and foreign politics, as in 1135, 1214, 1215, 1264.

At times, as in 1218, the Novgorod Democracy keeps a *Posadnik* in office, in defiance of the Prince. "He is blameless, and we will not give in to this." Yet next year the fickle monster may displace its favourite, only to replace him the same winter.

(iii) As everywhere in Old Russia, the Church in Novgorod is of the first importance. Vast as is the sphere of the Latin Church in Western history, the Greek Church in Russia is only less prominent because of the absence of Papalism, of religious war, and (in comparison) of ecclesiastical encroachment.

As early as 1034 *Nestor* mentions one of the *Vladykas* or Archbishops, whose succession is so carefully recorded, and in 1045 the historic Cathedral of the Holy Wisdom, the *Hagia Sophia* or *Sophiisky Sobor* of Novgorod, is built by Yaroslav the Lawgiver and his son Vladimir.

St. Sophia becomes the symbol of the freedom, prosperity, and powers of the city. "Where St. Sophia is, there is Novgorod," exclaims Prince Mstislav in 1215. "Come to your patrimony, to St. Sophia," the citizens beseech Prince Yaroslav. "With the aid of St. Sophia," Novgorod conquers in battle. Sooner than submit to the Mongol census (in 1259) the people resolve to "die honourably for St. Sophia." "I bow down to St. Sophia and to the men of Novgorod," says Mstislav, when negotiating for his installation as prince (in 1210). "I make my greeting to St. Sophia . . . and to you: God grant I may lie by my father in St. Sophia"—is the farewell of the same Prince to Novgorod. . . .

The Novgorod Chronicle, a work of ecclesiastics, abounds in references to church matters. Almost every other year we read of the consecration or adornment of a church or monastery, "a refuge for Christians, a joy to Angels, and ruin to the Devil." Often it is St. Sophia itself, Novgorod's Westminster, which is repaired or beautified, or which becomes the burial place of another prince. . . .

The Archbishops, usually chosen by the Prince and citizens—but needing confirmation by the "Metropolitan of all Russia" at Kiev, Vladimir, or Moscow —ultimately depend on popular favour. Thus in 1211 Mitrofan is exiled, "bearing this gladly, like John Chrysostom," and after eight years is recalled by the same popular voice (1219).

Monasticism, which began in the Eastern Church, and has always played so great a part in Russia, is strong at Novgorod. Many a time it is recorded how a bishop, abbot, prince, or rich man, founds a monastery—"a refuge for Christians and a delight to the faithful"; like the "Bishop's Court," the Russian monasteries serve at times as guardhouses for prisoners of state.

As in the West, so in the East. The greatest soldiers and statesmen may take refuge in the cloister. Alexander Nevsky himself, when he feels his mortal illness, is "shorn" as a monk (Nov. 14, 1263).

And abundant are the examples of prominent ecclesiastics of the Republic being "shorn into" (or "for") the *schema*, "choosing to lead a life of silence. . . ."

(iv) Beyond the ordinary business and business man of the average prosperous mediaeval town, the merchant and his trade play an exceptional part in Novgorod. For here was one of the four capital factories of the Hanseatic League in non-German lands.

Before, or during, the time of Frederick Barbarossa, foreign traders are noticed at Novgorod (1142); Bremen merchants appear in Livonia (1157); and direct commerce between Cologne and Russia is recorded (1165). The agreement concluded at the close of the Crusading Age (1269) between Novgorod, Lübeck, and Gothland, shows that the

Germans had long possessed a regular commercial status on the Volkhov. And the famous *Skra* or code of the German factory here goes back to the early thirteenth century (1225).

Half the town is known, we have seen, as the *Commercial Side*. Here the foreign traders had their quarters, their guildhall, their church (of St. Peter), their shops, stores, and dwelling-houses. This *Court of the Germans*, or *Court of St. Peter*, was built, like the Hansa settlements in Bergen and London, for defence as well as for trade, and was closed and guarded at night. At its head was a Council of Aldermen, with a President, the "[Chief] Alderman of St. Peter's Court." Common Rooms (very unlike those of Oxford) were maintained for all the Hanseatics, "summer and winter travellers" alike—both the privileged seafarers, and the landsmen who, as enjoying an easier life, had fewer privileges in the factory. The junior clerks and apprentices had plenty of freedom in the "children's room. . . ."

The growth of Hanse trade in Russia, during the Mongol Age (1220–1460), is not only due to the business ability of the German merchants. It is aided by the disasters (and consequent dependence) of the Russian people at this time —by Tartar, Lithuanian, and especially Teutonic, conquest.

Except in Flanders, no field of non-German trade gives so wide a Hanseatic picture, shows so many Hanse centres engaged in the local commerce. Merchants of Brunswick, Dortmund, Duisberg, Magdeburg, Munster, and pettier towns appear in Russia, especially in Novgorod, often travelling by the dangerous overland routes. And even mediaeval Russians sometimes ventured far overland in search of customers. . . .

Lastly, in the fifteenth century, foreign values and coined money are introduced into Novgorod traffic, and the old tokens superseded. Thus in 1410 "the men of

Novgorod began to trade in *Nemetski artugs* and Lithuanian *groshes* . . . doing away with skin-tokens," and in 1420 they "began to deal in silver coin," and sold the *Nemtsy* their *artugs* again.

(v) Every rank, power, and interest in Novgorod rests upon the sovereign people. As no dynasty can establish itself permanently, still less any aristocracy of western type, the Republic preserves with peculiar purity the ancient democratic ideas and institutions. Down to the Muscovite conquest, the city is more powerful than any of its lords, officials, or classes. The great popular assembly, comparable to that of Athens in power, is supremely characteristic of Novgorod among Russian states. The *Veche* invites a new prince, and arraigns, imprisons, or expels him when it pleases. It elects and deposes *Posadniks* and the lesser officers of state. Within the limits of the sacred lot, and of Orthodox feeling, it elects, as it can depose, the Archbishops. It decides peace and war, and punishes criminals. A bad character, or unpopular personage, may be hurled from the Great Bridge—or otherwise put out of the way—at the conclusion of a *Veche*.

Like the Polish Diets, the Novgorod *Veches* nominally respect the primitive Slavonic principle of necessary unanimity. But there is no real *liberum veto* on the Volkhov. Minorities in Novgorod are bludgeoned, ducked, drowned, "put to the edge of the sword," or expelled from the city. Prince or *Posadnik*—or any respectable party among the nobles or commons—can legally or practically summon the *Veche*, which usually meets either "at" (i.e. outside) St. Sophia, or in the *Court of Yaroslav* on the *Commercial Side*. Sometimes rival parties call rival *Veches*, which finish with a conference upon the Great Bridge, or with fighting. Matters of religion and morality are an important part of the work of the *Veche*, which banned pagan superstitions, punished the black art, designated the favoured few from whom a new archbishop might be chosen, or deposed an unpopular prelate.

2. THE EMPIRE OF NOVGOROD

. . . The first discovery of those two Siberias—European and Asiatic—which lay north and north-east of the primitive Russians, as far as the Polar Ocean and Tobolsk province, was the work of Novgorod. Probably about the time of the First Crusade (1096), and certainly before the Second (1147), the Republic had already come into touch with the country just beyond the Ural Mountains.

Long ere this, perhaps as early as the age of Cnut (1000–1030), the Novgorod pioneers had penetrated to Lapland, the White Sea, and even the Urals. One of the North Ural passes most likely corresponds to those Iron Gates where the men of Novgorod suffered disaster in 1032—"Few returned, but many perished there."

In 1079 we have the earliest reference of the Novgorod Annals themselves to these distant regions: "They killed Prince Gleb *beyond the Volok*" (in the Northern Dvina country) "on the 30th of May."

The time of Henry I of England shows Novgorod communicating with the Asiatic lands beyond the dividing range. Speaking of a year which apparently answers to A.D. 1112, the *Fundamental Chronicle*, usually known as *Nestor's*, tells how one Guryata Rogovishch of Novgorod sent his servant to the Pechora, how the Pechora folk then paid tribute to *Novgrad*, and how from the Pechora the messenger went on to Yugra. . . .

A tribute-gathering expedition in 1169 shows Novgorod active in the *Trans-Volok* or Northern Dvina basin, and may have been concerned with payments as far as Asia; and the foundation of Vyatka in 1174 carries permanent Novgorod settlement far nearer to Siberia, along a more southerly track. But in 1187, on the eve of the Third Crusade, *Yugra* appears tragically; both here and in lands west of the Ural the natives rise and massacre their Russian masters or customers. The punitive expedition of 1193–94 ends in disaster.

How and when intercourse with Asiatic Siberia is resumed we are not told; but this resumption possibly took place before the end of the Crusading Age, for in the agreement of 1264 between Novgorod and Prince Yaroslav, *Yugra*, like Perm and Pechora, appears among the domains or "claims" of the Republic. Sixty years later, in 1323 and 1329, Novgorod complains of outrages on its citizens travelling to *Yugra*. These outrages were often the work of Russian enemies (as at Ustyug) in the Northern Dvina basin, planted on the flank of the north-east trade-route from Novgorod, and a constant danger to its commerce. Again, the demand of Moscow, in 1332–33, for "tribute in silver" for the lands beyond the Kama—the first sign of coming Muscovite overlordship—probably has a special reference to the mines Novgorod had long exploited in the Northern Ural.

Lastly, in 1445, within a generation of the ruin of the Republic, we hear of a last vigorous effort to assert Novgorod rule in *Yugra*. Again the *Chronicle* tells of initial successes; then, as before, victory ends in ruinous defeat.

In 1471 Moscow crushes Novgorod, and takes over the Novgorodian empire. But even before this, the founder of the Moscow Tsardom, Ivan the Great, on his way to the subjugation of Novgorod, begins the conquest of the Asiatic Siberia with which Novgorod had dealt so long. . . .

Ivan Kalita had first turned Muscovite policy towards the Arctic Dvina; besides its wealth in furs and timber, he aimed at winning an outlet to the ocean. Some

seventy years later, his schemes are momentarily realized. In 1397 all the Dvina people are seduced from Novgorod, and "kiss the cross" to Moscow. The Grand Prince issues ordinances for his new subjects (in 1398–99),¸which are the earliest Muscovite laws known, and the first Russian laws preserved since Yaroslav [1016–54]. Yet in 1411, 1417, 1419, 1445, we find Novgorod again in possession of most of Siberia-in-Europe.

But finally the overmastering power of Moscow, which in 1452 chases an enemy through the Dvina lands, and in 1458–59 conquers Vyatka, achieves under Ivan the Great the complete destruction of Novgorod power on the Dvina, as elsewhere (1471). . . .

3. THE FOREIGN RELATIONS OF NOVGOROD

(a) *Novgorod and Kiev*

With Kiev, the so-called "Mother of Russian cities," the acknowledged head alike in politics and religion, during all the early centuries (*c.* 880–1169), the relations of Novgorod are naturally long and intimate. During most of this time the Grand Prince of Kiev nominates the Princes, and sometimes the *Posadniks*, of Novgorod, subject to the popular approval. And the Metropolitan of Kiev, with the same limitations, ratifies the episcopal elections.

Oleg, as Prince at Kiev, and chief of the Varangians in Russia, is said to have imposed a regular yearly tribute on Novgorod, about 881. His successor, Olga, "wisest of all persons," the pioneer of Christianity among the *Rus*, visits the city, from Kiev, in the next century, and establishes "depots for commerce" and "tolls and dues" on some of its waterways (*c.* 947–50?). Olga's son, the Great Vladimir, becomes Prince of Novgorod in 970, before he reigns in Kiev.

Through much of the eleventh and

twelfth centuries, the Novgorod Chronicle records events at Kiev (especially the succession of Kiev Princes and Metropolitans) or the embassies of Novgorod representatives as matters affecting the metropolis of Russia, and interesting to all Russians. The very name of *Rus* is long used to designate the Kiev region.

Yet the downfall of Kiev in 1169, when the Russia of the Forests humbles the Russia of the Steppes, is unnoticed in the Novgorod Annals. Even the final calamity, the Mongol storm of 1240, is only mentioned indirectly. On the other hand, the lesser disasters of 1203 and 1235, when heathen Kumans or Polovtsi, aided by traitor Russians, waste the city, are properly bemoaned by the Novgorod historian.

(b) *Novgorod and Moscow*

In 1325, we find the Archbishop of Novgorod visiting Moscow "for confirmation by the Metropolitan." For Ivan Kalita had just induced the Russian primate to move his seat from Vladimir, and Moscow had definitely taken the place of Kiev as the Canterbury or the Mainz of Russian Christianity.

In 1335, again, we find the Republic, despite "colonial" quarrels, recognizing the Prince of Moscow—this same "John of the Purse"—as Grand Prince, the secular head of the Russian people. Ivan visits Novgorod and "has a friendly talk"; Novgorod notables go to be honoured at Moscow.

In 1346 we first hear of the enthronement of the Moscow Grand Prince in Novgorod, as its Russian suzerain—though the Khan of the Golden Horde is still "Tsar," supreme even over Semeon the Proud, who after enthronement in Novgorod goes to "the *Low Country* on the Tsar's business." Yet Novgorod still struggles against Muscovite ascendency, appealing to the Tartar, on Semeon's death, to give the Grand Princedom to

Vladimir-Suzdal once more (1353); and though the intrigue is now unsuccessful, it momentarily succeeds a few years later (1360).

But in 1366 the Muscovite—now the famous Dmitri of the Don—is again Suzerain Prince, and quarrelling vigorously with the Republic about a Volga raid of Novgorod adventurers who had plundered Moscow merchants. Peace is made in 1367; the lieutenant of Dmitri is installed in Novgorod; and Novgorod helps Moscow against the hated Tver (1375), and accepts her decision in a dispute about the Metropolitan chair (1376).

On the other hand, Dmitri Donskoi confirms all the old rights of Novgorod in the year of his Tartar triumph at Kulikovo "in a clean field beyond the Don, on the birthday of the Mother of God" when, "preserved by God, he fought . . . for the Orthodox Faith, and for all the Russian land" (Sat., Sept. 8, 1380).

As the Tartar flood subsides, Moscow presses on Novgorod afresh, and in 1386 the Republic pays Dmitri a heavy fine (8,000 roubles) "for the guilt of the Volga men." Towards the close of the fourteenth century we find Novgorod (in 1391) again struggling to free itself, if not from political suzeraity, at least from the ecclesiastical jurisdiction, of Moscow. But before the end of 1393 (and this is prophetic) Novgorod yields, and concludes peace "on the old terms. . . ."

(c) *Novgorod and the Scandinavians*

. . . According to *Nestor*, Rurik settles first in Novgorod, when he enters Russia to rule the tribes that had invited the *Rus*. "And the Russian Land, Novgorod, was called [i.e., called *Rus*] after these Varangians; they [i.e., the *Rus*] are the Novgorodians of Varangian descent; previously the Novgorodians were Slavs."

The mastery of the *Rus* over the Slavs begins, therefore, with their settlement in Novgorod; but the great Northern town soon ceases to be their capital. After some twenty years, Rurik's successor, Oleg, takes Kiev and makes it his capital, and even the name of *Rus* now vanishes from Novgorod, and is usually, for centuries, connected with Kiev.

Yet, though abandoned by the sovereign clan of the *Rus*, Novgorod maintains its distinctive position. In reality it is the chief rival, and in commerce ultimately the superior, of Kiev among the early Russian states (880–1220). In Novgorod the Scandinavian element is stronger even than in Kiev—so strong indeed that Nestor considers it a Varangian town. Elsewhere we hear of the Varangian Church, of the Guildhall of the Gothlanders in twelfth-century Novgorod, and of other matters which prove the early prominence of Scandinavians, and especially of Swedes, in Novgorod traffic. But in the later Middle Ages the Scandinavians gradually give way to the Germans, and the Hansa comes to control Novgorod trade. . . .

And when we next hear of Scandinavian influence, as in 1142, it is purely hostile. Towards the close of the Crusading Age comes the decisive struggle of 1240, when, "through the power of St. Sophia and the prayers of the Mother of God," Swedes and Northmen are routed by that prince of Novgorod, who, from this day, is known as "Alexander of the Neva" (July 15, 1240).

After this Novgorod runs no serious danger from Scandinavia for another century, although at times there are rumours of wars. Thus in 1300 the Swedish attempts on the Neva are renewed: "The accursed came in strength, with . . . a special master from the great Pope of Rome, and they founded a town at the mouth of the Okhta, in the Neva, and strengthened it indescribably, calling it *Landskrona* [The Crown of the Land].

But by the power of St. Sophia . . . that fortress came to nothing," being captured by Novgorod men in 1301.

In the early fourteenth century, perhaps the greatest period of Novgorod power, the Scandinavian states secure the friendship of the Republic, at the cost of former ambitions. Thus, while Denmark concludes a treaty in 1302, Sweden, in 1323, acquiesces in a Novgorod colony at the Neva estuary on Orekhov island, and signs an "everlasting peace," which is renewed in 1338. . . .

(d). *Novgorod and the Mongol Tartars*

. . . Novgorod is the only Russian state, or city, of importance, which escapes full subjugation by the Mongols of the thirteenth century. And even Novgorod, saved from siege and sack behind her marshes, in a summer of providential wetness, becomes the vassal of the Tartars. . . .

But Novgorod, though saved for the moment, would soon have shared the fate of other Russian cities, if she had not averted the danger by prompt, ready, and undeviating submission. The princes and officials of the Republic now obey the "Tartar Tsar" in all things, visiting the Horde when summoned (as in 1247), doing homage, punctually paying tribute, admitting Mongol assessors and tax-gatherers (as in 1257). The orders of Batu brook no evasion or delay; and the hero, Alexander Nevsky, statesman no less than warrior, is specially prominent in his obedience. . . .

In 1315, after seventy years of peaceful, if hateful, vassalage, Novgorod is forced into momentary conflict with the Mongols, through the treacherous ambition of the rival Russian state of Tver. The Republic suffers a serious defeat, but repulses an attempt upon the city (1316). In the retreat the enemy lose their way among the lakes and swamps that protected Novgorod, and nearly perish of hunger, eating their horses and leather shields. Finally, an appeal to the Khan of the Golden Horde ends the trouble. In 1327 "a mighty Tartar host took Tver . . . and wasted all the *Rus* land, Novgorod alone being spared" —on payment of a round sum. . . .

(e) *Novgorod and the Lithuanians*

. . . In the fourteenth century the Lithuanians first become a serious political power under their Grand Prince Gedimin the Conqueror, who in 1326 appears as mediating between Novgorod and the Germans, and in 1331 as trying to appoint the bishop, as he had appointed the prince, of Pskov, "without regard to Novgorod . . . being carried away with presumption. . . ."

. . . With Vitovt, the last great Lithuanian conqueror (1392–1430), ends the brief hope that Lithuanian conversion might profit the Eastern Church. "For Prince Vitovt," the Novgorod Annalist bemoans in 1399, "had previously been a Christian . . . but he renounced the Orthodox Faith and adopted the Polish, and perverted the holy churches to service hateful to God. He thought," continues the Chronicler, "that he would conquer . . . the *Rus* land and Novgorod, but he thought not of the Lord's saying, A thousand shall flee at the rebuke of one." After his ill-starred conflict with Timur, he concludes peace with Novgorod "on the old terms" (1400).

Yet in the fifteenth century Lithuanian aggressions are again alarming. But for their preoccupation with the Germans, the Lithuanians might have attempted the conquest of all Russia. In 1404, Vitovt gains Smolensk; and in 1415 "by the sufferance of God," he reorganizes the Church in Little Russia, under a Latin Metropolitan. Again, in 1444, Vitovt's successor, Casimir, calls upon Novgorod to submit. The Republic "did not fall in with this," but the famine of 1445 aided his efforts; in their distress some of the Novgorod folk "fled to Lithuania," or "passed over to *Latinism*." More and more this is the danger at the end of the Middle Ages—leading to the conclusion, when Moscow destroys the Republic to keep it from "lapsing into *Latinism*."

(f) *Novgorod and the Germans*

The relations of Novgorod with the Germans are among the latest in historical order, on the political side—though of respectable antiquity on the mercantile. There is no clear reference in the *Chronicle* to the Teutons of the Continent, as opposed to the Scandinavians, before the time of the Third Crusade (1188). And, in the next century, the stirring events of 1201 and the years following —when the *Knights of the Order of Christ*, better known as the *Brethren* or *Bearers of the Sword*, are called in as temporal helpers by Bishop Albert of Riga; when historic Riga is thus founded; and when Riga Gulf lands and the country of the old heathen Prussians are conquered by these German Crusaders and by their colleagues of the *Teutonic Order* or *Order of St. Mary*— all pass unnoticed in the Novgorod Chronicle. . . .

But soon the Germans appear among the most dreaded foes of Novgorod and Russia. In 1242 the Swedish victory of Alexander Nevsky is followed by Alexander's revenge upon the German Order on the ice of Lake Chudskoe—"lest they should boast, saying, we will humble the Slovan race under us—for is not Pskov taken, and are not its chiefs in prison?" (April 5, 1242). . . .

Almost every decade of later Novgorod history gives us some notice of conflict, negotiation, treaty, or commerce with the Germans, mainly represented by the Teutonic Order and the Hanseatic League. But though lands and towns near or within the Novgorod frontiers are in German occupation throughout this period (*c.* 1200–1450) or a great part of it; though the whole Baltic coast, from Danzig to the Gulf of Finland, is at one time held by the order; and though such near neighbours as Pskov fall at intervals into the German grasp—yet the German peril is kept at arm's length, and Novgorod is never beleaguered (far less taken) by the Knights, even if her trade passes in great measure under Hansa control. . . .

THE CHRONICLE

And now let the Chronicle speak for itself.

A.D. 1016. . . . And at that time Yaroslav was keeping many Varangians in Novgorod, fearing war; and the Varangians began to commit violence against the wives of the townsmen. The men of Novgorod said: "We cannot look upon this violence," and they gathered by night, and fell upon and killed the Varangians in Poromon's Court; and that night Prince Yaroslav was at Rakomo. And having heard this, Yaroslav was wroth with the townsfolk, and gathered a thousand soldiers in Slavno, and by craft falling on those who had killed the Varangians, he killed them; and others fled out of the town. And the same night Yaroslav's sister, Peredslava, sent word to him from Kiev, saying: "Thy father is dead, and thy brethren slain." And having heard this, Yaroslav the next day gathered a number of the men of Novgorod and held a *Veche* in the open air, and said to them: "My beloved and honourable Druzhina, whom yesterday in my madness I slew, I cannot now buy back even with gold." And thus he said to them: "Brethren! my father Volodimir is dead, and Svyatopolk is Prince of Kiev; I want to go against him; come with me and help me." And the men of Novgorod said to him: "Yes, Prince, we will follow thee." And he gathered 4,000 soldiers; there were a thousand Varangians, and 3,000 of the men of Novgorod; and he went against him. . . .

And Yaroslav went to Kiev, and took his seat on the throne of his father Volodimir. And he began to distribute pay to his troops; to the *starostas* ten *grivnas* each, to the *smerds* one *grivna* each, and to all the men of Novgorod ten *nogaty* each, and let them all go to their homes. . . .

A.D. 1136. Of the year of the Indiction 14. The men of Novgorod summoned the men of Pskov and of Ladoga and took counsel how to expel their Prince Vsevolod, and they confined him in the Court of the Bishop, together with wife and children and mother-in-law, on May 28, and guards with arms guarded him day and night, thirty men daily; and he sat two months and they let him out of the town on July 15, and they received his son, Volodimir. And they made these his faults: I. He has no care for the serfs. II. Why didst thou wish to take thy seat in Pereyaslavl? III. Thou didst ride away from the troop in front of all, and besides that much vacillation, ordering us first to advance against Vsevolodko and then again to retreat; and they did not let him go till another Prince came. . . .

A.D. 1156. The men of Novgorod drove out Sudila from the *Posadnik-ship* and he died on the fifth day after that expulsion; and then they gave the *Posadnik-ship* to Yakun Miroslavits. The same spring, on April 21, Archbishop Nifont died; he had gone to Kiev against the Metropolitan; many others, too, said that having plundered St. Sophia, he went to Tsargrad; and they said many things against him, but with sin to themselves. About this each one of us should reflect; which bishop ornamented St. Sophia, painted the porches, made an ikon-case, and ornamented the whole outside; and in Pskov erected a Church of the Holy Saviour in stone, and another in Ladoga to St. Kliment?

And I think that God for our sins not wishing to give us his coffin for our consolation, led him away to Kiev, and there he died; and they placed him in Pechersk monastery, in a vault in the [church of the] Holy Mother of God. The same year the whole town of people gathered together, and decided to appoint as Bishop for themselves, Arkadi, a man chosen of God; and the whole people went and took him out of the monastery of the Holy Mother of God, both Prince Mstislav Gyurgevits, and the whole choir of St. Sophia, and all the town priests, the abbots and the monks, and they led him in, having entrusted him with the bishopric in the Court of St. Sophia, till the Metropolitan should come to Russia, and then you shall go to be appointed. The same year the oversea merchants put up the Church of the Holy Friday on the market place.

A.D. 1157. There was a bad tumult in the people, and they rose against Prince Mstislav Gyurgevits, and began to drive him out of Novgorod; but the Mercantile Half stood up in arms for him; and brother quarrelled with brother, they seized the bridge over the Volkhov, and guards took their stand at the town gates, and [so did] the others on the other side; and they were within a little of shedding blood between them. And then Svyatoslav Rostislavits and David entered, and that night Mstislav fled out of the town. After three days Rostislav himself entered, and the brothers came together, and there was no harm at all.

A.D. 1209. The men of Novgorod held a *Veche* over *Posadnik* Dmitri and his brethren, because they had ordered the levying of silver on the people of Novgorod, for collecting money throughout the district, fines from the merchants, for enforcing the collection of taxes at fixed times and everything bad. And they went to plunder their courts, and set fire to Miroshkin's court and Dmitri's, appropriating their effects, sold all their villages and servants, sought out their treasures, and took of them without number, and the rest they divided so that each got some, at three *grivnas* throughout the whole town, and took everything. God alone knows how much any took secretly, and many grew rich from this; and what was on the boards that they left to the Prince. . . .

A.D. 1224. The same year for our sins, unknown tribes came, whom no one exactly knows, who they are, nor whence they came out, nor what their language is, nor of what race they are, nor what their faith is; but they call them Tartars. . . . God alone knows who they are and whence they came out. Very wise men know them exactly, who understand books; but we do not know who they are, but have written of them here for the sake of the memory of the Russian Princes and of the misfortune which came to them from them. For we have heard that they have captured many countries. . . .

A.D. 1230. And we will turn to the preceding, to the bitter and sad memory of that spring. For what is there to say, or what to speak of the punishment that came to us from God? How some of the common people killed the living and ate them; others cutting up dead flesh and corpses ate them; others ate horseflesh, dogs and cats; but to those found in such acts they did thus—some they burned with fire, others they cut to pieces, and others they hanged. Some fed on moss, snails, pine-bark, lime-bark, lime and elm-tree leaves, and whatever each could think of. And again other wicked men began to burn the good people's houses, where they suspected that there was rye; and so they plundered their property. Instead of repentance for our wickedness, we became more prone to wickedness than before, though seeing before our eyes the wrath of God; the dead in the streets and in the market-place, and on the great bridge, being devoured by dogs, so that they could not bury them. They put another pit outside at the end of Chudinets Street, and that became full, and there is no counting [the number of bodies in it]. And they put a third at Koleno beyond the Church of the Holy Nativity, and that likewise became full, there was no counting the bodies. And seeing all this before our eyes we should have become better; but we became worse. Brother had no sympathy with brother, nor father with son, nor mother with daughter, nor would neighbour break bread with neighbour. There was no kindness among us, but misery and unhappiness; in the streets unkindness one to another, at home anguish, seeing children cry for bread and others dying. And we were buying a loaf for a *grivna* and more, and a fourth of a barrel of rye for one silver *grivna*. Fathers and mothers gave away their children into servitude to merchants for bread. This distress was not in our land alone; but over the whole Russian province except Kiev alone. And so has God rewarded us according to our deeds.

A.D. 1238. And the accursed ones having come thence took Moscow, Pereyaslavl, Yurev, Dmitrov, *Volok*, and Tver; there also they killed the son of Yaroslav. And thence the lawless ones came and invested Torzhok on the festival of the first Sunday in Lent. They fenced it all round with a fence as they had taken other towns, and here the accursed ones fought with battering rams for two weeks. And the people in the town were exhausted and from Novgorod there was no help for them; but already every man began to be in perplexity and terror. And so the pagans took the town, and slew all from the male sex even to the female, all the priests and the monks, and all stripped and reviled gave up their souls to the Lord in a bitter and a wretched death, on March 5, the day of the commemora-

tion of the holy Martyr Nikon, on Wednesday in Easter week. And there, too, were killed Ivanko the Posadnik of Novi-torg, Yakin Vlunkovich, Gleb Borisovich and Mikhailo Moiseivich. And the accursed godless ones then pushed on from Torzhok by the road of Seregeri right up to Ignati's cross, cutting down everybody like grass, to within 100 *versts* of Novgorod. God, however, and the great and sacred apostolic cathedral Church of St. Sophia, and St. Kyuril, and the prayers of the holy and orthodox archbishop, of the faithful Princes, and of the very reverend monks of the hierarchical *Veche*, protected Novgorod. . . .

A.D. 1240. In the winter of the same year Prince Alexander went out from Novgorod with his mother and his wife and all his court, to his father in Pereyaslavl, having quarrelled with the men of Novgorod.

The same winter the Germans came against the Vod people with the Chud people and ravaged them, and laid tribute upon them, and made a fort in the village of Koporya. Nor was this the only evil; but they also took Tesov and pushed to within thirty *versts* of Novgorod, attacking merchants, and hitherwards to Luga and up to [the village of] Sablya.

And the men of Novgorod sent to Yaroslav for a Prince, and he gave them his son Andrei. And then the men of Novgorod having taken counsel sent the Archbishop with others again for Alexander; and the Lithuanians, Germans and the Chud people invaded the Novgorod district and seized all the horses and cattle about Luga, and in the villages it was impossible for anyone to plough and nothing to do it with, till Yaroslav sent his son Alexander again. . . .

A.D. 1242. Prince Alexander with the men of Novgorod and with his brother

Andrei and the men of the Lower country went [in the winter in great strength against the land of the Chud people, against the Germans, that they might not boast, saying: "We will humble the Slav race under us," for Pskov was already taken, and its *Tiuns* in prison]. And Alexander occupied all the roads right up to Pskov; and he cleared, seized the Germans and Chud men, and having bound them in chains, sent them to be imprisoned in Novgorod, and himself went against the Chud people. And when they came to their land, he let loose his whole force to provide for themselves. And Domash Tverdislavich and Kerbet were scouring [the country] and the Germans and Chud men met them by a bridge; and they fought there, and there they killed Domash, brother of the *Posadnik*, an honest man, and others with him, and others again they took with their hands, and others escaped to the troops of the Prince. And the Prince turned back to the lake and the Germans and Chud men went after them. Seeing this, Alexander and all the men of Novgorod drew up their forces by Lake Chud at Uzmen by the Raven's rock; and the Germans and Chud men rode at them driving themselves like a wedge through their army; and there was a great slaughter of Germans and Chud men. And God and St. Sophia and the Holy Martyrs Boris and Gleb, for whose sake the men of Novgorod shed their blood, by the great prayers of those Saints, God helped Alexander. And the Germans fell there and the Chud men gave shoulder, and pursuing them fought with them on the ice, seven *versts* short of the Subol shore. And there fell of the Chud men a countless number; and of the Germans 400, and fifty they took with their hands and brought to Novgorod. And they fought on April 5, on a Saturday, the Commemoration Day of the Holy Martyr Feodul, to the glory of the Holy Mother of God. The same year

the Germans sent with greeting, in the absence of the Prince: "The land of the Vod people, of Luga, Pskov, and Lotygola, which we invaded with the sword, from all this we withdraw, and those of your men whom we have taken we will exchange, we will let go yours, and you let go ours." And they let go the Pskov hostages, and made peace. . . .

A.D. 1259. There was a sign in the moon; such as no sign had ever been. The same winter Mikhail Pineschinich came from the Low Country with a false mission saying thus: "If you do not number yourselves for tribute there is already a force in the Low Country." And the men of Novgorod did number themselves for tribute. The same winter the accursed raw-eating Tartars, Berkai and Kasachik, came with their wives, and many others, and there was a great tumult in Novgorod, and they did much evil in the provinces, taking contribution for the accursed Tartars. And the accursed ones began to fear death; they said to Alexander: "Give us guards, lest they kill us." And the Prince ordered the son of the *Posadnik* and all the sons of the *Boyars* to protect them by night. The Tartars said: "Give us your numbers for tribute or we will run away." And the common people would not give their numbers for tribute but said: "Let us die honourably for St. Sophia and for the angelic houses." Then the people were divided: who was good stood by St. Sophia and by the True Faith; and they made opposition; the greater men bade the lesser be counted for tribute. And the accursed ones wanted to escape, driven by the Holy Spirit, and they devised an evil counsel how to strike at the town at the other side, and the others at this side by the lake; and Christ's power evidently forbade them, and they durst not. And becoming frightened they began to crowd to one point to St. Sophia, saying: "Let us lay our heads by St. Sophia." And it was on the morrow, the

Prince rode down from the *Gorodishche* and the accursed Tartars with him, and by the counsel of the evil they numbered themselves for tribute; for the *Boyars* thought it would be easy for themselves, but fall hard on the lesser men. And the accursed ones began to ride through the streets, writing down the Christian houses; because for our sins God has brought wild beasts out of the desert to eat the flesh of the strong, and to drink the blood of the *Boyars*. And having numbered them for tribute and taken it, the accursed ones went away, and Alexander followed them, having set his son Dmitri on the throne. . . .

A.D. 1348. Magnus, King of the Swedes, sent to the men of Novgorod saying: "Send your philosophers to a conference, and I will send my own philosophers, that they may discuss about faith; they will ascertain whose faith is the better; if your faith is the better; then I will go into your faith, but if our faith is the better, you will go into our faith, and we shall all be as one man. But if you do not agree to uniformity, then I will come against you with all my forces." And Archbishop Vasili and *Posadnik* Fedor Danilovich and the *Tysyatski* Avraam and all the men of Novgorod having taken counsel together, replied to Magnus: "If thou wishest to know whose is the better faith, ours or yours, send to Constantinople to the Patriarch, for we received the Orthodox faith from the Greeks; but with thee we will not dispute about the faith. As to what grievances there may be between us, we will send about that to thee to the conference." And the men of Novgorod sent to Magnus the *Tysyatski* Avraam, Kuzma Tverdislav, and other *Boyars*. And Avraam and the others arriving at Orekhovets wished to go to Magnus, but Magnus was then on Berezov island with all his forces. And the men of Orekhov beat with their foreheads to Avraam not to leave their town,

but Kuzma Tverdislav with others went to Magnus; and Magnus replied to Kuzma: "I have no grievance whatever against you"; but he said thus: "Adopt my faith, or I will march against you with my whole force"; and he dismissed Kuzma and the others. On their return to Orekhovets they all shut themselves in the town, and Magnus came up against the town with his whole force, and began baptizing. . . .

A.D. 1397. The same year the Grand Prince Vasili Dmitrievich sent his *Boyars*, Andrei Alberdov with others, to the whole Dvina colony beyond the *Volok*, saying thus: "That you should give allegiance to the Grand Prince and leave Novgorod; and the Grand Prince will defend you against Novgorod and will stand up for you." And the men of the Dvina, Ivan Mikitin, the *Boyars* of the Dvina, and all the people of the Dvina gave their allegiance to the Grand Prince and kissed the Cross to the Grand Prince; and the Grand Prince against his kissing of the Cross to Novgorod seized Volok-Lamsk with its districts, Torzhok and its districts, Vologda and Bezhitsy; and then put off from himself his kissing of the Cross to Novgorod and threw up the sworn charter. And the men of Novgorod put off from themselves their kissing of the Cross, and threw up the charter they had sworn to the Grand Prince. . . .

And the men of Novgorod sent as envoys to the Grand Prince *Posadnik* Bogdan Obakunovich, Kyuril Dmitrievich, and other men of substance, with their Father the Archbishop.

And Archbishop Ioan gave to the Grand Prince his good word and blessing, and the envoys from Novgorod a petition, saying thus: "That thou, my Lord and son, Grand Prince, receive my benediction and good word, and the petition of Novgorod; that thou withdraw thy displeasure from thy free men of Novgorod, and receive them on the old terms; that there be no more shedding of blood among Christians, my son, during thy reign. And what thou hast taken from Novgorod against thy kissing of the Cross, the country beyond the *Volok*, Torzhok, Vologda and Bezhisty, that thou give up all that, and that it come to Novgorod as of old. And as regards the common jurisdiction on the borderland, forego, my son, that, for that, Lord Grand Prince, is not the old custom."

And the Grand Prince would not accept the blessing and the good word of the Archbishop, nor the petition from the Novgorod envoys; and he did not withdraw from Novgorod his displeasure, and he granted no peace, but the Metropolitan Kiprian dismissed his son Archbishop Ioan with honour and with his blessing. . . .

A.D. 1418. There was a sign in the Church of the Holy Martyr Anastasia: blood seemed to come from both sides of the robe of the image of the Holy Mother of God, on April 19.

The same month this happened in Novgorod at the instigation of the devil: a certain man Stepanko seized hold of the *Boyar* Danilo Ivanovich, Bozha's grandson, and, holding him, cried out to the people: "Here, sirs! help me against this miscreant." And seeing his cry folk dragged him like a miscreant to the people, beating him with wounds nearly to death, and they led him from the *Veche* and hurled him from the bridge. And a certain man of the people, Lichko's son, wishing him well, caught him up into his boat; but the people, enraged against that fisherman, plundered his house. And the aforesaid *Boyar*, wishing to avenge his dishonour, caught the impostor and put him to torture, and wishing to cure the evil, raised up still greater trouble; I will not recall the spoken words: "Vengeance is mine." And the people learning that Stepanko had been seized, began to summon a *Veche* in Yaroslav's Court, and a mul-

titude of people assembled, and they kept shouting and crying for many days: "Let us go against that *Boyar* and plunder his house." And they came armed and with a banner to Kuzma-Demyan Street, sacked his house and many other houses, and ravaged the quay in Yanev Street. And the people of Kuzma-Demyan Street became afraid at these robberies that worse would befall them, surrendered Stepanko, and coming to the Archbishop prayed him to send him to the meeting of the people. And the prelate heard their prayer and sent him with a priest and one of his own *Boyars*, and they received him. And again they became enraged like drunkards, against another *Boyar*, Ivan Ievlich, of Chudinets Street, and on his account pillaged a great many *Boyars'* houses, as well as the monastery of St. Nikola in the Field, crying out: "Here is the treasure house of the *Boyars*." And again the same morning they plundered many houses in the Lyudgoshcha Street, calling out: "They are our enemies." And they came to Prussian Street, but there they beat them off successfully. And from that hour the mischief began to increase. Returning to their own, the commercial side, they said: "The Sophia side is going to arm against us, and to plunder our houses." And they began to ring throughout the whole town, and armed men began to pour out from both sides as for war, fully armed, to the great bridge. And there was loss of life too. Some fell by arrows, others by arms, they died as in war, the whole town trembled at this terrible storm and great rebellion and a dread fell on the people on both sides. And Archbishop Simeon shed tears from his eyes on hearing of the internecine war between his children, and he ordered those under him to gather his congregation; and the Archbishop, having entered the Church of St. Sophia, began to pray with tears, and arraying himself in his vestments with his clergy he ordered them to take the Lord's Cross and the image of the Holy Mother of God, and went to the bridge, and there followed him the priests and servants of the church and all who called themselves Christians, and a great multitude, shedding tears and saying: "O Lord, make it to cease by the prayers of our lord." And God-fearing people fell in tears at the feet of the prelate saying "Go, Lord, and may the Lord cause this internecine war to cease, through thy blessing." And others said: "May this evil be on the heads of those who began the fighting." And on reaching the middle of the bridge the prelate raised the lifegiving Cross and began to bless both sides. And those who looked at the honourable Cross wept. The opposite side, hearing of the prelate's arrival, *Posadnik* Fedor Timofeich came with other *Posadniks* and *Tysyatskis* and bowed to the Archbishop; and he heard their prayer and sent the Archimandrite Varlam and his spiritual father, and an archdeacon to Yaroslav's Court to bestow the blessing on the acting *Posadnik* Vasili Esifovich and on the *Tysatski* Kuzma Terenteyevich, to go to their homes; and they dispersed through the prayers of the Holy Mother of God and with the blessing of Archbishop Simeon, and there was peace in the town. . . .

A.D. 1471. The Grand Prince Ioan Vasilievich marched with a force against Novgorod the Great because of its wrong doing and lapsing into Latinism. . . .

That tempter the devil entered in their midst into the wily Marfa Boretskaya, widow of Isaak Boretski, and that accursed [woman] entangled herself in words of guile with the Lithuanian Prince Mikhail. On his persuasion she intended to marry a Lithuanian *Boyar*, to become Queen, meaning to bring him to Great Novgorod and to rule with him under the suzerainty of the King over the whole of the Novgorod region.

This accursed Marfa beguiled the people, diverting them from the right way to Latinism, for the dark deceits of Latinism blinded her soul's eyes through the wiles of the cunning devil and the wicked imaginings of the Lithuanian Prince. And being of one mind with her, prompted to evil by the proud devil Satan, Pimin the monk and the almoner of the old Archbishop, the cunning [man], engaged with her in secret whispering and helped her in every wickedness, seeking to take the place of his lord as Archbishop of Great Novgorod during his life, having suffered much punishment for his rogueries; his desire had not been gratified, inasmuch as the Lord God had not favoured him in the drawing of the lot, and he was not, therefore, accepted by the people for the high office. . . .

This cunning monk Pimin sought his appointment by the apostate Grigori, spreading it among the people that he should be sent to Kiev where he would receive his confirmation, being unmindful of the words in the Holy Gospels spoken by the lips of our Lord: "He that entereth not by the door into the sheep-fold, but climbeth up some other way, the same is a thief and a robber." Now this cunning man not only sought like a wolf to climb over the fence into the sheep-fold of the house of Israel, but to scatter and to destroy God's church; and he in this wise ruined the whole of the Novgorod land, the accursed one. According to the Prophet: "He made not God his strength, but trusted in the abundance of his riches and strengthened himself in his wickedness." This Pimin did similarly trust in the abundance of his riches, giving of them also to the crafty woman Marfa, and ordering many people to give money to her to buy over the people to their will; and this accursed wicked serpent fearing not God and having no shame before man, has spread destruction throughout all the Novgorod land and destroyed many souls. . . .

The Grand Prince being informed of the unceasing evil doings of the men of Novgorod, dispatched to Novgorod the Great a challenge in writing, exposing the malpractices of the people and their treason, and announcing that he was himself marching with a force against them. The Grand Prince had first sent his *Voyevodas* Vasili Fedorovich Obrazets and Boris Matveyevich Tyushtev with his men of Ustyug, of Vyatka and of the Vologda district, to the Dvina and the country beyond the *Volok,* and into all the territories of Novgorod in those parts. In advance of his own force the Grand Prince sent an army under his *Voyevodas,* Prince Danilo Dmitrievich Kholmski and his *Boyar* Fedor Davidovich, accompanied by many others of his court; they were ordered to scour the country around Novgorod, towards Russa beyond the Ilmen lake and to burn all places of habitation. To his patrimony Pskov the Grand Prince sent to say that the men of Pskov should release themselves from their engagement on oath to Great Novgorod, and take to horse in his service against Novgorod which had abjured Orthodoxy and was giving itself to the Latin king. They issued forth at once with all the men of the country of Pskov, and at the instance of the Grand Prince they revoked their oath on the Cross to Novgorod the Great. . . .

The Novgorod country is filled with lakes and swamps, for which reason mounted forces were never employed against Novgorod by former Grand Princes and the wicked people in their wonted contumacy dwelled in security during the summer after, following their own evil ways from the autumn to the winter, and even up to spring time, by reason of the inundation of the lands.

By the beneficence of God, vouchsafed by God from on high to the Grand Prince Ioan Vasilievich of all Russia to the detriment of the Novgorod land, not a drop of rain had fallen during the summer, from the month of May to the month of September the land was dry and the heat of the sun had dried up all the swamps. The troops of the Grand Prince found no impediments and could ride in every direction over the country, driving the cattle over dried ground; thus did the Lord God through this desiccation punish the men of Novgorod for their evil-doing and subject them to the strong hand of the pious sovereign and Grand Prince Ioan Vasilievich of all Russia. When the men of Novgorod heard that the Grand Prince was marching upon them with a large army, those cunning men sent to him professions of duty and again asked for guarantees of security while proceeding with their evil doing. At the same time they sent forces from Novgorod the Great by the Ilmen lake in boats against the advancing columns of the Grand Prince, and fought them; but God aided the *Voyevodas* of the Grand Prince, and 500 men of Novgorod were killed and others were captured or drowned, while others fled back to the town informing the townsmen that they had been defeated by the *Voyevodas* of the Grand Prince. . . .

The pious Grand Prince was gladdened by the unspeakable mercy of God in the aid given to him from on high against his cunning enemies. Praising God and the most pure Mother of God for having frustrated their wicked design of corrupting the sacred churches of God, of causing agitations and of producing hostilities between great sovereigns to the utter discomfiture of all Orthodoxy. He found among the documents the draft of a treaty with the king, by the terms of which the men of Novgorod agreed to surrender all the towns and districts of the Grand Prince, with his lands and waters and with all the taxes of Novgorod the Great, setting forth the names of the envoys to be sent to the king—Panfili Selifontov and Kurila Ivanov, son of Makar—and naming him "our honourable king and sovereign." It is written, that their sickness shall turn upon their heads and their untruth shall descend upon them. So may it be with them for their craftiness and evil counsels. . . .

When the men of Novgorod were brought before the Grand Prince, he, the pious one, with a godly wisdom accused the crafty men of their cunning and dishonourable proceedings, of departing from the light of true worship and giving themselves up to Latinism, of surrendering themselves to the Latin king while being the patrimony of him the Grand Prince; and of surrendering to the Latin king according to the draft of a treaty with him all the towns, districts, lands and waters which belonged to him the Grand Prince of Moscow together with the taxes. Having found them guilty of all this, and being thus stirred against the men of Novgorod, he ordered them to execution by the sword, the chief *Posadniks*, among whom was Dmitri the eldest son of the charming Marfa, the town *Posadnik*; and she was also to lose her life by decapitation. . . .

4

THE DIG AT NOVGOROD

By Valentin L. Yanine

During the Second World War Novgorod was damaged by the invading Germans who, in addition to bombing and occupying the city, engaged in willful destruction of churches and other monuments. Nevertheless Novgorod remains a treasure house of the Russian past. It has also been the site of the largest archeological excavations undertaken during the Soviet regime. The author of the article below, a young Soviet archeologist who participated in the excavations, writes about the fascinating finds which have been unearthed there over the past decades.

An early Soviet historian who wrote about the city and its life was Mikhail Pokrovsky in his *History of Russia from the Earliest Times*. More recent Soviet accounts are by Mikhail Tikhomirov, *The Towns of Ancient Rus*, and Boris Rybakov, *The Early Centuries of Russian History*. There is a brief account by Robert Smith, "Some Recent Discoveries in Novgorod," *Past and Present*, May, 1954. The latest study, richly illustrated, is M. W. Thompson, *Medieval Novgorod*. On Soviet archeology in general see Alexander Mongait, *Archaeology in the USSR*, and Mikhail Miller, *Archaeology in the USSR*. An American comment is in Frederick Starr, "Archaeology in the Soviet Union," *Yale Review*, Winter, 1965. The quarterly *Soviet Anthropology and Archaeology* has appeared since 1962.

The study of the Russian Middle Age, utilizing archeology as a key, has scored great successes at Novgorod during these last years. The thick historical layer formed there over a period of a thousand years is at present being sifted by an important group of Soviet archeologists.

This focusing of attention on ancient Novgorod is explained principally by the outstanding role the city played in Russian history. Here were concentrated in earlier days the industrial, commercial, cultural, and military life of the vast regions of northwestern Russia. Novgorod was a center of the greatest importance, where, for centuries during its development, the principal historic laws governing the formation of Russian feudalism revealed themselves with the maximum of clarity.

The particular aspects of the social regime of Novgorod during its evolution led to the emergence of a state where characteristic signs of a republican order were in constant progress, to the detriment of the monarchical power of the

From *Midway* (Chicago), No. 5 (1961,) pp. 2–25.

47

prince, the former finally predominating over the latter in the fourteenth and fifteenth centuries.

Novgorod is a veritable treasure house of documentation which can be verified by cross-checking. There the writing of annals was traditional, and many local chronicles have come down to us, setting forth in consistent fashion the events of the eleventh to the fifteenth centuries. By virtue of the strict system followed, writings concerning affairs of state as well as private documents having an official character were carefully preserved, including a certain number of official documents which have also been preserved. The fact that Novgorod was not subjected to the Mongol invasion permitted its old artistic monuments to survive. Finally, the fact that, in the sixteenth century, Novgorod lost some of its importance and became a small provincial town preserved in the best possible way its architectural unity, its monuments, and its soil, despite the extensive construction carried on from the eighteenth to the twentieth centuries.

With its unprecedented collection of historical monuments, Novgorod offers enormous advantages to the archeologist. Certain factors, notably the high humidity of the soil, have influenced the formation of its historical layer. A constant humidity helps considerably to preserve ancient objects. Metal objects found in the soil are covered with a thin layer of corrosion which can easily be removed or regenerated, while organic materials totally penetrated by humidity keep their form entirely. This is the reason the many wooden remains of roadbeds, buildings, palisades, household utensils, etc., as well as grains, leather, and birch-bark articles, shreds of cloth, and chips of wood, are completely intact in the soil. In many Russian towns where organic refuse has decomposed, the depth of the historical layer is likely to be no more than one or two meters, while in Novgorod the stratification of the historical layer often reaches a thickness of six to eight meters. Since the city has existed for a thousand years, we may say that the top layer has risen on an average of about one meter a century.

The high soil humidity has had another important consequence. Before the eighteenth and nineteenth centuries, the inhabitants generally refrained from digging cellars for storing and preserving food beneath their houses, built principally of wood, as these were constantly threatened with flooding. Consequently, the top layer was not subjected to any important disturbances, and its exceptional thickness protected it against the excavating done in the nineteenth and twentieth centuries, which generally affected only the most recent levels of the historical layer. Moreover, in the Middle Age, Novgorod did not know the use of excavated foundations for wooden buildings, a process which always damages the historical layer in towns built on dry soil.

Thanks to these circumstances, Novgorod's historical layer, in contrast with that of many other Russian cities, is easily divisible into relatively thick levels of twenty to twenty-five years each. These levels are rich in ancient objects, whose dating is thus facilitated. The great number of finds which have been made here allows the use of statistics and affords constantly repeated verifications of the date obtained by stratigraphic observations. The Novgorod excavations permit the establishing of a precise chronological scale of the different categories of ancient objects; thus, these objects serve to date finds which until recently demanded far more complex procedures.

The work has a decisive importance for researchers still to be undertaken in Novgorod, for this is the first time that archeological chronology has acquired a precision equal to that of written sources.

The work is important also for the study of other cities of the Middle Age. Articles found in Novgorod may be local products, or they may come from Kiev, Smolensk, or Moscow, to say nothing of the Orient, Byzantium, and the West. Whereas at the site of their production many of these articles are dated within a period of one or two centuries, those taken from the Novgorod historical layer can be dated with greater precision.

The good preservation of wooden architectural remains allows us to reconstruct the plans of ancient dwellings with their outbuildings, including the slightest modifications made in them over the centuries; moreover, these remains allow us to state precisely, in correlation with the established buildings, the purpose of the series of objects found there and, using these as keys, to learn the character and the ownership of the dwellings.

The Novgorod diggings have been considerably facilitated by the fact that the present plan of the city goes back only to the eighteenth century and that its street pattern does not coincide with the ancient one. Vestiges of former streets and their buildings have remained separated from the new arteries of the community underground pattern, which can be extremely complicating in archeological work.

DIGGING UP A MEDIEVAL SUBURB

The systematic excavations at Novgorod began in 1929. They were undertaken on the initiative of Professor A. Artsikhovsky, who later became the permanent head of the expedition. Before the war, excavations were conducted on a small scale in different quarters of the city, with the essential purpose of determining beforehand the particular aspects of the historical layer to be explored and the vestiges that it might yield.

During work carried out in 1947–48,

on the site of the residence of Prince Yaroslav (eleventh century), and later on the site of the Novgorodian people's assemblies, excavations in one sector extended over 836 square meters. These allowed us for the first time to study in detail an important fraction of the former city and provided information from which could be drawn some very interesting conclusions. Nevertheless, their importance is relatively small in comparison with the large excavations undertaken in 1951 in another quarter of Novgorod, the suburb of Nérévo.

The noteworthy discoveries of 1951 clearly demanded a concentration of all efforts upon a single sector. Since then, the work has been resumed each year. The radius of the diggings extends to an ordinary quarter of town, which in the Middle Age was built over with dwelling houses. In eight years the excavations have involved a sector whose total area is more than 7,300 square meters. The exposed quarter is outlined precisely on the old medieval map of Novgorod, particularly because the arrangement of this part of the city goes back to the tenth century and remained unchanged up to the eighteenth century.

The plan of this sector is perfectly verified. Novgorod's streets have always been paved with large circular blocks, of a diameter up to a meter, set on crossbeams. So well preserved are these street foundations that they can still carry heavy loads. The lower circular blocks of the old wooden buildings and the buried part of the palisades are also well preserved.

The vertical section of the digging area is characterized by the same precision. The foundation of Novgorod's streets was renewed as the earth layer built up around it and was kept clean. Nevertheless, that layer, rising around the foundation, finally became higher than the street level. A new foundation of circular blocks was then installed, right on top of the old one, which could still give many years of service. Thus, the street beds of the fifteenth century had a number of older ones as their foundations. During excavations in the suburb of Nérévo, twenty-eight of these street beds were uncovered, the oldest dating from the tenth century, the most recent from the sixteenth.

These street foundations allow us to divide the historical layer chronologically, and the study of the successive layers of wood shavings, ashes, etc., allows us to establish a correlation between the foundation and a determined level with all the objects and remains of buildings found in it. Each level thus constitutes an archeological whole, which is the principal objective of the researches conducted at Novgorod. On the maps the excavation area can be shown as many times as there were roadbeds, that is to say, once in the space of a minimum of twenty-five years, and, in going over the maps, we see in succession the way in which the arrangement of the city has evolved from its beginnings.

The following figures give some idea of the extent of the diggings. The average thickness of the historical layer in the suburb of Nérévo is from seven to seven and a half meters. Toward the end of 1955, the remains of more than 5,500 buildings of different periods had be brought to light.

In the twelfth century and in the first half of the thirteenth, Novgorod received many objects originating in Kiev, notably certain articles of glass, wines contained in pottery vessels from the south, and objects made of Volhynie slate. Production of these articles stoped completely toward the middle of the thirteenth century, when the workshops at Kiev and in the other southern Russian cities were destroyed by the Mongols and the artisans were killed off or were taken away to Tartar cities. In Novgorod, half of the thirteenth century is marked by a reduction, which can be followed, in the quantity of objects of southern origin. Other dates are determined by means of coinage and of lead seals used by known historical persons (in eight years more than sixty seals were found), by means of articles bearing heraldic and other markings, found in different levels.

To cite a few examples: In Novgorod the production of ornaments in Baltic amber was highly developed, a fact confirmed by numerous finds of the remains of this production. Now the statistics of the finds show a remarkable decrease of these vestiges in the thirteenth century, which, indeed, was the period of the most intensive military clashes on the western borders of the territory and, naturally enough, had repercussions on the general state of Novgorod's trade with the West. Another example is the dating of the twenty-seventh level. Stratigraphically, it had been set provisionally in the seventh decade of the tenth century. In the following years, two treasures of coins from Central Asia were found, each one containing about nine hundred coins coming for the most part from Samarkand. One treasure, according to the least ancient coin, was dated as of 972, the other as of 975, thus confirming that the whole level had been correctly dated. Still another example: An analysis was made by Artsikhovsky of the twenty-three spurs which were found and which reproduced exactly by their form those used in the West and dated by means of the sculptures of the tombs of the kings where they were fashioned. In each case, the stratigraphical dating coincides exactly with the Western dates. Writings on birch bark, discovered during the excavations and bearing the names of historical persons, also give eloquent confirmation of the stratigraphic dating. We shall discuss this in greater detail below.

The scope of this article does not allow us to acquaint the reader with all the aspects of the study of Novgorod's antiquities, and we are therefore focusing only on the most important ones.

REVEALING ANCIENT PROFESSIONS

The foundation of feudal relationships throughout the territory of central and southern Russia, a foundation recognized without reservation, is the landed property of the princes and the boyars; and the foundation of city life, the development of trades. Now certain researchers considered Novgorod exclusively as a center of European commerce, and commerce for them was the unique basis of its historical development. It seemed that trading substituted completely for the professions and agriculture, since a market located at the crossroads could furnish all indispensable products. Only such industries as fishing, hunting, and the like appeared to be incontestably forms of the economic activity of the citizens.

It is evident that an exact idea of the economic life of Novgorod could be had only through excavations, for only the study of the numerous objects they revealed could help in fixing the production site. By comparing the quantity of objects brought into Novgorod and the products of the city itself, by comparing the importance of the different categories of imports, by clarifying the categories of objects needed most by the Novgorodians and which they had to import, we can finally determine the relationship which obtained at that time in the city's economy between the professions and commerce. The excavations permitted us to establish, first of all, that professions did exist in Novgorod, that they were varied, and that they had reached a high technical level.

Many and varied instruments used by artisans were discovered—not only instruments of general use but special ones as well, for working metals, wood, jewelry, leather, for engraving on bone, for weaving and shoemaking. The remains of artisans' shops and of the raw materials used, unfinished articles, and production wastes have all been found.

It is known that the working of iron is the principal trade—it produces not only items of daily use but, more importantly, work tools. Iron is the only metal whose deposits lie everywhere in eastern Europe (in the form of limonite). The discovery of iron blooms was often noted during the excavations at Novgorod. Nevertheless, that does not indicate the level reached by iron metallurgy in Novgorod itself. It was important to determine in what proportions they used their own iron production and that of other cities. Spectral analysis has shown that in the iron objects discovered during the excavations in southern Russian cities we constantly see the presence of titanium and chrome, whereas nickel and molybdenum are typical of the iron of Novgorodian origin. These latter elements are found in seventy-four out of eighty-two sample articles of iron from the Novgorod collections, selected for analysis, whereas traces of titanium and chrome are found in only a few.

The study of the structure of iron undertaken by Koltchine has shown that the artisans of Novgorod made a variety of instruments and utensils and practiced a large number of technological operations: hammering, forge welding, thermal treating, lathe shaping, cold-cutting, polishing, soldering, coating with non-ferrous metal, incrusting non-ferrous and precious metals, and art-forging. They made, in addition, different kinds of steel articles. The chronological study of the development of this technology has revealed that all those processes were already current in the second half of the tenth century and in the beginning of the eleventh, a period when a high-level technique had been attained, one which was maintained through the sixteenth century. Moreover, the artisans of Novgorod simplified their technology knowingly when they had to produce en masse for the market.

In contrast to ironwork, the production of articles of non-ferrous metals and of jewelry could not make use of local raw materials and had to have recourse to importation, first from the East (in the tenth and eleventh centuries) and later from the West (after the eleventh century). Novgorod did not, however, import the finished articles but rather the raw material. The many finds of crucibles and foundry forms, and the particular form of non-ferrous and precious metal objects, show that they were made in Novgorod.

The same rule is applicable when we study the work done in amber. This substance is not of local origin and reaches Novgorod and all of Russia through trade with the Baltic countries. But the work itself is specifically Russian, principally Novgorodian, as is shown by the discovery of a large number of discards, as well as crosses and the beads of semi-finished amber necklaces.

Perhaps the most striking example is furnished by the study of wooden objects. In the Novgorod historical layer combs are constantly being found—760 of them in 1956. Most of the wooden ones go back to the tenth, eleventh, thirteenth, and fifteenth centuries, while combs made of bone are dated, as a general rule, to the twelfth century. Ac-

cording to Vikhrov's researches, the wood of these combs is largely the box-wood which grows on the northern slopes of the Caucasus and on the Caucasian shore of the Black Sea, and the ornamentation on them is of Novgorodian origin. The absence of wooden combs in the twelfth-century levels is explained by history—at that time the trade routes between Novgorod and the south had been cut by the Polovetzs. Novgorod's artisans, no longer receiving their customary raw material, had to replace it with bone.

Novgorod had its own important handicraft base, and its development was much less linked with external trade than we were led to believe before the excavations.

AN EDUCATED POPULACE

Before the Novgorod excavations our idea of the level of education in the Middle Age was far removed from reality. Researchers tended to compare this level for city-dwellers from the eleventh to the fifteenth century with that of the rural area in the eighteenth and nineteenth centuries and assumed that only the richest urban circles, principally the clergy, knew how to read and write. The diggings have caused a revision of this idea. Objects marked with the names or initials of their owners were found successively on different levels. Inscriptions have been found on cobblers' lasts, fishing leads and floats, cask covers, distaffs, and wooden dishes. The diversity of these articles, spread over a wide area, indicates that a vast circle of persons knew how to write. When we take into account the fact that objects were marked not so much for the purposes of the owners as for their neighbors, we must conclude that this circle of literate persons was still wider.

More exhaustive information has

been supplied by the discovery of writings on birch bark, the principal find of the Novgorod archeological expedition. It seemed, before this discovery, that the written source of the history of the Russian Middle Age before the fifteenth century had been completely exhausted. The chronicles and official documents only depicted the history of the Middle Age in a clearly limited way, relating principally the political and military activity of the Russian sovereigns. The annals were in large part a chronicle of aristocratic families and could serve only to a slight degree as ethnographical documents. While we were able to establish the detailed biography of certain princes, hierarchical chiefs, and boyars, the simple citizen or the peasant lost even his name.

Now the individuality of a man with some education leaves traces in history: it is encountered again and again in his inscriptions, his letters, and his memorandums. Archeologists have long wondered whether the soil could preserve such documents down to our times. We have the answer. Parchment and paper generally decompose in the ground, and the text written in ink is lost. But such writings were not the only kind in the Middle Age. Moreover, they were costly, and their use was limited. Study of the writings of a more recent period (seventeenth and eighteenth centuries) has shown that in Russia a cheaper, and consequently more accessible, material was used—birch bark. Certain sources indicate that its use goes far back.

At Novgorod, birch-bark sheets are perfectly preserved and have attracted attention from the very beginning of the diggings. Each piece of birch bark— and tens of thousands are encountered —was studied. At the time this was prompted by a fact which appeared to be incontestable—that, if damp soil

preserves birch bark, the inscriptions carried on the bark cannot, on the contrary, subsist in any clear manner, and one can only reconstitute them according to the faint traces left by ink which has been leached out by water. On July 26, 1951, the first inscription on birch bark was discovered, and it gave totally different evidence. It was seen that the inscriptions were made, not with ink, but with a stylus, just as inscriptions are lightly engraved on wax tablets or as graffiti are done on plaster. The instruments used for writing, which were bone or metal points, are sometimes highly ornamented. Dozens of examples have been found so far and are under special study.

This was a historical source in principle entirely new, for in the majority of cases the writings consisted of letters on the most varied and often most insignificant subjects. The oldest so far discovered has been dated as middle eleventh century, the most recent as belonging to the end of the fifteenth century. The character of these documents shows that they come from the most diverse milieux of Novgorod's society— from the *possadnik,* chief of the boyar republic, down to the simple weaver, anxious to ship out the order she has filled.

It is extremely important that these writings on birch bark do not in their assemblage constitute archives. They are constantly being found on different levels and in different sectors of the diggings. Just as today we throw away our notes and our rough drafts of accounts which we no longer need, so did medieval Novgorodians dispose of their useless notes.

Since we raised earlier the question of the extent of education, let us note two circumstances. First, a considerable percentage of the writings stems from peasants and artisans. The author's profession is clearly indicated in them, and certain letters give technical recipes (for example, Document No. 288 contains a recipe for dyeing silks) or we find accounts relating to a craftsman's order for raw materials, or, again, notes about soil cultivation. In the second place, the authors or recipients of numerous documents are women, which can be an eloquent indication of the high level of education.

We have already mentioned the letter of a female weaver of the fifteenth century; here again are letters sent to Nastassia and those which she wrote. The first is from her husband, Boris, requesting that she send him his shirts which he has forgotten to take with him; the second, written by Nastassia, tells her parents of Boris' death. A letter from Piotr to Maria (fifteenth century) is important also for the economic history of Novgorod. Piotr has gone to Poozérié (on the shore of Lake Ilmen, southwest of Novgorod) to cut hay, but the residents of the area have seized his hay, and he begs his wife to send him a document confirming his rights to the piece of land. Evidently, Piotr was not one of the great landowners, in which case the villagers would not have dared to enter into conflict with him.

It is very interesting, in judging the development of education, to look at a whole series of birch-bark writings going back to the end of the twelfth century and the beginning of the thirteenth. They come from a small boy, from six to ten years of age, named Onfim, who was learning to write. We have fifteen letters containing the alphabet, lessons in writing by syllables, and the first model letters. Being a schoolboy, he divided his attention during the lessons between his work and his penchant for drawing in the blank corners of his

sheet of birch bark—he draws little men, men on horseback riding down their enemies, and even a portrait of himself, disguised as a fantastic animal. These sketches gave the clue to his age. The expedition has collected other remains of schoolwork—exercises for boys studying in other grades, the cover of a penbox showing a model alphabet and belonging to the end of the thirteenth century or the beginning of the fourteenth, and even a silly schoolboy joke of the time, a cryptographic inscription on birch bark. The abundance of these documents clearly indicates that the teaching of reading and writing to children was one of the major concerns of medieval Novgorod.

The birch-bark documents collected so far have now become a base from which we may draw important historical conclusions. Through topographical study of them, we can learn the names of the owners of the sites where the excavations are made. Often writings addressed to the same individual are found in the limits of the same piece of ground. Analysis of certain writings has permitted us to establish the fact that two large pieces of property belonged to the family of the boyars Ontsiforovitch, known through the annals and other documents. From this family there came eminent *possadniks* of Novgorod, among them Ontsifor Loukitch, famous in the city's history toward the middle of the fourteenth century, and his son, Youri Ontsiforovitch, a *possadnik* at the beginning of the fifteenth century. Writings sent to Ontsifor and to Youri, as well as to other members of this line of boyars, were found.

All the writings connected with this family offer great interest, since for the first time the researcher is led into the circle of the daily preoccupations of the boyar aristocracy when it was in power.

Analysis indicates clearly the real basis on which the boyars' power and that of the state of Novgorod rested. Not once do these writings treat of mercantile matters—on the contrary, all have more or less to do with great landed property.

Document No. 94 is addressed to Youri Ontsoforovitch by the peasants, who complain to their master about his overseer: "Nothing pleases him," they write. No. 97, also sent to Youri, concerns the sale of rye. No. 167 is sent by the miller of the village of Zlostitsy which belongs to the *possadnik;* he begs Youri to take pity on him and not to send another miller to replace him.

A complete series of writings is addressed to Mikhail, the son of Youri Ontsiforovitch. In No. 157 the peasants object to an order issued by the boyar concerning the transfer of an inclosed piece of land. No. 242 does not bear the addressee's name, but it was found on property belonging to Mikhail. It concerns dependent peasants, subject to state labor, who are awaiting the boyar's orders for threshing rye and who complain about the poor condition of draft animals: "Those who have horses have poor ones; others have none." Document No. 297 indicates that a certain Serguéi is informing Mikhail Yourievitch of the theft of a millstone for milling rye. No. 301 reminds us of the doleful state of the peasant class, announcing to Mikhail, who is called here the son of the *possadnik,* that half his domain is empty and that the other peasants are making ready to flee and are begging the boyar to reduce taxes. Document No. 311 describes the whole system for us, indicating particularly that between Mikhail Yourievitch and the peasants there is a small feudal holder.

We have cited here several documents sent to persons already known from other sources. The list of writings concerning real estate can be made many

times longer. Land is the principal preoccupation, and this interest is not limited to the boyar aristocracy of Novgorod. By studying documents of this kind, Artsikhovsky has come to the conclusion that *the major portion of the population of this city was composed of feudal holders, large and small. They resided in Novgorod, where they were citizens and belonged to the popular assembly* (*vetché*). In our opinion, this circumstance explains in large measure the particular forms of the state of Novgorod, which rested on a wide base, composed of many classes of large, average, and small landowners.

Writings dealing with commerce offer much interest, particularly those which show that the specialization of trade was quite advanced. The merchants of Novgorod in the fourteenth and fifteenth centuries were going through an important stage which led them from highly diversified into *extremely specialized commerce.* For example, writings concerning the fish trade show an *exclusive interest on the part of some dealers in lake trout, while others specialize in sturgeon.* Dealers have a large number of professional fishermen under their control.

Certain documents bring in new and interesting information on Novgorod's trade with the outside. Document No. 125 (end of the fourteenth century), for example, is the request of a certain Marina to her son to buy her some *zendien*—the term used for a cotton stuff woven in the village of Zenden near Boukhara in Central Asia. A document from the early twelfth century concerns far-ranging journeys of Novgorod merchants into the interior of the Russian territories.

Other writings mention political events of the history of Novgorod. The owner of an inclosed piece of land, where excavations are now being conducted, was a tax farmer for the lands of Karelia, which paid tribute to Novgorod. In the levels corresponding to his time (first half of the fourteenth century) several documents were found bearing Karelian names, as well as letters sent to Novgorod by Karelians. One of these documents can be dated exactly, for it mentions the peace just signed between Novgorod and Sweden, in the days of Prince Youri. With the same expressions, the annals relate the peace of 1338, whose conclusion did not definitively decide the political affiliation of certain frontier tribes of Karelia. And, in fact, the writing in question, sent to the tax farmer before his departure for the north, urges him to exercise extreme prudence and compliance in levying tribute on those territories.

Other documents concern justice and discuss questions of depositions or tell of punishments which have been inflicted. Another series consists of wills of different persons.

The terminology found gives a wealth of information important for understanding the system of measures and especially the history of the circulation of money in the Middle Age, for monetary units are constantly mentioned, and certain of the terms have not been known before. The writings on birch bark have enriched knowledge with a long series of unknown names; they have also taught us many new words which were not listed in vocabularies of the medieval Russian language. But their principal value lies in the fact that they are unique documents on mores and customs of the period, and they bring the researcher into the area of the daily interests of people who disappeared many centuries ago. Thus they bring an epoch back to life.

THE "MUSEUM CITY"

Novgorod is often called a "museum

city." It is indeed an original and unprecedented museum of medieval art, its many old churches constituting the principal element of its whole. The succession of architectural styles can be followed almost uninterruptedly over a long period, from the eleventh century to our own day. The icons and frescoes created by Novgorodian painters are universally known, as well as the magnificent examples of the chiseler's art, preserved on chasubles. During the Middle Age, Novgorod attained one of the highest points in Russian art. However, its art monuments were subject to the same influence as the annals. The churches and their ornamentation, the icons and artistic vessels, were ordered by the boyars and the higher clergy of the city. Thus they show not only the masterful skill of Novgorod's artists but also the tastes of distinct social levels. To what extent was aesthetic perception common to medieval Novgorodians? That question has appeared to be insolvable.

Excavations carried out in other Russian cities had led to the deduction that there was a deep contrast between the people's artistic taste and the aesthetic concepts of the richest segment of the society. The reason for this had been the absence of art objects in the archeological finds of ancient Russian dwellings. An important circumstance, however, was overlooked—man of the Middle Age was surrounded by a world of wooden objects which could not be preserved unless the historical layer met the requisite conditions. Through diggings in cities located on dry ground, archeologists were unable to get any idea of the ornamentation and the furnishing of the dwellings or of the utensils and household items then in use. It is precisely the ornamentation of objects used by man during his whole lifetime which can best reveal the level of his aesthetic education.

The Novgorod excavations have allowed us to amass a huge collection of the most diverse objects, all having the common feature of ornamentation. Most of the objects made of wood—whether spoons, combs, bowls, parts of wagons, or furniture—are covered with sculptured designs. Often an engraved tracery design completely covers the article and in most cases is executed with a sure and accustomed hand and with a developed sense of composition. The excavators found a large number of decorated door frames and tapestries in birch bark, set off with ornamentation. Highly worked are the cradles and the birch-bark fishing floats and basket covers. The desire to embellish often gave birth to true works of art which became a part of the daily life of the simple city dweller.

In this connection we can cite certain remains of wooden flatware from the twelfth and thirteenth centuries on which dragons and other monsters are perfectly depicted, a wooden spoon bearing a finely executed design of a horseman, and dippers with handles worked into the shape of monsters. A true masterpiece is the sculptured wooden head of a clean-shaven man, apparently a portrait, going back to the twelfth or thirteenth century.

Bone objects offer the same interest. In the eyes of a Novgorodian of the Middle Age, work in bone, like that in wood, offered an opportunity for applying his artistic skills. At present, a large collection of bone plates of different uses has been assembled. Perfectly depicted on them are dragons and other monsters, and there are bone handles in the form of stylized birds' heads, etc.

A highly important analogy is seen in the way in which ordinary objects and religious objects are ornamented.

We find again the same motifs in the interior ornamentation of stone church walls and windows. As for book ornamentation, it derives entirely from that of ordinary wooden objects.

A most interesting find, and one which has profoundly modified the ideas we had of the character and the ways of the development of Russian art, is that of two wooden columns found in the level corresponding to the middle of the eleventh century. They had served first to support the flooring of a house in the early part of the century and had then been cut into circular blocks to serve as street paving, the form in which they were discovered. The surface of the columns is entirely covered with a chiseled design of wide interlacing bands in which are set medallions, one showing a centaur, another a griffin.

While the tracery on the columns is a current motif with the Slavs and is well known on Balkan stone monuments and on numerous objects coming from the Novgorod diggings (beginning at the earliest levels), the figures on the medallions reveal a detailed analogy with the chiseling on stone in the churches of Vladimir-Souzdal at the end of the twelfth century and in the early thirteenth, and particularly with the designs of monsters found on the walls of the cathedral of Saint George in Youriev-Polski, built in 1234. These analogies show an artistic unity, a close bond between outstanding architectural monuments and ordinary objects which have artistic interest. And their importance is considerable for still another reason.

The stone reliefs of the churches of Vladimir-Souzdal belong to the great creations of Russian medieval art and have long had the effect of magnificent flowers sprung forth in a desert, for their originality did not seem to have been nourished by the sap of Russian art. We found no close analogy with other more recent Russian monuments. For that reason many scholars tended, in the course of discussions on the origin of these reliefs, to establish a correlation with Western or Caucasian art. It has now become evident that these works of art are bound to the Russian soil, for their prototype is being rediscovered repeatedly in the chiseling on wood which researchers had almost never seen prior to the excavations at Novgorod. The Novgorod column with its griffin and centaur is two hundred years older than the reliefs of Vladimir-Souzdal. In Novgorod, wood-chiseling was not transformed into stone-chiseling, since the material used for the construction of Novgorodian churches was the soft milling stone from Ilmen. The Vladimir architecture makes use of a harder stone, better suited to artistic chiseling.

The Novgorod excavations also afford interesting results under the heading of "methodology." Their scope has always posed many problems in connection with the organizing of the work. During archeological diggings over a large surface, the evidence-bearing cover being quite thick, the greatest efforts and costs have to do with the removal of earth which has been examined. Its transportation becomes more difficult as the diggings extend in breadth and in depth.

That is why the Novgorod expedition insisted from the very beginning on mechanizing the work to the greatest possible extent. It goes without saying that the only "mechanism" acceptable for actual digging is, and will always be, human hands. To facilitate the work, a large number of conveyor belts is used to remove earth from the interior of the excavation and bring it to the

outside. At great depths, the earth is removed by means of carts and electric skip hoists. The surface is cleared of mounds of debris from the preceding year by the most efficient means, the bulldozer. The expedition's experience in applying mechanization has been described in detail in Soviet archeological literature and is being adopted by other expeditions. The collections assembled during the diggings, because of their great size, permit the application of scientific methods, such as spectral and structural analysis of objects of antiquity.

In recent years an effort has also been made to verify chronological conclusions through the study of the magnetic property of the old ceramics. The study of numerous vestiges of old revetments and constructions will also make possible the establishment of a dendrochronological dating system for Novgorod and the surrounding areas.

The expedition has important tasks to finish. In particular, it must complete the diggings in the suburb of Nérévo. We should also like to terminate researches on the site of the ancient domains where only partial excavations have been conducted, especially on the properties of the two *possadniks*. The expedition plans next to transfer digging to another quarter of the city, where an important sector must come under research. By comparing the results obtained, we will be able to state definitely those conclusions already reached in a general way concerning the character of this medieval city. Finally, there is a great need for augmenting the Novgorod excavations by archeological study of the medieval rural area of the state of Novgorod. This will be one of the next important tasks.

The time is fast approaching when medieval Novgorod will be, for the most part, an open book, making known to us the names of its former residents, their thoughts, their way of life, and the insights we have, until recently, so greatly lacked.

5

RUSSIAN EPICS

The pages which follow are a sample of the *byliny*. These are epic folk songs loosely connected with some historical person or event and much embellished with fantasy. The name *bylina* ("what happened") is a scholarly term coined in the 1830's; peasants call these songs *starina* ("what is old"). These epics are old, as old as the dawn of Russian history, but they were first recorded only in the sixteenth century, ironically enough by an Englishman, Richard James. They were chanted by narrators (*skaziteli*) without musical accompaniment. Such narrators are still found in the Russian Far North and in parts of Siberia. Most *byliny* are connected with Kiev and the reign of Vladimir (978–1015); the Novgorod cycle is less prominent.

It appears that the merchant Sadko was a historical personage. The Novgorod chronicle records in 1167 that one Sadko raised a stone church in the city to the saints Boris and Gleb. Vasili Buslaev seemed to have been his contemporary; the same chronicle records under the year 1171 the death of one "Vaska Buslaevich," who is referred to as a *posadnik*, not a *tisiatskii*. Kirsha Danilov, mentioned below, collected *byliny* in the eighteenth century.

In addition to the collection we have used, there are anthologies of *byliny* by Leonard Magnus (*The Heroic Ballads of Russia*) and by Isabel Hapgood (*Epic Songs of Russia*). Carl Stief is the author of *Studies in the Russian Historical Song*. H. M. and N. K. Chadwick discuss the *byliny* in *The Growth of Literature* (Vol. II). Serge Zenkovsky's *Medieval Russia's Epics, Chronicles and Tales* should also be used. For a Soviet interpretation, see Yuri Sokolov's *Russian Folklore*, pp. 291–341, and the chapter on Novgorod literature, pp. 278–95, in N. Gudzy's *History of Early Russian Literature*. The Sadko legend has been turned into an opera by Rimsky-Korsakov and filmed in color by the Soviets. The film *Sadko* is available from Brandon Films (offices in New York, Chicago, and San Francisco). There is much interesting information on the *byliny* as a genre in C. M. Bowra's *Heroic Poetry*. See also George Fedotov's *Russian Religious Mind*, Vol. II. Alexander Kaun's *Soviet Poets and Poetry* has samples of twentieth-century *byliny* with Lenin and other Communist notables as the heroes.

SADKO, THE RICH MERCHANT OF NOVGOROD

RECORDED BY KIRSHA DANILOV

As over the sea, the blue sea,
There sailed, there sped thirty ships,

From N. K. Chadwick, *Russian Heroic Poetry* (New York: Cambridge University Press, 1932), pp. 134–55. Reprinted by permission of the publisher.

Thirty ships, one falcon ship
Belonged to Sadko, the rich merchant.
And while all those ships were flying like
falcons,
One falcon ship was becalmed on the
sea;
Sadko the trader, the rich merchant,
spoke:
'Ho you clerks, you hired men,
You hired men, subordinates!
Assemble all of you in your places
And carve lots in heavy wood blocks,
And all of you write your names on
them,
And throw them into the blue sea.'
Sadko threw a light one made of hops,
And on it he had inscribed his signa-
ture,
And Sadko himself pronounced judg-
ment:
'Ho you clerks, you hired men,
Hearken to my just words:
Let us fling them into the blue sea.
Those of us which float upon the sur-
face—
Theirs must be righteous souls,
But whichever of them sink into the
sea—
We will drown them into the blue sea.'
But all the lots floated on the surface,
As if they had been ducks bobbing on
the water.
One lot only sank into the sea,
Into the sea sank the lot made of hops,
The lot of Sadko, the rich merchant.
Sadko the trader, the rich merchant,
spoke:
'Ho you clerks, you hired men,
Hired men, subordinates,
Cut lots made of willow,
And write all your names upon them;
And I pronounce this judgment upon
them:
Whichever lots sink into the sea—
Theirs must be righteous souls!'
But Sadko threw in a steel lot,
Even of blue steel from beyond the sea,
A whole twenty pood in weight.

And all the lots sank in the sea.—
One lot only floated on the surface,
The lot of Sadko, the rich merchant.
Then spoke Sadko the trader, the rich
merchant:
'Ho you clerks, you hired men,
You hired men, subordinates,
I myself, Sadko—I know, I see—
I have traversed the sea for twelve years.
To the Tsar beyond the Sea
I have never paid tribute, or duty,
And in the blue Khvalinsk Sea[1]
I never threw bread and salt.—
Upon me, Sadko, has death fallen;
And do you, ye traders, rich merchants,
You, my dear sworn companions,
All of you good vendors,
Bring me my cloak of sables.'
And hastily Sadko arrayed himself,
He took his resounding gusli,
With splendid strings of gold,
And he took his precious chessboard
With its golden pieces,
Its precious carved pieces,
And they lowered the gangway of silver,
Of silver covered with red gold.
Sadko the trader, the rich merchant,
walked along it,
And let himself down into the blue sea;
He seated himself on his golden chess-
board;
And the clerks, the hired people,
The hired people, the subordinates
Drew back the gangway of silver,
Of silver covered with red gold,
Drew it on to the falcon ship,
And Sadko was left in the blue sea.
And the falcon ship departed over the
sea.
And all the ships flew like falcons;
But one ship sped over the sea
Like a white hawk,—
The ship of Sadko, the rich merchant.
Loud were the prayers of the father and
mother

[1] This name occurs very commonly in the *byliny*, and appears to be used of different seas. Here the geography of the poem makes it clear that the reference is to the Baltic.

Of Sadko, the rich merchant.
Calm weather set in
Bearing along Sadko, the rich merchant.
Sadko the trader, the rich merchant, . . .
Saw neither mountains nor shore. . . .
Sadko was carried to the shore,
And there he, Sadko, marvelled.
Sadko emerged on the steep strand,
Sadko walked beside the fiery[2] sea,
He . . . came upon a grand izba,[3]
A grand izba, built entirely of wood;
He found the doorway and he entered
    the izba;
And there lay the Tsar of the Sea on a
    bench:
'All hail to you, trader, rich merchant,
God has granted me my heart's desire.'
And Sadko remained there for twelve
    years.
And then the Tsar of the Sea bethought
    him of Sadko.
'Play, Sadko, on the resounding gusli.'
And Sadko began to entertain the Tsar,
He began to play on the resounding
    gusli,
And the Tsar of the Sea began to caper
    and dance.
He plied this Sadko, the rich merchant,
With drinks of every kind;
Sadko drank his fill of all kinds of
    drinks,
And Sadko fell down, for he was quite
    drunk.
And Sadko the trader, the rich mer-
    chant, fell asleep,
And in his sleep Saint Nikolai appeared
    to him,
And addressed him in the following
    words:
'Hearken, Sadko, trader, rich merchant!
Rend asunder your golden strings,
And cast away your resounding gusli.
Your playing has plunged the Tsar of
    the Sea into a fit of dancing,

2 I.e., with the rays of the setting sun.—Ed.

3 The *izba* is the wooden hut of the Russian
peasants.

And the blue sea has grown rough,
And the swift streams have overflowed.
Many falcon ships are sinking,
Many sinful souls are sinking,—
Souls of our orthodox people.'
At this Sadko, the trader, the rich mer-
    chant,
He rent asunder his golden strings,
And cast away his resounding gusli;
The Tsar of the Sea ceased capering and
    dancing,
The blue sea grew calm,
The swift streams became tranquil,
And in the morning the Tsar of the Sea
    began,
He began to exhort Sadko:—
For the Tsar of the Sea wished to marry
    Sadko,
And he brought before him thirty maid-
    ens.
Nikolai enjoined him in his sleep:
'Hearken, you trader, you rich mer-
    chant,
The Tsar of the Sea is about to marry
    you,
He is bringing thirty maidens.—
Do not take a fair, white, rosy one,
Take a kitchen wench,
The foulest kitchen wench of all.'
And then Sadko, the trader, the rich
    merchant,
He made his choice and did not hesitate,
And he took a kitchen wench,
The foulest kitchen wench of all.
Sadko awoke from his sleep.
He found himself close to the city of
    Novgorod,
And his left foot was in the River Vol-
    khov;
And Sadko leapt up; he was startled;
Sadko cast his eyes on Novgorod
He recognised the church, his own par-
    ish,
That of Nikolai Mozhaiski.
He crossed himself with his cross,
And Sadko gazed on the River Volkh.—
From the blue Khvalinsk Sea,
Over the glorious mother, the River

Volkh,
There sped, there flew towards him thirty ships.
One was the ship of Sadko himself, the rich merchant;
And Sadko the trader, the rich merchant, welcomed them,
His dear sworn companions.
All the ships came to shore.
They cast their gangways on the steep strand.
The sworn companions stepped forth on to the steep strand,
And there Sadko gave them greeting;
'All hail to you, my dear sworn companions,
And worthy clerks!'
And then Sadko the trader, the rich merchant,
Made valuation from all the ships in the customs office
Of his twenty thousand treasures—
The estimate was not completed in three days.

VASILI BUSLAEV

SUNG BY FEDOTOV

Buslaev lived in Novgorod,
Buslaev lived for ninety years,
Buslaev ruled as *tysyatski*,
But as long as he lived he was never too old to rule,
He was never too old to rule, he was never displaced.
Buslaev never wrangled with the citizens of Novgorod,
He never disputed with stone-built Moscow.
He left behind him a beloved son,
Young Vasili Buslaevich.
And Vasili began to walk abroad in the city,
He began to play pranks on the children;
Whoever he pulled by the arm, the arm came off,
Whoever he pulled by the leg, that leg was no more.

Their mothers began to pursue Vasili,
They began to pursue him and make complaint:
'Hearken, honourable widow Amelfa Timofeevna!
Take away your dear son:
If you do not take away Vasili Buslaev,
We will duck him in the River Volkhov.'
In bitter sorrow
Vasili distilled green wine,
Vasili brewed sweet mead,
Vasili prepared an honourable feast
For the company of princes and boyars,
And for the citizens of Novgorod.
And Vasili spoke as follows:
'Whoever will empty a cup of green wine,
A cup containing a huge measure,
A cup weighing a heavy weight,
And whoever can endure my club of red elm-wood,
Let such come to my feast!'
Young Potanyushka came to the feast,
Young Potanyushka the valiant,
He came with limping gait and looks askance,
He took the cup in one hand,
He drained the cup at one draught.
Vasili Buslaevich beat him
About his rebellious head,
But Potanyushka endured it, he did not quail.
His golden curls were not ruffled,
He made his bow and went to the feast.
Kostya Novotorzhenin also came to the feast.
Then Vasili Buslaevich,
He set out the table of oak,
He spread it with sugared foods,
He spread it with honeyed drinks,
With mead which was quite mellow;
He rolled out casks into the fortified court-yard.
'Eat your fill of my food
And drink yourselves drunk on my drink,
Only do not take to quarrelling among yourselves.'
Then the citizens of Novgorod,

They ate their fill,
And they drank themselves drunk.
The red sun sank towards evening,
The honourable feast waxed merry,
And they all became merrily drunk,
And took to quarrelling among themselves.
And Vasili seized his club of red elmwood,
And began to lay about him right and left,
And took to belabouring the guests.
And the guests left the honourable feast all maimed.
'Devil take you and your feast, Vasili!
There has been too much eating and drinking at the feast,
And we have been crippled for life.'
Then the citizens of Novgorod,
They prepared their own honourable feast
For the company of princes and boyars,
And the mighty Russian heroes.
Vasili set off to the honourable feast;
But he did not go alone, he took his druzhina.
And his dear mother said to him:
'Hearken, my dear son,
Young Vasili Buslaevich!
You are going to an honourable feast
Where all the guests have been invited,
While you are going as an uninvited guest.'
'Hearken, dear mother,
Honourable widow Amelfa Timofeevna!
Even if I go as an uninvited guest,
Where there are seats, there I sit,
And what I can reach with my hand, I eat and drink.'
And Vasili went to the honourable feast;
But he did not go alone, he took his druzhina.
He held the cross in the manner prescribed,
He made his bow as it is enjoined:
'Greetings, Mikula Selyaninovich!
Greetings, Kozma Rodionovich!'
'Come along, Vasili Buslaevich,
Take a seat, Vasili, at the table of oak.'

Vasili took his seat in the place of honour;
Not alone did he seat himself, but his druzhina with him.
Then the guests who had been invited protested,
'Ho, Vasili Buslaevich,
You seat yourself in the place of honour
Though you are an uninvited guest,
And we other guests were invited.'
'Even if I am an uninvited guest,
Where there are seats, there I sit,
And what I can reach with my hand, I eat and drink.'
The red sun sank towards evening,
The honourable feast waxed merry,
And they all became merrily drunk,
And began to boast of this and that.
Then Vasili Buslaevich
In his drunken folly,
He laid a great wager,
To go at daybreak to the Volkhov,
To go with his druzhina,
And to fight against all the men of Novgorod.
Then Vasili left the honourable feast,
His head drooped over his right shoulder,
His eyes were downcast towards the damp earth.
He went to the princely palace,
His dear mother greeted him:
'Alas, my beloved son,
Young Vasili Buslaevich.
Why are you distressed and afflicted?
Was the place assigned to you not according to your rank,
Or did they pass you by when handing round the cup,
Or have the citizens mocked you in their drunkenness?'
Vasili could not give his mother
Either response or greeting.
But his bold druzhina spoke:
'The place assigned to Vasili was according to his rank,
And they did not pass him by when handing round the cup,
Nor did the citizens mock him in their

drunkenness;
But Vasili has laid a great wager
With the citizens of Novgorod,
To go at daybreak to the Volkhov,
To go with his druzhina,
And to fight against all the men of Novgorod.'
Then his dear mother,
The honourable widow Amelfa Timofeevna,
Thrust her shoes on to her bare feet,
Flung her sable cloak over one shoulder,
Took her golden keys,
And went into her deep cellars,
Filled a bowl with red gold,
And another bowl with pure silver,
And a third bowl with round pearls,
And came to the citizens at the honourable feast.
She held the cross in the manner prescribed,
She made her bow as it is enjoined:
'Greetings, Mikula Selyaninovich,
Greetings, Kozma Rodionovich!'
And she placed her gifts on the table of oak.
'Accept these gifts from Vasili
And pardon Vasili his fault.'
The citizens of Novgorod made answer:
'We will not receive gifts from Vasili,
And we will not pardon Vasili his fault.
Rather may God help us to overcome Vasili,
And to ride his good steeds,
And to wear his patterned robes,
And to take his golden treasure by force.'
Then the honourable widow Amelfa Timofeevna
Turned away from the honourable feast,
And kicked with her right foot
That cudgel of maple-wood—
And the cudgel flew away behind the fence,
Behind the fence, scattering everything in its course.
Vasili slept till dawn and took his ease,
Unconscious of the misfortunes which
had befallen him.
But a serving-maid approached him,
Coming for water to the spring,
And she addressed him thus:
'Alas, Vasili Buslaevich!
While you sleep and take your ease,
You are unconscious of the misfortunes which have befallen you:
Your bold druzhina are fighting
On the bridge over the Volkhov,
Their rebellious heads broken,
Their eyes all bandaged with kerchiefs.'
Then Vasili Buslaevich,
Very quickly he awoke from his heavy sleep,
Thrust his shoes on to his bare legs,
Flung his sable cloak over one shoulder,
And seized his club of red elm-wood,
And sped to the bank of the Volkhov.
And an old monk from the Andronova[4] monastery encountered Vasili,
On the bridge over the Volkhov,
Wearing on his head the great bell of St. Sophia.
And Vasili Buslaevich addressed him:
'Ho, you old monk of Andronova,
My godfather!
You did not receive an egg on Easter Sunday,
So I will give you an egg on St. Peter's day.'
And he belaboured him with his club of red elm-wood
About the great bell of St. Sophia,
And killed the old monk of Andronova, his godfather.

And he ran to the bank of the Volkhov,
And began to lay about him with his club:
Where he struck, a street was formed through the fallen,
Where he brandished his club a lane

[4] Again the singer has omitted several details of the story. When Vasili had been fighting for some time, and dealing great slaughter among the men of Novgorod, they went to intercede with his mother, who advised them to persuade his godfather, an old monk, to come and appease him.

was made,
And he slew all the citizens of Novgorod.
And the citizens went to Vasili's mother.
'We pray you, dear mother of Vasili,
Honourable widow Amelfa Timofeevna!
Take away your dear son,
Leave enough of the citizens to carry on
   the race.'
Then his dear mother,
The honourable widow Amelfa Timo-
   feevna,
She thrust her shoes on to her bare feet,
Flung her sable cloak over one shoulder,
And spend to the bank of the Volkhov,
Enveloped Vasili in her sable cloak,
And bore him off to her palace of white
   stone,
And cared for and tended the bold noble
   youth.

VASILI BUSLAEV, A VARIANT VERSION

RECORDED BY KIRSHA DANILOV, FROM
THE MINERS IN PERM

In glorious Novgorod the Great,
Buslaev dwelt for ninety years;
He dwelt with the people of Novgorod
   and never gainsaid them;
To the citizens of Novgorod
He never ventured a word of opposition.
Buslaev lived to a good old age,
A good old age, and at last he died.
After his long life
He left his property
And all his noble estate;
He left a venerable widow,
The venerable Amelfa Timofeevna,
And he left a little child,
His young son, Vasili Buslaevich.
When Vasili was seven years old,
His dear mother sent him—
The venerable widow Amelfa Timofeev-
   na—
To learn the art of reading.
And he mastered the art of reading.
She set him to writing with his pen,
And he mastered the art of writing.

She sent him to learn church singing,
And he mastered the art of singing.
And never had we had singing
In glorious Novgorod
To compare with that of Vasili Buslaev.
But Vasili Buslaevich began to consort
With drunkards and fools,
And the joyous, bold, fine youths.[5]
Then he took to drinking himself drunk,
And roamed about the city maiming
   people;
Whoever he caught by the arm—
He wrenched off that arm at the shoul-
   der,
And whoever he seized by the spine,
That person shrieked, roared, and crept
   about on all fours.
There arose a great outcry,
And the citizens of Novgorod,
The burgesses and the merchants,
They lodged a great complaint
With the venerable widow Amelfa Timo-
   feevna,
Against this same Vasili Buslaev;
And his mother proceeded to chide and
   rebuke him,
To chide and rebuke him, and to teach
   him sense;
But scolding was not to Vasili's liking.
He took himself off to an upper room,
He seated himself on a leather chair,
And he wrote proclamations in hand-
   writing,
And the matter was set down skilfully:
'Whoever wished to drink and eat at
   pleasure,
Let them throng to Vasili's broad court-
   yard,
And there drink and eat at will,
And receive patterned garments of all

---

[5] I think that this is a reference to the *veselÿe
lyudi* (lit. "joyous people"), a powerful guild
or body of popular entertainers, who, together
with the *skomorokhi*, played a prominent part
in Russian social life from the late Middle Ages
down to the close of the seventeenth century.
Numerous ecclesiastical proscriptions were
published against them, and they were finally
suppressed.

kinds.'
He dispersed the proclamations by the hand of his servant,
In the broad streets,
And in the narrow alleys,
And then Vasili stationed a vat in the midst of the court,
And filled the vat with green wine,
And dipped in it a goblet of huge measure.
Now in glorious Novgorod
The people were educated;
They read the writing of the proclamations,
And went to Vasili's spacious court,
To the vat of green wine;
First of all came Kostya Novotorzhenin.
Kostya entered the spacious court
And Vasili made trial of him,
He began to beat him with a club of red elm,
With a core in the centre
Of weighty lead from the east.
This elm club weighed twelve pood
And he beat Kostya over his rebellious head;
But Kostya proved his worth, he did not flinch,
And on his rebel head the curls did not stir;
Vasili Buslaevich spoke:
'Hearken, Kostya Novotorzhenin!
Be my sworn brother,
More to me than a brother born.'
And when they had lingered together for a short time
There came two brothers of boyar class,
Luke and Moses, a boyar's sons.
They came into Vasili's spacious court.
Young Vasili Buslaevich,
At once he welcomed and made merry with these youths.
Then came citizens from Zaleshen,
But Vasili did not dare show himself to them.
Moreover there came the seven brothers Sbrodovichi;
There collected and assembled
Thirty youths save one,

And Vasili himself made the thirtieth;
Whoever came their way, him they felled,
They felled him and flung him forth.
Vasenka Buslaevich heard
That among the men of Novgorod
The vigil-ale was brewed, the barley brew.
So Vasili set off with his druzhina,
He went to the guild of St. Nikolai:
'We will not pay you a paltry fee;
We will pay five roubles for every brother.'
And for himself Vasili gave fifty roubles.
And the churchwarden
Received them into the guild of St. Nikolai.
Then they began by drinking the vigil-ale,
This same barley brew.
Then young Vasili Buslaevich
He made off to the royal inn[6]
With his bold druzhina;
Here they drank their fill of green wine
And returned to the guild of St. Nikolai.
The day drew towards evening,
From young and old
The boys then began wrestling,
And boxing in the ring.
From this wrestling of the boys,
From this fighting with fisticuffs,
A mighty brawl arose;
Young Vasili tried to part the combatants,
But a certain fool obstructed him,
And boxed his ears.
Then Vasili cried out in a loud voice:
'Hearken, Kostya Novotorzhenin,
And Luke, Moses, boyar's sons,
They are beating Vasili here.'
The bold noble youths came hurrying up,
They soon made a clearance,
Many they beat to death,
They maimed them two and three at a

[6] Spirits were regarded as a monopoly of the Crown in Russia and formed a part of the royal revenues. The inns bore the royal arms, the Russian eagle.

time,
Breaking their arms and legs.
The burghers of the city screamed and
   roared,
Then Vasili Buslaevich spoke:
'Hearken ye, citizens of Novgorod,
I will lay a great wager with you,
I will attack all Novgorod,
Fighting and contending,
I and all my bold druzhina.
If you men of Novgorod should over-
   come me and my druzhina,
I will pay you tribute from now until
   my death,
Three thousand roubles every year;
But if I should overcome you
And you have to yield to me,
You must pay me the same tribute.'
And to this compact they set their hands.
Then a mighty onset took place between
   them. . . .
Vasili went along the River Volkhov.
And as he came along the River Volkhov,
Along the Volkhov street,
The noble youths descried him,
Even his bold druzhina,—
They saw young Vasili Buslaev.
Wings grew on the bright falcons,[7]
Hope dawned for the youths.

[7] This is a figurative expression common in
the *byliny*. The explanation follows in the next
line.

Young Vasili Buslaevich,
He came to the rescue of the youths.
With those citizens of Novgorod
He fought and contended all day till
   evening,
And then the citizens yielded,
They yielded and made peace.
They took binding documents
To the venerable widow Amelfa Timo-
   feevna,
They filled a bowl with pure silver,
And another bowl with red gold,
And went to the noble dwelling,
Beating the ground with their foreheads
   and bowing low.
'Venerable lady,
Accept our precious offerings,
And take away your dear son,
Young Vasili and his druzhina;
And we will gladly pay
Three thousand roubles every year,
And every year we will bring you
Bread from the bakers,
Rolls from the confectioners
And offerings from the young married
   women,
From the unwed maidens,
From tradesmen and everybody
Except priests and deacons.'
Then the venerable widow
Amelfa Timofeevna
Despatched a serving-maid
To fetch Vasili and his druzhina, etc.

6

FEUDALISM IN RUSSIA

By George Vernadsky; L. V. Cherepnin

In the West there is little agreement on the problem of defining Russian feudalism. Needless to say, Soviet scholars have their own interpretation of the matter. In this item we reprint the analysis of one of the most distinguished students of the subject in the West and a rebuttal by a leading Soviet medievalist. The second contribution comes from a volume entitled *A Critique of Bourgeois Conceptions of Russian History in the Feudal Period*, published by the Soviet Academy of Sciences in 1962.

For a Soviet work dealing with part of the problem under discussion here, see Boris Grekov's *Kiev Rus*. See also Alexander Vucinich, "The Soviet Theory of Social Development in the Early Middle Ages," *Speculum*, XXVI, 243–54. There are two articles on feudalism in Russia in Rushton Coulborn's volume *Feudalism in History*. For some comparisons, see L. Ignatieff, "Rights and Obligations in Russia and the West," Canadian *Slavonic Papers*, II, 26–37, and A. Miller's "Feudalism in England and Russia," *Slavonic and East European Review*, XIV, 585–600. See also V. Tschebotarioff-Bill, "National Feudalism in Muscovy," *Russian Review*, IX, 209–18. Another article by Vernadsky is "On Feudalism in Kiev Russia," *American Slavic and East European Review*, VII, 3–14. Horace Dewey writes on "Immunities in Old Russia" in the *Slavic Review*, December, 1964. Peter Struve discusses Russian feudalism in the *Cambridge Economic History of Europe*, Vol. 1. There is a chapter on "Feudalism in Early Rus" in Mikhail Pokrovsky's *History of Russia from the Earliest Times*, which represents the first Soviet interpretation of the subject dating from the 1920's. For a very recent Soviet view see Militsa Nechkina, " 'Ascending' and 'Descending' Stages of Feudalism," *Soviet Studies in History*, Vol. III, No. 1.

VERNADSKY: FEUDALISM IN RUSSIA

. . . There were undoubtedly present in the Russian socio-political background some of the prerequisites for feudalizing processes. There was a certain fusion of public and private law; there was a far-

From George Vernadsky, "Feudalism in Russia," *Speculum*, XIV, 302–23. Footnotes have been omitted. Reprinted by permission of the Mediaeval Academy of America.

From L. V. Cherepnin, *Kritika Burzhuaznykh Kontseptsii Istorii Rossii Perioda Feodalizma* (Moscow, 1962), pp. 83–90. Translated by Charlotte Feinberg. Footnotes have been omitted.

reaching dismemberment of political authority; there was to a certain extent an interdependence of political and economic administration. As to the Russian economic background, one has, however, to take into consideration that along with primitive rural economy the development of commerce in mediaeval Russia should not be underestimated.

In order to approach the problem of the origins and development of the social structure of mediaeval Russia we have first to examine both the geo-political and the historical background of the early Russian state. In both these respects the foundations of Russian state and society differ considerably from those of the countries of Central and Western Europe. . . .

During the period from the sixth to the eighth century A.D., East Slavic tribes expanded over most of the Russian plain, from the lower Dnieper and lower Don to the banks of the Lake Ilmen and the Upper Volga. Considerable portions of these tribes, including the remnants of the Antae, were by the beginning of the ninth century controlled by the Khazars. It seems that by this time the bulk of the Eastern Slavs were organized in clan communes (*zadrugi*) and that little was left of the aristocratic groups of the period of the Antae. There were, however, princes or chiefs at the head of some of the tribes, and the Varangian princes of Kiev in the ninth and the tenth centuries encountered considerable resistance on the part of some of these local chiefs. The period of Khazar domination must have resulted in a considerable influence of Khazar institutions upon those of the Eastern Slavs. Unfortunately, little is known about the organization of the Khazar state. Speaking generally, the Khazar domination followed the same general lines as that of the Scythians and the Sarmatians. Like the latter, the Khazars were originally nomads who

organized and exploited the neighboring agricultural peoples. The Mongol state of the Golden Horde was of the same type.

We may well believe that the Varangians after their conquest of the Eastern Slavs changed but little in the administrative system established by the Khazars. The taxation system of the Russian principalities of the Kievan period was probably based on the Khazar practice. As to the social structure of Khazar society, it is now common in Soviet historiography to label it as feudal. While such terms cannot be accepted without reservations, it seems that there was a deep social cleavage between the upper and the lower classes in the Khazar state. Wealthy Khazar lords owned slaves and used bonded laborers. On the other hand, there apparently was no far-reaching dismemberment of the political power, and the central government of the Khazars must have enjoyed considerable authority. The supreme power had, however, a dual aspect, divided as it was between the *Kagan* (Khan) and the *pekh* (*bek*). It is characteristic that the first Kievan princes assumed the Khazar title of *Kagan* with the apparent intention of enforcing their prestige.

The coming of the Varangians in the ninth century A.D. and the formation of the Kievan state brought about important changes in the social and political structure of Russia. The Varangian princes were followed by their retinue (*druzhina*), which formed the ruling class of the new state and in the same way as did the *Gefolgshaft* (*antrustiones*) of the German kings and dukes who established their control over Central and Western Europe in the course of the period from the sixth to the tenth century. It was the *antrustiones* who contributed most toward the establishment of the feudal régime in most of the countries of mediaeval Europe. The *druzhina* of the Kievan princes can be expected to have played the same rôle in Russia, and to a certain extent they actually did play such a rôle. It was chiefly from the *druzhina* that the land-owning aristocracy of mediaeval Russia, the boyars, emerged.

While the first members of the *druzhina* were Varangians, later on native Slavs as well as Turks and Iranians (Alans) were admitted, and by the eleventh century the *druzhina* as a whole became thoroughly russianized as the princes likewise were. The members of the *druzhina* were provided with offices and lands. The *druzhina* members who received land grants were in certain cases simultaneously invested with authority to collect taxes from and to administer justice to the neighboring population.

That feature alone might predispose the student of the period to draw parallels between the social tendencies of mediaeval Russia and those of mediaeval Europe, and we see that both Yushkov and Grekov have attempted to represent the social structure of Kievan Russia as a typical feudal régime. The existence of feudalizing processes in Kievan Russia cannot be denied. And yet one wonders whether the Kievan state and society taken as a whole could be called 'feudal.' Let us first examine the Russian political structure of the Kievan period. The starting point of Russian political development of this period was an attempt to organize a united state under the authority of the Kievan *Kagan*. After the death of Yaroslav I (1054), however, the process of dismemberment made rapid progress and resulted in the establishment of a loose confederation of princes ruling each in a principality of his own.

We must bear in mind, however, that in spite of the dismemberment of the political authority the power in that period belonged to the princes of the one ruling house only, that of Vladimir I (972–1015), that is, the so-called Rurikides. This ruling clan as a whole was considered to possess exclusive princely authority and no outsiders were admitted. It was only in the westernmost part of Russia, in Galicia, that a boyar once attempted to seize the princely throne (1213). But he was able to hold it for a brief term only.

Within the ruling house of Vladimir all princes were considered equal. No hierarchy of greater and lesser princes was established in this period in spite of the attempts on the part of some stronger princes, e.g., Andrei Bogolyubski, to introduce such régime.

On the other hand, in the western Russian principalities, some influence of the Romano-Germanic feudal concepts was noticeable. Prince Izyaslav I of Kiev, after losing his throne and being obliged to go into exile to secure the aid of the West in recovering his principality, pledged vassal allegiance to the Pope (1075). In the twelfth and early thirteenth centuries the principality of Galicia was subject to claims on the part of both Hungarian and Polish rulers offering their suzerainty over it. The intense intercourse between Galicia and the West can also be illustrated by the fact that a detachment of Galician troops participated in the Third Crusade (1190). The Byzantine Empire as adapted to a certain extent to the feudal concepts of the Comneni in the twelfth century was another source for the penetration of feudal ideas into Russia. Prince Vladimirko of Galicia was induced to recognize himself a vassal of the Emperor Manuel Comnenus.

With princely authority concentrated in the ruling clan, the political rôle of the boyars remained rather restricted throughout the whole period. It was in Western Russia only that the boyar aristocracy assumed greater importance. But even there, with one known exception, as referred to above, the boyars were excluded from enjoying princely power. At this period a boyar could become an influential agent of the princely administration, but he was not a ruler by himself. He was an assistant to the prince, but not his vassal in a political sense. There was no formal reciprocal contract which would bind a prince and a boyar. The boyar was free to shift from one prince to another.

We turn now to the social and economic aspect of Kievan Russia. The growth of large estates of the manorial type is an important trait of this period. Both the princes and the boyars owned land. The church, and particularly the monasteries, rapidly accumulated land estates as well. The labor was supplied partly by slaves, and partly by indentured laborers (*zakup*) as well as by free peasants of somewhat restricted legal status (*smerd, izgoi, sirota*, etc.) As yet there was no serfdom as a legal institution. The church as well objected to the institution of slavedom, and apparently succeeded in the gradual reduction of the number of slaves used in agriculture by both princes and boyars. The manor, however, did not become a universal institution in the Kievan period. The famous feudal rule *nulle terre sans seigneur* could certainly not be applied to the conditions of Kievan Russia. The bulk of the population were full-fledged free men (*lyudi*) owning their own land (*svoezemtsy*). Some of them were organized in communes, but each member of a commune controlled his particular field. Generally speaking, land at that period was owned as private property and was both bought and sold without restrictions. Such transactions were regulated by Byzantine Law, that is, fundamentally by Roman Law. The boyar's right on his land was not dependent on his service to the prince. The boyar would join a *druzhina* of another prince without losing his estate. The latter was

thus not a fief. It was a patrimonial estate, and if we look for a parallel western term for it we can rather call it an allodium. Under such conditions it hardly would be possible to characterize the régime prevalent in Russia of the Kievan period as a feudal one. It is of the existence of some feudalizing tendencies only that we can speak with regard to the Kiev state and society.

The Mongol invasion of 1237–40, which for some time thereafter subjugated all Russia to the authority of the Khan, exerted a paramount influence on the further development of the Russian state and Russian society. This influence had more lasting results in Eastern Russia than in Western Russia, since the Mongol domination over the latter was replaced in the fourteenth century by that of Lithuania and Poland. The Mongol Empire was a peculiar political formation, combining various factors and tendencies. The Khan's imperial power was superimposed upon the clan society of a nomadic people. With the growth of the Empire, the Khan extended his authority over peoples of settled agricultural or semi-agricultural civilization as well. Among such were the Uigurs in Eastern Turkestan. By conquering China, Mongol Emperors opened the way to Chinese influences on the administration of the Empire. The conquest of Western Turkestan, Iran, and part of Hither Asia added countries of Islamic culture to the roll of imperial provinces.

Owing to this historical background of the Mongol Empire its structure was a heterogeneous one. The Mongol Imperial Law, as reflected in the Great Yasa of Chingis Khan, tended to establish a régime of autocracy. The Khan was the supreme authority in the Empire and no feudal lords were recognized. On the other hand, tribal and clan customary law was not abrogated by the Great Yasa. While the Mongols were a nomadic people, there were many tendencies in their social organization which can be compared with social trends in mediaeval Europe. For that reason it is now customary in Soviet historiography to speak of 'nomadic feudalism.'

Feudalizing trends are also characteristic of the Uigur social structure of the Mongol period (eleventh to fourteenth century). We observe in Eastern Turkestan of this period the growth of large landed estates. Some of them constituted the Khan's domain or the appanages (*inchu*) of the members of the Khan's family. Local princes (*bek*) dependent on the Khan had estates of their own. Immunity privileges assured the power of the big landowners. The peasant population, partly organized in communes for the purpose of taxation, supplied their agricultural labor. There also developed the institution of indentured labor which probably served as a pattern for the so-called *kabalnoe kholopstvo* in Muscovite Russia.

Because of the facts that lands of Islamic law were incorporated into the Mongol Empire and that later on the Khans of the Golden Horde became converts to Islam, we may expect to find some influences of so-called Islamic feudalism at work in Russia of the Mongol period. The institution of *ikta*, which has been sometimes compared to the western fief, might have been partly instrumental for the growth of the *pomestie* régime in Russia.

The unity of the Mongol Empire did not last long. After Chingis Khan's death, his descendants each received an appanage (*ulus*) of his own. It was Djuchi's *ulus*, known as the Golden Horde, to which Russia was attached. Theoretically, the *ulus* Khans recognized the authority of the Great Khan as paramount. Actually, during the reign of the fifth Great Khan Kubilay (1259–94), the Khans of the western *uluses* (Iran and Kipchak, i.e., the Golden Horde) became, for practical reasons, independent. In spite of the fact that Hulagu, the Khan of Iran, and Barka, the Khan of Kipchak, were second cousins and both considered Kubilay their common suzerain, they started a stubborn war for control of Transcaucasia. The partition of power in the Mongol Empire was similar to that in Russia of the Kievan period. The Khans had to belong to the House of Chingis, just as the Russian princes of the Kievan period had to belong to the House of Vladimir. The power as a whole was vested in the ruling clan which, as we have just seen, did not prevent individual Khans and princes from quarrelling among themselves.

Within the boundaries of each *ulus* or Khanate the same process of partition was gradually developing,. The Khan would apportion suitable shares as appanages to his cousin and his descendants and in some cases to his favorite wives as well. High officers of the Khan's army, both of Mongol and of Turkish blood, were little by little assuming more authority of their own. This process resulted in the establishment of a hierarchy of princes and lords not dissimilar to the feudal hierarchy of the West. There was still, however, a great difference between the two, since the principle of the supreme authority of the Khan's power (as now applied to the local Khanates) continued to be legally valid. . . .

In the next section we shall deal with the developments in Eastern Russia, and now confine our comments to Western Russia. The period of Mongol domination in Western Russia lasted a little over one hundred years. In the middle of the fourteenth century, most of the West Russian provinces recognized the authority of the Grand Duke of Lithuania in order to escape that of the Khan. The grand duchy of Lithuania was, politically speaking, a loose federation of both Lithuanian and West Russian principalities and provinces organized along lines strikingly similar to the feudal patterns of the Romano-Germanic countries.

In order better to understand the graduation of dependency of the local princes and lords (*pany*) on the Grand Duke, it would not be amiss to state briefly the territorial division of the grand duchy of Lithuania with respect to the distribution of political authority of the Grand Duke. There was, first, the grand duchy of Lithuania proper, composed of those lands which came under the sway of the Grand Duke in the period of the original formation of the grand duchy. This original domain was comprised of most of the Lithuanian and of some of the West Russian lands incorporated into the grand duchy at the end of the thirteenth and in the beginning of the fourteenth century. It was divided into two duchies: that of Vilno and that of Troki. The second group of lands was the federated principalities which recognized the authority of the Grand Duke in the second half of the fourteenth century or in the first half of the fifteenth. One of such affiliated dominions was the Lithuanian province of Zhmud. All of the others were West Russian principalities as follows: Polotsk, Vitebsk, Smolensk, Kiev, Volyn, Podolie and Chernigov-Sever. It was only within the grand duchy proper that the Grand Duke was able to exercise his immediate control. Even within the boundaries of the grand duchy proper only part of the territory was left to the Grand Duke as his own domain. The other part was held by feudal lords—princes and boyars.

Though pledging an oath of personal fealty to the Grand Duke, each local prince was a ruler over his own province. As to the boyars, the Grand Duke granted them the control of their estates on condition of military service as well as the performance of some other duties as provided in the patents (*privilei*). In addition to the patrimonial boyar estates, there also developed another type of conditional grants of land either for life or for the term at the Grand Duke's discretion. Such lands were known as *pomestie*. Similar régimes came into being in each of the federated principalities. Some of the provincial princes were descendants of the Grand Duke Gedymin (1316–41); others belonged to the old house of Kiev. The provincial prince, himself a vassal of the Grand Duke, had his own vassals, both the local princes and the *pany* (boyars). The provincial prince was a seignior in his own domain and a suzerain with regard to the minor local princes, each of whom had his *votchina* as well.

As a result of such arrangements, a feudal scale of greater and lesser rulers bound by a mutual contract established itself in the grand duchy as a whole. The Grand Duke was the supreme suzerain, comparable to a feudal king of continental Europe or even to the King of England. His higher vassals, the provincial princes, corresponded to the German and French dukes; both the local princes and the major boyars constituted the bulk of the feudal landowning class comparable to the counts, barons, and knights of Central and Western Europe.

It is necessary to bear in mind that Latin was one of the two official languages of the Grand Duke's chancery, the other being Russian. The Grand Duke's charters, when issued in Latin, adapted Western feudal terminology to the political régime of the grand duchy. In that way the feudal aspects of the political and social structure of the grand duchy were even more sharply emphasized.

Turning to social conditions, we notice the establishment of the typical manorial régime throughout the country. The legal status of the peasants was subject to gradual restrictions, both with regard to those peasants who cultivated the Grand Duke's domanial estates and those who were laboring on the princely and boyar estates. In 1447 the Grand Duke issued a patent forbidding the peasants to shift from a princely or a boyar estate to that of the Grand Duke. This amounted to the official recognition of serfdom.

While we have sufficient reason to call the socio-political régime of the Grand Duchy of Lithuania feudalism, we now point to some divergent tendencies in its development. The owners of the larger feudal estates, both princes and boyars, attempted gradually to enforce their respective authority over their lands in such a way that they would receive full property rights over their estates not subject to any restrictions with regard to their suzerain. On the other hand, the political authority of the Grand Duke was more and more limited by the parliament (*Seim*). By the middle of the sixteenth century, this twofold transformation of the political and social structure of the grand duchy went a considerable distance toward undermining its feudalizing tendencies. The union of Lublin with Poland (1569) was an important landmark in this regard, signalizing the increase of the patrimonial rights of the gentry. The Commonwealth which resulted from the political union of the Crown (Poland) and the grand duchy (Lithuania) was an aristocratic republic, but it was no more a feudal confederation.

While the Mongol domination in Western Russia was in the fourteenth century replaced by the control of the Grand Dukes of Lithuania, Eastern Russia continued to remain under the Khan's authority for one more century, and it was not until the middle of the fifteenth century that the Grand Duke of Moscow emancipated himself from the Khan's control. The princes of Eastern Russia lost their independence after the Mongol conquest and recognized the Khan's suzerainty, or, as the contemporary terms put it, placed themselves under the Khan's hand, became his *podruchniki* (literally 'underarmmen,' i.e., vassals).

As has been already mentioned, the Khan issued patents (*yarlyk*) to the native princes in Russia. A prince provided with such *yarlyk* enjoyed the Khan's support against other claimants. In case such prince would apportion part of his principality to his son or his younger brother, the latter would rule over his portion as a subordinate (*podruchnik*) of the main prince of the province. In that way there was established a hierarchy of princes within each province. At the head of it was the Grand Duke (literally, Grand Prince, *veliki Knyaz*, in Turkish *ulug beg*), provided with the Khan's patent. The local princes were subordinated to the Grand Duke, some of them directly, others indirectly.

The main grand-ducal provinces of Eastern Russia were Vladimir, Tver, Ryazan, Suzdal, Nizhni Novgorod. From the end of the thirteenth century the princes of Moscow advanced their claims to the grand duchy of Vladimir. Their aspirations collided with those of the princes of Tver. A stubborn struggle started between the princes of Moscow and Tver for obtaining the Khan's patent (*yarlyk*) covering the grand duchy of Vladimir. From 1329 the grand duchy remained in the hands of the Prince of Moscow. The next move of the princes of Moscow, now Grand Dukes of Vladimir, was to extend their suzerainty over the Grand Dukes of other provinces of Eastern Russia as well. Since the Grand Duke of Moscow and Vladimir succeeded in receiving the Khan's commission to collect taxes for the Khan's treasury, he had ample opportunity to improve his own financial affairs considerably, which placed him in an advantageous position with regard to the other princes.

According to the treaty of 1375, the Grand Duke of Tver, Michael, recognized himself a *podruchnik* of the Grand Duke of Moscow, Dimitri. The result of this policy was the gradual concentration of political authority over most of the East Russian principalities in the hands of the Grand Duke of Moscow. While Moscow was in ascendancy, the Golden Horde was in decline, and in the middle of the fifteenth century the former became practically independent of the latter. Owing to the disintegration of the Golden Horde at that time, part of the Tatar princes now recognized the suzerainty of the Moscow Grand Dukes. The creation of the vassal Tatar principality ('Tsardom') of Kasimov (about 1452) was a masterpiece of Moscow policy. In that way, the political and social intercourse between the Turko-Mongol world and Eastern Russia was only strengthened. To the princes of the Kiev house a number of Mongol and Tatar princes ('Tsars' and 'Tsareviches') were now added as vassals of the Grand Duke of Moscow and Vladimir.

The political structure of Eastern Russia thus assumed some aspects of similarity to both Western Russia and Europe. It is necessary to bear in mind, however, that a boyar, Russian or Tatar, still could not become a prince. On the other hand, the authority of a boyar as a landlord was increasing. The manor as an institution gradually consolidated itself. The manor administration and the manor courts claimed authority over the peasant population originally not connected with it. Reservation should be made, however, that the typical boyar *votchina* (patrimonial estate) of the pe-

riod was a manor of a simple type and not a developed seigniory. The *votchina* consisted of the boyar's demesne and of the plots of land settled by peasants, the latter being subject to some control by the boyar. This in itself presented but a nucleus of a developed seigniory if compared with the Western patterns. As has been already mentioned, a fully developed Western seigniory used to comprise not only the seignior's demesne and the village community, but the vassal fiefs as well.

Now it was not so common for a boyar to apportion part of his *votchina* estate as a *pomestie* (land grant under provision of service) to one of his servitors. Such practice was indeed usual with the princes and ecclesiastical lords or monasteries. We have, however, to keep in mind that the institution of *pomestie* in itself was not identical with that of the fief. The boyar's authority over his manor, as well as that of the ecclesiastical dignitaries and monasteries over the church *votchina*, was strengthened by the practice of the Grand Dukes in granting immunity charters to the *votchina* owners, guaranteeing them the privilege of manorial justice and exemption from taxation. Such immunity charters were often known as *tarkhan*, which implies the presence of the Turko-Mongol roots of this institution in Eastern Russia. The patents, or *yarlyk*, granted by the Khans of the Golden Horde to the Russian church formed the background for the *tarkhan* charters of the Moscow Grand Dukes in favor of the monastery *votchina*.

As to the peasants tilling the lord's land, they were not yet his serfs, and the peasant commune had as yet not become a universal institution. Some tendencies may, however, be noticed as preparing the ground for the coming of serfdom. In case a peasant's family stayed on the lord's land for more than a generation, they were considered 'old settlers' (*sta-rozhiltsy*) and were not expected to leave the manor freely and without notice. The indebtedness of the peasant who would need a loan for buying cattle and farming implements was another way in which the peasant lost his freedom. The institution of indentured labor assumed stricter forms under Turko-Mongol influence. The man receiving a loan had to work for his creditor until the loan was paid back. According to the new type of agreement, his work covered only the interest on the loan, not the principal. It is obvious that under such arrangements the debtor had to work for life and never was able to repay the principal unless he received a new loan from another creditor. This was known as *kabala* slavedom, which developed in Eastern Russia under the apparent influence of Uigur law.

While the manor type of agriculture was making rapid progress in Eastern Russia of the Mongol period, the smaller farms of the freemen (*lyudi, svoezemtsy*) were still existent, although their numbers steadily decreased. It was in the province of Novgorod that they stood their ground more firmly, but in 1479 Novgorod was annexed to Moscow and all private land estates in Novgorod were confiscated by the Moscow Grand Dukes, who granted these estates to Moscow nobles as *pomestie*. While both the hierarchical organization of the princely power and the growth of the manor were important features of feudalizing tendencies in Eastern Russia during the Mongol period, no comprehensive feudal régime was established. The very essence of the feudal nexus was lacking. There was no implicit connection between the institutions of 'political feudalism' and those of 'economic feudalism.' The authority of the boyar as the lord of his manor was not dependent upon his service to the prince of the Grand Duke. The Russian manor of this period was

the boyar's patrimonial estate (*votchina*) and not his fief. The boyar would not lose his estates in case he left his prince and enrolled in the service of another prince.

In order to tighten their control over the administration of their state, the Moscow Grand Dukes attempted, from the early fourteenth century, to build up a new class of servitors to whom land would be granted upon condition of service only. Such lands became known as *pomestie*. The *pomestie* system, however, assumed no general significance before the sixteenth century, and accordingly will be dealt with in the next section.

By the beginning of the sixteenth century the Grand Duke of Moscow and Vladimir had extended his control over all Eastern Russia. This meant the political unification of the so-called Great Russian branch of the Russian nation. In 1547 Ivan IV assumed the title of Tsar to emphasize both his independence from outside rulers and his sovereignty at home. The Tsardom of Moscow absorbed in itself the remnants of the former grand duchies and principalities of Eastern Russia. The former provincial Grand Dukes and local princes lost their independence or even their autonomy. They now became known as mere *knyazhata*, 'the princes' sons,' and joined the ranks of the Moscovian boyardom. The central power was rapidly concentrating in the hands of the Tsar. The *knyazhata* made a disorganized attempt to recompense themselves for the loss of political power in the provinces by claiming their share in the central government. In that they were supported by some old Moscow boyar families. The Moscow Duma did not succeed, however, in establishing itself as a constitutional council similar to the *Pany-Rada* of the grand duchy of Lithuanian and Western Russia.

Tsar Ivan the Terrible ruthlessly

crushed the boyar opposition by organizing the so-called *oprichnina*. As a result of the *oprichnina* terror, part of the
princely and boyar families were deprived of their patrimonial estates. The
boyar class was badly shaken, thus opening the way for the ascendancy of the
new class, that of the *pomeshchik*. The
pomestie was a land grant issued by the
Tsar on condition of the military service
of the recipient of the grant (the *pomeshchik*). In case no service was rendered
by the recipient the grant was revoked.
Not all of the boyar patrimonial estates
(*votchina*) were confiscated during the
oprichnina régime, and part of those
confiscated were later returned to the
former owners or their descendants.
New *votchina* grants were also made for
some special service, e.g., to reward officers of the army for defending the city
of Moscow against the Poles in 1618.
Thus patrimonial estates were not entirely replaced by *pomestie* estates even
in the seventeenth century. But the *pomestie* now became the standard type of
land grant and the patrimonial estates
(*votchina*) were now more or less ad-
justed to the *pomestie* type. In that way
military service was required by the
Tsar from the owners of the *votchina*
estates to the same extent as from the
holders of the *pomestie* estates.

The discretionary powers of the owner
of the *votchina* with regard to his landed
property were likewise somewhat limited, as for example in the matter of
inheritance. On the other hand, the social authority of the *pomestie* holder
within his estate was gradually increasing on the basis of the privileges possessed by the *votchina* owner, with the
result that from the point of view of
social and economic function the *pomestie* was gradually merging with the
votchina.

Freedom of the peasants, on both
votchina and on *pomestie* estates, was
restricted by the ukas (1581) forbidding them to quit the landlords' estates
on certain years proclaimed as 'prohib-
itive' (*zapovedny*). By the middle of the
seventeenth century, serfdom became a
universal institution in the Tsardom of
Moscow.

We may notice that the régime of
serfdom established itself in Eastern
Russia almost two centuries later than
it did in Western Russia, but even there
it came later than in Romano-Germanic
countries. The Russian peasants became
serfs at a time when there were only
remnants of serfdom in both France and
England. It is for this reason that some
scholars speak of an 'inverted process'
in the social developments of Russia and
Eastern Europe.

The Moscow *pomestie* régime has
many traits in common with western
feudalism, especially with the centralized feudalism of the Norman period in
England. In the sixteenth and the seventeenth centuries we have in Moscow what
seems to be one of the essential features
of a feudal régime, i.e., holding of land
estates by members of the military class
on condition of service rendered. For
that reason P. B. Struve even considers
the sixteenth and the seventeenth centuries as the actual period of the establishment of feudalism in Moscow Russia.
His argument is hardly valid. The similarity between the Moscow *pomestie* régime and the regulated feudalism of the
English type is an outward one only.
The Moscow régime, while establishing
the nexus between military service and
landholding, lacked another essential
trait of western feudalism. There was no
reciprocity of contract between the Tsar
and the *pomeshchik*. The latter was not
the Tsar's vassal; he was merely the
Tsar's servitor.

Such similarity as there was between
the Russian *pomestie* régime and feudalism came to a close in the eighteenth
century. The essential trend in Russian
social development from the semi-feudal

monarchy of the seventeenth century toward the absolutist Empire of the eighteenth century was the gradual merging of the original two different types of landholding, the patrimonial estate (*votchina*) and the conditional grant (*pomestie*) into one new type— that of the real estate (*nedvizhimoe imenie*) owned on a full property basis.

If, as has been mentioned, the Tsar intended to equate the patrimonial *votchina* to the *pomestie* in requiring equal military service from both, the *pomestie* holders attempted to increase their discretionary powers over the *pomestie* land they held in such a way that they would enjoy at least some of the authority of the *votchina* owners. According to the original plan, a *pomestie* grant was strictly personal. However, the recipient of such a grant usually attempted to secure it to his descendants. A *pomestie* could not be, strictly speaking, a subject of legacy, but it soon became customary that, in case the holder had male descendants, the *pomestie* grant was transferred to the name of his eldest son when the original holder became too old for military service. In case the *pomestie* holder died during his service term and left no male heirs, the estate or any portion of it could be left to his widow for her use until she died or married again, or to his daughter until her marriage. In this latter case the daughter's husband could expect that the estate would be given to him to hold on condition of his service to the Tsar.

By the slow process of such gradual adjustment there was established, by the end of the seventeenth century, a habit of leaving the *pomestie* for the use of the same family whenever there was the slightest pretext for arranging it. To all practical purposes, there was at the beginning of the eighteenth century little difference between the rights of a *pomestie* holder and those of a *votchina* owner with respect to their respective estates.

Important changes in the land régime resulted from Peter the Great's thorough reconstruction of both the military and civil service statutes. He required personal service from all members of the gentry class without any discrimination by virtue of the type of their landholding. On the other hand, Peter to a recognizable extent considered all types of land estates as being subject to direct control of the government. All timber on private estates, as on crown lands, was under option to the government for the building of the navy. The owner had no right to cut it without governmental permit. The same was true with regard to mining. It would not be an undue modernization to suggest that Peter intended to establish what is now termed a totalitarian state. However, following his death (1725) the gentry attempted to recover their individual freedom and property rights, in which effort they finally succeeded.

By the law of 1731, the legal distinction between *pomestie* and *votchina* was finally abolished and the real estate (*nedvizhimoe imenie*) was recognized as the property of the owner. The estates were still for some time liable to state encroachments, e.g., for timber and mining. These were cancelled by Catherine II, and by her Charter of the Gentry (1785) she solemnly guaranteed full property rights to the gentry on their land. Meanwhile, the gentry were excused from obligatory service to the state (1762).

The authority of the gentry over the peasant population, however, was not yet abrogated. In the sixteenth and seventeenth centuries the gentry used laborers of two different categories. Some of the laborers were slaves (used chiefly for household service), the others were serfs (used exclusively for tilling the land). The serfs were considered bound to the estate, but not to the owner of the estate personally. The slaves were the private property of the owner. The distinction between the two groups was abolished by Peter the Great, who ordered both serfs and slaves drafted into his army. This resulted in the merging of the two groups into one, that of the serfs.

While slavedom was thus abrogated, the position of the serfs was not improved. With the expansion of gentry privileges in the course of the eighteenth century the authority of the landlord over his serfs even tended to increase. There was some inner contradiction in granting to the gentry full property rights on their estate while the serfs legally were still considered as attached to the estate and not to the person of the owner.

Serfdom was originally introduced in Russia in order to supply the military landholders (the *pomeshchiki*) with labor, and thus enable them to devote themselves to the Tsar's service. Now that obligatory service was abrogated, the land estate became full property of the former owner. There seemed to be no logical ground for continuing to keep the peasants in the state of serfdom. It was not, however, until 1861 that the peasants were emancipated. By the provisions of the emancipation act each estate was divided into two parts, one retained by the lord and the other transferred to the peasants. In this way the legacy of the *pomestie* régime was at last liquidated.

We now have to sum up the main results of the preceding argument.

Three distinct types of socio-political structure may be taken into consideration when discussing the problem of feudalism in Russia. These are: (1) the *votchina* régime; (2) the *pomestie* régime; (3) standard feudalism of the western type.

1. The *votchina* régime is characterized by the growth of the manorial power of the lord of the estate over the laboring population working on the estate or merely settled around it. Such power could be enforced by immunity privileges. The *votchina* estate may be owned by a political ruler (prince) or by private persons, or else by the church. While representing to a certain extent the social aspects of feudalizing processes the *votchina* régime has no direct political counterpart for it.

The political power superimposed upon the *votchina* plan of society might assume feudalizing traits, such as the building up of the scale of suzerain and local rulers, but there is no formal connection between the vassal's service and the control of the land.

2. The *pomestie* regime tends to make the control of the land dependent upon service rendered to the state by the holder of the land estate. There is no partition of political power in this régime as it grew up in the Muscovite state of the sixteenth and seventeenth centuries. The power was concentrated in the person of the supreme ruler, the Tsar.

3. For the development of the standard type of feudalism in which some characteristics of both the *votchina* and the *pomestie* régimes are combined, certain traits are essential which are lacking in either the *votchina* régime or the *pomestie* régime, or in both.

Like the *votchina* régime, the standard type of feudalism presupposes the expansion of manor and the growth of the manorial rights of the lord. On the other hand, like the *pomestie* régime, feudalism of the standard type is characterized by the conditionality of rights on the land. The control of the land by the lower class landlord is dependent on his service rendered to the seignior.

The important point of difference between the *pomestie* régime and feudalism of the standard type is that, while in the former the political power is concentrated in the hands of the supreme ruler, for the latter the partition of political authority is typical. Greater and lesser rulers each have their respective share in it. The suzerain, the vassals, and the subvassals form a continual political chain, all bound as they are by reciprocal feudal contracts.

It is only in Western Russia as organized by the Grand Dukes of Lithuania in the fourteenth and to the sixteenth centuries that we have been able to establish this existence of the standard feudalism of western type. The *votchina* régime was existent in the Kievan period but was not prevalent then. It is in Eastern Russia of the Mongol period (thirteenth to fifteenth centuries) that the *votchina* régime assumed full significance.

While the *pomestie* régime first took root in the Mongol period, its full development occured in the Muscovite Tsardom of the sixteenth and the seventeenth centuries. By the eighteenth century the *pomestie* system, as has been seen, was dead, and only some scanty repercussions of it can be traced as far down as the middle of the nineteenth century.

CHEREPNIN: BOURGEOIS HISTORI- OGRAPHY ON FEUDALISM IN RUSSIA

The development of feudal relations and the process of enserfment of the peasants in Russia are examined in the works of George Vernadsky. The author points out that there is a possible twofold approach to the definition of feudalism. In the widest (sociological) sense, the understanding of the word "feudalism" includes the most typical characteristics which took place in different countries and in different times. It follows, according to Vernadsky, that feudalism, in a more specific sense, supposes a clear, distinct complex of events

characteristic of the Romano-Germanic countries of medieval Europe. This complex may be elevated to the "standard," that is, the "ideal type" of feudalism. Vernadsky himself deems it more expedient to choose the second way. Marking these features as belonging not only to the Romano-Germanic "standard type" of feudalism, he thinks that they will also help to solve the problem of the question concerning the character of the social development of Russia.

These judgments are farfetched, and it is difficult to agree with them. The task of the historian consists not in the construction of "ideal types," but in the study of objective, historical reality. The social development of distinct countries and peoples depends on the general historical laws and on their specific rules, which, in turn, depend on the concrete conditions of their history. Of what use is it to establish some extrahistorical "standards" or to look for some yardstick? A comparative-historical method ought not to stretch the historical past of one people to a previously chosen model, but ought to facilitate the explanation of the general as well as of the particular in the life of different peoples. An understanding of this general and particular should help toward the understanding of objective historical laws, and not toward the construction of abstract concepts. Feudalism is not an ideally typical construction, not a scheme of development to which the concrete historical paths of separate peoples either correspond or from which they deviate. Feudalism is a socio-economic formation which represents a natural stage in the development of all nations, each of which passed through this stage in its own specific way, and not according to some standard pattern. It is characteristic that some bourgeois historians (Alexander Eck, for example), spoke against the tendency of making the features of Western European feudalism into a standard.

Vernadsky, in defining this "standard," which in his opinion is represented by "Romano-Germanic feudalism," points out four prerequisites for the growth of feudal institutions: (1) a fusion of public and private law; (2) a dismemberment of political authority; (3) the predominance of a natural economy; (4) the interdependence of political and economic power.

Dealing with the development of the feudal régime, Vernadsky points out three of its most important elements: (1) "Political feudalism," characterized by the appearance of a number of interdependent links in the structure of the supreme authority by the establishment of a scale of higher and lower rulers (suzerains, vassals, subvassals) bound together by a mutual, contractual relationship; (2) "Economic feudalism," or the establishment of the manorial régime with its limitations on the legal status of the peasant, and with its distinction between the right of direct possession of the land and the right of using it; (3) Under the feudal régime, there occurs the fusion of personal and land rights; the transfer of land into the management of the vassals is conditioned by their service to the seignior.

On the basis of these general maxims, Vernadsky tries to uncover the specifics of feudal society. According to him, the seignior is the local cell of feudal society. It is headed by the seignior on whom depend the vassals, bound to him by military service, and the peasants, who work the land and fulfil a number of obligations as its users. The different seigniories are linked together by a chain of vassal contracts. Less influential seigniors become the vassals of the more powerful ones; the vassals of the former become the subvassals of the latter. Thus evolves a scale of seigniories. The feudal world assumes a more complex appearance.

Vernadsky's construction (which reproduces the usual bourgeois conception of feudalism) is unacceptable because it neither uncovers nor explains the real contradictions of social life and the dialectics of their development. The author's thoughts rotate mainly in the plane of political, legal aspects, while even here he is mainly interested in their form and not in their inner essence. Vernadsky's attention is attracted to the outer features, but not to the substance of the social relationships which he studied. Instead of revealing the inner relationships of the development of feudal society, the author lists different "aspects" of feudalism, without grasping the true interrelations, not distinguishing the main from the secondary, the fundamental from the derivative.

Only in the realm of the productive relationships lies the substance which defines the antagonistic structure of feudal society. It is a fact that the direct producers did not own the principal means of production—the land—and that such ownership, even of the labor and the person of the peasant, was, to a great extent, concentrated in the hands of the ruling class. In the defense of the feudal landowning rights and privileges lies the main inner function of the feudal state which unites the class in its own peculiar hierarchy of landowners of various titles and ranks. Through contracts, these privileged landowners formulate their interrelationships, which deal with the distribution of economic goods and political authority (which is partitioned) and at the same time legally confirm their unity as a class opposing the peasantry.

Feudalism develops under the domination of a natural economy (Vernadsky is right in this), but it is the mode of production which defines the essence of the feudal social order. The fusion of public and private law, the interdependence of political and economic power—all these points (shown by Vernadsky) are important not in themselves but as an expression of the class nature of the feudal society and state. For the condition of the domination of the privileged feudal lords over the masses of the socially underprivileged and the serfs was the concentration in their hands of certain political rights along with rights of land ownership.

Turning from the theoretical deliberations on feudalism, Vernadsky applies the question of whether one can speak of feudal relationships in Russia to specific periods of Russian history. Turning to Kievan Rus of the tenth through eleventh centuries, he points out that it is impossible to deny that in this period "processes of feudalization" were becoming distinguishable. At the same time, he considers, "the Kievan State and society, taken as a whole, cannot be called feudal." In his opinion, there was no feudal society in Kievan Rus because, at this time, one princely family as an entity directed the state, and within that "ruling house" there was no hierarchy. All the princes were considered equal. The boyars could not aspire to obtain princely authority. Not only were they not princely vassals, but no contract existed between them and the princes.

A typical characteristic of Vernadsky's methodology, which illustrates his helplessness, strikes one's eyes: the author is interested in the form and not in the substance of historical phenomena (in this case, the state). It is not accidental that he begins with an analysis of the phenomena of the superstructure. But it is possible to understand the class essence of the state as a political superstructure only by being aware of what its corresponding base was.

The ancient Russian state with its center in Kiev, independent of its form, was feudal because it was the organ of

the power of the feudal landholders dominating over and dependent upon the peasants. And in this respect, there was no principal difference between Kievan Rus and the medieval states which emerged in the Romano-Germanic countries adopted by Vernadsky as a prototype. In its form, the ancient Russian state had, of course, its own peculiarities. One of these was that many of the princes who ruled in Kievan Rus (although not all by far) did come from one and the same family. However, these princes and boyars had their own system of interrelationships and the scope of political authority of each of them depended in one degree or another on the totality of his landholding rights. Just as in other countries, the feudal property in land bore a partition character and medieval Rus had a ladder of privileged feudal lords of different ranks. Doubtless, contracts also existed among them.

Turning to the socio-economic characteristics of Kievan Rus, Vernadsky points out the indisputable fact of the growth of landowning—on the part of the princes, boyars, and the church. At that time, according to Vernadsky, the rural population consisted of slaves as well as of freedmen who paid taxes to the state. The latter category, Vernadsky says, had arisen in Russia in an earlier period of the history of the eastern Slavs as the result of the conquest by the Alans, Goths, and Hungarians, who levied tribute from the different Slavic tribes. With the emergence of the ancient Russian state, with its center in Kiev, the remnants of these communities which were obliged to pay tribute (Vernadsky arbitrarily names them "the serfs of the state") were transferred to the jurisdiction of the Kievan princes and received the name of *smerdi*. Consequently, unlike Eck, Vernadsky considers the *smerdi* to have been dependent people. But the author presumes that in Kievan Rus there was no real serfdom, for he conceives serfdom as being defined by law (in contrast to slavery) as being an institution of private law. The bulk of the population was composed, Vernadsky assures us, of free landowners who cultivated their own possessions. It is impossible to apply the rule, "No land without a seignior," to Kievan Rus. Meanwhile, the right of the boyars to their land, according to Vernadsky, was not dependent on serving a prince. Therefore, the boyar land possessions cannot be called a fief.

First of all, it is necessary resolutely to refute Vernadsky's thesis about the freedom of a considerable number of rural inhabitants in Kievan Rus; nor did this group consist of petty landholders. The facts show that in the process of feudalization, the free communes (*liudi*) were losing their lands, becoming *izgoi*, and then became peasants dependent on the state or on private landholders (both secular and ecclesiastical), receiving the names of *smerdi*, *zakupi*, and later on, *siroty*, etc. This dependence was economic (because the peasants received land portions and often a loan from the landholders) as well as personal (because the peasants' position was reduced to that of persons without full rights who were limited in their right of departure, managing their own property, coming under the *votchina* jurisdiction of the lord, etc.). Of course, in the tenth through the twelfth centuries, and even later, serfdom had still not attained the forms which became the rule in the centralized Russian state of the sixteenth through seventeenth centuries. But serfdom as the condition of peasant bondage was being formed in practice and was fortified by law (for example, the *Russkaia Pravda*). And the development of serfdom signifies the development of feudalism.

As for the connection of landownership with service of the landowner to the seignior, it is by no means obliga-

tory that it should appear identical in form to the Western European fief (although it is mainly from this term, "fief," that "feudalism" took its name). It is incontestable that princely grants of land for service not only took place but were common in Rus.

As is well known, Vernadsky, in all of his works, argues the point of view that the Tartar-Mongol yoke had a great influence on the social development of Rus (how much more conservative he is than Eck on this point!). Vernadsky says that the immunity of the church lands points up the influence of deeds by the Mongol khans and that the influence of Tartar-Mongol law can be found in the "kabala" form of "kholop." Finally, he considers that due to the Tartar-Mongolian yoke, there arose new types of "serf communities" charged with specific services to the Golden Horde. At the same time the bulk of the population remained, according to Vernadsky, free.

It is hardly necessary to stress that it is not scholarly to derive from an alien conquest such institutions as immunity or debt *kabala* which existed in Rus even before the Tartar-Mongolian invasion and which continued to exist and develop, acquiring new features primarily under the influence of the inner process of social development. What is incontestable is the role of the Tartar-Mongol conquest in imposing certain services and obligations to the Horde on certain sections of the population. Most important is the fact that the oppression of the Horde was experienced by the entire Russian people and not only by certain separate strata.

Analyzing the social development of Russia in the period of its partition and the emergence of the centralized state (thirteenth through seventeenth centuries), Vernadsky, in order to ascertain whether or not feudal relationships existed then, considers it necessary first to delineate the character of the *vot-*

china and later the *pomestie* regime, and then to compare these with the "standard feudalism of the Western type." The general conclusion of the author is: both the *votchina* and *pomestie* had some feudal characteristics, but it is nevertheless impossible to speak about feudalism of the "standard type" in Rus, because only the combination of a number of features characteristic of the *votchina* and *pomestie* systems separately or together could produce the image of a feudal régime.

Here, the anti-historical, scholastic character of Vernadsky's methodology is most apparent. Having worked out a "standard" notion of "feudalism" and surveyed actual historical reality, he artificially derives from it this or that preconceived notion and then goes on to derive arbitrary combinations from them, adjusting these to his "standard." It would seem that the task of the historian consists of something else: he must understand and explain the objective, historical reality without deviating from its concrete nature and not raising it to a standard, but finding in this concrete situation the manifestations of general laws.

The *"votchina"* régime," according to Vernadsky, approaches feudalism because of the fact that it presents a widening of the rights of the landholder over the population, which is aided in no small degree by a number of immunity privileges. But the ownership of the *votchina* is not connected with military service and therefore the multiple relationships of the suzerain-vassal do not arise. The *"pomestie* régime" is characterized as typical for feudalism, because of its connection between landownership and military service obligations, but the *pomestie* system cannot constitute the foundation of the feudal régime because the latter requires the partition of sov-

ereignty, while the full supreme power in Rus during the growth of the *pomestie* system belonged to the tsar. In the last analysis, Vernadsky is inclined to believe that in Muscovite Rus there was no feudalism of the "western type." Closer to this type, he says, were the social relations formed in the western Russian lands which were part of the Grand Duchy of Lithuania.

Vernadsky's conclusions are unwarranted. The *votchina* and *pomestie* are a variety of feudal landownership and share many characteristics, although they do have a diversity of features. It is quite impossible to contrast the *votchina* with the *pomestie* in the sense that owning a *votchina* allegedly did not impose on the *votchinik* (the princely servant or boyar) any service obligations toward his suzerain (the prince, the Grand Prince), while the *pomeshchik* did carry such obligations. The problem of the juridical basis of *votchina* landownership is complicated. But it is indisputable that, in a number of cases, *votchinas* were confirmed by the princes for service and did oblige the recipient to serve. It is impossible to agree with the statement that the *pomestie* system cannot be called a phenomenon of the feudal order, because its political order is not characterized by the partitioning of sovereignty. Of course, the hierarchy, manifesting itself in the system of the service "ranks" of the landowners in the period of the centralized Russian state (sixteenth to seventeenth centuries), among which the *pomeshchiki* occupied a prominent place, bears a centralizing character. Nevertheless, it is a feudal hierarchy because it defines the system of relationships between the privileged landed property owners, economically and politically dominant over the peasants attached to the land.

7

THE KURBSKY–IVAN THE TERRIBLE
CORRESPONDENCE EXCERPTS

It was from enemy territory that Prince Andrey Kurbsky (1528–83) wrote the first of his five letters to the Tsar in 1564. The ensuing correspondence, which lasted until 1579, is one of the important historical documents of the Russian sixteenth century. Since it throws more light on the character and thinking of the Tsar, a word should be said about Kurbsky. He was a boyar and a leading general who had helped Ivan win at Kazan and in other battles. But having been defeated on the Western frontier, he deserted to the Polish-Lithuanian forces, fearing punishment for his failure from his dreaded master. He was never to return to his homeland. Only his first letter and the reply are reproduced here, the latter much abridged.

Kurbsky's *History of Ivan IV* has been translated into English recently by J. L. I. Fennell. For another sample of Kurbsky's writing see Nikolay Andreev's "Kurbsky's Letters to Vasyan Muromtsev," *Slavonic and East European Review*, Vol. XXXIII. An older interpretation of the Tsar is in Vol. II of Vasily Kliuchevsky's *A History of Russia*. Among the many biographies of Ivan, the most recent and most brilliant is Bjärne Noerretranders, *Ivan Groznyj and the Shaping of Tsardom*. For a study of the Livonian wars see Walter Kirchner, *The Rise of the Baltic Question*. See also Thomas Esper, "Russia and the Baltic, 1494–1558," *Slavic Review*, September, 1966.

FIRST EPISTLE OF PRINCE AN-
DREY KURBSKY, WRITTEN TO
THE TSAR AND GRAND PRINCE
OF MOSCOW IN CONSEQUENCE
OF HIS FIERCE PERSECUTION

To the tsar, exalted above all by God, who appeared [formerly] most illustrious, particularly in the Orthodox Faith, but who has now, in consequence of our sins, been found to be the contrary of this. If you have understanding, may

From J. L. I. Fennell (ed. and trans.), *The Correspondence between Prince Kurbsky and Tsar Ivan IV of Russia, 1564–1579* (New York: Cambridge University Press, 1955), pp. 3, 5, 7, 9, 11, 13, 15, 17, 19, 23, 27, 69, 71, 73, 75, 77, 79, 81, 83, 85, 87, 89, 91, 93, 95. Reprinted by permission of the publisher.

you understand this with your leprous conscience—such a conscience as cannot be found even amongst the godless peoples. And I have not let my tongue say more than this on all these matters in turn; but because of the bitterest persecution from your power, with much sorrow in my heart will I hasten to inform you of a little.

Wherefore, O tsar, have you destroyed the strong in Israel and subjected to various forms of death the *voevodas* given to you by God?[1] And wherefore have you spilt their victorious, holy blood in the churches of God during sacerdotal ceremonies, and stained the thresholds of the churches with their blood of martyrs? And why have you conceived against your well-wishers and against those who lay down their lives for you unheard-of torments and persecutions and death, falsely accusing the Orthodox of treachery and magic and other abuses, and endeavouring with zeal to turn light into darkness and to call sweet bitter? What guilt did they commit before you, O tsar, and in what way did they, the champions of Christianity, anger you? Have they not destroyed proud kingdoms and by their heroic bravery made subject to you in all things those in whose servitude our forefathers formerly were? Was it not through the keenness of their understanding that the strong German towns were given to you by God?[2] Thus have you remunerated us, [your] poor [servants], destroying us by whole families? Think you yourself immortal, O tsar? Or have you been enticed into unheard-

of heresy, as one no longer wishing to stand before the impartial judge, Jesus, begotten of God, who will judge according to justice the universe and especially the vainglorious tormentors, and who unhesitatingly will question them "right to the hairs [roots?] of their sins," as the saying goes? He is my Christ who sitteth on the throne of the Cherubims at the right hand of the power of the Almighty in the highest—the judge between you and me.

What evil and persecution have I not suffered from you! What ills and misfortunes have you not brought upon me! And what iniquitous tissues of lies have you not woven against me! But I cannot now recount the various misfortunes at your hands which have beset me owing to their multitude and since I am still filled with the grief of my soul. But, to conclude, I can summarize them all: of everything have I been deprived; I have been driven from the land of God without guilt, hounded by you. I did not ask [for aught] with humble words, nor did I beseech you with tearful plaint; nor yet did I win from you any mercy through the intercession of the hierarchy. You have recompensed me with evil for good and for my love with implacable hatred. My blood, spilt like water for you, cries out against you to my Lord. God sees into [men's] hearts—in my mind have I ardently reflected and my conscience have I placed as a witness [against myself], and I have sought and pried within my thoughts, and, examining myself, I know not now—nor have I ever found—my

---

[1] A reference to the first wave of Ivan's persecutions, which, according to Kurbsky, began "shortly after the death of Aleksey [Adashev] and the banishment of Sylvester," i.e., in 1560.

The expression "the strong in Israel" echoes the current panegyrical political literature of the sixteenth century, extolling the absolutism of the grand prince and the supremacy of Moscow, "the Third Rome," "the New Israel."

Voevoda—commander of troops, general.

[2] The "proud kingdoms" destroyed by the "strong in Israel" in the fifties of the sixteenth century were the Tatar Khanates of Kazan' (captured in 1552) and Astrakhan' (captured in 1556).

The "strong German towns" refers to the Baltic towns captured during the first three years of the Livonian War (1558–60): Narva, Neuhausen and Dorpat (1558); Marienburg, Ermes and Fellin (1560).

guilt in aught before you. In front of your army have I marched—and marched again; and no dishonour have I brought upon you; but only brilliant victories, with the help of the angel of the Lord, have I won for your glory, and never have I turned the back of your regiments to the foe. But far more, I have achieved most glorious conquests to increase your renown. And this, not in one year, nor yet in two—but throughout many years have I toiled with much sweat and patience; and always have I been separated from my fatherland, and little have I seen my parents, and my wife have I not known; but always in far-distant towns have I stood in arms against your foes and I have suffered many wants and natural illnesses, of which my Lord Jesus Christ is witness. Still more, I was visited with wounds inflicted by barbarian bands in various battles and all my body is already afflicted with sores. But to you, O tsar, was all this as nought; rather do you show us your intolerable wrath and bitterest hatred, and, furthermore, burning stoves. . . .[3]

Deem not, O tsar, and think not upon us with your sophistic thoughts, as though we had already perished, massacred [though we are] by you in our innocence and banished and driven out by you without justice; rejoice not in this, glorying, as it were, in a vain victory; those massacred by you, standing at the throne of Our Lord, ask vengeance against you; whilst we who have been banished and driven out by you without justice from the land cry out day and night to God, however much in your pride you may boast in this temporal, fleeting life, devising vessels of torture against the Christian race, yea, and abusing and trampling on the an-

gelic form,[4] with the approbation of your flatterers and comrades of the table, your quarrelsome boyars, the destroyers of your soul and body, who urge you on to aphrodisiacal deeds and, together with their children, act more [viciously] than the priests of Cronus. So much for this. And this epistle, soaked in my tears, will I order to be put into my grave with me, when I [shall be about to] come with you before the Judgment of my God, Jesus Christ. Amen.

Written in Wolmar, the town of my master, King Augustus Sigismund, from whom I hope to receive much reward and comfort for all my sorrow, by his sovereign grace, and still more with God's help.

I have heard from sacred writings that a destroyer will be sent by the devil against the human race, a destroyer conceived in fornication, the Antichrist, hostile to God; and now I have seen a counsellor, known to all, who was born in adultery and who today whispers falsehoods in the ears of the tsar and sheds Christian blood like water and has already destroyed the strong and noble in Israel, as one in agreement with the Antichrist in deed.[5] It is not befitting, O tsar to show indulgence to such men! In the first law of the Lord it is written: "A Moabite and an Ammonite and a bastard to the tenth generation shall not enter into the congregation of the Lord."

---

[3] Evidently one of the commonest forms of torture employed by Ivan IV. . . .

[4] The Russian expression "to accept the angel's form" is the equivalent of "to take the monastic vows. . . ."

[5] Ustryalov considers this to be a reference to Fedor Alekseevich Basmanov, who was a favourite of Ivan at the time. He was, indeed, renowned for his cruelty and is alleged by Kurbsky to have murdered his father. There is, however, no confirmation of his illegitimacy.

EPISTLE OF THE TSAR AND SOVEREIGN TO ALL HIS RUSSIAN KINGDOM AGAINST THOSE THAT VIOLATE THE OATH OF ALLEGIANCE, AGAINST PRINCE ANDREY KURBSKY AND HIS COMRADES, CONCERNING THEIR TREACHERIES

The autocracy of this Russian kingdom of veritable Orthodoxy, by the will of God, [has its] beginning from the great tsar Vladimir, who enlightened the whole Russian land with holy baptism, and [was maintained by] the great Tsar Vladimir Monomach, who received the supreme honour from the Greeks, and the brave and great sovereign, Alexander Nevsky, who won a victory over the godless Germans, and the great and praiseworthy sovereign, Dimitry, who beyond the Don won a mighty victory over the godless sons of Hagar,[6] [and autocracy was handed down] even to the avenger of evils, our grandfather, the Grand Prince Ivan, and to the acquirer of immemorially hereditary lands, our father of blessed memory, the great sovereign, Vasily—and [autocracy] has come down even to us, the humble sceptre-bearer of the Russian kingdom. And we praise [God] for his great mercy bestowed upon us, in that he has not hitherto allowed our right hand to become stained with the blood of our own race; for we have not seized the kingdom from anyone, but, by the grace of God and with the blessing of our forefathers and fathers, as we were born to rule, so have we grown up and ascended the throne by the bidding of God, and with the blessing of our par-

ents have we taken what is our own, and we have not seized what belongs to others; [from the ruler] of this Orthodox true Christian autocracy, which has power over many dominions, a command [should be sent to you]; but this is our Christian and humble answer to him who was formerly boyar and adviser and *voevoda* of our autocratic state and of the true Christian Orthodox faith, but who is now the perjurer of the holy and life-giving Cross of the Lord and the destroyer of Christianity, the servant of those enemies of Christianity who have apostatized from the worship of the divine icons and trampled on all the sacred commandments and destroyed the holy temples and befouled and trampled on the sacred vessels and images, like the Isaurian and the one who is called Putrefaction and the Armenian—to him, who has cast in his lot with all these, to Prince Andrey Mikhailovich Kurbsky, who with his treacherous ways wished to become master of Yaroslavl';[7] let [this] be known. . . .

Consider not that it is right to give offence to God, having fallen into wrath against man. It is one thing [to give offence to] a human even if he wears the purple, but it is another thing [to offend] God! Or do you think, accursed one, that you will protect yourself from this [i.e., from offending God]? By no means! If you wage war together with them, then will you also destroy churches and trample on icons and annihilate Christians; and even if you do not dare [to act] with your hands, still with your deadly poisonous thoughts will you cause much of this evil. Consider how in a battle attack the soft limbs of infants are crushed and maimed by the legs of horses! And if

---

[6] The "Sons of Hagar," or "Ishmaelites," was the common Russian appellation for all Mohammedans, more particularly for the Tatars. In 1380 Dimitry Donskoy defeated the khan of the Golden Horde, Mamai, on the field of Kulikovo.

[7] Yaroslavl', the patrimony of the Kurbskys since the end of the thirteenth century, had been annexed by Moscow in 1463.

the attack is in winter, then is the evil wrought still worse! And this your devilish scheming—how can it not be likened to the fury of Herod, manifested by his massacre of the innocents! Do you consider this—the perpetration of such evils—to be piety? Should you accuse us of warring against Christians —namely, against Germans and Lithuanians—then your accusations are groundless. [For] even if there were Christians in those lands, we would [still] wage war according to the customs of our forefathers, just as has happened many times before now; but now we know that in those lands there are no Christians except for a very few ministers of the Church and secret servants of the Lord. Furthermore, even the Lithuanian struggle began because of your treachery and malevolence and your inconsiderate carelessness.[8]

You, however, for the sake of your body have destroyed the soul and for the sake of short-lived fame have scorned imperishable glory, and having raged against man, you have risen against God. Consider, wretch, from what heights and into what depths you have descended in body and soul! On you have come to pass the words: "from him . . . shall be taken away even that which he hath." Is this then your piety, that you have destroyed yourself because of your self-love and not for the sake of God? Those who live there [i.e., in your new fatherland] and those who have understanding can understand

your evil poison, how, desiring short-lived glory and wealth, and not in order to escape from death, you have done this deed. If you are just and pious as you say, why did you fear a guiltless death, which is no death but gain? In the end you will die anyhow! If you did fear a false death sentence against you owing to the villainous lying of your friends, the servants of Satan, then is your treacherous intention clear from the beginning up to now. Why did you despise even the apostle Paul? For he said: "Let every soul be subject unto the higher powers. For there is no power ordained that is not of God. . . . Whosoever, therefore, resisteth the power, resisteth the ordinance of God. . . ."

But for the sake of temporary glory and self-love and the delights of this world, you have trampled down all your spiritual piety together with the Christian faith and law, and you have become like unto the seed falling on stone and springing up, and when the sun shone scorchingly, then were you, because of a false word,[9] led astray and you fell away and bore no fruit. . . .

How were you not shamed by your servant, Vaska Shibanov?[10] For he pre-

---

[8] The Lithuanian war did not, in fact, begin until 1561, when Livonia, as a country, ceased to exist. However, in view of the military pact concluded between Livonia and Lithuania in 1557, war with Lithuania was virtually declared in 1558 when Livonia was invaded by the Muscovites. Ivan's accusations to the effect that Kurbsky's clique was responsible for the war are, therefore, somewhat illogical—especially in view of the fact that he later upbraids "the Priest Sylvester and his counsellors" for advising against the "German" (i.e., Livonian) war.

[9] I.e., because of alleged rumour that I was plotting your death.

[10] According to a seventeenth-century source, Kurbsky, after his flight from Dorpat, sent his servant, Vaska Shibanov, with his letter to the tsar. Shibanov's encounter with Ivan is described as follows: "Vaska Shibanov handed to the tsar . . . the letter from his prince. And the tsar asked him: 'Who are you and whence have you brought this writing?' And he answered the tsar, saying: 'I am the servant of your traitor, Prince Andrey Kurbsky, and this letter which I have given you is from him.' Then the tsar was filled with wrath, and calling this servant unto him, transfixed his foot with the sharp end of his staff. Then he lent upon his staff and ordered him to read the letter. . . ." However, according to a more reliable source of the sixteenth century, Shibanov was not sent as an emissary by Kurbsky but was arrested by Ivan's *voevodas* and despatched by them to the tsar.

served his piety, before the tsar and before all the people, standing at the gates of death; and because of his oath on the Cross he did not renounce you, but, praising you, he did hasten to die for you. But you have not imitated his piety. Because of one small angry word you have destroyed not only your soul but the souls of your forefathers, for by the will of God, they were placed by God in the service of our grandfather, the great sovereign, and, having sacrificed their souls, they served unto their death and ordered you, their children, to serve even the children and grandchildren of our grandfather. And you have forgotten all that; in your houndish, treacherous manner you have broken the oath on the Cross and joined the enemies of Christianity; and furthermore, paying no heed to your wickedness, with such pusillanimous words, like one "that casteth a stone on high," you utter foolish things and you feel no shame before the piety of your servant, and you have refused to do things similar to this [i.e., to what he did] for your master.

So much for worldly matters; as for spiritual [matters] and [for matters] concerning the Church, if there [is any question of] small sin[s] [to be imputed to me], then this is [only] because of your corruption and treachery; still more so because I am only human; for there is no man without sin, only God alone; but not like you [am I human], for you think yourself the equal of the angels. And as for the godless peoples—why mention them? For none of these rule their own kingdoms. As their servants order them, so too do they rule. But as for the Russian autocracy, they themselves [i.e., the autocrats] from the beginning have ruled all the[ir] dominions, and not the boyars and not the grandees. And this you have not been able to appreciate in your wickedness, calling it "piety" when the autoc-racy is under the power of a certain priest and at the mercy of your impious commands. While this, according to your understanding, is evil—namely, that we ourselves rule[d] [with] the power given us by God and had no desire to be at the mercy of the priest and of your wicked designs! Is this then what we are to understand by "Contrary [to Orthodoxy]," that, by the Grace of God and the intercession of the most pure Mother of God and the prayers of all the Saints and with the blessing of my forefathers, I did not at that time suffer myself to be destroyed by your devilish scheming? Yet what evil did I suffer at your hands! Of this will my word[s] from now on most amply inform you. . . .

As I have said above, I will prove in the greatest detail what evil I have suffered from my youth even unto the present day. For this is clear [even if you were young in those years, yet none the less this you can know]: when, by the decree[s] of God, our father, the great sovereign, Vasily, having exchanged the purple for the angel's form,[11] had left all that was perishable and the fleeting earthly kingdom and come to the heavenly [realm], to that everlasting eternity, to stand before the Tsar of Tsars and the Lord of Lords, I remained with my only brother Georgiy, who has departed this life in sanctity, I was then three years old and my brother was one, and our mother, the pious Tsaritsa Elena, was left in such miserable widowhood—as though in the midst of flames, she suffered on all sides now unmitigated strife stirred up against her by all peoples—by the foreign peoples encircling [our realm], Lithuanians, Poles, Perikopians, Nadchitarkhan, and No-

11 Lit. "having exchanged the purple with the angelic transformation," i.e., when the grand prince had received the tonsure. It was the custom of the Muscovite grand princes to accept the monastic tonsure on their death-beds.

gais,[12] and Kazan',—now manifold misfortune[s] and suffering[s] [inflicted by] you traitors; for, like unto you, you mad dog, Prince Semen Bel'sky and Ivan Lyatsky ran away to Lithuania; [from there] whither did they now run like men possessed? To Tsargrad and to Crimea and to the Nogai [Tatars] and on all sides they raised strife against the Orthodox.[13] But they had no success. Thanks to the intervention of God and the most pure Mother of God and the great miracle-workers, and because of the prayers and the blessing of our parents, all these things, like the counsel of Ahitophel, were scattered. In like manner later did the traitors raise up our uncle, Prince Andrey Ivanovich, against us, and with those traitors did he go to Novgorod, [so, these are they whom you praise! You call them our "well-wishers" and "those that lay down their lives for us"!]. And at that time did these [traitors] secede from us and adhere to our uncle, Prince Andrey, and at their head was your brother [i.e., cousin], Prince Ivan, the son of Prince Semen, the son of Prince Petr Romano-

12 The "Perikopians" was the name frequently given by the Muscovites to the Crimean Tatars.
"Nadchitarkhan" is presumably a corruption of "Hadji-Tarkhan," the Tatar name for Astrakhan'. The Nogai Tatars were a nomadic race in the steppeland north of the Caspian Sea.

13 In 1534 Prince Semen Fedorovich Bel'sky, owing to his dissatisfaction with the government of Elena Glinsky and her favourite, Prince Ivan Fedorovich Telepnev-Obolensky, fled to Lithuania, where he took part in various campaigns against the Muscovites. Owing to the failure of these campaigns, which Sigismund, grand prince of Lithuania and king of Poland, attributed to the Russians in his service, Bel'sky fled to Constantinople and thence to Crimea (1537), where he vainly attempted to incite the Khan against Russia, in the hope of retrieving his mother's principality of Ryazan'. He was subsequently captured by the Nogai Tatars and later ransomed by the Crimean Khan. Ivan Vasil'evich Lyatsky fled to Lithuania together with S. F. Bel'sky.

vich Lvov, and many others.[14] And likewise with the help of God did this plot miscarry. . . . Well then, is that the "well-wishing" of those whom you praise? Thus do they "lay down their lives for us" by wishing to destroy us and raise our uncle to the throne? But later, in their treacherous manner, they began to hand over our patrimony to our Lithuanian enemy—the towns of Radogoshch, Starodub, Gomel'[15]—thus do they "wish us well"? . . .

Thus by God's will did it come to pass that our mother, the pious Tsaritsa Elena, went from the earthly kingdom to the heavenly; and we and our brother Georgiy, who has departed this life in

14 In 1537 Ivan IV's uncle, Prince Andrey of Staritsa, frightened by current rumours of impending arrest, fled to Novgorod, notwithstanding various assurances and admonitions of the Metropolitan Daniel and the senior clergy. His sister-in-law, Elena, dispatched her lover and favourite, Prince Telepnev-Obolensky, to Novgorod, where, according to the most probable of the two versions of the story, he succeeded in persuading Andrey to return to Moscow. There Andrey was perjurously arrested and thrown into prison where he died in the same year. Prince Ivan Lvov, a distant cousin of Kurbsky, is not mentioned in the chronicles as a partisan of Andrey Staritsky.

15 Ivan's allegations, which refer to the Russo-Lithuanian campaigns of 1534–35, do not appear to be entirely justified. In the autumn of 1534 the *voevoda* of Kiev, Andrzej Niemirowicz, burned Radogoshch, but was forced to withdraw from Starodub and Chernigov with heavy losses. In the following year a Lithuanian army under the command of Jerzy Radziwill, Andrzej Niemirowicz, the Polish Hetman Tarnowski and the fugitive Russian, Semen Bel'sky, again invaded the surrounds of Novgorod-Seversky. Owing to the pusillanimity of the local commander, Prince Obolensky-Shchepin, who fled to Moscow with all his troops and weapons, Gomel' surrendered without a struggle. But in Starodub the local *voevoda*, Prince Fedor Telepnev-Obolensky, resisted manfully, and it was only after the fiercest of struggles that the Lithuanians succeeded in blowing up and occupying the town. During the battle for Starodub the *voevoda* was captured and 13,000 of the inhabitants were killed.

sanctity, remained as orphans, [having lost] our parents and receiving no human care from any quarter; and hoping only for the mercy of God, we put our trust in the mercy of the most pure Mother of God and the prayers of all the Saints and the blessing of our parents. But when I had entered upon my eighth year of life and when thus our subjects had achieved their desire, namely, to have the kingdom without a ruler, then did they not deem us, their sovereigns, worthy of any loving care, but themselves ran after wealth and glory, and so leapt on one another [in conflict]. And what did they [not] do then! How many boyars and well-wishers of our father and *voevodas* did they massacre! And the courts and the villages and the possessions of our uncles did they seize and they set themselves up in them! And [the majority of] my mother's treasure did they transfer to the Great Treasury, furiously kicking out [at each other] and stabbing with sharp implements; but the remainder they shared amongst themselves. Your grandfather, Mikhailo Tuchkov did this. And so Prince Vasily and Prince Ivan Shuisky of their own accord did appoint themselves to the throne; and all those who had been our father's and our mother's main traitors did they release, one after the other, from imprisonment and win over to their side. And Prince Vasily Shuisky began to live in the court of our uncle, Prince Andrey Ivanovitch, and in that court—as it were in a Jewish synagogue[16] —they seized Fedor Mishurin, the private *d'yak*[17] of our father and of us, and having put him to shame they murdered him. And they banished Prince Ivan Fedorovich Bel'sky and many others to various places and rose up in arms against the Church and, deposing the

Metropolitan Daniel from the metropolitanate, they sent him into banishment; thus did they achieve their desire in all things and themselves began to rule. But as for us, together with our only brother Georgiy, who has departed this life in sanctity—they began to feed us as though we were foreigners or the most wretched menials. What sufferings did I [not] endure through [lack of] clothing and through hunger! For in all things my will was not my own; everything was contrary to my will and unbefitting my tender years. I [will] recall one thing: whilst we were playing childish games in our infancy Prince Ivan Vasil'evich Shuisky is sitting on a bench, leaning with his elbows on our father's bed and with his leg up on a chair; and he did not even incline his head towards us, either in parental manner, or even as a master—nor was there any element of servility to be found [in his attitude to us]. And who can endure such arrogance? How can I enumerate such countless sore sufferings as I put up with in my youth? Many a time did I eat late, not in accordance with my will. But what of the treasures inherited by me from my father? With their cunning scheming they seized it all, as though it were pay for the boyar children;[18] but from them they took it all

16 The expression "in the manner of a Jewish synagogue"—is used by Ivan to signify bedlam, utter confusion.

17 In the thirteenth and fourteenth centuries the term *d'yak* or "scribe" signified merely a personal servant who, by virtue of his ability to read and write, assisted his master in any matters connected with correspondence or finance. With the formation of *Prikazy* (ministries) and the centralization of the administration in the fifteenth and sixteenth centuries, however, the *d'yaki* assumed a far more important role in society, becoming not only members of the various ministries, but even secretaries, ministers and Privy Councillors of the grand prince.

18 "Boyar children" was the name given to that class of society which consisted of the descendants of boyars who had lost the title of boyar.

for themselves for their own profit, rewarding them [the boyar children] not according to their service and recompensing them not according to their merits; and they appropriated the incalculable treasure of our grandfather and of our father; and so from this treasure did they forge for themselves golden and silver vessels and upon them they inscribed the names of their parents as though they had been the possession of their parents. . . .

And when they had lived thus for a long time and when I was growing up physically, I did not wish to remain in servile submission [lit., under servile power] and for this reason I sent away [from myself] Prince Ivan Vasil'evich Shuisky to service and ordered my boyar, Prince Ivan Fedorovich Bel'sky, to be beside me. And Prince Ivan Shuisky, having united all the people beneath his banner and led them to the oath of allegiance [lit., to the kissing of the cross], marched in arms on Moscow and his advisers, Kubensky and others, before his arrival seized our boyar, Prince Ivan Fedorovich Bel'sky, and other boyars and *dvoryane*[19] one after the other and exiled them to Beloozero and murdered them; yea, and they drove Metropolitan Ioasaf with great indignity from the metropolitanate. Then Prince Andrey Shuisky together with his partisans came into our refectory and in frenzied manner having seized and put to shame before us our boyar, Fedor Semenovich Vorontsov, they bore him out from our refectory and intended to kill him. . . .

But when we reached the fifteenth year of our life, then did we take it

upon ourselves to put our kingdom in order and thanks to the mercy of God our rule began favourably.[20] But since human sin ever acerbates the Grace of God, it came to pass that—because of our sins and the intensification of God's wrath—a fiery flame burned the ruling city of Moscow, and our treacherous boyars, who are called martyrs by you (their names will I intentionally pass over), seized the moment which appeared [lit., as it were] favourable to their treacherous wickedness [and] incited the feeblest-witted of the people [by saying] that the mother of our mother, Princess Anna Glinsky, together with her children and her retinue extracted human hearts and with such magic set fire to Moscow and that we had knowledge of this their counsel;[21] and owing to the incitement of those traitors, the people, raising a cry and having seized in frenzied manner our boyar, Prince Yury Vasil'evich Glinsky in the chapel of the holy martyr Dimitry of Salonica, and having dragged him

---

[19] The term *dvoryanin* implied in the sixteenth century a member of the new class of minor nobility (as opposed to the boyars, the hereditary aristocracy), the "Service People," who acquired position and property by virtue alone of their service either in the armed forces or in the government.

[20] According to the chronicles, 1545 saw the beginning of a peculiarly fierce period of persecution and cruelty. One Ivan Kubensky, a relative of the tsar, was imprisoned and beheaded. Afanasy Buturlin had his tongue cut out for impertinence. Two of the Vorontsov family were executed. In 1547 Ivan chose to punish a deputation from Pskov, who came to complain of their governor, Prince Turuntay, in the following manner: "He poured boiling wine on them, singed their beards and set fire to their hair with a candle and bade them be laid naked on the ground."

[21] After the murder of A. M. Shuisky in 1543 the Glinsky family appears to have assumed control of the State. But their sway was short-lived. In 1547 after the terrible fire of Moscow a group of boyars, determined to put an end to the power of the tsar's relatives, incited the mob to frenzy by telling them that the fire had been started by Anna Glinsky (Ivan IV's grandmother), who with her children "had extracted human hearts and put them in water; and ridden through Moscow, sprinkling [the streets] with that water. And as a result Moscow burned down."

out, inhumanly slew him in the apostolic cathedral of the Assumption of the most holy Mother of God opposite the throne of the metropolitan, and filled the church with his blood; and they dragged his dead body into the porch of the church and laid him, like one condemned [to death], in the market place, And this his murder in the church is known to all, and not as you lyingly assert, you cur! [Now] while we were living in our village of Vorob'evo these traitors stirred up the people to kill us too, on the grounds that we were hiding from them the mother of Prince Yury [Glinsky], Princess Anna, and his brother Prince Mikhail.[22] How can one help but deride such sophistries! For what reason, pray, should we ourselves be the incendiary of our own kingdom? Indeed, so many possessions—the legacy of our forefathers—did we lose as could not be found again in the whole universe. Who could be so insensate or wild as to destroy his own possessions when in anger with his servants? He would burn down their [houses], but would preserve himself. In everything is your currish treachery brought to light. And how could one sprinkle water to such a height as [the church of] St. John? This is indeed clear madness.[23] ... Now at this time that cur, Aleksey, your chief, was in the court of our kingdom during our youth, and I know not by what means he was promoted from *batozhnik*;[24] but we, having seen such

treachery on the part of our grandees, thus took him from the dung-heap and placed him together with the grandees, hoping for faithful service from him. What honours and riches did I not heap upon him—[and] not only upon him, but also upon his family! Yet what true service did I get from him?[25] Listen further. Afterwards, for the sake of spiritual counsel and the salvation of my soul, I took [into my service] the priest Sylvester, thinking that he, because of his ministry at the altar of the Lord, would have care for his soul; but he, having trampled under foot his priesthood vows and his ordination [and] all that [appertains] to service with the angels at the altar of the Lord, "which things the angels desire to look into," where the Lamb of God is ever sacrificed for the salvation of the world and is never consumed—he, indeed, whilst still in the flesh, was deemed worthy [to perform] the Seraphic service with his own hands; and all this he trampled down in his cunning way; yet at first it

[22] When Prince Yury Vasil'evich Glinsky heard the rumours spread against his mother he came to Moscow to reason with the mob, only to be murdered by them. His mother, Princess Anna, and his brother Mikhail escaped a similar fate by being in Rzhev at the time. Three days after Yury's murder the mob came to Ivan IV at Vorob'evo (on the outskirts of Moscow) to demand Mikhail and Anna, whom they claimed he was hiding. In answer to their demand Ivan had as many of the mob as could be caught arrested and put to death. The remainder escaped.

[23] This obscure passage is clearly a refutation of the rumour spread by the boyars to the effect that the Glinskys dipped human hearts in water with which they sprinkled the streets of Moscow and thus set the city on fire. How, Ivan asks, could anyone possibly reach so tall a building as the church of St. John with water from the streets of the city?

[24] The *batozhniki*, or "stick-bearers," were those servants of the tsar who walked before him, clearing the people from his path with their sticks.

[25] Aleksey Adashev's origins appear to have been humble. His father, Fedor Grigor'evich, was promoted *okol'nichy* (a rank in the court hierarchy directly below that of boyar) in 1548, and boyar in 1553. Aleksey Adashev is first mentioned in 1547 as the tsar's *postel'nik* (keeper of the bed-chamber). Although he only reached the rank of *okol'nichy* in 1555, he appears to have won the tsar's confidence and to have excercised a beneficial influence over him from the time of Sylvester's appearance. He was at once entrusted with the task of receiving and dealing with petitions to the tsar and later with important diplomatic functions.

seemed as though he had begun in a righteous manner, following the Holy Scriptures; [and] when I saw in the Holy Scriptures that it is right to submit to good preceptors without any consideration, then, willingly, but through ignorance, did I obey even him for the sake of spiritual counsel. But he was carried away by power like Eli the priest [and] began to form friendships[26] as laymen do. Then we assembled all the archbishops and the bishops and all the holy synod of the Russian metropolitanate, and as for what befell us in our youth, the digraces inflicted by us upon you, our boyars, and likewise too the hostility towards us and the misdemeanours committed by you, our boyars— for all these things did we ourselves publicly ask forgiveness before our father and interceder, Makary, Metropolitan of All Russia. And [to] you, our boyars, and to all our people did I grant [forgiveness] for your misdemeanours and [decreed] that henceforth all memory of them be obliterated; and so then did we begin to treat you all as [though you were] good men.[27]

But you did not abandon your first cunning habit[s], but returned again to your former ways and thus began to serve us with cunning counsel and false, and to do all things with scheming and not with simplicity. And so the priest Sylvester joined Aleksey too in friendship and they began to hold counsel in secret and without our knowledge, deeming us to be incapable of judgment;[28]

26 I.e., to form his own party.

27 This "summoning of the clergy" refers either to the sacred council convened in February, 1549, or to the Council of the Hundred Chapters (Stoglavy Sobor) of 1551. At the first the tsar addressed the assembled hierarchy and nobility, accusing the boyars of the disorders during his minority, ordering them to settle peacefully all disputes and finally granting a general amnesty. At the second the tsar repeated his reconciliatory remarks concerning the boyars.

and thus did they begin to give worldly counsel in the place of spiritual, and thus did they begin little by little to lead all the boyars into contumacy, taking the splendour of our power from us and leading you into opposition, and in honour almost levelling you with us, while they made the young boyar children your equals in honour. . . .

And so neither in external affairs nor in internal affairs,[29] nor in the smallest and pettiest things [and (I refer to such things as) footware and sleeping]—was anything according to my will; but everything was done according to their desire, while we remained, as it were, a child. Now is this "Contrary to reason" that I, having reached man's estate, did not desire to be a little child? Likewise afterwards this too became a habit: if we had at that time to contradict even one of the most insignificant counsellors, then all these [my words] were interpreted as impious, as is written in your calumnious epistle; but if any of his most inferior advisers were in their madness to utter haughty words to us, not as to a master or as to a brother, but as to the most inferior thing, then all these things too were reckoned to be pious; and whoever provided us with a little obedience or peace, to his lot fell persecution and torment. And should anyone annoy us in aught or cause us to

28 It is hard to assess the full extent of the influence of the "Izbrannaya Rada" or Chosen Council (the name given by Kurbsky in his *History* to Sylvester and his associates) on the tsar in matters of governmental policy during the fifties of the sixteenth century. It seems, however, probable that the majority of the great administrative, legal and military reforms of the fifties were designed by and executed at the instigation of Sylvester's clique. Yet it is hardly likely that the young tsar allowed himself to be pushed into the background or to be "deemed incapable of judgment" to the extent that he here suggests.

29 I.e., neither in affairs of State nor in personal affairs.

suffer any oppression, to his lot fell wealth, glory and honour. . . .

Likewise, when we had arrived in the ruling city of Moscow God increased his mercy towards us and gave us at that time an heir, our son Dimitry. But after a short time had passed [it fell to our lot]—as indeed it falls to the lot of [all] men—to be afflicted with sickness and to be sorely ill; and then did those who are called by you "well-wishers" rise up like drunken men with the priest Sylvester and with your chief Aleksey, thinking that we were no longer alive, having forgotten our good deeds and even their own souls too, and [having forgotten] that they had kissed the Cross [in allegiance] to our father and to us, [vowing] to seek no other sovereign but our children. Yet they desired to raise to the throne Prince Vladimir, who is far removed from us in the line of succession; while our infant, given to us by God, did they, like Herod, desire to destroy [and how could they fail to destroy him!], having raised Prince Vladimir to the throne. For even though it was said in the ancient secular writings, yet none the less is [the following] fitting: "Tsar does not bow down to tsar; but when one dies, the other rules." [If] then we, while still alive, enjoyed such "well-wishing" from our

subjects, what will it be like after our death! But again thanks to God's mercy we recovered, and thus was this counsel scattered. But the priest Sylvester and Aleksey ceased not from that time forth to counsel all that was evil and to inflict [on me] still harsher oppression, conceiving persecutions of various kinds against our [true] well-wishers, while indulging every whim of Prince Vladimir; and likewise they stirred up great hatred against our tsaritsa Anastasia and likened her to all the impious tsaritsas; as for our children, they were not able even to call them to mind.[30]

---

[30] According to the *Tsarstvennaya Kniga*, Ivan fell seriously ill on his return from Kazan' and nominated his infant son, Dimitry, as heir apparent. He then requested his cousin, Prince Vladimir Andreevich Staritsky, and the boyars to swear allegiance to Dimitry. Vladimir, however, and many of the boyars refused, not wishing to have an infant on the throne. Aleksey Adashev's father, Fedor, explained the reason to the tsar: "Your son is still in swaddling clothes; the Zakhar'ins will rule us." Among the other supporters of Vladimir Andreevich were Sylvester, Kurlyatev, Paletsky and Funikov (but not Aleksey Adashev or Kurbsky). The "rebellious" boyars were, however, eventually persuaded by the "true boyars" (Mstislavsky, Vorotynsky, Sheremetev and others) to kiss the Cross in allegiance to Dimitry. The Soviet critics tend to doubt the authenticity of the information contained in the *Tsarstvennaya Kniga*.

8

IVAN GROZNY EXCERPTS

By Robert Wipper

Wipper's book was first published in 1922, long before the formulation of any official Soviet views on Russian history. The author (1859–1954) was not a Marxist but, according to the first edition of the Great Soviet Encyclopedia, "a most talented representative in historical science of the Russian petty bourgeois intelligentsia." He taught ancient history at Moscow University from 1899 to 1924, when he emigrated to his native Latvia. There he taught at the University of Riga until 1940 when the country was annexed by the Soviet Union. He then returned to Moscow and in 1942 issued a revised edition of the present work which was welcomed by Soviet reviewers. An officially ordered new trend in historical writing resulted in the glorification of such Russian rulers as could be considered useful precursors of the Soviet state. Ivan the Terrible was one of those figures.

Wipper's work was accorded the privilege of being translated into English for foreign consumption. The author became a member of the Soviet Academy of Sciences, the highest scholarly honor in the USSR. Since the rejection of "the cult of the individual," however, the party has admonished historians to revise the hitherto standard idealization of Ivan the Terrible, known in Russia as Ivan Grozny.

The works of Peresvetov and Schlichting are not available in English. There is a new translation of Staden in Thomas Esper's *The Land and Government of Muscovy: A Sixteenth Century Account*. Volumes I and II of the newly reissued *Voyages* of Richard Hakluyt include several accounts by English visitors to Russia during the reign of Ivan. A deservedly famous account by a contemporary of Ivan is Giles Fletcher's *Of the Russe Commonwealth*, recently reissued in two new editions with commentary. Ina Lubimenko comments on the letters of Ivan to Elizabeth of England in her article, "The Correspondence of Queen Elizabeth with the Russian Tsars," *American Historical Review*, XIX (1914), 525–42. There is an analysis of the popular image of Ivan the Terrible during his lifetime and after in Michael Cherniavsky's *Tsar and People*. See also Jack Culpepper, "The Kremlin Executions in 1575 and the Enthronement of Simeon Bekbulatovich," *Slavic Review*, September, 1965.

From R. Wipper, *Ivan Grozny* (Moscow, 1947), pp. 91–100, 103–8, 134–41, 144, 156–61, 234–43.

It has long been the custom in Russian historiography to depict the institution of the Oprichnina primarily as a gesture of horror and despair, which conformed to the high-strung character of Ivan IV, before whom yawned a chasm of disloyalty and treachery among what had seemed his best servants and counsellors.

This naïve and romantic presentation of the subject must be abandoned once and for all. It is time to understand that the institution of the Oprichnina was primarily a great military-administrative reform, called forth by the growing difficulties of the great war for access to the Baltic Sea and for the opening of intercourse with Western Europe. Present-day historians, whose world outlook was moulded in the period between the two world wars of 1914–18 and 1939–45 will also abandon the mistaken method of relating the events of foreign policy, wars and international relations divorced from social and political movements and changes at home.

It seems to me that historians must note the fact that the Livonian War gave rise to a number of difficulties not encountered in previous wars; and to remove these difficulties it was necessary to employ new military-technical methods. During the conquest of the Volga region the Moscow cavalry armies fought against warriors like themselves in conformity with strategy and tactics of an extremely simple nature. It was quite different, however, in the western war, in which the Moscow forces encountered the intricate military art of the commanders of European trained mercenaries. An extremely important defect from which the Moscow forces suffered was the absence of discipline and solidarity. The army did not represent a uniformally organized tactical entity. The effect was felt of the remnants of the independence exercised by the former appanage princes and big boyar owners of patrimonies who still maintained their local courts, administered justice, collected dues for themselves and granted patrimonies and manors to their dependents as if they were their own lieges. They joined the Tsar's levies together with their own units of serf soldiers whom they had placed on their lands; with their own "liverymen," as they would have been called in England during the Wars of the Roses. . . .

In introducing, in 1550–56, the reforms for improving the military-manorial system, the government, on this question, as in others, permitted the presentation of petitions containing schemes and advice. Among the latter is that signed by Ivashka Peresvetov, which amazes one for the talent and publicist zeal it reveals. In his petition Peresvetov proposed that the reorganization of the armed forces go hand in hand with an increase in the power of the monarch. Peresvetov describes himself as a public servant of Lithuanian-Russian extraction who had been in foreign, i.e., Hungarian, Polish and Walachian service, and had voluntarily chosen service in Moscow. He refers with emphasis and pride to his poverty, to the fact that he had risen from obscurity. He compares himself to the "warriors of needy appearance" who came to Augustus Caesar and to the great Alexander and gave these rulers wise counsel.

Peresvetov, in a very peculiar way, combined the exaltation of monarchical power with defence of the interests of the lower public servants, among whom he included himself. He detested the higher aristocracy, wished to have complete equality among all servants of the state, and opportunity for the free development of their talents also for the common gentry. Only monarchical power could create such opportunities for the lower aristocracy. On the other hand, it was in the monarch's interest to gain the services of all strata of the aristocracy in order to improve the military system and to create a flexible, vigorous and invincible military force. Peresvetov combines all the ideas in a general political maxim: "Above all else a Tsar should love his troops." He was of the opinion that the notables in Moscow wanted to take the care of the army out of the Tsar's hands, to divorce him from it, to leave only civilian affairs in his hands. He advised the Tsar not to yield to such treacherous designs, for his safety depended on the loyalty of the army.

Peresvetov urged that the state should be reorganized on the lines of strict military discipline. The administration must be strict and justice stern and swift, like courts-martial. The main point of the reform, in his opinion, was to deprive the notables of the right to have their private military retinues. He advised the Tsar to choose the best of the soldiers who were subordinated to the nobles and to form them into a picked corps of his own. After that he was to rule untrammelled and remorselessly crush all resistance. . . .

Comparing the advice offered by Peresvetov with the institution that became known as the Oprichnina one must admit that the publicist had made a number of proposals which the reformer accepted.

We shall observe that no little time intervened between the proposal of the various schemes and their execution. Peresvetov wrote his petition before the capture of Kazan. He had in mind only the struggle on the eastern front and had no knowledge whatever of the Baltic War. All the more interesting, therefore, is the light he throws on the political situation. When he referred to the intention of the notables to divorce the Tsar from his troops and to prevent him from playing an active part in the government of the country, he had in mind

nothing more nor less than the close Duma, or Council, which had surrounded Ivan IV since 1547, and which, in the period of the Hundred Chapter Council and the Kazan campaign, exercised unlimited authority.

Thanks to Kurbski's testimony, this Duma, which was headed by Sylvester and Adashev, enjoys a high reputation among historians; the beginnings of Ivan IV's cruelties and caprices are usually ascribed to the decline of its influence. There can be no doubt, however, that in this too much attention has been devoted to personal conflicts and private grudges and too little to the political aspect of the matter. It would have been worth noting that, quite characteristically, Kurbski called the close Duma, of which he himself was a member, the "Elected Rada." No other writer called the Duma by that name; and this reactionary Russian boyar did not use that term fortuitously. His eyes were turned to the "Pans' Rada," the Supreme Council which limited the power of the Polish King. This representative of an ancient princely line and the peer of the Lithuanian and Polish Pans was naturally attracted by the example of the western neighbour's oligarchy. By applying to the close Duma of the Moscow Tsar the title of the Upper Chamber of the aristocratic Rzecz Pospolita, he merely proved that Ivan IV was justified in complaining that his counsellors had divorced him from public affairs, had restricted his power, had encouraged the boyars to "gainsay," had distributed rank and lands without authorization, and so forth. Peresvetov, the bitter enemy of the aristocracy, throws unexpected light on the activities of the "Elected Rada" when, quite early in the period when the Tsar reposed the fullest confidence in his counsellors, he advised the Tsar to lean on the mass of minor aristocracy and resolutely break the power of these counsellors. . . .

Kursbki's ambitions were fully satisfied when, as a member of the supreme government council, he found the Moscow Tsar's will subordinated to his own and that of his colleagues. But when this situation was shaken he could find only one way out, viz., to betray his country, to desert the state. His views fully coincided with the world outlook of the big Polish Pans, of the German Fürsts and of the French seigneurs of the sixteenth century, who either compelled the monarch to submit to their governmental pressure or, if they failed to do so, betrayed their respective countries and proclaimed themselves free and independent leaders, or sovereigns, as it were. In 1521, Bourbon, Constable of France, a Prince of the royal blood and a kinsman of the king, in revenge for personal wrongs, deserted to the side of Charles V, Emperor of Germany, and took command of troops which were fighting against his country; and Kurfürst Maurice of Saxony, a faithful servant of Charles V in 1548, deserted the latter in favour of France in 1552. These are striking western parallels of Kurbski's conduct. In this respect Muscovy neither lagged behind nor ran ahead of the West European states. . . .

Attention must be drawn to a characteristic item which reveals how Peresvetov's views coincided with those of Ivan IV. Enumerating the various misdemeanours committed by the notables against the monarch, the publicist called them "magicians and heretics who robbed the Tsar of his happiness and of his royal wisdom." The charge was a terrible one for those times. Never, perhaps, was belief in witchcraft, black magic and evil charms so widespread, and never were there so many witchcraft trials in the West and in Moscow as in those days. It is difficult to say to what extent Ivan Grozny was inclined to believe in the power of witchcraft and black magic; perhaps, in attempting to rouse his suspicion that the people around him were designing to use black magic against him, Peresvetov resorted to an extremely dangerous weapon against them. Kurbski relates that in 1560 Sylvester and Adashev were convicted without an opportunity to defend themselves because they were regarded as miscreants and magicians. He also relates that in Moscow a woman of high virtue and ascetic life was put to death because her extraordinary spiritual qualities gave rise to the suspicion that she was a witch who was capable of causing the Tsar's death by her charms.

In their characterization of Ivan Grozny most historians lump all his executions together and point to them indiscriminately as proof of his cruelty. A distinction should be drawn, however, between political and witchcraft trials. The former expressed white-hot wrath against traitors and were prompted by motives of a rational nature; the latter expressed something elementary, manifested when Ivan IV shared the superstitions of his contemporaries. It would be interesting to know what Kurbski himself would have done in Ivan Grozny's place. He implicitly believed in the power of witchcraft, and he ascribes the change in the Tsar's temper, his turn towards cruelty, to the power of magic expressed by the Tsar's "evil" counsellors who had taken the place of the "good" ones.

Again we take the opportunity to remind the reader that as regards superstition sixteenth-century Muscovy was not far behind the West. The period of humanism and the Reformation was the period when witch-hunting was most rampant; and it was the Puritan sects, who prided themselves on having purged Christianity of paganism, who engaged in this most. . . .

If we regard the institution of the Oprichnina in 1564 as a military-organizational measure we will realize that it was a continuation of the reform of 1550. At that time one thousand men of the new service were granted estates around Moscow. Now, Ivan Grozny, too, chose "princes and nobles and sons of Boyars, Court and Town, a thousand head," but he settled them in the districts around and beyond Moscow— Galich, Kostroma and Suzdal—and in the towns on the other side of the River Oka. The reformer, however, went much further in developing military technique. It is very interesting to compare Peresvetov's counsels with the way the army reform was carried out.

The author of the petition urged the formation of a picked corps of twenty thousand "young men, brave and skilled in the use of firearms." He had in mind the difficult and heroic struggle waged against the Crimeans in the South. He conceived of a tireless warrior Tsar who lived heart and soul with his army; and it is not surprising that he was inspired by the personality of Mohammed II. The Turkey of his day had produced another restless conqueror of the same stamp in the person of Suleiman II (1520–66). For this role, however, Ivan IV was not quite suited. . . .

Although lacking the gifts of a military leader, Ivan IV possessed technical talent in engineering and building and a wide and practical outlook on questions of military organization. The division in 1564 of the lands and the people into an Oprichnina and Zemshchina, i.e., civil provincial government, was carried out in conformity with a well thought-out plan. In the Zemshchina the old caste arrangements and service ranks remained. In the Oprichnina, however, the Tsar gathered all the elements that he regarded as suitable for his purpose, irrespective of birth, precedence, class prejudices and claims, and in placing men in different ranks he was guided exclusively by their military abilities, their talents and their merits. Step by

step he collected under his personal, purely military, administration a central group of lands, and placed the Oprichnina in control of the most important state roads that led from the capital to the frontiers. The "Zemshchina Service" was shifted to the outlying regions, where it functioned under the surveillance of the central military administration.

There can be no doubt that the real arrangements of 1564 were affected by the irritation caused by the military setbacks and the first betrayals. They represented a sort of temporary structure erected with great haste. Later, the content of this original framework was constantly changed. Ivan Grozny himself expressed the significance of this reform in the following words written in an ironic petition he submitted to Simeon Bekbulatovich,[1] the baptized Tatar in whose favour he temporarily abdicated in 1574: "Sort out men, boyars and nobles, and the sons of boyars and domestics." Indeed, he seems to have been continuously sorting out the members of the serving class and its domains, shifting and re-shuffling its individual representatives, distributing and redistributing them without end. . . .

Ivan Grozny's policy, both foreign and domestic, clearly expressed the *class* character of the rising monarchy. Moreover, the definite social change that was exceptionally marked by the institution of the Oprichnina in 1564 should be noted. The Tsar acted mainly in the interests of the middle landed gentry,

[1] Simeon Bekbulatovich, Khan of Kasimov, who adopted Christianity. In 1574, when misfortune pressed heavily upon Ivan Grozny, he formally abdicated and proclaimed Bekbulatovich Grand Prince of All the Russias, although actually ruling behind the scenes. Two years later he banished Bekbulatovich from Moscow and gave him the administration of Tver and Torzhok. He was recalled from banishment only when Dmitri the Pretender ascended the throne.

from whose representatives he formed what was, to use J. V. Stalin's classically precise term, an *aristocratic military bureaucracy.* . . .

Most of the historians of the nineteenth century were wont to regard the Oprichnina exclusively, or mainly, as an instrument of nascent despotism. It is true, of course, that in 1558–64 Ivan IV made a series of extremely vigorous efforts to throw off the oligarchy that had grown up around him; he strengthened the monarchy, however, not only by means of terrorism, but also by the methods which had been recommended to him by Peresvetov and Yermolai-Erasmus, i.e., by drawing closer to the army and recruiting for it men from different classes of society. The impression of such an appeal to the patriotism of wide sections of society is created by the Zemski Sobor, or National Assembly of 1566, which was convened not long after the institution of the Oprichnina, and was intended to demonstrate, as it were, the importance the government attached to the temper of the army.

Russian historians are now agreed that the Assembly of 1566 was the first real Zemski Sobor (the latest attempt to depict the Assembly of 1550, with the Tsar's speeches to the people, as a Zemski Sobor is now unanimously relegated to the realm of fantasy). Scholarship has discovered the predecessors of "the council of all the land." These are the assembly of various ranks of the army, an example of which was given by Ivan III in 1471, and, on the other hand, the Sanctified Assembly, the council of the supreme hierarchy. In the period of the tutelage the government combined both forms of assembly for the discussion of the church reform, and the Stoglavi Sobor of 1551 was a combination of the "authorities" (the clergy), the "Synkletos" (the Boyars' Duma) and representatives of the army. In 1566 Ivan IV revived the form of the Assembly of 1551 for secular purposes. He gathered together the clergy, the Boyars' Duma in full strength with its secretaries, the dyaks of the various government departments, and representatives of the higher ranks of the government service; but he introduced an important innovation by inviting, for the first time, merchants and traders. As for the motives which prompted the convocation of this assembly, Ivan IV, in this case, reverted to the traditions of his grandfather. Just as Ivan III had consulted his troops before launching the campaign against Novgorod, so Ivan IV submitted to the assembly of military men and merchants the question as to whether they were willing to continue the war for the possession of the whole of Livonia, considering that Poland had proposed the partition of the country on terms which practically meant that Riga would remain in her hands.

In addition to the presence of merchants, whose appearance for the first time at a great state conference indicated their growing importance in the state, the Assembly of 1566 possessed other original features. Among the lower ranks of government servants, which constituted a separate group, mention is made of squires from Toropets and Lutsk. Evidently, these were members of the minor aristocracy from the most immediately threatened border regions who served in the forces directly engaged in the war and who happened to be in Moscow during the negotiations with Poland. Although few in number, they occupied a prominent place in the assembly, and their opinion was canvassed separately. The government of Ivan Grozny permitted the free exchange of opinion. We learn that among the views expressed at the assembly was the dissenting opinion of the Dyak Viskovati, the director of foreign policy, who proposed that the assembly should consent to the partition of Livonia, with the stipulation, however, that the king should withdraw his garrisons from the occupied towns.

The Assembly of 1566 was a peculiar combination of the ancient and the new, of tradition and political ingenuity. V. O. Kluchevski called attention to the predominance at this assembly of representatives of the celebrated "thousand" which had been recruited in 1550 and had settled in the environs of Moscow to be ready to carry out the government's commissions. On the other hand N. Myatlev has shown that the aristocracy elected in 1550 occupied in subsequent decades a large part of the important posts in the army command, in home administration and in diplomacy. We see, therefore, that in spite of the acuteness of the crisis of 1564–65, in spite of the banishments and executions, Ivan Grozny retained the old, tried cadres, which he had enlisted for his administration, and even surrounded himself with their representatives at an important assembly to discuss an extremely important question of policy. . . .

If we may speak of inventions in politics, Ivan Grozny deserves to be regarded as the inventor of the Zemski Sobor, just as Simon de Montfort was the inventor of Parliament, and Philip IV the Handsome the inventor of the States General. . . .

The *Memoirs of Muscovy* by two Germans, the Westphalian Staden and the Pomeranian Schlichting, belong to the category of "foreigners' narratives," but they differ very sharply from those other memoirs and descriptions that come within this category by Herberstein, Chancellor, Fletcher, Possevino, and others. The latter were written by men who had come on official missions for short periods. Their observations could not be other than superficial, the more so that they were closely watched, and much was carefully concealed from them. The former, however, were written by men who had lived in the Moscow State for long periods (Staden lived in Russia for twelve years, from 1564 to 1576, and during this period he served for six years in the Oprichnina). They were right in the thick of events, watched things unobserved, freely mixed in the most intimate circles of high society, close to the Court and the Tsar's person, and at the same time mixed with wide circles of the people. Unfortunately, the advantages which these secret witnesses of events and customs enjoyed are converted in their writings almost entirely into handicaps, and their evidence, therefore loses a great deal of its value. Both were men of low character; they were ungrateful and were destitute of honour and conscience. Having acquired by force and fraud much wealth in Moscow, having been not only witnesses of but also participants in the horrors and crimes they described, they entertained for the people and the sovereign who gave them asylum no other sentiments than those of contempt and hatred.

After safely slipping out of the country they wrote malicious lampoons about Muscovy and its Tsar, each with a definite object, and in conformity with definite instructions. When, in 1570, Pope Pius V thought of sending Portico, his Polish Nuncio, to Moscow to conduct negotiations with the object of bringing about reconciliation between Moscow and Poland, Sigismund II, who was afraid that friendship inimical to the interests of Poland might spring up between Moscow and the Papal Curia, instructed Schlichting, the fugitive from Moscow, to write a tract exposing the crimes of the "Moscow tyrant." This document the king handed to the Nuncio to present to the Vatican, where it made a very powerful impression. As a result, Portico received the following instructions from the Pope: "We have made ourselves familiar with what you have communicated to us about the Moscow

State; don't take any more trouble and stop the preparations. Even if the King of Poland himself now approved of our journey to Moscow and facilitated it, even then we would not enter into intercourse with such barbarians and savages."

Staden too, like Schlichting, wrote an indictment against the Moscow Tsar, with this difference, however, that being a man of greater and more independent mind, he set out to achieve an object of his own by means of a grandiose plan. His bulky manuscript is divided into three parts, the most important being a project for the military occupation of Moscow which he, a fugitive, in 1578, decided to present to the Hapsburg Emperor Rudolf II through the medium of the Pfalzgraf Georg Hans. The other two parts, containing "a description of the country and administration of the Muscovites" and Staden's autobiography, constitute, as it were, appendices to this military-political plan. They were intended as a means of throwing light on the weak point of Moscow's policy and of proving that its system of government, which, the author alleged, was based on naked violence and the plunder of the subjects, was unsound.

Both authors, never calling Ivan IV Tsar, but applying to him only his previous title of Grand Prince, tried to rouse the public opinion of Western Europe against him and to incite the rulers to fight the eastern "infidels." The denunciations of Schlichting and Staden fully achieved their purpose. They contributed a great deal to create Ivan IV's unfavourable reputation in diplomacy, politics and literature in the West. In passing, their "revelations" cast a shadow upon the entire Russian people. As a result of their malicious descriptions, the Muscovites were reputed to be ignoramuses whom anybody could deceive and lead by the nose, a savage mob, with proclivities for plunder and violence.

Here the similarity between the two authors ceases. The difference between them is much more marked, and the value of their testimony varies in proportion to the difference in their personal qualities and talents, their conduct and the scope of their activities. The difference in their careers begins with the fact that Schlichting found himself in Moscow not by his own choice, but as a prisoner of war after the fall of the Lithuanian Fortress of Ozerishche in 1564, whereas Staden, deliberately following the fortune of war, left the Polish for the Russian service after the capture of Polotsk by Ivan Grozny.

In Moscow Schlichting, who knew Russian and Latin, occupied the post of servant and interpreter to the Court physician Albert, whom he erroneously calls an Italian, whereas he was actually a Belgian. In this obscure position he remained during the whole of the seven years (1564-71) that he lived in the Moscow State. He describes himself as a soldier. His own aristocratic origin causes him heartily to sympathize with the boyars, whom Ivan Grozny was persecuting. His world outlook was very primitive. In his opinion the fury of the "tyrant" and of his Oprichniks were due to the bad nature of the Russians. "The Muscovites suffer from a sort of innate ill will, as a result of which it has become a habit of theirs mutually to denounce and slander each other to the tyrant, and to burn with hatred against one another, so that they kill each other by mutual slander. The tyrant loves all this, and there is nothing that he listens to more eagerly than informers and slanderers, not caring whether they speak falsely or truly, as long as they provide an opportunity to put people to death, although many of them never even thought of committing the crimes that were attributed to them. . . ."

Of quite a different character is the work of Heinrich Staden, which may boldly be called a first-class document of the history of Muscovy and of the Moscow State of the sixties and seventies of the sixteenth century. It is necessary, however, to adapt oneself to the study of this peculiar monument to the past, in which profound observation, wit and striking and vivid descriptions are interwoven with the author's cynical admissions of his own mean conduct. In general, this German, Staden, creates the awful impression of a person gifted with brilliant talents and at the same time obviously vicious and criminal.

To what class of society did he belong? The fact that his parents were burghers in an obscure provincial town tells us little. His career was very wide and varied. Of more importance is his own characterization of that section of the vagrant soldiery which he joined early in life when obliged to leave his country to escape punishment for some crime he had committed. In his plan for the conquest of Muscovy he says: "For this a preliminary sum will be needed of 100,000 thalers. And the soldiers must be equipped so that when they arrive in the country [of the Grand Prince] they may be able to serve as horsemen. They must be soldiers *who have left nothing in Christendom, neither hearth nor home.* There are many such in Christendom. I have seen multitudes of such vagrant soldiers, enough to conquer more than one country. If the Grand Prince had in his country all the vagrant soldiers that are wandering through Christendom—*many of whom are thieves, for which some are hanged* —he would be able to seize all the surrounding rulerless countries whose thrones are vacant and take possession of them." (Italics in this fragment mine.—R.W.)

Perhaps Heinrich Staden was one of the most brilliant of the "vagrants," but he was not a great man; his goal was never higher than "thieving, for which some are hanged."

Indeed, what amazing talent Staden revealed, and to what miserable and revolting objects he employs it! After wandering through the homesteads of Livonia and serving in the ranks of the volunteers of the Polish Commandant of Fellin, Polubinsky, he, a lad of twenty-two, decides to flee "in fear of the gallows," as he himself puts it. Posing as a *pod-dyak,* or clerk, and displaying brazen effrontery, he, from the frontier, sent Mikhail Morozov, the Russian Lieutenant-Governor in Dorpat, a letter in which he wrote: "If the Grand Prince offers me good pay, I shall be ready to serve him, if not I shall go to Sweden. I must receive a reply forthwith." The Lieutenant-Governor was impressed by this insolent epistle, and believing that this foreigner was a military expert, of which the country was in great need, he sent a mounted escort to him with the following message: "The Grand Prince will give you all you ask for."

At his first appearance Staden charmed Morozov. The latter urged him to remain in Livonia, as he was familiar with men and affairs in that country; but Staden, screwing his price up still higher, demanded an audience with the Moscow sovereign himself, and Morozov immediately dispatched him post-haste to the capital. He covered the distance of 200 Prussian miles (1,400 kilometres) in six days. On his arrival in Moscow he was presented at the Posolski Prikaz (Department for Foreign Affairs). "Dyak Andrei Vasilyevich questioned me about various affairs and my answers were at once written down for the Grand Prince," writes Staden. "Immediately afterwards I was given a note, or memorandum, with which I could demand and receive at the inn every day one and a half vedros of mead and four dengas as food money. I was also presented with a silken gown, cloth for garments, and also a gold piece.

"On the Grand Prince's return to Moscow I was presented to him as he passed from the church to his Palace. The Grand Prince smiled and said: 'Eat bread,' which was an invitation to his table. Then I was given a note, or memorandum, to the Pomyestni Prikaz [Estates Department] and I received the village of Tesmino with all the hamlets attached to it. . . . Thus I entered on a great career. The Grand Prince knew me and I knew him. I then commenced my studies; I already knew Russian fairly well. . . ."

After the burning of Moscow in 1571, which the troops of the Oprichnina failed to prevent, and the second raid by Devlet-Ghirai in 1572, which was repulsed by the Zemshchina *voyevodas*, the Tsar's confidence in the Oprichnina was shaken. A new "sorting out of men," as Ivan Grozny called it, was undertaken, i.e., a revision of the army service lists, and, in connection with it, the confiscation of the manors of the banished Oprichniks and the reinstatement of the former patrimony owners who had been banished in the institution of the Oprichnina. Staden was not included in any of the new lists and was deprived of all his possessions; but thanks to his resourcefulness, he escaped direct proscription. He abandoned all his Moscow affairs and undertakings and went to live in the North. First he built a flour mill in Rybnaya Sloboda (Rybinsk) and later, planning "how to get out of this country," he went further north to Pomorye, where he engaged in the fur trade. His escape was facilitated by his connections with powerful people, his histrionic talents, and his experience in commercial affairs. "I was well acquainted with David Kondin, who collects tribute from Lapland," he writes. "When I arrived

there I stated that I was waiting for a merchant who owed me a sum of money. Here I met some Dutchmen. I posed as a wealthy merchant and acted as a middleman between the Dutch, the English, the Bergeners from Norway, and the Russians."

In 1576 he boarded, at Kola, a Dutch ship that was carrying 500 centners of stone cannon balls for the Dutch insurgents who were fighting against Spain. He himself carried a large cargo of furs which he profitably disposed of at the Leipzig Fair in partnership with a Russian merchant. . . .

. . . In S. B. Vesselovsky's researches on the Synodics we have a new document, which is included in the scientific handbook of collected data on the history of the military and civil administration of the Moscow State. . . .

Further on in these researches on the Synodics we find references to a number of men of prominence and merit who were executed either for attempts to flee, or for the flight of their kinsmen.

To the same category of complicity in flights, or preparation for such, belong all those persons, and their number is fairly large, who had gone bail for the noble Princes Mstislavskys, Pronskys, Prozorovskys and others who had broken their vows "to serve the Moscow Tsar faithfully well. . . ."

Was not flight to Lithuania, individually and in entire groups, not only by ordinary government servants accused of committing crimes, but of high-placed commanders and administrators, and this during a war, the most heinous state crime which Ivan Grozny was obliged to combat? Was it not a gaping wound in the body politic, a catastrophe, to which the Tsar reacted by banishments and executions, by ever new "sorting out of men," by dismissing some of his servants and taking others into favour?

There may have been cases of excess, of hunting after imaginary traitors; there may have been the personal intrigues of rivals, as for example in the case of Viskovati, who, evidently, was squeezed out of his post by his rival Shchelkalov, who at once acted as his accuser.

On the other hand it must be admitted that in his struggle against treason, Ivan Grozny underrated the danger which threatened him and failed to pick out the real traitors in his entourage. He did not suspect how many men he still had in his service of the type of Staden, in whose head was maturing not only the idea of flight abroad, but far wider plans of foreign intervention, of a coalition attack on Muscovy, for the execution of which he was secretly collecting the necessary information. . . .

In addition to the most glaring cases of actual treason there were other cases of secret and undetectable desertion from state service, of the shirking of duty to the country and the people. We obtain a striking picture of one of the forms of this "internal flight" in S. B. Vesselovsky's essay on *Monasterial Landownership in Moscow Rus in the Latter Half of the Sixteenth Century.*

The investigator examined 657 cases of donations to large monasteries made in the Zamoskovni region in the period from 1552 to 1590. These donations took the form of gifts of patrimonial and manorial lands by men in the military service. Most of these gifts consisted of estates of medium size ranging from 200 to 500 dessiatins (450 to 1,240 acres). Appended to this analysis we have a skilfully drafted diagram showing that the curve of monasterial acquisitions rose exceedingly in the period 1569–78, reaching its peak in 1571.

What motives can be ascribed to the flight of landowning government servants to seek the protection of the monas-

teries?

Some of these may have been religious. The gift of property, movable or immovable, was one of the terms on which the monks undertook to pray for the peace of departed souls, and often gifts of land were made for the burial of the donor and the members of his family. During the period of banishments and executions the sudden turn of fate among government servants may have increased the necessity of making provisions for burial places within monastery walls, and also for the long journey beyond the grave.

The chief motives for this feverish haste and zeal in making gifts of land to the monasteries were of a practical character, however.

Ruined landowners, or such patrimony owners as were in danger of losing their possessions, sought the protection of the richest, privileged monasteries, which enjoyed right of sanctuary, and by transferring part of their property to the monasteries, tried to save the rest. . . .

The motives which prompted the landowning government servants to donate lands to the monasteries varied, but from the point of view of the interests of the state, these transactions were unpatriotic, for they represented attempts to remove the land from the state's control, which meant a diminution of the country's military and financial resources for defence. The possessions of the monasteries, which thanks to their privileged position played only a small part in the military organization, grew at the expense of the possessions of the military serving class.

During the period of the ruinous foreign wars there was an increase in the wealth of the parasitic section of society, under whose wing those whose duty it was to perform military service sought refuge. . . .

In so far as they trusted the thoughts

of the opposition of the sixteenth century the Russian historians of the nineteenth century were obliged to reconcile the stern judgment of the contemporaries of that period with a generally favourable appraisal of the Great Power policy pursued by the Moscow government. It seemed as though the solution of this contradiction lies in the assumption that the cautious system introduced by the founder of the state was upset by the arbitrary conduct of his grandson, the last autocrat but one of the Rurik dynasty. Hence the outrages committed by Ivan Grozny's Oprichnina and his queer and restless administration had to serve as an explanation for the ensuing "disruption." All the great work that was performed during his youth seemed to have been eclipsed and upset by his frenzied caprices. V. O. Kluchevsky regards the institution of the Oprichnina as a struggle not against the social system but against persons, and he appraises Ivan IV himself merely as a gifted dilettante. S. F. Platonov admits that the institution of the Oprichnina was part of a broad and in many respects expedient military-administrative plan, but he condemns Ivan Grozny's nervous activity in shifting people from one place to another, changing them from one office to another, constantly dispersing them and breaking up institutions, thus preventing people from establishing themselves in a given office and from settling down to their administrative affairs, all of which, in the end, wrecked the foundations of the system he had built up in his early years and brought nearer the "time of troubles."

In their judgments, however, these writers lost sight of a very important circumstance, viz., that Ivan Grozny's greatest social and administrative reforms—his struggle against the minor princes, his elevation of common people at the expense of the ancient boyars, his tightening up of military service and increasing of public burdens and the centralization of administration—were introduced not in peacetime, but amidst great military upheavals. Virtually, Ivan IV's reign was an almost incessant war. In 1551–56 there was the war for the Volga region, and in 1558 commenced the greatest war in Russian history which lasted twenty-four years—the war for Livonia, for an outlet to the sea, complicated by fierce collisions with the Crimea, Poland and Sweden.

The situation was very similar to that of Peter I, whose object in life was also to gain this "Window into Europe."

At all events history's verdict on Ivan Grozny should not be sterner than that on Peter I, bearing in mind that the conditions under which the Moscow Tsar operated in the sixteenth century were ever so much more severe than those under which Peter I operated. If Ivan Grozny is to be condemned, then he must be blamed either for the very idea of waging the war, or at least for having failed to abandon this unsuccessful undertaking in time, for having wasted the best forces of his state in Livonia. But the more we insist on accusations of this kind the further we get away from the characterization of Ivan IV as a capricious tyrant. . . .

The limited judgment of Ivan Grozny that is characteristic of the historians of the nineteenth century is partly to be explained by their ignorance of numerous extremely important sources which have been discovered during the past two decades and partly to the fact that most of them belong to the liberal bourgeois school. . . .

9

THE DEBATE ON
IVAN THE TERRIBLE IN 1956

Since the death of Stalin, Soviet historians have been unwilling to accept views such as those of Robert Wipper reproduced above. Individual scholars tend to offer interpretations which differ quite drastically from the uniformity which characterized the Stalinist era. Below is part of an account of a meeting of Soviet historians called to discuss the errors of the past in regard to interpretations of Ivan IV. The original article, which appeared in the leading Soviet historical journal, is entitled "On Evaluating the Activities of Ivan the Terrible." One is tempted to hope that the study of Russia's medieval period, unlike that of more recent centuries, has largely been lifted from the sphere of ideology to that of scholarly debate. That there is continuing interest in Ivan is attested by the recent excavations in the Kremlin. In 1964 Soviet archeologists exhumed Ivan's body in order to look for answers about his person and his time. For an account of this undertaking see *The Current Digest of the Soviet Press*, April 29, 1964.

For a general study of Russian historiography see Anatole Mazour's *Modern Russian Historiography*. A pre-revolutionary Russian historian, Sergei Platonov, offers a survey of the views on Ivan in "Ivan the Terrible in Russian Historiography," reprinted in the first volume of Sidney Harcave's *Readings in Russian History*. A British account of the same subject is in G. H. Bolsover, "Ivan the Terrible in Russian Historiography," *Transactions of the Royal Historical Society*, Series 5, VII (1957), 71–89. There is an article on the changing Soviet interpretation of Ivan in Cyril Black's *Rewriting Russian History* (paperback). An early Soviet view is available in Mikhail Pokrovsky's *A History of Russia*. Konstantin Shteppa's *Russian Historians and the Soviet State* relates the general fortunes of the Soviet historical profession. *History in the USSR* is a new anthology of readings by Marin Pundeff. Eisenstein's famous film on Ivan, in two parts, is available from Brandon Films (offices in New York, Chicago, and San Francisco).

On May 14–15, 1956, a conference on the feudal period of Russian history was held at the Institute of History of the USSR Academy of Sciences. Sergei Dubrovskii delivered a paper entitled "On the personality Cult in Some Historical Works." The report attracted a great many Moscow historians of the most varied specialties.

Sergei M. Dubrovskii (of the Institute of History of the Academy of Sciences) noted that our historical literature contains serious deviations from Marxist evaluations of many figures of the past.

From *Voprosy Istorii* (Moscow), September, 1956, pp. 195–203. Translated by Sylvia Fain.

Some historians began to put very great emphasis on the role of individual princes, tsars, and commanders, building personality cults around them. Thus, some described Ivan IV as a superman. The monstrous crimes of this tsar were justified by arguments for the progressive nature of the measures he employed. Dubrovskii opposed descriptions of Ivan IV as a "Tsar of the People." He was, rather, a tsar of the serf-owning landlords, a dictator over the peasants.

Ivan IV and his followers have usually been described as representatives of progressive forces, fighting for a centralized Russian state, while Ivan's opponents are described as representatives of reaction who wished to re-establish the fragmented feudal system. In Dubrovskii's opinion this is an erroneous conception. He considers that the question of the re-establishment of feudal fragmentation was not a real one in the middle and especially in the latter half of the history of the Russian state. A centralized Russian state had been formed and basically consolidated in the second half of the fifteenth century, although the struggle against survivals of the feudal system continued until the seventeenth and even the eighteenth centuries. Dubrovskii showed that other problems were at hand in the sixteenth century, such as the growth of the labor dues system of the serf economy; the question of the nature of the dictatorship to be established by the landlords— whether in the direction of unlimited power to Ivan and his *oprichniki,* or in the direction of some form of limited monarchy; expansion of the Russian state to the east and to the Volga region (annexation of the Kazan and Astrakhan Khanates, and penetration into Siberia); and a struggle for an outlet on the Baltic Sea.

Dubrovskii considers it impermissible to evaluate all proponents of limitations on the tsarist autocracy as reactionary. Autocracy was not the only progressive form of state power for Russia at that time. There could have been an unlimited monarchy, or there could have been a monarchy limited by a boyar duma or parliament, as it was in England and elsewhere. Dubrovskii also noted the error of the proposition that the *oprichnina* was directed against the boyars. One cannot lose sight of another fundamental aspect: the *oprichnina* represented a special form for the coercion of the peasants by the serf-owning landlords. The *oprichniki* seized lands and peasants from the boyars, and if the peasants resisted, they took them forcibly, burned their houses, and so forth. Peasants fled in all directions. It is common knowledge that the *oprichnina* resulted in a large-scale depopulation of farms and villages. The *oprichnina* was above all a means for purging the land to pave the way for serfdom, and was an important stage in preparing for wholesale enserfment of all the peasants. A second result of the *oprichnina* was the weakening of the boyars and strengthening of the tsarist autocracy—that is Russian absolutism.

In examining the foreign policy of Ivan IV, Dubrovskii notes the progressive character of the annexation of the Volga region and of the struggle for an outlet on the Baltic Sea. But he suggests we should not forget that tsarism also practiced predatory expansionist policies and oppressed the Russian and other peoples. We should not overlook the atrocities committed in the taking of Kazan, or forget that the march to the Baltic Sea was accomplished by barbaric means which were characteristic of the serf-owning landlord class.

In Dubrovskii's opinion, creating a cult of Ivan IV was facilitated by insufficiently critical attention to the sources.

For instance, the whole of the correspondence between Ivan and Prince Kurbski, as well as Ivan's diplomatic correspondence, was attributed without argument to Ivan himself, although not one line written by Ivan personally has come down to us. Some historians have taken the education and literacy of persons who wrote for Ivan and prepared materials for him to be that of Ivan himself.

Dubrovskii's paper devotes a great deal of space to criticism of the views of Robert Wipper, Sergei Bakhrushin, and Ivan I. Smirnov. In Dubrovskii's opinion, these historians have idealized Ivan the Terrible in their works as a political and military figure, and as a diplomat. The historical development of Russia in the second half of the sixteenth century gives way to praise for Ivan's deeds, whereas the negative aspects and consequences of some of Ivan's measures are ignored in the works of these authors. The social nature and character of the centralized Russian state is covered over by general arguments concerning its progressive character. Some historians, criticizing the mistakes of Mikhail Pokrovskii and his school, have in fact turned to Dmitrii Ilovaiskii and other pre-revolutionary historians.

Ivan Ivanovich Smirnov (of the Institute of History of the Academy of Sciences) then spoke in opposition to the basic propositions of Dubrovskii's paper. He agreed that roles of individual figures of the past have been incorrectly interpreted in our historical science. Class evaluations of their activity have been nearly completely rejected, and attempts have been made to describe them as popular heroes. Smirnov considers it deeply mistaken to find personality cults in all works and researches devoted to individual historical figures. Such an approach to historical works

would only be going from one extreme to the other, from an anti-Marxist personality cult to an anarchic negation of the will of leaders and commanders.

In Smirnov's opinion, instead of evaluating sixteenth-century absolutism and the activity of Ivan IV by proceeding from the knowledge that all historical development is governed by regular laws, Dubrovskii mechanically applies to the period propositions and values of Marxist theory which are related to the imperialist era or even to the present time. Dubrovskii considers that there was no need for violence or for civil war in the sixteenth century, and he expressed the opinion that Russia could even develop politically into a parliamentary monarchy of the English type. This way of thinking, says Smirnov, very much recalls Mikhail Pokrovskii's formulation of "history as past politics." Dubrovskii, Smirnov notes, ignores the fact that absolutism appears as a logical stage in the history of feudal society and plays a progressive role in the process of eliminating the fragmentation of the feudal system.

Smirnov considers erroneous Dubrovskii's position that feudal fragmentation had already been overcome and that the centralized Russian state was significantly consolidated in the second half of the fifteenth century. The sixteenth century was the most important stage in the process of the creation and consolidation of the centralized Russian state. The *oprichnina* terror was a definite manifestation of the struggle against the princes and boyars, and not a senseless extermination of people from all classes of society, uncalled for by any objective necessity, as Dubrovskii asserts. Smirnov pointed out that "a terribly bloody struggle" is characteristic of the creation of an absolutist state and is not exclusive with and peculiar to Russian history. Still less was it a product of Ivan the Terrible's individual qualities but rather an example of a general feature of a certain historical period (e.g., the Wars of the Roses in England, the Bartholomew's Eve Massacre in France, "the Stockholm Blood Bath"). The bloody deeds of the *oprichnina* must not overshadow its objective progressive historical significance as a form of the struggle for a centralized state.

In Smirnov's opinion, Dubrovskii has not understood the mutual ties and interdependence between the cutting-edge side of the *oprichnina*, which was directed against the boyars, and its policy toward the peasantry. Strengthening the centralized state as a dictatorship of serf-landowners reinforced the class positions of feudal lords and laid the groundwork for attacks on the peasantry, and for the strengthening of the bondage system. In his domestic and foreign policy Ivan IV acted as a representative of his class, the class of feudal lords, whose class position he strengthened. Moreover, in his struggle for the liquidation of feudal fragmentation, the struggle against the reactionary feudal aristocracy, Ivan's policies relied on the support of the wide masses of the people, who also had an interest in liquidating the feudal fragmentation and the intestine war. A tsarist policy in the struggle for the creation of a national state could and did use the support of the broad popular masses.

Smirnov noted that Dubrovskii's views on serfdom as a special form distinguished from feudalism are a repetition of his old erroneous conception of serfdom, which was stated in his work *On the Nature of the Asiatic Means of Production, Feudalism, Serfdom, and Mercantile Capital.* Smirnov denied that there is any cult of Ivan the Terrible in his own book. Such "cults" are found only in literary works and in films.

A lively discussion developed on the questions which Dubrovskii and Smirnov raised. . . .

Isaac Budovnits (of the Institute of History of the Academy of Sciences) attacked Dubrovskii's assertion that the formation of the centralized Russian state was already completed in the fifteenth century and that the measures taken by Ivan the Terrible to centralize the government were superfluous. He also disagreed with Dubrovskii's assertion that the *oprichnina* was a historically unjustified means and that its cruelties and extremism actually brought on the events of the Time of Troubles. These thoughts permeate all of aristocratic and bourgeois historiography (Karamzin, Pogodin, Kliuchevsky, *et al.*) The Time of Troubles was above all a peasant war. To represent it as a consequence of the *oprichnina*, which was a manifestation of the evil will of Ivan the Terrible, means to make the Tsar a super-hero. But this is not combatting a personality cult: on the contrary, this amounts to supporting one.

Basing himself on the researches of P. A. Sadikov, Budovnits showed that as a result of the *oprichnina* activities, the great landowners of various provinces were deprived of land. There is no data to support the assertion that in these seizures peasants were driven from their land, although they did suffer from the *oprichnina*. If the *oprichnina* had been thought of as a means for taking land from the peasants and for enserfing them, then it would have been used in the first place not on the large estates where the peasants were already bound to the land in one way or another, but in the black lands. From a moral point of view, Ivan must be strictly condemned, but the means he employed, including the *oprichnina*, cannot possibly be presented as senseless, unjustifiable creations of a petty tyrant.

Assertions of this kind cannot be supported by concrete material. . . .

Sigurd O. Shmidt (of the Archival Institute) remarked that the problems raised in Dubrovskii's paper go beyond the question of personality cults of Ivan the Terrible. He talks about deviations from Marxist understanding of our history—about distortions of historical truth. Some historians approach the study of outstanding personalities of the past from a class point of view. They lose sight of the fact that, for instance, Alexander Nevsky put down an uprising of the Novgorodians, and Suvorov smashed a peasant war led by Pugachev and an uprising in Poland. Rightly noting Ivan IV's contribution to the formation of a centralized Russian state, and his military achievements, historians have forgotten about his harmful activities and his personal cruelty. Russian history has often been confused with the history of tsars. This is reflected even in the titles of books written by Robert Wipper, Sergei Bakhrushkin, and Ivan I. Smirnov.

Shmidt feels that it is necessary to examine the question of the Livonian war, which is generally viewed as a just war. It is not completely true that the nobles and Ivan personally were active advocates of a war in the west, while the boyars wished to fight in the south. The idea of continuing the Livonian war was supported by everyone in the Sobor of 1566, and not just the nobles. Adashev, who was in charge of all diplomatic negotiations in the first period of the Livonian war, was not against this war in the west. He thought the war should stop after taking Narva and winning a sea outlet. He also thought it was impossible to continue the Livonian war, in which he proved himself a more frightened and wiser politician than Ivan.

Shmidt thought Dubrovskii justified in the way he posed questions about the *oprichnina's* dark side, and about its role in the enserfment of the peasants. But Shmidt finds insupportable the proposition that the purge of the lands to pave the way for serfdom during the *oprichnina* years was like the purge of lands which took place in England during the phase of primary capital accumulation. In Russia there was merely a struggle for redistribution of lands among feudal lords, including land with peasants.

Agreeing with Dubrovskii that a centralized monarchy was not the only form of state possible in the Middle Ages, Shmidt pointed to the relatively progressive character of a centralized monarchical state in comparison to state systems in the period of feudal fragmentation. In Dubrovskii's opinion, the sixteenth-century Russian state could have come to resemble the Novgorod republic. But this Novgorodian system was weakly centralized, somewhat like medieval Poland. By asserting that the Russian centralized state was already formed in the fifteenth century, Dubrovskii confuses the question of the reinforcement of the sovereign's power and the unification of the lands around Moscow by the creation of a single state apparatus. This process was completed at best only at the end of the sixteenth century. By then the first Zemskii Sobors had appeared, as well as the basic organs of central administration (the *prikazi*) and provincial and rural institutions.

Shmidt acknowledged the utility of Dubrovskii's critical remarks. However, the majority of the positive propositions he had advanced were weakly argued and could not be accepted. Shmidt also pointed out that there was no basis for praising the work of the Metropolitan Makarius as Smirnov had done, for Makarius had participated in the suppression of the 1547 Moscow uprising, actively opposed many reforms directed at further state centralization, and was a staunch defender of extensive ecclesiastical land ownership. . . .

Aleksandr A. Zimin (of the Institute of History of the Academy of Sciences) noted that the study of sixteenth-century Russian history has been significantly advanced by the works of Soviet historians and that this work should continue. There had indeed been excessive praise of the work of Ivan the Terrible in many Soviet historical works published from 1942 to 1944, but especially in literary and film productions. In Zimin's opinion, Dubrovskii's serious mistake was to see Tsar Ivan's deeds as the cause of the most important phenomena of sixteenth-century history, just as Wipper had done. While Wipper considered Ivan's deeds productive, Dubrovskii considers them harmful or senseless. Dubrovskii attributes all Russia's military failures to Ivan's military decisions. He sees Ivan the Terrible as a creative diplomat, although an unsuccessful one, and as an author of an ideology of autocracy. It was Ivan who enserfed the peasants and created an unlimited absolutism. Yet Dubrovskii criticized the works of Wipper, Bakhrushin, and Smirnov for excessive exaggeration of Ivan's role in Russian history.

In the popular mind, Ivan IV is viewed as a dread but just monarch. Folk songs clearly sympathize with him in his struggle with the boyars, thus revealing the monarchist bias in peasant thinking. Zimin stated that literary historians have actually succeeded in identifying Ivan's unique literary style and thus have established that he is the author of the correspondence which Dubrovskii discussed. This is confirmed also by the writings of some of his contemporaries about Ivan's "education."

Had Ivan not been the author of the letter to Kurbski, Kurbski would have tried to make use of that fact in his polemics with the Tsar. But Kurbski aptly did not doubt that this correspondence came directly from Tsar Ivan himself.

In Zimin's opinion, the process of binding the peasants to the land was continuous during the years of the *oprichnina* as well as subsequently (the laws of the 1580's, the land census, the rule of St. George's Day). There was no reason for the *pomeshchiks* to "drive" the peasants from their estates, inasmuch as they now owned all their land anyway. As Boris D. Grekov and Ivan I. Smirnov have shown in their works, in the late 1500's the process by which the peasants eventually became landless took the form of a reduction in the size of peasant holdings. At that time, only a part of the peasantry became completely landless. The *oprichnina* helped to transfer boyar lands to the *pomeshchiks,* and contributed to the growth of feudal exploitation of the peasantry. But this does not mean that it was directed above all against the peasants, and was a tool for driving them from the land. Its chief task was to crush the feudal aristocracy, to struggle with the survivals of feudal fragmentation, and the means used to accomplish these ends were barbaric and medieval. The splitting of the country into two political units, one of which took the form of an imperial appanage system, also had many serious consequences. But of course, one must not confuse the form of the *oprichnina* and the methods it employed with its objectively progressive content. . . .

Serafim A. Pokrovskii (of the Law Institute of the Academy of Sciences) noted that Dubrovskii's basic mistake was his attempt to doubt the historical orthodoxy of the struggle which the late sixteenth-century nobles undertook against the reactionary boyars and to attribute the entire matter to the personality of Ivan the Terrible. But Dubrovskii is right in one thing: there have been very serious mistakes in the characterization of Ivan IV in our literature in the spirit of a personality cult. Smirnov does not wish to admit his own mistakes, and he declares that such errors appeared only in films and folk songs. Zimin says these mistakes were committed only in popular literature. In fact, there were also mistakes in scholarly researches, including Grekov's work *The Peasantry in Russia*.

Pokrovskii admitted his own mistakes in assessing Ivan the Terrible. He stated that at one time he supported the assertion made by Budovnits in his *Sixteenth Century Publicists* that ideologically Ivan IV revealed a sense of a tsar's responsibility to the people. Dmitrii S. Likhachev had advanced the same idea in the preface to his book on Peresvetov. Zimin regarded Ivan Peresvetov (Ivan's reform ideologue) as a freethinking heretic. In the *Essays on the Feudal Period in the History of the USSR*, the tsarist monarchy of the sixteenth century is described as a lawful state, in which norms of criminal law were strictly observed. None of these assertions agrees with reality and all are clearly deviations from Marxism. We must seriously examine all established views on Russian history of the second half of the sixteenth century. . . .

Vladimir T. Pashuto (of the Institute of History of the Academy of Sciences) emphasized that Soviet historical science had accomplished much in the correct interpretation of the Russian past and in the study of the work of many progressive persons of the past. The struggle with cosmopolitanism and bourgeois objectivism had aided in the consolidation of Marxist understanding of the role of personality and in clarifying the national origins and class character of the activities of individuals in history. But it would be incorrect not to see the dark side of these successes. We must eliminate the remnants of the personality cult; yet our struggle against them must not be nihilistic. Pashuto expressed his agreement with Smirnov's criticism of Dubrovskii's paper. He emphasized that historians have a responsibility for what is done in literature, films, and the arts, for historians provide the foundation for the interpretation of historical subjects. He pointed out the necessity for studying historical materialism, which would help us understand such complicated problems as the genesis of capitalism in Russia, the Russian variant of primary capital accumulation, the uniqueness of Russian humanism, and so forth. In Pashuto's opinion mistakes had been made most frequently in the interpretations of Russia's foreign policy. Historians now face the problem of delving more deeply into the socioeconomic foundations of war and foreign policy. . . .

Dubrovskii, in a concluding word, said that the discussion was interesting and helpful, and many correct ideas had been expressed. But he did not agree with a number of the critical remarks. He pointed out that some historians (like Smirnov) were continuing to defend erroneous views on the interpretation of Ivan the Terrible's autocracy and the historical events of the sixteenth century. He noted that the process of the formation of the centralized Russian state was complicated and prolonged and was determined by profound socioeconomic causes, and not simply by the chopping-off of some boyar heads in the days of Ivan and his *oprichnina*.

Summing up the results of the discussion, Lev V. Cherepnin noted Dubrovskii's initiative in raising an important question. The resulting debate had testified to the interest in his subject. The majority of the comrades present thought Dubrovskii had not presented the scholarly foundations of the propositions he advanced, but some of his opinions were supported by those who spoke. Unquestionably, Ivan and his policies have been wrongly idealized in our literature, scholarly as well as artistic and popular. Mistakes along these lines have been widespread. Moreover, there was much that was unconvincing in Dubrovskii's paper, although he has refuted the criticism in his final address. There is a whole series of questions which demand further study, but such study must proceed on the basis of the results which scholars have already achieved. We must be very clear in our minds concerning what must be avoided. Historians examining the feudal period are faced with several tasks: (1) continuing the study of the concrete forms of the growth of serfdom in Russia, and related questions about the role of the labor dues system and the *pomestie* system, and so forth; (2) investigating the objective regularity of Russian socioeconomic development, and the formation of the centralized Russian state which conditioned this process; (3) studying the social and political nature of the *oprichnina*, the nature of Russian tsarism, its foreign policy, wars, social thought, and a whole series of other important problems. Re-examination of these questions must be serious and creative.

10

THE LIFE OF ST. SERGIUS   EXCERPTS

By St. Epiphanius

Sergius of Radonezh (1314–92) was perhaps the most popular of Russia's saints and was considered her patron after the Russian victory over the Mongols at Kulikovo (1380) which raised him to eminence as a national hero, a builder of the Moscow state. His influence on the growth of the monastic movement was immense. During his lifetime, in the fourteenth century, 42 monasteries of the common life type were founded. There were 57 new ones in the fifteenth century, and 51 were added in the sixteenth century. Thus, by 1600, there were 150 monasteries of the type favored by Sergius as against 104 of the old type.

Below are excerpts from the saint's biography by his disciple Epiphanius, who became a monk at the Trinity monastery during the saint's lifetime. Lives of the saints were very popular reading in old Russia. Of the eight hundred saints recognized by the Russian church two hundred have been honored by lives. These sources are particularly important for men such as Sergius who left behind no written records.

For an account of monasteries in the Kievan period see George Fedotov, *The Russian Religious Mind*, Vol. I (paperback), and the article by R. Casey, "Early Russian Monasticism," *Orientalia Christiana Periodica*, XIX (1953), 373–423. The monasteries of the Moscow period are discussed in George Fedotov's *The Russian Religious Mind*, Vol. II; in James Billington's *The Icon and the Axe*; in Vasily Kliuchevsky's *History of Russia*, Vol. II; and in Nicolai Andreyev's "The Pskov-Pechery Monastery in the 16th Century," *Slavonic and East European Review*, XXXII, 318–43. For other examples of lives of saints see George Fedotov, *A Treasury of Russian Spirituality* (paperback); Sergei Zenkovsky, *Medieval Russia's Epics, Chronicles, and Tales* (paperback); and in "Two National Saints," *Russian Review* (London), II, No. 3 (1913), 21–44, which deals with Prince Michael of Chernigov and Father Irenarch the Hermit. The genre of hagiography is analyzed in Dmitrij Cizevskij, *History of Russian Literature*. On St. Sergius in particular see the inspired essay by Vasily Kliuchevsky reprinted in Sidney Harcave's *Readings in Russian History*, Vol. I (paperback), as well as a chapter in Constantin de Grunwald's *The Saints of Russia*. On St. Epiphanius see Michael Dane's "Epiphanius' Image of St. Stephen," *Canadian Slavonic Papers*, V (1961), 72–86. An abbot very different from Sergius is described by Marc Raeff in "An Early Theorist of Absolutism: Joseph of Volokolamsk," *American Slavic and East European Review*, Vol. VIII. For a review of a Soviet work highly critical of the role of Russian monasteries see George Orchard, "The 'Wasteland' Monasteries: An Historical Revision," *Canadian Slavic Studies*, Vol. II (1968).

Our blessed Father Sergius was born of noble, faithful and devout parents. His father was named Cyril and his mother, Mary. They were pleasing to God and righteous in the sight of God and men, having in abundance the virtues which God loves. . . .

Cyril, servant of God, had three sons. The eldest was Stephen, the second Bartholomew, and the third Peter. . . .

The aforenamed servant of God, Cyril, had led the life of a wealthy man in the principality of Rostov, being one of the distinguished and prominent boyars of that region, but in his old age, he was reduced to poverty. Why and how did he become poor? This too we shall tell: he was ruined by the frequent visits he made in the company of the prince to the Tartar camp in order to pay homage and tribute; by the frequent Tartar raids which laid waste to Russia; by the exactions of many Tartar embassies, by heavy taxes and bad harvests; but most of all by the great Tartar war and the period of upheaval which followed it. When the prince of Moscow, Ivan Danilovich, became Great Prince, Moscow extended its domination to the principality of Rostov. Alas, woe befell the city of Rostov then, and its princes and boyars suffered most of all. They lost their power and authority, their estates, their honor, their distinction; everything now was in subjection to Moscow. They left Rostov by the order of the Great Prince; a governor, Vasily Kocheva by name, and another one, called Mina, were sent from Moscow to Rostov. And when they entered the city, they inflicted oppression upon its population. It was a time of persecution, and many citizens of Rostov were forced to surrender their estates to the men of Moscow, receiving only insults and wounds in exchange. They went away empty-handed as the least of beggars. No use to dwell on this! The

abuses heaped upon the people of Rostov went to such lengths that the governor himself, a boyar named Averky, was hung head downward, and his body insulted and cast away like refuse. Horror spread among all who had witnessed and heard of this, not only in the city of Rostov, but in all the neighboring districts. Because of these disastrous events, the servant of God, Cyril, left his Rostov estate with all his kith and kin, and settled in Radonezh [forty miles northeast of Moscow]. He chose for his abode a place near the church of Christ's Nativity, which stands in Radonezh even to the present day, and there he lived henceforth with his family.

Cyril's sons Stephen and Peter married, but the third son, the favored youth Bartholomew, was loath to take a wife, for he aspired to the religious life. Many a time he begged his father to let him be a monk, but Cyril said to him: "My child, wait a little and be patient for our sake; we are old, poor and sick, and there is no one to care for us, since your brothers are married." The excellent youth gladly promised to serve his parents as long as they lived, and from that day on endeavored in all ways to please them, until at last they entered the religious life, each retiring to a monastery. When they had spent a few years in the monastic observance, they passed away to God. The consecrated youth, having taken his parents to their graves, spent forty days praying for their souls, and then returned to his home. Calling Peter, his younger brother in the flesh, he gave him the whole of his father's legacy, taking nothing for himself. The wife of Stephen, his eldest

From Nicolas Zernov, *St. Sergius, Builder of Russia* (London: Society for Promoting Christian Knowledge, 1939), pp. 117–38, 140–44, 146–50. Reprinted by permission of Nicolas Zernov.

brother, had died, leaving him with two sons, Clement and John; later John, changing his name to Theodore, became an archimandrite of the Simonov monastery. Stephen himself had left the world and become a monk of the monastery of the Mother of God at Khotkov.

After his parents' death, the dedicated Bartholomew went to Stephen and asked that he should accompany him in his search of a wilderness. Stephen acceded to the request of the saint. They roamed the woods for a long time, and finally came to a deserted spot in a thicket near a stream. They explored this place and found it suitable, for God had inspired their choice. After they had prayed, they began to fell the trees with their own hands and to bear the trunks away on their shoulders. First they built a shack and a hut, then a cell, and they constructed a chapel. When the chapel was ready and it was time to consecrate it, the holy youth said to Stephen: "My lord, you are my elder brother in the flesh and the race, but even more in the spirit. Tell me, to what saint shall we dedicate this shrine?" Stephen answered: "Why do you question me and tempt me? God chose you in your mother's womb, giving a sign before your birth, that the infant should one day be the disciple of the Holy Trinity. Not only should he himself have a devout faith, but he should bring many others to believe in the Holy Trinity." So the holy youth went to the bishop for the blessing and the consecration of the chapel. The priests came, and the chapel was consecrated by them in the name of the Holy Trinity. This was done by permission of Theognostus, Metropolitan of Kiev and of all Russia, under the rule of the Great Prince Simeon (1343–53)—we believe, at the beginning of his rule. As for Stephen, after he had built the chapel, he did not remain long in the desert with his

brother. He saw the trials of the desert: the lonely, rigorous life, the poverty and the privations which must be undergone, since food, drink, and the bare necessities of life were nowhere obtainable. No man came near them or brought them food, for at that time there were as yet no villages, no houses, no inhabitants whatsoever in the vicinity of the desert cell; no man-made path led to the hermitage, only the forest stretched out on every side, and everywhere was wilderness. Dismayed by all these things, Stephen resolved to leave the desert, and forsook his brother, the saintly hermit and desert-lover. He went to Moscow, and established himself in the monastery of the Epiphany; he found a cell there, and lived in it, acquiring great virtue. He led a laborious life, one of severe mortification, prayer and fasting; he denied himself even beer, and was clad in poor garments. At that time, there lived in the monastery the monk Alexis, who was later to become Metropolitan; he had not yet been consecrated bishop, but faithfully observed the monastic rule. He and Stephen led the spiritual life together and sang side by side in the choir. The Great Prince Simeon heard of Alexis' saintly life; he ordered Metropolitan Theognostus to ordain him priest and later abbot of the aforesaid monastery. Seeing his many virtues, the prince then chose him for his spiritual father.

As for our blessed father, he had not, at that time, entered the angelic [monastic] state, for he was not yet perfected in the knowledge of the monastic life and rule, and all that is required of a monk. When the time came, he called to his hermitage a certain elder on whom ordination had been conferred, and who was an abbot, one Metrophanus. Humbly falling at the elder's feet, he pleaded with him:

"Father, in the name of God's love, give me the tonsure. I have loved the religious order from my very childhood, and have desired it for a long time, but my parents' advanced age and their indigence kept me at home. Now, however, I am free, my Lord and Father, and I am athirst, as the heart thirsts for living waters." The abbot at once entered the chapel and gave the tonsure to the young hermit, thus introducing him to the angelic state. This was on the seventh day of October, on the feast of the holy martyrs Sergius and Bacchus, and he was given the name of Sergius in religion, since it was the custom in those days to give a monk the name of the saint honored on the day of his profession. When he became a monk and took the name of Sergius, Bartholomew was twenty-three years old. . . .

Who can relate his works, who can enumerate the trials he underwent, living alone in the wilderness? Often the beasts prowled around him, not only at night, but in the daytime. There was a pack of howling wolves, and sometimes bears approached the hermitage. The saint, though fearing them a little because of human frailty, fervently sent up his prayers to heaven, and spiritually armed, remained unhurt, by God's grace; the beasts withdrew from him and did him no harm. . . .

At different times, the saint had to wrestle with the devil in various forms and apparitions, but he and his demons struggled in vain. Whatever the delusions he produced, he did not succeed in striking terror to the resolute and courageous heart of the hermit. Sometimes he suffered the assaults and the terrifying devices of the demons themselves, sometimes he was vexed by beasts. For, as has been said, many wild animals roamed in the wilderness at that time. Some of them prowled at a dis-

tance, others drew near to the saint, surrounded him, even sniffed at him. A bear had taken to coming every day to the hermitage. Seeing that the beast came with no evil design, but in order to obtain some morsel, the saint would fetch a piece of bread from his hut and place it on a tree-stump or block of wood; finding that food had been provided for him, the bear would take it in his jaws and go away. But when the hermit had no bread and the bear found nothing at the usual place, he would not go away for a long time, but would stand there, looking right and left and watching, like a ruthless creditor waiting for his due. At that time Sergius had no varieties of food in his hut but only the bread and the water which he got at the spring, and even bread was scarce. Often there was no bread at all, and both the man and the beast went hungry. At other times there would only be one piece of bread left, and the saint would fling it to his beast, so as not to disappoint him. . . .

Whether he lived two years or more alone in the wilderness, I cannot tell, only God knows. And then, seeing the saint's great faith and patience, the Lord had pity on him. Seeking to make the saint's life in the desert less difficult, He inspired and guided the hearts of certain God-fearing monks, who began to come into the wilderness. . . .

A small number of brethren, about twelve in all, gathered around him. They built cells, and enclosed the grounds, which were of no great area, by a fence, at whose gates they placed a gate-keeper. Sergius built four cells with his own hands, and he did other monastery chores to serve the brethren. He brought fire-wood from the forest, carrying it on his own shoulders; he chopped the logs and took them to the cells. Wonderful to behold was the monastery at that time. The forest was not at a distance from it, as it is today; the trees stood right over the place where the cells were being built, the wind rustling through the branches. There were stumps and blocks of wood all around the church, and the monks had sown the seeds of various vegetables in that place.

But let us return to the good works of Saint Sergius. He pounded and ground the grain under the mill-stone, he baked the bread and cooked the food, he cut and sewed the clothes and the foot-wear; he went to fetch water at the spring, and carrying it in two buckets, climbed the hill to the monastery, and placed a jug of water in every cell. The night he spent in prayer, without sleep; he lived on bread and water, and even that in small quantity. He never spent a single hour in idleness.

A year later, the abbot who had conferred the tonsure on the saint fell sick and passed away. And God moved the brethren to approach Sergius with their petitions: "Father, we cannot live without an abbot. We want you to be our abbot and the guardian of our souls and bodies." Saint Sergius, sighing from the depths of his heart, answered: "I had no thought of being an abbot, and it is the desire of my soul to die as a monk in this place." The brethren insisted, and finally he let himself be convinced, inspired by brotherly love; so, with a deep sigh, he said to them: "Fathers and brothers, I will not oppose you but will obey the will of God, who searches the hearts and souls of men. Let us go to the city and consult the bishop." Metropolitan Alexis of Russia was at that time in Constantinople; in his place he had appointed Bishop Athanasius Volynsky in the city of Pereyaslavl. Our venerable father Sergius visited this bishop, accompanied by two elders. Entering, they bowed low before the bishop, and he, joyfully welcoming them, gave them the kiss of peace. He had already heard of Sergius and of his life in the desert, and he conversed with him concerning spiritual matters. Our blessed father Sergius then implored the bishop to give them an abbot to guide their souls. The venerable Athanasius replied: "My son and brother, God called you when you were in your mother's womb; henceforth you shall be father and abbot of the brethren." The venerable Sergius refused, stressing his unworthiness, but Athanasius went on: "Beloved, you have acquired all virtues, but you still must learn obedience." The saint bowed low and said: "As God wishes it to be, so let it be; glory be to the Lord in all eternity." And all responded: "Amen." The saintly bishop Athanasius took Sergius to the church and ordained him subdeacon, then deacon. The next morning he ordained him priest. And then, taking him aside, he imparted to him the apostolic rule and the teaching of the Fathers concerning the edification and instruction of souls. And giving him the kiss of peace, he let him go, truly an abbot, a pastor and guardian, a spiritual physician of the brethren. The saint had not seized authority on his own initiative, God had entrusted him with it; he had not thrust himself forward to receive it, he had not wrested it from others; he had not offered any compensation for it, as do certain ambitious men who enter into competition, whirling hither and yon and snatching power from one another. God Himself raised His saint to the rank of abbot. . . .

Who shall relate the true story of his virtuous life, and of the grace flowering in his soul? In the beginning of his abbacy, there were twelve brethren in the monastery, and he, the abbot, was the thirteenth. This number did not increase or diminish until Simeon, the Archimandrite of Smolensk, joined them, and one more was added to their company. From that day on, their numbers grew constantly. . . .

At the time when this monastery was being built, there were many needs and privations. The highway was at a great distance, and the desert stretched on all sides. They lived under these conditions, we think, for some fifteen years. Later on, peasants began to flock to the monastery and to settle all around it. They cut down the trees, and no one forbade them; they cleared the woods and disfigured the desert; indeed they did not spare it, but turned it into open fields, as we see them in our day. The newcomers built homesteads and villages and began to visit the monastery, bringing many offerings. But at the time of its founding, the community suffered great poverty. Sometimes there was no bread, no flour, wheat or any other grain; sometimes there was no wine for Mass, no incense, no wax. In the night, Matins were sung without candles, and the monks would be content with the light of a splinter of wood, birch or fir.

One day the abbot had neither bread nor salt, and the monastery was in great need of food. However, the saint had forbidden the brethren to leave the monastery and to ask help from the lay folk; the monks were to remain patiently in the monastery, awaiting God's mercy. Thus he spent three or four days, eating nothing himself. On the fourth day at dawn, he took an ax and went to one of the elders, Daniel by name. Sergius said to him: "I have heard, elder, that you want to build a porch for your cell. Well, I have come to build it, so that my hands should not remain idle." Daniel answered: "Yes, this has long been my intention, but I am waiting for the carpenters from the village, and I dare not hire you; you will demand a high price." Sergius said to him: "I will ask but a small reward. Have you got any old, mildewed loaves? I would very much like to eat some. I shall ask for nothing else. And where shall you find another such carpenter?" Elder Daniel brought him a sieve of mildewed loaves, saying: "This is all I have." Sergius answered: "It will be more than enough. But put them away till the ninth hour. I accept no pay till the work is done." So saying, he girded his loins and started to hew from morn till night. He hewed all the boards, chiseled the pillars, and set up the porch. When evening came, Daniel brought him the sieve with the promised loaves. Sergius said grace, blessed the loaves and began to eat. He drank only water; there was no soup and no salt. And this was both his dinner and his supper. Some of the brethren saw something like a whiff of smoke issuing from his mouth. Nodding toward each other, they said: "O brethren, how great is the patience and the abstinence of this man!" But one of the monks then murmured against Sergius. He had not eaten for two days. Drawing near to Sergius, he exclaimed boldly: "What! Mildewed loaves? Why should we not go out into the world to beg for bread? Because we obey you, we are dying of hunger. Tomorrow morning we shall leave this place and not return. We can no longer suffer this need and poverty!" Not all of them murmured, but only one brother. On his account, Sergius assembled the entire community. Seeing them weak and troubled, he taught them from Holy Scriptures: "Not without temptations is God's Grace given; but we must expect joy after sorrow. It has been said: In the evening there is weeping, and in the morning joy. You too are now suffering from the need of bread and other food, but tomorrow you shall delight in many good things." He was still speaking, when someone began to knock at the gate. The gate-keeper, putting his eye to the chink in the boards, saw that a great quantity of food had been brought. Overjoyed, he did not trouble to open the gates, but rushed to the abbot to tell him what he had seen. The saint commanded: "Make haste to open the gates and let them enter." He told the monks to invite those who had brought the food to share their meal, and he himself had the bell sounded, and went with the brethren to the church to sing a *Te Deum*. After this, they sat down to their meal, and loaves of fresh bread were placed before them. These breads were warm and tender, and their taste was exceedingly sweet, as if they had been baked in honey and seed-oil and spices. Afterward they tried to discover from whom this bread came and who had sent it. Those who had brought it said: "A certain pious man, who is very rich and lives far away, has sent this bread to Sergius and his brethren." Once again the monks, in obedience to their abbot's orders, went to invite the men to share their meal, but the men did not come, for they said that they must hasten on their journey. The next day, more food and drink were brought to the monastery, and again on the third day, this time from another region. The abbot Sergius, seeing and hearing all this, praised God with all the brethren, saying: "You see, brothers, that God, who provides for all, will never forsake this place. . . ."

The clothes he wore were so shabby—far shabbier than those of the other monks—that some of the visitors who did not know him were misled by his appearance. One day a peasant came to the monastery who had never seen Sergius. At that hour the saint was working in the vegetable garden. The peasant looked about for him, asking: "Which of the monks is Sergius? Where is that wonderful and famous man?" The brethren said to him: "He is working alone in the kitchen-garden. Wait for a while, till he has finished his work." But the peasant, becoming impatient,

looked through the chink in the fence and saw the saint, in his torn and patched old cassock, working in the sweat of his brow, and he could not believe that this was the abbot about whom he had heard such extraordinary accounts. When the saint came to join them, the brethren pointed to him, saying: "Here is the man whom you wished to see." The peasant turned away, laughing. "I have come to see a prophet," he exclaimed, "and you show me a beggar!" The brethren related this to the abbot: "We do not dare tell you all he says, venerable Father, but we would like to send this visitor away as a good for nothing, churlish fellow. He does not bow to you or render you the honors due to your rank. He rebukes us and will not listen to us." But the man of God, seeing the perplexity of the brethren, said: "Do not do that, brothers, for he did not come to you, but to ask for me." And not waiting to receive the peasant's obeisance Sergius bowed low before him; when he had given the man his blessing, he praised him for the correctness of his judgment concerning himself. Taking the visitor's hand, the saint had him sit at his right hand, and persuaded him to taste of the food and drink. But the peasant went on protesting that he deplored the absence of Abbot Sergius, whom he had come to see, but with whom he had been denied an interview. The saint said to him: "Do not be troubled; so great is the grace of God in this place that no one leaves here with a sad heart." And while he was speaking, a prince arrived at the monastery in great pomp and splendor, surrounded by a vast retinue of boyars and servants. The soldiers who went before the prince took the peasant by the shoulders and pushed him away from Sergius and the prince. The noble visitor bowed low before Sergius, even before he had approached him. The abbot blessed him and gave him the kiss of peace, after which they both sat down, while all the others remained standing. Meanwhile the peasant had made his way back through the crowd, and inquired of one of the attendants: "Tell me, who is this monk, sitting on the right hand of the prince?" The man, looking at him in astonishment, exclaimed: "Are you a stranger in these parts? Have you never heard of the blessed Sergius? It is he who is conversing with the prince." Hearing this, the peasant was shaken with fear and remorse. He fell at the saint's feet, crying: "Oh, how greatly I have sinned, wretch that I am! Forgive me and help my unbelief." The saint forgave him, gave him his blessing, and having spoken words of comfort to him, let him return to his home. . . .

On another occasion there came to him some Greeks from Constantinople, who had been sent by the Patriarch. They bowed before him, saying: "The Ecumenical Patriarch of Constantinople, Philotheus, sends you his blessing." And they gave him a letter. The saint said: "Have you not made a mistake? Who am I, a sinner, that such favors should be brought to me from the holy Patriarch." "We have been sent to you, venerable Sergius," the messengers answered. The saint bowed low before them and went himself to Metropolitan Alexis, bearing the letter from the Patriarch. The Metropolitan had this letter read to him, and it ran as follows: "By the grace of God, the Archbishop of Constantinople, the Ecumenical Patriarch Philotheus, to our son and fellow in service, Sergius. Grace, peace and our blessing be with you. We have heard of your virtuous life consecrated to God, and we have greatly praised and glorified God for it. There is still one thing lacking: you have not as yet attained to a life in common with others. You

know, most venerable one, that the prophet David himself, whose mind has embraced all things, could find no higher praise for this common life than when he chanted: 'Behold how good and how pleasant it is for brethren to dwell together in unity.' Therefore I too give you this salutary advice, to establish a community, and God's mercy and the blessing of God will abide with you."

Sergius asked the Metropolitan: "And you, holy father, what do you order me to do?" The Metropolitan answered: "We strongly advise you and offer our thanks." From that day on, a community life was established in the saint's monastery. The venerable and wise pastor entrusted the brethren with various duties; that of cellarer, cook, baker, infirmary-brother, and the various guardians of liturgical order. He commanded the brethren to live strictly according to the rule of the holy Fathers, not to acquire property, to call nothing their own, but to have everything in common. When the glorious saint had accomplished the establishment of his community, the number of disciples began to multiply. And the more the gifts poured into the monastery, the greater number of guests and pilgrims were received. No beggar left the monastery with empty hands; the saint had ordered the brothers to give comfort to the poor and the wanderers, always to give to beggars. And this is done even to the present day.

After a time discord arose. The enemy, who hates good, inspired the monks with the thought that they could no longer tolerate the primacy of Sergius over them. One Saturday they were singing Vespers, and Abbot Sergius was in the sanctuary in his sacerdotal vestments. His brother Stephen, who was standing in the left choir, inquired of the Canonarch: "Who gave you this book?" The Canonarch replied: "It was

Life of St. Sergius

given to me by the abbot." Stephen asked: "Who is abbot in this place? Was I not the first to sit here?" And he added other unreasonable remarks. The saint in the sanctuary heard this, but said nothing. When they went out of the church, he did not enter his cell, but leaving the monastery secretly, set out alone from that place. Proceeding to the monastery of Makhristcha (twenty miles away), he asked the abbot of that monastery to grant him the assistance of a brother who could show him some desert places. Having visited various sites, they found one which was beautiful, near the river Kerzhach. When they heard of the saint's presence, the brethren began coming to him by twos and threes. Sergius sent two of his disciples to Metropolitan Alexis to request his blessing for the building of a church. And thus, with the grace of God, a church was soon erected and a multitude of brothers gathered there. Meanwhile, some of the monks of the Holy Trinity, unable to suffer a long separation from their spiritual teacher, had gone to the city and said to the Metropolitan: "Holy Father! We are like sheep without a shepherd. Order Sergius to return to his monastery, so that we shall not be entirely undone by the sorrow of being without him." The Metropolitan sent two archimandrites, Gerasimus and Paul, who were enjoined to say to Sergius: "Your father, Metropolitan Alexis, sends you his blessing; he rejoices because of your life in this remote desert. However, you must return to the monastery of Holy Trinity. As for those who have annoyed you, I shall send them away from the monastery." Hearing this, the saint answered: "Say this to my Lord, the Metropolitan: 'All that comes from your lips I shall accept with joy, as from the lips of Christ, and I shall disobey you in nothing.'" The Metropolitan, pleased with such ready

obedience, quickly sent his priests, who consecrated the new church in the name of the Annunciation of our Pure Lady, the Mother of God. Sergius chose one of his disciples, Roman by name, and sent him to the Metropolitan, and thus having blessed him for the priesthood and as prior of the new monastery, the saint returned to the Holy Trinity. . . .

Now the rumor spread that by God's will and because of our sins, Prince Mamai had mustered a great army, the entire host of the infidel Tartars, in order to attack the Russian land. And all men were seized with terror. The ruling prince, who at that time held the scepter of the Russian lands, the praiseworthy and victorious great Dimitry, came to Sergius, for he had great faith in the saint. He asked whether Sergius would command him to march against the infidels. The saint gave him his blessing, armed him with his prayers, and said: "My Lord, it behooves you to guard the worthy flock entrusted to you by God. You must march against the infidels, and with God's help you shall defeat them and return unhurt to your native land, and you shall merit great praise." The prince replied: "If God lends me His help, I shall found a monastery in the name of the Most Pure Mother of God." And having received the saint's blessing, he hastened away. Mustering all his warriors, he marched against the godless Tartars; but when he saw their powerful host, he held back from the assault, and many in his camp were in the grip of fear, not knowing what to do. At that very moment, a messenger suddenly appeared, bringing word from the saint: "My Lord, do not hesitate. March boldly on against the fierce enemy. Fear nothing, for God will help you." Prince Dimitry and his army were inspired with great courage; they attacked the infidels and fought, and many fell, and God helped the great and victorious Dimitry; the Tartars were defeated. At that time the saint, who had the gift of supernatural sight, was praying with the brethren before God for the victory over the pagans. And at the very hour when the infidels were finally routed, Sergius foretold the whole event to the brethren. He spoke of the victory, and of the courage displayed by Prince Dimitry, and he named those who were slain and prayed for their souls to the all-merciful God. Prince Dimitry returned joyfully to his country and hastened to Sergius. He thanked him for his prayers and for those of his brethren, bestowed a generous gift upon the Holy Trinity, and, in fulfilment of his promise, took steps to found a monastery in the name of the Most Pure Mother of God in whatever suitable place should be found. Father Sergius found this place on the river Dubenka, and in accordance with Prince Dimitry's wish, he built there a church dedicated to the Mother of God. . . .

The blessed Metropolitan Alexis, conscious that his strength was declining through old age, summoned Saint Sergius. As they conversed, the Metropolitan ordered the cross and the passion cloth, adorned with gold and precious stones, to be brought to him; and he gave it to the saint. Sergius bowed humbly, saying: "Forgive me, my Lord, but from my youth I have never worn any gold on my person. All the more do I want to remain in poverty in my old age." The Metropolitan said to him: "I know, beloved, that you observe this rule, but prove your obedience by accepting the blessing we bestow on you." And he went on: "Do you know, venerable father, why I have called you here? While I am still living, I want to find a

man capable of tending Christ's flock. I mistrust all others, I have chosen you as the only one worthy. I know for certain that all want you, from the ruling lords to the least servant." Hearing these words, the saint was deeply troubled, considering this proposal to be a great occasion of vanity, so he answered: "Forgive me, my Lord, but what you offer me is beyond my strength, you will never find me suitable for this. Who am I, but a sinner and the least of men?" The Metropolitan quoted many things to the elder from the Holy Scriptures, yet the saint vowed to humility did not give in, but said: "Holy Lord, if you do not want to drive my poverty away from your holiness, cease to speak of this thing to an unworthy man, and do not permit anyone else to do so, for no one can prevail upon me to accept this." Seeing the saint's inflexible resolution, the Metropolitan let him return to his monastery. Soon after this, in the year 1377, the saintly Alexis died, and again the princes implored Sergius to accept the succession; but he was adamant and would not yield. An archimandrite named Michael was raised to the metropolitan seat and dared to vest himself in the prelate's vestments and to place the white cowl on his head. He armed himself against the saint, believing that Sergius would seek to combat his presumption and mount the metropolitan's throne himself. Hearing of Michael's threats against him, Sergius told his disciples that the man who had designs against Holy Trinity would not obtain his wish, and would be defeated by his own pride. And his prophecy came true. While his ship was sailing to Constantinople, Michael fell sick and died. Hence all venerated Sergius as a prophet. . . .

11

AVVAKUM'S AUTOBIOGRAPHY

EXCERPTS

At the time of Tsar Alexis (1645–76) a group of zealots brought about the revival and enforcement of strict ecclesiastical rules of prayer, fasting, and personal morality. Avvakum, then a country priest in Nizhni Novgorod on the Volga (now Gorky), gave his support to this program. But Patriarch Nikon had other ideas of religious reform which involved bringing the Russian church closer to the practices of Greek Orthodoxy. Many faithful, led by Avvakum and other conservatives, refused to adopt Nikon's changes and became known as Old Believers. Eventually they were excommunicated by the Church Council of 1666. For fifteen years Avvakum languished in the subterranean prison at Pustozersk in the Far North, on the Pechora River, where he wrote his autobiography. Ten years after its completion, in 1682, he was burned at the stake.

George Fedotov writes that Avvakum was "an author of genius, undoubtedly the best writer among the Muscovites, and certainly, in the daring venture of writing his spiritual autobiography, unique in old Russia. Old Believers consider him a canonized saint of the Church." For an assessment of Avvakum as a writer, see N. Gudzii's *History of Early Russian Literature*, pp. 378–96. For another sample of his writing, see H. Lanz, "Selections from Avvakum's Book of Discourses," *Slavonic and East European Review*, December, 1929. For a biographical study of the man, see Sergei Zenkovsky's "The Old Believer Avvakum," in *Indiana Slavic Studies*, Vol. I. George Lantzeff has written a useful monograph, *Siberia in the Seventeenth Century*. The entire Avvakum autobiography has been translated by Jane Harrison as *The Life of Archpriest Avvakum by Himself*. For one aspect of the Nikon-Avvakum controversy, see Nikolay Andreyev's "Nikon and Avvakum on Icon Painting," *Revue des Etudes Slaves*, Vol. XXXVIII. There are some very interesting remarks on Avvakum in James Billington, *The Icon and the Axe*. See also Catherine Caut, "The Archpriest Avvakum and His Scottish Contemporaries," *Slavonic and East European Review*, July 1966, pp. 381–402.

I was born in the region of Nizhny-Novgorod, beyond the river Kudna, in the village of Grigorovo. My father, Peter by name, was a priest. My mother, Maria, took the veil under the name of

From *A Treasury of Russian Spirituality*, compiled and edited by G. P. Fedotov, translated by Helen Iswolsky, Copyright 1948, Sheed & Ward, Inc., New York. Pp. 137–48, 150–52, 154–56, 159–67, 170–74. Reprinted by permission of the publisher.

Martha. My father was given to drink, but my mother practised prayer and fasting and constantly taught me the fear of God. One day I saw a neighbor's ox fall dead, and that night I arose and wept before the holy icon, sorrowing for my soul and meditating upon death, since I likewise should die. From that time on it became my custom to pray each night. Then my mother was widowed and I became an orphan in my early days, and we were exiled by our kin. My mother decided that I should marry. I besought the Mother of God to give me a wife who would help me to attain salvation. In that same village there was a maiden, also an orphan, who was wont to go frequently to church, and whose name was Anastasia. Her father was the blacksmith, Marco, a rich man; but after his death his whole substance was wasted. The maiden lived in poverty, and she prayed to God that she might be united to me in marriage; and it was God's will that this should come about. Then my mother returned to God after a life of great piety, and as for me, being turned out, I went to live in another place. I was ordained deacon at the age of twenty and priest two years later. I exercised the functions of ordinary priesthood for eight years and was then made archpriest by the Orthodox bishops, and that was twenty years ago; and I have now been in holy orders for thirty years.

Since the early days of my priesthood I have had many spiritual children, until now, some five or six hundred. I, miserable sinner, labored without rest, in churches and in houses, at the crossroads, in villages and towns, and also in the capital of the Tsar and in the Siberian land, preaching and teaching the word of God for some twenty-five years. . . .

After a short time, as it has been written, "the sorrows of death compassed me, and the perils of hell found me. I met with trouble and sorrow." An officer took away a maid, the daughter of a widow, and I implored him to give the orphan back to her mother. But he disdained our importunities and raised a storm against me. His men came to the church and crushed the life out of me; I lay senseless on the ground for half an hour or more. I came back to life by the will of God, and he, seized with fear, gave up the maid to me. Then the devil prompted him and he came to the church and beat me, and dragged me, in my vestments, on the ground, and I recited a prayer all the while.

Afterwards another officer found occasion to be moved with fury against me; he came running to my house, beat me, and buried his teeth in my finger like a dog. And when his throat was filled with gore, he released my hand from the clutch of his teeth and, leaving me, went home. As for me, I thanked God, bandaged my hand with a piece of linen, and betook myself to Vespers. As I was on my way that same man attacked me once more, with two small pistols. Standing close to me, he fired one of them. By the will of God, although the powder exploded in the pan, the pistol did not go off. He flung it on the ground and fired the other pistol, and the will of God was exercised once more and the pistol did not go off. I continued on my way praying fervently, and raised my hand to bless the officer and bowed to him. He cursed me, and I said to him: "Let grace be on your lips, Ivan Rodionovich." He was enraged with me because of the chanting in church; he wanted it to be done with dispatch, and I sang the office according to the rule, without haste. Then he deprived me of my house and drove me out onto the road, plundering everything and giving me no bread for the journey.

At that time my son Procopy was born, the one who is now imprisoned underground with his mother. I took my staff, and she the unbaptized child, and we went wherever God should speed us; on our way we baptized the child as, of old, Philip had baptized the eunuch. When I arrived at Moscow and went to the Tsar's confessor, Archpriest Stephen, and to Archpriest John Neronov, they both told the Tsar about me, and from that time on the Tsar knew me. The Fathers sent me back a certificate of safe-conduct, and I dragged myself home; but the very walls of my house were destroyed, and I began to establish myself afresh, and again the devil raised a storm against me. . . .

Soon after this, others drove me out for the second time from this place. I dragged myself to Moscow, and by the will of God the Tsar ordered that I should be installed as Archpriest at Yurievets on the Volga. There too I remained but a short time, only eight weeks. The devil inspired the priests, .the peasant folk and their women; so they came to the Patriarchal Chancery, where I was attending to ecclesiastical affairs, and they dragged me out of the chancery (they were about fifteen hundred strong); they beat me with rods in the middle of the street and trampled me on the ground, and the women beat me with oven-forks; for my sins I was beaten almost to death, and they threw me against the corner of the house. The governor came rushing up with his cannoneers and, seizing me, carried me off on horseback to my poor home; and he placed his men around the yard. Meanwhile the mob marched to the house, and they raised a great tumult in town; especially did the priests and the women whom I had warned against fornication shout, "Kill this thief and son of a harlot, and throw his body to the dogs in the ditch!"

As to me, having rested a while, I left my wife and children on the third day and fled by night up the Volga to Mos-

cow with two companions. I should have liked to stop at Kostroma, but there too they had driven out Archpriest Daniel. Ah me, the devil stirs up trouble everywhere.

I got to Moscow, and went to Stephen, the Tsar's confessor: he too made a wry face, saying, "Why have you abandoned your church?" So there was more trouble at hand. Then, in the middle of the night, the Tsar came to visit his spiritual father and to receive his nightly blessing, and he found me there, and there was more woe, since he asked, "Why have you left your city?" My wife and children and some twenty retainers had remained in Yurievets; I knew not whether they were alive or dead, and that was another calamity.

Soon after this Nicon, our friend, brought the relics of Metropolitan Philip from the Solovki Monastery to Moscow. Before he arrived, Stephen, the Tsar's confessor, spent a week in prayer and fasting with the brethren on behalf of the Patriarch (and I was with them), that God should grant us a pastor for the salvation of our souls. Together with the Metropolitan of Kazan, we wrote, and signed with our own hand, a petition which we presented to the Tsar and Tsarina in favor of Stephen, that he should be made Patriarch. But Stephen would not have it so, and suggested Metropolitan Nicon. The Tsar followed his advice. He sent a letter, to be delivered on his way to Moscow: "To Nicon, the Most Reverend Metropolitan of Novgorod and Velikia Luki and all of Russia, greetings," and so on. And once he was there, he was all bows and compliments with us, like a fox. He knew that he was going to be Patriarch and feared lest some obstacle should arise. There would be much to tell about these wily dealings. And when he was installed Patriarch, he would not even let his friends enter his chapel, and soon he spewed forth all his poison.

During Lent (in 1653) he sent a letter to the Cathedral of Our Lady of Kazan, addressed to John Neronov. The latter was my spiritual father; I lived at his church and took charge of it when he was absent. It was said that I should have been appointed to the post of the late Silas at the Savior's Church in the palace, but God had not willed it, and I myself had no great desire to be sent there. I loved the church of Our Lady of Kazan and was content to serve in it. I read holy books to the faithful, who came in great numbers. In his letter (dated such and such a year and month), Nicon wrote: "According to the tradition of the holy apostles and fathers, it is not fitting to make genuflections; suffice it to bow from the waist; and the sign of the cross must be made with three fingers."[1] We assembled and reflected upon this. We saw that winter was near; our hearts were frozen, and our limbs shaking. Neronov entrusted the church to me and hid himself in the Chudov Monastery, where, in a cell, he spent a week in prayer. As he prayed, a voice came from the icon: "This is the time of tribulation: you must suffer without weakening." He related this to me, weeping, also to Bishop Paul of Koloma, whom Nicon afterwards had burned at the stake at Kostroma; then he likewise told all the brethren about it. With Daniel, I copied excerpts from the Holy Fathers concerning the fingers used in the sign of the cross and the bows to be made during prayer, and these were submitted to the Tsar. There were a great many of these excerpts, but I know not where the Tsar hid them; I believe he gave them to Nicon.

Soon after this Nicon ordered Daniel to be seized and had his head shorn[2] in the Monastery at the Tver Gates, in the Tsar's presence. They tore his cassock from his back, and, heaping insults on him, took him to the Chudov Monastery and locked him in the bakery. After many torments had been inflicted on him, he was banished to Astrakhan; there he was crowned with a wreath of thorns, and they let him die in a dungeon. . . .

I too was arrested at Vespers by Boris Neledinsky and his musketeers. About sixty persons were arrested with me and taken to prison. As for me, I was put in chains and taken for the night to the Patriarch's Court. And on Sunday, as soon as it was day, I was placed in a cart with my arms outstretched and driven from the Patriarch's Court to the Monastery of Saint Andronicus. And I was thrown in chains into an underground cell. I spent three days in the dark, without food or drink, and in my chains I bowed in prayer, but whether to the west or to the east, I know not. Nobody came to my cell, only mice and cockroaches and chirping crickets and hordes of fleas. On the third day I was moved by the desire to eat—in other words, I was hungry—and, after Vespers, I saw someone standing before me; but whether it was man or angel I could not say, and cannot say even to this day, save that he uttered a prayer in the dark, and laying his hand on my shoulder, led me on my chains to a bench. He had me sit down and placed a spoon in my hand, and he gave me a little bread and some cabbage soup to eat, and it tasted good. Then, saying to me: "Enough. This will suffice for thy sustenance," he vanished: though the door did not open, he was no longer there. This would have been a strange thing, had it been a man, but for an angel 'tis no wonder, since he can be

---

[1] The main point of difference between the old and the new rites is the number of fingers used in making the sign of the cross: two for the Old Believers, three for the Established Church.

[2] This is part of the rite of the degradation of a priest.

stopped by no barrier. . . .

Afterwards I was taken from the monastery and led on foot, arms outstretched, to the Patriarch's Court. After a great deal of heckling, I was returned to my cell in similar fashion. On St. Nicetas' day there was a procession, and I was taken out in a cart to meet it; and I was brought to the cathedral to be shorn, and during Mass, they kept me for a long time on the parvis. The Tsar left his throne and, going up to the Patriarch, asked him not to have me shorn. I was taken to the Siberia Office, where I was placed in the custody of the secretary, Tretiak Bashmakov (now Father Savvaty), who today is also suffering for Christ's sake, imprisoned in an underground cell at the New Monastery of Saint Savior, may God save him. Even at that time he did me a kindness.

I was sent to Siberia with my wife and children. It would be a long tale, if I related all the tribulations we endured on our way; suffice it to say a little about them. During the journey Dame Avvakum gave birth to a child, and she was driven, sick, in a cart to Tobolsk. We travelled three thousand versts in thirteen weeks or so; we were dragged by cart, by boat or, half of the way, by sleigh.

In Tobolsk the Archbishop appointed me to a church,[3] and there I suffered great trials. In a year and a half, I was accused five times of treason against the Tsar. . . .

There came a ukase ordering that I should be taken away from Tobolsk, because I had condemned Nicon for his heresy, speaking from the Scriptures. At that time I received a letter from Moscow, informing me that two of my brothers, who lived in the palace in the Tsarina's apartments,[4] had died of the plague, with their wives and children;

and many others among my kinsmen and friends had also died. God had let flow on the Kingdom the vial of His wrath, and the wretched ones did not repent; they continue to cause trouble in the Church. Neronov had often warned the Tsar: There will be three visitations resulting from the schism in the Church: plague, the sword, division. And this is what has happened today. . . .

Once more I sailed in my ship, as had been shown to me in the vision already described. I made my way to the Lena River. When we reached Yeniseisk there came another ukase ordering me to Dauria,[5] twenty thousand versts and more from Moscow; I was to be given over to Afanasy Pashkov and his regiment. He had six hundred men under his command. He was a rough man, for my sins, and he burned, flogged and tortured people unceasingly. I had often tried to stay him, but finally I had fallen into his hands. From Moscow he had received Nicon's orders to torment me. . . .

Ah, poor me! the mountains were high, the forest dense; the cliffs stood like a wall, one could break one's neck looking up at them. In these mountains live great snakes, and geese and ducks with red feathers fly overhead, black crows and grey jackdaws. In these mountains there are also eagles and hawks and gerfalcons and guinea-fowl, pelicans and swans, and other wild birds of different kinds in great numbers. And many beasts roam likewise in these mountains: wild bucks and deer, aurochs, elks, boars, wolves, wild sheep, which

[3] Since Avvakum had not been degraded (shorn) like his colleagues, he was accepted in Tobolsk as a parish priest.

[4] The Tsarina Mary Miloslavsky, the first wife of Alexis, was in sympathy with the Old Believers.

[5] Dauria was the name given in the seventeenth century to the country on the left bank of the Amur River. The Russians had recently undertaken the conquest of this country, and Pashkov was the captain of the expedition.

are plainly to be seen but cannot be captured.

Pashkov wanted to cast me out into these mountains, to live among the birds and beasts. So I wrote him a short letter, and it started thus: "Man, fear God, Who sits on the Cherubim and Who watches over the abyss, before Whom tremble the heavenly powers and all creatures, including man. You alone despise Him and cause disturbance," and so on. There was much I wrote in that letter, and I had it taken to him. About fifty men came running, and they took my barge and towed it to where he was, about three versts away. I cooked some porridge for the Cossacks and fed them, poor souls; they were eating and trembling at the same time and some of them wept out of pity for me.

When the barge was towed ashore, the executioners seized me and led me before him. He stood, sword in hand, and shaking. First he asked me: "Are you a true priest or an unfrocked one?" I answered: "I am Avvakum, Archpriest. Speak, what is it you want of me?" He roared like a wild beast and struck me on one cheek and then on the other and beat me on the head, and knocked me down, and seizing his battle-axe, he struck me three times on the back, as I lay there. Then, tearing off my garment, he applied seventy-two strokes of the whip on that very same back of mine. And I cried: "Lord Jesus Christ, son of God, help me!" And I repeated these words unceasingly, and he was sorely vexed, because I did not say: "Have mercy." At each stroke of the whip, I recited the prayer; then, in the middle of the thrashing, I cried out: "Enough of this beating," and he ordered the thrashing to be stopped. I asked him: "Do you know why you beat me? Why? . . ."

Then I was taken to Fort Bratsky and thrown into jail, and given a little straw. I remained there till St. Philip's fast,[6]

in a frozen tower; it is already winter at that time in this land, but God warmed me in want of clothing. I lay like a dog on the straw; some days they would feed me and some days not; there were a great many mice, and I hit them with my biretta—the fools would not even give me a stick. I lay all the time on my belly: my back was sore, and there were many fleas and lice. I wanted to cry out to Pashkov: "Pardon!" but God's will forbade it and ordered me to be patient. Later I was transferred to a warm house, and there I spent the winter in chains with the hostages[7] and the dogs. My wife and children had been sent far from me, some twenty versts away. And all that winter she was plagued and rebuked by her servant Xenia. My son Ivan, a small lad, came to stay with me for a while after Christmas. Pashkov had him thrown into the cold cell where I had lain. He spent the night there, poor dear lad, and almost froze to death. In the morning, he was sent back to his mother. He reached home with his hands and feet frozen. . . .

That spring we began to sail on rafts down the Ingoda River. This was my fourth year of navigation since I had left Tobolsk.

We floated lumber for the building of houses and forts. There was nothing to eat; men died of hunger, and from working in the water. Shallow was the river and the rafts heavy, the taskmasters pitiless, the sticks hard, the cudgels knotty, the whips cutting, our sufferings cruel: fire and rack and people starving! One more stroke and a man would fall dead. Alas, what times were these! I know not how he could lose his mind in this way. . . .

I also lost two small sons in those hard days. They roamed the hills with

[6] November 15, in 1656.

[7] Hostages from the native tribes (in Bratsky it was the Buriats) were kept in Siberian forts to secure the payment of tribute.

the others, naked and barefoot on the sharp stones, feeding on grass and roots as best they could. I myself, miserable sinner, had to eat that horse-flesh and the foul carcasses of bird and beast. Alas for my sinful soul! Who shall freshen my eyes with the source of tears, that I may weep over my poor soul, for having lost itself to the delectations of the world!

But we were helped in Christ by the lady Eudokia Kirillovna, daughter-in-law of Afanasy, the governor, also by his wife, Fekla Semenovna. They preserved us secretly from starvation and death by sending us, without his knowing anything about it, now a piece of meat, now a loaf of bread, sometimes a little flour and oats, whatever she could gather, ten pounds, and some money, and even sometimes as much as twenty pounds. Or else she would scrape up some food from the chickens' trough.

My daughter, the poor maid Agrippina, would secretly go up to her window. It made us feel like weeping and laughing at the same time. Sometimes they would drive her away, without the lady being warned, but sometimes she would come home with an armload. She was then but a small child; she is twenty-seven today and still a maid, living in Mezen with her two younger sisters, in grief and uncertainty. Her mother and brother are imprisoned underground. But what can be done about it? Let them all suffer bitterly for Christ's sake. So be it, with God's help. It is fitting to suffer for the Christian faith. This Archpriest formerly enjoyed intercourse with the great, and now, poor wretch, let him delight in suffering to the end; for it has been written: Blessed is not he who begins, but he who perseveres to the end. But enough on that subject. Let us resume our previous topic. . . .

From the Nercha River we turned back once more to Russia. For five weeks we drove on icy roads in our sleighs. They gave me two nags to draw the children and the baggage. Dame Avvakum and myself journeyed on foot, stumbling on the ice. We travelled through a barbarous land, the natives were hostile; we dared not lag behind and could not keep up with the horses. We were hungry and weary. Dame Avvakum, poor thing, tramped on and on, and then she would fall. It was exceedingly slippery, and once another man, no less weary, stumbled over her and fell too. Both cried out and could not get to their feet again. The man cried: "Oh, good mother, dear lady, pardon me!" And she: "Do you want to crush me?" I came up to her, and she, poor lady, put all the blame on me: "How long, Archpriest, are we to suffer thus?" I answered: "Until our very death, Markovna!" And she replied, with a sigh: "So be it, Petrovich, let us plod on. . . ."

Then we journeyed back to the Lake Irgen. My lady took pity on us, and sent us a pan of wheat, and we had pudding to eat. Eudokia Kirillovna was our true provider, but with her too the devil prompted me to quarrel, and this is how it happened. She had a son, Simeon, who was born in that land. I had churched the mother and baptized the child, and each day she sent her son to me, that I should bless him; I would bless him with the cross and sprinkle him with holy water, and kiss him and let him go. The child was healthy and strong, but one day, when I was away, he became sick. The lady, angry with me and faint of heart, sent the baby to a witch-doctor. When I was informed of this, I was angry with her in turn, and so there was a bitter quarrel between us. The child grew worse, his right arm and leg became like sticks. Seized with remorse, she knew not what to do, and God struck even more heavily. The child was well-nigh dead, and the nurses came to me weeping, and I said: "Since she's a wicked woman, leave her alone!" And I waited for her repentance. I saw that the devil had hardened her heart, and I prayed for her, asking the Lord to bring her back to reason. And the Lord, God of mercy, freshened the arid fields of her heart; in the morning, she sent me her second son, John. Weeping, he begged my forgiveness for his mother, bowing low by my stove. I was lying on the stove, naked under some birch-bark; Dame Avvakum was in the stove, and the children lying about here and there. It was raining, and we had nothing to cover ourselves with, and water was leaking through the roof into our shack. We were managing as well as we could. In order to mortify the lady, I sent this message to her: "Tell your mother to beg Aretha, the witch-doctor, for this grace." Then they brought the child to me; she ordered him to be laid before me. They were all weeping and bowing. I rose, picked up my stole from the mud, and found the holy oil; having prayed and incensed the child, I anointed him and blessed him with the cross. And he —it was God's action—was healed, and his hand and leg became sound. I gave him holy water to drink and sent him back to his mother. Observe, you who listen to me, how great a virtue there is in a mother's contrition; she healed her own heart and restored her child's health. But what of that? 'Tis not only from this day that there is a God for penitents.

In the morning, she sent some fish and pies for us, who were starving; indeed it was a timely gift. From that day on, I made my peace with her. After she came back from Dauria, she died in Moscow, dear little lady, and I buried her in the Assumption Monastery.

Pashkov had heard the story of the child; she had told him about it. Then I went to him and he said, bowing low: "God save you, you have been a father to us, you have forgotten our evil do-

ings." It was his favorite grandson; he had baptized the child and had been deeply grieved on his account. And at that time he sent us much food. . . .

For ten years he tormented me—or I him, I know not which! God will decide on the day of judgment. Then he was appointed to a new post, and I received a letter; I was to return to Moscow. Pashkov left but did not take me with him. He said to himself: "If he journeys alone, the natives will kill him." He sailed in boats with men and weapons, and I learned from the natives that he was shaking with fear. One month after his departure, I gathered the old, the sick and the wounded, who were of no use over there, about ten men—with my wife and children, seventeen persons in all—and we got on a boat; trusting in Christ and with a cross on our prow, we sailed by the grace of God, afraid of nothing. . . .

Thus we left Dauria. Food became scarce, so I prayed to God together with my companions, and Christ sent us a buffalo, a huge beast. Thanks to this we reached Lake Baikal. A number of Russians had come to the shores of this lake, sable-hunters and fishermen. They were glad to welcome us, and they dragged our boat high onto the rocky shore. The good Terenty and his companions wept at the sight of us, and we looked at them. They gave us plenty of food, as much as we needed, about forty fresh sturgeons, saying: "Let this be your share, Father, God put them in our nets, take them all." I bowed to them, blessed the fish, and told the fishermen to take it back. What should I do with so much food? After we had stayed with them for awhile, I had to accept some of their supplies, and having repaired our boat and rigged up a sail with a woman's old smock, we started across the lake.

During the crossing the wind fell, and we had to use our oars. In that place the lake is not very wide, only eighty to one hundred versts or so. When we reached the other shore, a storm began to blow up, and we could scarcely land because of the waves. From the shore rose steep hills and sheer cliffs. I have dragged myself twenty thousand versts and more, but never have I seen such high mountains. And their summits are crowned with halls and turrets, pillars and gates, and walls and courts, all made by the hand of God. In those hills grow garlic and onion, the bulbs larger than those of Romanov onions, and very sweet. And there is also hemp, sown by God's hand, and in the courts, beautiful grass and sweet-smelling flowers. There are wild fowl in great number: geese and swans floating on the lake, like snow. And there are also fish: sturgeon and salmon-trout, sterlet and omul and white-fish, and many other kinds. This is a fresh-water lake, but great seals and sea-hares live in it. I never saw the like in the great ocean, when I lived on the Mezen River. And the fish is abundant; the sturgeon and salmon-trout are so fleshy, one cannot fry them in a skillet, it would be nothing but fat. And all this has been created by Christ for man, that he should find pleasure in it and praise God. But man, who is enslaved by vanity—his days pass like a shadow; he leaps, like a goat; he puffs himself out, like a bubble; he rages, like the lynx; seeks to devour, like a serpent; at the sight of another's beauty, he neighs like a foal; is wily, like the devil; having had his fill, he falls asleep without observing the rule of prayer. He puts off repentance until the day when he shall be old, and then he is vanished, I know not where, into the light or into the darkness. It shall be revealed upon the day of Judgment. Pardon me, I have sinned more than any man.

Then we reached the towns of Russia, and I became aware, concerning the Church, that "it prevailed nothing, but rather a tumult was made." I was sad-

dened, and sitting myself down, I reflected: What am I to do? must I preach the word of Christ or go into hiding? For I was bound to wife and children. Seeing my distress, Dame Avvakum came up to me respectfully and asked: "What troubles you, my lord?" And I told her everything in detail: "Wife, what shall I do? 'Tis the winter of heresy. Shall I speak or be silent? You have shackled me." And she replied: "God forgive! What say you, Petrovich? Did you not read the words of the Apostle: 'Art thou bound to a wife, seek not to be loosed. Art thou loosed from a wife? Seek no wife.' I and the children bless you. Continue to preach the word of God as fearlessly as before, and be not concerned about us, as long as God shall allow it. If we are separated, then do not forget us in your prayers. Christ is mighty and will not abandon us. Go, go to church, Petrovich, and convict the heretics of their whoredom!"

At these words, I bowed to her, and, having shaken off my grievous blindness, I began once more to preach the word of God and to teach in towns and everywhere, and boldly to condemn Nicon's heresy. . . .

Then I arrived in Moscow and the Tsar received me joyfully, as if I were an angel of God. I went to Fedor Rtishchev;[8] he came out of his chamber to meet me, asked for my blessing, and we talked for a long while: he would not let me go for three days and three nights, and then he announced my presence to the Tsar. The Tsar immediately received me in audience and spoke to me kindly: "How fares it with you, Archpriest? God has let us meet once more." I kissed his hand and pressed it, answering: "God lives and my soul lives, Tsar, my Lord! From now on, It will be as God ordains." And he, dear soul,

[8] Rtishchev was an influential boyar and one of the most cultivated and tolerant statesmen in the seventeenth century.

sighed and went to attend to some business. We had spoken a few words more, but it is no use recalling them, it all belongs to the past. He ordered that I should be given lodgings in a monastery in the Kremlin; when he passed my house, he would bow to me, saying: "Bless me and pray for me." One day, as he rode by on horseback, he took off his hat. And when he drove in a carriage, he would lean out of the window to see me. And all the boyars did as much, each one bowing to me: "Archpriest, bless us and pray for us."

How should one not pity such a Tsar and such boyars? Yes, indeed, they are to be pitied. See how good they were, offering me parishes to choose from, and even suggesting that I should become confessor to the Tsar, if only I would consent to be reunited to them. I counted all this as dung, that I might gain Christ, thinking of death, for all these things pass away. . . .

They saw that I was not going to be reconciled with them. So the Tsar ordered Rodion Streshnev to persuade me to be silent. And I did so, in order to please him. He was the God-established Tsar, and good to me. I hoped he would advance little by little. On St. Simeon's Day[9] I was promised an appointment to the Printing Office, to correct the books, and I was extremely pleased; I liked this better than being confessor to the Tsar. He did me a favor, sending me ten rubles, and the Tsarina gave me ten rubles; and Lucas, the Tsar's confessor, ten; and Rodion Streshnev, ten. As for my old friend Fedor Rtishchev, he told his treasurer to put sixty rubles in my bonnet—to say nothing of the others. Each one brought me something or other.

I spent all my time with my dear Feodosia Prokofievna Morozova, for she was my spiritual daughter; and so

was her sister, Princess Eudokia Prokofievna, dear martyrs in Christ! I likewise visited Anna Petrovna Miloslavsky constantly, and I went to Fedor Rtishchev, to have disputes with the apostates. I lived in this manner for about half a year.

Then I saw that "it availed nothing" in the Church, "but that rather a tumult was made," and so I began once more to grumble. I wrote a long letter to the Tsar, asking him to re-establish the old ways of piety, to defend our common mother, Holy Church, against heresy, and to place on the patriarchal throne an Orthodox pastor instead of the wolf and apostate Nicon, scoundrel and heretic. . . .

From that time on the Tsar was hostile towards me. He did not like my speaking again. He wanted me to be silent, but this did not suit me. And the bishops sprang on me like goats. They wanted to exile me once more from Moscow, for many came to me in Christ's name, and, when they had heard the truth, gave up attending their mendacious services. The Tsar reprimanded me: "The bishops complain of you, they say you have emptied the churches. You shall be exiled once more." It was Boyar Peter Mikhailovich Saltikov who brought me the message. They took me to Mezen. The good people had given me many things in the name of Christ, but I had to leave everything behind and was accompanied on my journey only by my wife, children and family. And again I taught the people of God in the towns and condemned the piebald beasts. So they brought me to Mezen.[10] After holding me there a year and a half, they took me back to Moscow with two of my sons, Ivan and Procopy. Dame Avvakum and all the others remained at

9 September 1, 1662, the day of New Year in old Russia.

10 The Mezen is a river discharging itself into the White Sea eastward from Arkhangelsk. There, on the sea coast, was a small Russian settlement (now the town of Mezen).

Mezen. Having brought me to Moscow, they first took me to the Monastery of St. Paphnutius. And there they sent me a message, always repeating the same thing: "How long will you torment us? Reunite yourself with us, dear brother Avvakum." I rejected them like the devils, and they flew into my eyes. And I wrote a long and wrathful declaration and sent it through Cosmas, deacon of Yaroslavl and clerk in the Patriarch's chancery. This Cosmas was I know not what kind of man. In public he tried to persuade me, and in private he upheld me, saying: "Archpriest, do not renounce the old [way of] piety. You will be a man great in the eyes of God if you suffer to the end. Do not heed us if we perish." And I said to him that he should return to Christ. He answered: "This I cannot do; Nicon has caught me in his snares." To say the truth, the poor man had renounced Christ for Nicon and could not get back on his feet. I wept, blessed him, poor wretch; that was all I could do for him. God knows how it will go with him.

Thus, after I had spent ten weeks in chains at the Monastery of St. Paphnutius they took me back to Moscow, an exhausted man on an old nag; a guard behind me, a guard in front of me. Whip your horse and on you ride! At times, the horse would fall into the mud, its four legs in the air, and I tumbling over its head. One day we galloped ninety versts and I was half dead at the end of it. In Moscow, at the Patriarch's chapel, the bishops held a disputation with me. Then I was led to the cathedral, and after the Great Entry I was shorn, together with Deacon Theodore; they cursed me, and I cursed them. Great indeed was the tumult at that Mass. Having stayed some time at the Patriarch's Court, I was taken by night to the Chamber of the Palace. There a colonel examined me and sent me to the Secret Gates on the Waterfront. I supposed

that they would throw me into the river, but here Dementy Bashmakov, the man of Private Affairs and the agent of Antichrist, awaited me. He said to me: "Archpriest, the Tsar ordered me to tell you: 'Fear no one; place your trust in me.'" I bowed to him, saying: "My thanks for his favor. What security has he for me? My trust is in Christ." Then they led me over the bridge to the other bank of the river, and on my way, I said to myself: "Put not your trust in princes, in the children of men in whom there is no salvation."

Then officer Joseph Salov and his musketeers took me to St. Nicholas' Monastery at Ugresha. They sheared off my beard, the enemies of God! And why not? They are wolves and have no pity for the sheep. They tore off all my hair—the dogs!—leaving but a forelock, such as the Poles have on their heads. They drove us to the monastery, not along the roads, but through marshes and mire, so that people should not see us. They were well aware of their folly, but were unable to give it up. The devil had clouded their minds. How can we blame them? Were it not they, it would be others. The time is at hand when, according to the Gospels: "It must needs be that scandals come." And the other evangelist teaches us: "It is impossible that scandals should not come. But woe to him through whom they come."

Take heed, you who listen to me: Our misfortune is inevitable, we cannot escape it. If God allows scandals, it is that the elect shall be revealed. Let them be burned, let them be purified, let them who have been tried be made manifest among you. Satan has obtained our radiant Russia from God, so that she may become crimson with the blood of martyrs. Well planned, devil! It pleases us, too, to suffer for our dear Christ's sake.

At St. Nicholas I was locked up in a cold hall above the ice-cellar for seventeen weeks. There I had a vision sent by

God. You may read about it in my letter to the Tsar. And the Tsar came to the monastery and walked around my prison and sighed, but did not come in to see me. They had prepared the road and sprinkled it with sand. He thought and thought, and did not come in. I think he pitied me, but such was the will of God. When I had been shorn, there had been a great dispute at the palace between the Tsar and the late Tsarina. The dear lady was at that time on our side, and she had preserved me from mutilation. . . .[11]

And now I shall tell you again about my tribulations. From St. Paphnutius, they took me back to Moscow and placed me in the court of the Monastery. And they dragged me many times to the Chudov Monastery, before the ecumenical patriarchs; and our bishops all sat there like foxes.[12] I discussed many things with the patriarchs in the words of the Scriptures. God opened my sinful lips and Christ confounded them. Their last words to me were: "Why are you stubborn? All our people of Palestine, and the Serbs, and the Albanians and Valachians and Romans and Poles, all cross themselves with three fingers. You alone in your obstinacy cross yourself with two fingers. This is not fitting." And I, miserable wretch, how bitter I felt! But I could do nothing. I reproved them as well as I could, and my last word was: "I am uncorrupted, and I shake the dust from my feet, for it is written: 'Better is one that feareth God, than a thousand ungodly.' " So they cried out even louder against me: "Take him, take him, he has dishonored us all." And they began to shove me and

[11] The companions of Avvakum had their tongues cut off before they were sent into their place of deportation.

[12] The famous council of 1666–67 in which two Greek patriarchs participated. The council condemned the schism of the Old Believers and deposed the Patriarch Nicon himself.

beat me. And the patriarchs themselves rushed at me; about forty of them, I believe—'twas a great army of the Antichrist that had mustered. Ivan Uvarov seized me and dragged me along; and I cried: "Hy, wait, don't beat me!" They staggered back and I said to the interpreter, an archimandrite: "Tell the patriarchs: Paul the Apostle says: 'It was fitting that we should have such a highpriest, holy, innocent,' and so forth. But you, how shall you celebrate Mass after beating a man?" Then they were seated, and I retired to the door and lay down on my side, saying: "Stay seated, and I shall lie down for a while." They laughed and said: "This Archpriest is a fool, without respect for patriarchs." I answered: "We are fools for Christ's sake . . . we are weak but you are strong, you are honorable, but we are without honor." Then the bishops returned and began to discuss the *Alleluia*, and Christ helped me to confound their Roman heresy with the help of Dionysius the Areopagite. And Euthymius, the cellarer of the Chudov Monastery, said to me: "You are right; it is of no use to discuss anything further with you. . . ."

Then we were returned to Moscow, to the court of the St. Nicholas Monastery, and again they sought from us a profession of orthodoxy. And the gentlemen of the bedchamber, Artemon and Dementy, were sent to me many a time, and they repeated the Tsar's words to me: "Archpriest, I know your innocent, spotless, and godly life. I ask your blessing, together with the Tsarina and my children. Pray for us." Thus spoke the messenger, bowing, and I always wept for the Tsar. I had the greatest pity for him. And he went on: "I pray you, listen to me, reunite yourself with the ecumenical patriarchs, at least in part." I answered: "Let me die if God wills it so, but I will not be reunited with the apostates. You are my Tsar—but they?

—what have they got to do with you? They have lost their own Tsar, and now they drag themselves here to devour you! I will not lower my arms, which are lifted to heaven, until God shall give you back to me!" There were many messages of this kind. One thing and another was discussed. Their last word was: "Wherever you are, do not forget us in your prayers." Even today, miserable sinner that I am, I pray for him as well as I can.

Then, after mutilating our brothers, but not me, they banished us to Pustozersk. From there I wrote two letters to the Tsar, the first one short, and the second, longer. I told him various things, among them, of certain signs that God had shown me in my prisons. Let him who reads understand. Moreover, I and the brethren sent, as a gift to the followers of the true faith in Moscow, the Deacon's manuscript entitled *Answer of the Orthodox,* along with a condemnation of heresy and apostasy. It declared the truth about the dogmas of the Church. And two letters were also sent to the Tsar by the priest Lazarus. And for all this, we too received some gifts in return: in my house on the Mezen they hanged two men, spiritual children of mine, Theodore, the fool in Christ already mentioned, and Luke Lavrentievich, servants of Christ. . . .

After that, the same officer Ivan Yelagin who had been with us at Mezen came to Pustozersk, and he received from us a profession which ran thus: "Such and such a year and month. We inalterably observe the traditions of the Holy Fathers, and we anathematize the heretical assembly of Paisius, the Patri-

arch of Palestine, and his followers." And this profession declared many other things, and Nicon, the maker of heresies, received his share in it. For this we were taken to the scaffold, and the verdict was read to us; I was taken to prison without mutilation. The verdict stated: "Let Avvakum be imprisoned in a wooden framework underground and be given only bread and water." In answer I spat. I wanted to starve myself to death, and did not eat for eight days and more, until the brethren ordered me to eat again. . . .

Then they covered us with earth. They placed a wooden framework under the earth and another one nearby, and a common enclosure around them with four locks, and guards were placed before the prison doors. And we, imprisoned here and everywhere—sang before our Lord Christ, Son of God, a canticle such as Solomon sang as he looked upon his mother, Bathsheba.

Having first gone from us to Mezen, Yelagin journeyed to Moscow. And in Moscow the rest of us were roasted and baked. They burned Isaiah and they burned Abraham, and a great many other champions of the Church were annihilated. God will count their numbers. It is amazing that the Niconians refuse to regain their senses: they propose to establish the faith through fire, whip and gallows. Who were the apostles that taught them these things? I do not know. My Christ did not order His apostles to teach in this way, to lead men to the faith with fire, whip and gallows. He commanded the Apostles: "Go ye into the whole world and preach the gospel to every creature. . . ."

12

THE RUSSIAN CHURCH SCHISM

By Serge Zenkovsky

One of the most neglected topics of prerevolutionary Russian history is the development of the Russian church. Perhaps the most dramatic chapter of that story is the cruel struggle within the church which took place in the second half of the seventeenth century. Our author, professor of Russian history at Stetson University, Florida, has succeeded in placing the schism into a wider framework of internal and foreign policy and has traced the story up to 1917.

For the early stages of the controversy, we have the testimony of an important eyewitness, Paul of Aleppo, in his *The Travels of Macarius* (2 vols.). There are two monographs which deal with the schismatics: Sergei Bolshakoff's *Russian Nonformity* and F. Conybeare's *Russian Dissenters*. The largest work on Patriarch Nikon is W. Palmer's *The Patriarch and the Tsar* (6 vols.). For an interpretation of the schism, see Kluchevsky's *History of Russia*, III, 292–330. For the influence of the Ukraine, see W. E. D. Allen, *The Ukraine*, and D. Doroshenko, *History of the Ukraine*. For a brief study of the church-state relationship during this period, see Matthew Spinka, "Nikon and the Subjugation of the Russian Church to the State," *Church History*, X, 347–66. See also L. R. Lewitter, "Poland, the Ukraine and Russia in the 17th Century," *Slavonic and East European Review*, XXVII (1948), 157–71, 414–29. An over-all view of Russo-Ukrainian relations in this period is available in *Muscovy and the Ukraine* by Carl O'Brien. There are several chapters on the schism in James Billington's *The Icon and the Axe*. The beliefs of the Old Believers are analyzed in Sergei Zenkovsky's "The Ideological World of the Denisov Brothers," *Harvard Slavic Studies*, Vol. III, and in Michael Cherniavsky's "The Old Believers and the New Religion," *Slavic Review*, March, 1966. On the role of the Old Believers in industry see Valentine Bill's *The Forgotten Class* and William Blackwell's "Old Believers and the Rise of Private Industrial Enterprise in Early 19th Century Moscow," *Slavic Review*, September, 1965.

Deacon Paul of Aleppo, a Christian Arab who accompanied his father, Macarios, Patriarch of Antioch, on a journey to Muscovy, tells in his memoirs of Macarios' participation in a council of the Russian church in 1656. This council convened to condemn a rebellious Russian archpriest who refused to obey Nikon, Patriarch of Russia. "After the council"—on the Sunday after the Ascension, May 18—relates the Arab clergyman, "our master celebrated with

From the *Russian Review*, XVI, 37–58. Reprinted by permission of the *Russian Review*. Footnotes have been omitted.

Patriarch Nikon in the cathedral, where they anathematized the priest. . . . Following the liturgy the Patriarch of Antioch gave a sermon concerning the priest, through an interpreter, and likened him to Arius, archpriest in Alexandria—for this man was archpriest in Moscow. The Patriarch then excommunicated the Moscow archpriest together with all his followers, and the singers and clergy chanted against him thrice 'Anathema.' After the liturgy we went to dine with the Patriarch of Moscow."

The excommunicated archpriest was a certain Ivan Neronov, the most popular and ardent preacher of the Russian moral and religious revival in Nizhni-Novgorod and Moscow during the period 1630–50. Neronov had rebelled against some ritualistic innovations introduced in the Russian Church by Patriarch Nikon, and remained the latter's adamant and implacable adversary. His excommunication was the first instance of the Church Council's condemnation of the supporters of the old rites, and led later to the formation of a schism within the Russian church which undermined Russian cultural unity and resulted in an irreconcilable cleavage of Russian Orthodoxy which has lasted to the present time.

Prior to this rupture in the Church, the Muscovite state had succeeded in preserving a cultural and ideological harmony. Neither the heresy of the Judaizers during the reign of Ivan III nor occasional conversions to Protestantism and Catholicism in the time of Ivan IV and during the Times of Trouble seriously affected Russian spiritual unity. Understandably, because of her geographical situation, Russia did not participate in the European cultural evolution but formed her own national type of civilization. Muscovy, however, was not seeking isolation from Europe,

and the first Russian autocrats did not shun dynastic ties with the West. Ivan III married Sophia Paleologue, a Catholic princess of Byzantine origin, educated in the Latin tradition. His son, Basil III—father of Ivan IV—chose for his wife Elena Glinsky, a Lithuanian princess whose uncle, Prince Michael Glinsky, was one of the most influential feudal lords of the Polish-Lithuanian condominium and a brilliant condottieri well known in Germany and Italy. Ivan IV once proposed to Lady Mary Hastings of England, while Boris Godunov planned the marriage of his daughter to a Danish prince. The politics of both Ivans and of Basil III reflected the prevailing European methods during the Renaissance, and their deeds, in fact, often smacked of the precepts of Machiavelli. The Livonian wars of Ivan III and Ivan IV were conducted with the purpose of establishing direct contact with the West. At that time numerous Europeans visited and lived in Russia; even among the *oprichniki* of Ivan IV could be found numerous Germans and other West Europeans. After the reign of Boris Godunov a great many European military specialists, mercenaries, merchants and physicians came to Moscow. The False Dimitri, imbued with the Western culture of Poland, had been enthusiastically received by the Russian people, and after his accession successfully initiated measures aimed at the extension of Western culture to Russia. The assassination of this enigmatic impostor was due not to an outbreak of popular indignation at his policies and cultural innovations but to the conspiracy of the boyars, and to the tactlessness of the Poles who accompanied Dimitri's bride to Russia.

The Muscovites and the Russian government, however, ceased to accept foreigners tolerantly after the Times of Trouble, when Russian national feeling was aroused by Polish and Swedish interventions. The attempt of the Catholics to conquer Russia for Rome, the pillages of the Lithuanian and the Zaporozhie bands, the occupation of Moscow by the Poles, the outrages of the Russian sanctuaries, and the loss of the Western provinces—all constituted a threat to Russian independence. The sharpening of Russian national feeling led to an intensification of Muscovy's cultural alienation and to general xenophobia.

These tribulations of the Times of Trouble were accepted by devout Russians as a manifestation of the wrath of God, and there came about a renewal of religiosity. In the 1630's and 1640's a new and unique religious movement, that of the Zealots of Piety, came into being. The Zealots were people who had witnessed the massacres and the conflagrations of the Times of Trouble in their childhood and who were now seeking the rebirth of Orthodoxy. Their aims were a moral reformation of the clergy and the people, a liturgic revival, and renewed piety. They also preached Christian assistance to the needy and weak, whom they tried to protect from injustice. They wanted to permeate the life of the nation with the teachings of Christ, to realize the ideal of an Orthodox tsardom.

At the core of this movement were representatives of the White Clergy, non-regular priests and archpriests. Their leader was Archpriest Neronov, who later was anathematized and excommunicated by the Russian and Syrian Patriarchs in Moscow. The movement had the support of Tsar Alexis and his close advisers, the pious boyars Morozov and Rtishchev, as well as Archbishop Nikon, who later became Patriarch. The Zealots of Piety carried the words of the Gospel and the Church fathers, particularly St. John Chrysostom's, the protector of the persecuted and the poor, to the people, who responded to these Russian Savanarolas and followed them. These preachers did not hesitate to challenge the Patriarch and the bishops when they found the hierarchy lax.

A harmonious relationship between the government and the leaders of the Zealots of Piety existed until 1653, although certain bishops found the movement's passionate sermonizing disturbing and a threat to their authority. In 1652 Nikon became Patriarch. Together with stricter discipline in the church and the introduction of various measures meant to improve the moral condition of the population, Nikon sought to increase the influence of patriarchal power in Church and state affairs. This theocratic tendency had probably grown under the influence of Kievan monks who were invited to Moscow as translators and teachers, and of the Greek clergy, many of whom were educated in Rome, whose representatives were frequently sent to Russia to seek financial support for their church. From both the Kievan monks and the Greeks Nikon may have learned of the independent and influential position of the Italian and Polish Catholic hierarchy and the power of the Pope. Also, the example of Patriarch Philaret (1619–33), a dominating personality and brilliant statesman who became co-ruler with Tsar Michael, Alexis's father, might have suggested the idea of ruling the Church autocratically and playing a stronger role in state affairs. But Nikon, the son of a Russian-Mordvinian peasant, overlooked the fact that Philaret's position was due primarily to the fact that he was the father of Tsar Michael, and that despite his unusual power Patriarch Philaret had always acted very cautiously in Church affairs, never undertaking any important decision without consulting the Church Council.

In early spring, 1653, Nikon decreed

the first changes in the ritual of the Church service and prescribed the use of three fingers instead of two in making the sign of the cross. This innovation, issued solely by the Patriarch himself with no accompanying explanation and without the consultation of the Church Assembly, met with the vigorous opposition of the Zealots of Piety as well as the disapproval of Tsar Alexis. Nikon did not immediately try to enforce the decree, but proceeded first to settle with the opposition.

Ivan Neronov was sent to the far north, Archpriest Avvakum was exiled to Siberia, and others were transferred to remote provincial towns. Thus free to act unhindered, Patriarch Nikon in 1654–56 carried through a number of innovations which brought the practices of the Muscovite Church closer to those of the Greek and other eastern Orthodox churches. The Church books, which contained discrepancies from the Greek versions, were corrected according to the Greek originals. The Muscovite Church agreed to the changes and subordinated itself in all details to the Greek standards accepted by the Eastern Patriarchs of Constantinople, Alexandria, Antioch, and Jerusalem. Opposition—which had issued from the Zealots of Piety—was unbroken, however. Supporters of the Muscovite traditions in the capital, in the north and in Siberia, on the Volga, and on the Don, continued to defend in their writings the two-fingered sign of the cross and the old Muscovite church rites. At the same time they challenged the discriminatory authority of the Patriarch and became increasingly bitter in opposing him.

What were the real causes of this contention over the reforms? The Patriarch and the Tsar wanted to remove the discrepancies which had crept in over the centuries; they wanted to introduce a common Orthodox ritual. Opponents of reform regarded the Muscovite practices as an inseparable part of the Russian Orthodox way of life—as, indeed, sanctified by generations of Muscovite clerics, saints, and laymen. When in 1656 and again in 1667 the adherents to the old Muscovite traditions were finally excommunicated they asked, not unjustifiably, "How can it be that the Muscovite saints, who crossed themselves with two fingers and sang 'Alleluia' in the old way, have erred and thus been anathematized?" In their view, as formulated by Spiridon Potemkin, the Muscovite Church was right and could never sin in word, customs or writings, for the Church was sacred and nothing in its practice and doctrine could be suppressed or altered. For these traditionalists, or as they are now called, Old Believers, a strict observance of doctrine and rite was a prerequisite for salvation and attainment of the Kingdom of God. Since the Kingdom of God could be reached through the permeation of life by Orthodox principles and by strict observance of the liturgy and rites, they regarded any modification of the church service as a sin which obstructed the way of salvation.

Furthermore, since the late fifteenth century the Russian people had been told, both by their own ideologists and by visiting Eastern Patriarchs, that Muscovite Russia, the "Third Rome," was the sole remaining stronghold of the true faith in the world. Suddenly, it appeared that Russia was not the bearer of piety and the true faith but rather the guardian of foolish errors, for which they were now anathematized and excommunicated. For the Old Believers the Nikonian reform signified the disintegration of the Muscovite Church and the old way of life, the collapse of the state ideology of the Orthodox tsardom.

The Council of 1666–67 condemned not only the old Muscovite church books, rituals, and two-fingered sign of the cross, but also the *Stoglav*—the decisions of the Church Council of 1551, which had been Russian canonic law for a century and the symbol of pure Orthodoxy. Old Muscovy was dethroned, deprived of its halo and glory. The "Third Rome" was demolished not from without but from within, by its own hierarchs, the Ukrainian monks, and the Greek prelates.

It is not difficult to picture the despair felt by the faithful Russians. Were they to relinquish the old ideals by which they and their fathers had lived, and accept damnation by submitting to the discriminative decision of the state power and the Church hierarchy? It was a particularly difficult situation for those enthusiastic sermonizers who had but recently called the people to a spiritual rebirth, to increased veneration for the Church and the Muscovite Orthodox way of life. The majority of them could not accept the prescribed changes and found themselves in opposition to the Church and State.

Here, then, the question might be asked, why did the Church and the Muscovite ruling elite embark upon a path of reform which could lead only to the creation of a profound conflict in the hearts of the Russian people? The reasons were not only religious, but also political and personal. There was no real necessity for the Church's denial of Muscovite religious traditions. True, the requirements of printing demanded conformity of text in the Church books and the elimination of contradictions or errors; but Nikon's peremptoriness in initiating these changes was extreme. He issued his first directives upon the advice of the Greek and Ukrainian monks and bishops, while, at the same time, his measures were not condoned by the Patriarch of Constantinople, who wrote him that every local church could have its particular customs, provided only that it preserve the purity of Orthodox teaching and the fundamental dogmatic truths.

The Councils of 1666–67 were inspired beyond merely correcting books and rites. These Councils, as well as that of 1682, undertook a substantial reorganization of Church life, and, contrary to centuries-old tradition, control over parochial life was tightened. New bishoprics were created and the parishes, formerly democratic in structure, were deprived of independence. The election of priests was replaced by their nomination by the bishops. Where the Zealots of Piety had sought to reinforce the influence of priests among the parishioners, the Church and state now aimed at destroying the independence of the local religious communities. Thus the decisions of the Councils paved the way for the future reforms of Peter I, who placed Church life entirely under the tutelage of the state.

Considerations of foreign policy played no less important a role in the state's acceptance of Patriarch Nikon's reforms. In the 1650's, recovering from the Times of Trouble, Moscow renewed its political interest in Poland, the Ukraine, and Turkey. The government, alarmed by the appeals of the Cossacks and the South-Western Russian clergy, decided to initiate the unification of those Russian territories which had been annexed to Lithuania and Poland during the centuries of the Tartar yoke. As early as 1624 Isaaky Borisevich, Bishop of Lutsk, apparently representing Metropolitan Iov Boretsky of Kiev, had come to Moscow to persuade the Tsar to liberate the southern and western territories from the oppression of the Poles. In 1632 the Ukrainian Cossacks had met with Bishop Jonas Konissky in the city of Korsun and resolved to request Tsar Michael to accept them as his subjects if the Poles continued their persecution. From the very beginning of the rebellion of the Cossack leader Khmelnitsky against the Poles, petitions to the Tsar

for help came more and more frequently from the Russian Orthodox population of the Polish and Lithuanian Territories. Khmelnitsky and the Ukrainian
Cossacks asked the Muscovite government to incorporate the Ukraine into its
realm, but under the pressure of conservative elements this action was post-
poned by the Muscovite Land Assembly until 1653, when Polish successes in
the Ukraine seemed to endanger the
very existence of Orthodoxy. The reuni-
fication of all the former lands of the
late Rurik dynasty, those Russian territories which had been a part of the domain of the Grand Duke of Kiev, became the primary concern of the Muscovite policy with the reign of Ivan III.

With Muscovite Russia's decision to
intervene in the civil war in the Ukraine
a new political perspective came to the
view of tsarist statesmen. The reunifica-
tion of all the Ukrainian territories with
Russia would bring the new Russian
borders closer to the Orthodox population of the Balkans, the former territories of the Byzantine Empire. The possibility of new contacts with the Orthodox world of the Near East kindled
hope for the liberation of the ancient
Imperial city of Constantinople from
Moslem rule. This hope was expressed
by Tsar Alexis to Greek merchants re-
siding in Moscow in 1656, and it was
reflected in verses written by Simon
Polotsky, the ideologist of the Muscovite government and the court poet to
Tsar Alexis, on the occasion of the birth
of Peter I:

The month of May brings us new hopes
Since the Tsarevich Peter was born.
Yesterday Constantinople was taken by
    Turks,
Yet its liberation appears imminent.
The deliverer is here and intends to re-
    venge;
The Imperial city will soon be freed.
O enjoy this news, City of Constantinople,
And thou, Holy Sophia, hast bright pros-
    pects—

An Orthodox prince has been born,
The Great Duke Peter of Muscovy.

During these years the famous "Greek
Project," which took final shape under
Catherine II, was initiated. The Russian Tsar was envisioned as the protector of the entire Orthodox world. It
should be pointed out, however, that the
initiative for this grandiose Near Eastern project belonged not to the Muscovites but to the Greeks. As early as 1590
the Ecumenical Patriarch Jeremiah had
expressed the hope that "all pious lands
will be united under the Tsar, and you
[the Tsar] will be the only true Christian monarch of the universe." The continuous pilgrimage of Near Eastern Patriarchs to Muscovy and their acceptance of the Tsar's protection and political guidance only strengthened the conviction of Nikon and Tsar Alexis that
the time had come for Russia to play a
decisive role in the Orthodox world, and
thus the reforms of Patriarch Nikon coincided with the activization of Muscovite policies in southern Russia.

The reunion of the Ukraine and
White Russia with Muscovy and the
plans for the eventual unification of all
Orthodox peoples under the aegis of the
Russian Tsar required the unification
of Orthodox practices and the adaptation by the Russian Church of the ritual
and the customs common to Greek-
Orthodox tradition, which had been introduced in the Ukraine in the mid-
seventeenth century. The innovations of
Patriarch Nikon in 1653, which were
actually an introduction of the Greek
ecclesiastical pattern in Russia, almost
coincided with the Ukrainian Cossack
Assembly in Pereyaslav, which decided
to accept the suzerainty of the Russian
Tsar. Once the decision to readjust
Russian Orthodoxy to the Greek pattern
was taken, the Muscovite statesmen, on
the advice of the Greeks, proceeded to
disavow the essence of "ancient Russian
tradition," the exclusiveness of Musco-

vy's mission as guardian of the "true Christian faith" and bearer of the idea of a Christian state, as well as local Great Russian nationalism.

In these fateful years of the 1650's and 1660's Moscow relinquished its traditional ideology and ceased to be a purely Great Russian state, in order to become an All-Russian Empire. The Tsar and his advisers repudiated the policy of Muscovite cultural and religious isolation, the 200-year-old tradition of Russia's exclusive historical mission, and the messianic theory of the Third Rome. For the sake of imperial expansion as well as intellectual and technical cooperation with the outside world, the Russian government decided to abandon its old myths and beliefs and with them the entire pattern of the indigenous Muscovite civilization. The Grand Duke and Sovereign of Muscovy became Tsar of Great, Little and White Russia, a title which clearly indicates a transition toward imperial goals. Half a century later Peter I was officially crowned as Emperor.

The change from the old Muscovite to the new "All-Russian" cultural patterns occurred with astonishing rapidity—a sign, perhaps, that the old traditions no longer corresponded to the needs of an expanding, new, powerful state. Almost overnight monks from Kiev and Polotsk replaced the former Muscovite cultural leaders. The old Muscovite missal was re-edited by Kievan monks, and the Polish-educated White Russian monk, Simon Polotsky, became the recognized state ideologist and educator of the Tsar's children. Kievan choirboys replaced the Muscovite singers in the Tsar's and the Patriarch's churches, and the Tsar organized a Western-style theatre in his formerly pious palace. Soon Ukrainian bishops invaded Moscow, introducing their Catholic and Protestant "heretical" teachings and replacing the Great Russian hierarchs;

even the Muscovite literary and Church language underwent the influence of the Kievan dialect. Tsar Alexis' son, Peter the Great, less than half a century after the beginning of the reform, would follow his father's policies closely, order the beards and long coats of the boyars to be cut, conquer the Baltic, and strengthen the army. The odor of tobacco would replace that of incense in the Tsar's palace, and the nobility would soon not only become secularized but would completely forget their bearded and pious ancestors.

However, neither the decisions of the seventeenth-century Councils nor the ensuant persecution by the state broke the supporters of the Old Faith, and their newly-found leaders. Among the opponents to the state's new policies were not only mere obscurantists and enemies of enlightenment, but also the majority of traditional Muscovites, the main part of its "intelligentsia," and its recent spiritual elite. While the court, officers, and some of the landed gentry supported the reforms, a part of the aristocracy also opposed the new order. Great Russian intellectual opposition to Westernization and their refusal to bow to the new "general line" was so unanimous that for three-quarters of a century, from 1660 to 1735, almost no Great Russian names appear on a list of the writers, educators, and theologians of the official "governmental" cultural school. This is a phenomenon which has been overlooked by historians, but nevertheless it remains undeniable that among the cultural leaders of Imperial Russia in the late seventeenth and early eighteenth centuries there were very few Great Russians.

Until 1702, the year of the death of Adrian, the last Patriarch, the Church still remained in the hands of the Muscovites. With the exception, however, of Sylvester Medvedev and the monk Eutymios, there were no outstanding personalities in its ranks, and even these two men did not play roles of any importance in the further evolution of Church and state. From the beginning of the eighteenth century, the hierarchy of the young Empire's church leadership consisted primarily of Ukrainians. The state did not accept Great Russians into the higher administration of the Church, suspecting them of sympathy with the Old Believers, while the Old Believers themselves avoided joining the "Nikonian," established Church clergy. In 1722 there were five Ukrainians and four Great Russians in the Holy Synod; by 1725 there were two Great Russians and five Ukrainians; and by 1751, nine Ukrainian bishops and one Great Russian priest. The same predominance of Little Russians could be observed in the seminaries, in the ranks of provincial bishops, and among the court clergy. The former Muscovite elite was no longer represented even in the Church hierarchy.

A similar situation existed in the schools and in literature. Textbooks of Russian literature mention no Great Russian names between the death of Alexis and the reign of Anna, and until the time of Sumarokov in the 1750's only two Great Russian names of importance stand out—Lomonosov and Tretiakovsky. Even Pososhkov and Tatishchev remained unknown to their contemporaries, their works being published only many years after their deaths.

Of those names well known in Russian literature of the early imperial period, such as Simon Polotsky, Feofan Prokopovich (the main ideologist under Peter the Great), Stefan Yavorsky, Dimitri Tuptallo (bishop of Rostov), Kantemir, Mons, and Puass—all were of Little or White Russian, Moldavian, or German origin. Long before them the Kievan monks Epiphany Slavenetsky, Damaskin Ptitsky, and Arseny Satanovsky had begun to introduce stylistic and linguistic novelties in Muscovite writings.

It is not surprising that the privileged position of west Russians (Ukrainians and White Russians) and foreigners in fields of cultural endeavor and the church administration irritated the Muscovites. Their exclusion from the cultural and spiritual leadership of the land during the early decades of Westernization—which had already begun under Tsar Alexis—led to antagonism between the old and new citizens of the Empire and strengthened the Muscovites' hostility toward Westernization. It was not fear of novelty but rather offense at the defamation of ancient traditions and repudiation of the Old Russian ideology which brought about opposition to cultural reform and to the new policies of the Empire.

Imperial Russian policy toward the populations of the newly incorporated territories was crowned by a long-lasting success. Little Russia, today's Ukraine, found a field of endeavor for its intelligentsia. Career opportunities greatly facilitated the ideological integration of the Empire's new subjects, for the state rejected Great Russian nationalism for the sake of the imperial idea. Feofan Prokopovich, the closest collaborator of Peter the Great in the field of cultural reform, and a Ukrainian by birth and education, wrote, "In our fatherland we can now observe differences in clothes, houses and names, but there is no discrimination before the law; all are equal." It was Prokopovich who, in his sermons, created and popularized· the word *"Rossianin"* ("imperial Russian"), and there is little doubt that his grief at the death of Peter the Great was genuine, for Peter had created a genuinely multi-national empire. Many "imperial Russians" from Kiev or Poltava were attracted by the growth of this Empire, and even the tumultuous Cossack leaders forgot their dreams of independence and served the Tsars faithfully, particularly upon receiving privileges of nobility and the right to introduce serfdom on their estates. For two hundred years—from Mazepa to Petliura—the Ukraine remained the most tranquil part of the Empire. The agrarian disturbances there in the nineteenth and twentieth centuries were directed against local landlords, not against the integrity of the nation.

The political and intellectual integration of the leading strata of other recently acquired territories proceeded with the same rapidity. The Baltic barons rushed with the greatest joy to Petersburg, and for a period in the 1730's even dominated the Russian court and Russian policies. Later, Georgians, Armenians, Poles, and Tartars also appeared at court and in the higher administration posts. The names of Razumovsky, Bezborodko, Rodzianko, Skoropadsky, Loris-Melikov, and Kutaisov, Czartoryski and Wielopolski, Tsitsianov and Bagration, Khan Nakhichevansky, and Mahmendarov all point up to the success of the imperial idea during the first two centuries of the Empire's existence. Later, in the Duma period, the Russian and non-Russian intelligentsias collaborated in a most friendly way.

Thus, while the Empire was expanding and integrating its new citizens, a part of the Great Russian, former Muscovite, population remained in opposition to the cultural and political activities of the state and became increasingly isolated from it. The traditionalists refused to cooperate with the Empire, and the state, for its part, eliminated them from the political and cultural mainstream of the nation's life. For two centuries these nonconformist communities lived apart from the Westernized body of the nation. At best their churches were merely tolerated, for they were not officially recognized by the tsarist government until 1906, and their preachers

were arrested or exiled. Persecuted for their religious nonconformity, these traditionalists, faithful to their beliefs and traditions of their Great Russian ancestors, lived in a state of internal emigration and created their own cultural world in which life was neither Westernized nor secularized but patterned after the old Muscovite ways. In their independent communities the Old Believers preserved the ancient customs, ideology, and family structure. Their preachers exalted the virtues of the purest Orthodoxy, their writers defended the principles of their faith, cautioning them against the dangers of secular and cosmopolitan culture. Many were executed during the first century of the schism; thousands died in prison or in exile, and tens of thousands preferred to immolate themselves in the fires of the Self-Burners rather than submit to the schismatic state. The publication of their books was prohibited by the tsarist authorities, who sought to preserve Westernized society and culture from the poison of old Muscovite thought and traditionalist literature. It seems incredible now that the most brilliant writer of Muscovite origin, the Archpriest Avvakum, an unexcelled master of the Russian colloquial tongue and creator of an artistic Russian prose more than a century before Karamzin, remained totally unknown to Westernized Russians until the 1850's. The *Encyclopedia of Brokhaus and Efron*, a standard prerevolutionary Russian work, ignores Avvakum as a writer and devotes fewer lines to him than to a forgotten Algerian rebel, Abd-el Kader.

Avvakum was not the only outstanding writer among the Old Believers. Epiphany, Deacon Theodore, Avraamy, the Denisov brothers, Ivan Filipov, and many others were the representatives of Great Russian literature during the time of cultural upheaval from 1660 to 1735, while successive generations of Old Be-

lievers in the late eighteenth and nineteenth centuries produced others. Their
works, however, were not better known
to the Westernized landlord, enlightened
courtier and early intellectuals than are
the works of such present-day émigré
Russian writers as Nabokov, Berdiaev,
or Bulgakov known to Soviet readers.

Despite persecution, however, the Old
Belief spread. Thousands, at times tens
of thousands, of Great Russians were
converted to the Old Faith by its mis-
sionaries. N. Melinikov, a tsarist official
responsible for carrying out the government's policies toward the Old Believers
and himself a specialist in the history of
the schism, considered that in the
1860's over one-quarter of the Great
Russian people belonged to the Old
Faith—about one-sixth of the total Orthodox population of Russia. Other in-
vestigators in the nineteenth and early
twentieth centuries believed that as
much as one-third of the Great Russian
population still adhered to the old rites
and thought. Melnikov, in a report to
the Minister of the Interior in 1857,
bluntly stated that if the persecution
were to cease and the Old Faith were to
be officially recognized, the entire Great
Russian population would probably revert to the Old Belief.

As is frequently true of religious
minorities, the Old Believers demonstrated their spiritual and social vitality.
Most researchers investigating the history and evolution of the schism have
agreed that the Old Believers were
stronger economically than the rest of
the non-Westernized population and that
literacy among them was greater than
among supporters of the established
church. The Old Believers' discussions
of theological and ritualistic problems
of dogma served them as a kind of mental discipline, while persecution hardened their character, enabling them to
persist in the preservation of their national traits and traditions. Toward the

end of his career Melnikov wrote, surprisingly, that in his opinion the spiritual revival of Russia would be possible
only on the basis of the Old Believers'
mode of life and way of thinking. He
added, however, that this evolution
would occur only after the schismatics
joined the mother church and ceased to
be schismatics.

Propagation of the Old Faith was
especially successful in the borderlands
of the Empire, where the state's control
had always been looser than in the central region. That part of northern Russia between the Volga and the White
Sea—where local self-government and
free parochial organization were preserved till the beginning of the eighteenth century—was the first stronghold
of the Old Believers. In the forests were
hundreds of Old Believer hermitages
and monasteries, from which the fanat-
ic and tenacious preachers carried their
teachings to all parts of Russia. Siberia,
parts of the Don, and the lands of the
Ural and Terek Cossacks—regions in-
habited by independent and energetic
people who had escaped serfdom and the
state's strict regulation—became predominantly non-conformist quite early.
In the latter half of the eighteenth century, when Catherine II reduced persecution of the Old Believers, the latter began to move from the country and forests to the cities, where they became
tradesmen and industrialists. In the late
eighteenth and early nineteenth centuries the Rogozhsky and Preobrazhen-
sky communities of dissenters in Moscow controlled the largest concentrations
of capital in Russia, and such Old Believer bourgeois families as Morozov,
Riabushinsky, Guchkov, Soldatenkov,
Prokhorov, Kokorev and others played
leading roles in the economic evolution
of nineteenth-century Russia. In the
1830's and 1840's, alarmed at the rapid
extension of Old Believer teachings and
growth of their economic power, the

government renewed its persecution. By 1853, on the eve of the Crimean war, all Old Believer centers and monasteries were closed. The priests were exiled; their books and ancient, often priceless, ikons were deposited in government warehouses or burned. While Catholics, Protestants, Moslems, and Jews in the Russian Empire were accepted as legal religious bodies by the state, the Old Believers—the representatives of Muscovy —were denied recognition as an organized religious community. At the end of the nineteenth century, for instance, the Moslems in Russia, whose number was probably close to that of the Old Believers, had 25,000 parochial and private schools, while the Old Believers, the most Russian of Russians, officially had none. They remained without bishops until the end of the 1840's, and when, with the help of a retired Greek metropolitan, they succeeded in organizing their hierarchy, the administration refused to legalize its existence.

After the death of Nicholas I persecution diminished under the liberal government of Alexander II. A decree of 1863 granted the Old Believers some civil and economic privileges, and in 1874 another decree permitted them to register their marriages with the police. Finally, in 1883, the Old Believers were granted most civil rights, including the right to obtain identification papers and to change professions on the same bases as members of other denominations. Still, they were strongly limited in admission to government service, the army, and educational institutions. During the Russo-Japanese war the Old Believer archbishop of Nizhni-Novgorod was drafted as a private and sent to the front, while the clergy of all other confessions was exempt from compulsory military service. In 1905, of the 174 Old Believer communities in the region of Nizhni-Novgorod, only twelve were registered and officially recognized by the government. The final granting of all civil rights, which put the Old Believers on an equal footing with other confessions, came with the act of religious tolerance of April 17, 1906. For the next eleven years Russian Old Believers would congregate freely, open schools, print their books, and organize congresses. It was a shortlived period of revival. In 1917 came a new era of trial.

These were the conditions in which the most conservative and traditional part of the Great Russian population lived and developed. Economically they were probably the most prosperous segment of the Great Russian people, and probably the staunchest morally and psychologically, with strong family ties, well-organized communities, and a spirit of active mutual aid. Yet persecution prevented these substantial and conservative citizens from sympathizing with the tsarist government and its policies. Forced isolation, restrictions, offences against their beliefs and the periodic curtailment of their economic activity under threat of confiscation resulted in the alienation of this traditionalist group from the politics of the Empire, and helped cause the split of Russian conservative forces into two irreconcilable sectors. In one group were the Westernized pro-government bureaucracy and nobility, which throughout the last two reigns were strong neither culturally nor economically. After the emancipation of the serfs in 1861 the nobility rapidly lost its wealth, and with it its influence, while the steadily growing and ambitious intelligentsia gradually dislodged it from the role of cultural leadership of the Empire. In the other sector were the traditionalist peasants, tradesmen, and industrialists who underwent Westernization to a much lesser degree than the upper classes. Among these, the Old Believers constituted the most cohesive and dynamic element. But in view of tsarist

policies toward them, they could hardly
be supporters of anything but a more
tolerant and liberal policy on the part of
the government. In many respects their
attitude was similar to the oppositional
attitude of the Catholic minority in the
German Reich during Bismark's rule, in
the era of *Kulturkampf*. After many
years of opposition, the German Catholics also slipped to the left, and their
party, "the Center," became a solid pil-
lar of the Weimar Republic. Likewise,
the French Huguenots, strongly traditional socially and economically, after
two centuries of persecution supported
liberal political parties.

Thus, the Old Believers' political op-
positionalism, rooted in the North Russian democratic tradition and intensi-
fied by two centuries of persecution,
conflicted with the political conservatism
of the government and nobility. In the
1840's one of the pillars of the Orthodox
Church, the brilliant Metropolitan
Philaret of Moscow, proclaimed that in
spite of the Old Believers' religious tra-
ditionalism, their democratic and social
nature was incompatible with the ideological basis upon which the Russian
imperial system was founded. A quarter
of a century later K. Pobedonostsev, the
notorious adviser to Emperor Alexander
II and supervisor of ecclesiastic affairs,
maintained that the schismatics were
more dangerous than the revolutionaries.
In the early twentieth century there
were, at the head of the liberal bourgeoisie, such leading Muscovite bankers
and industrialists as Riabushinsky,
Konovalov, Morozov, and Guchkov—all
of whom were of Old Believer descent.

In the local government, in the Zem-
stvos and municipalities, in the Duma,
and in political congresses, the traditionalist groups of northern, central and
eastern Russia usually sided with the
liberals rather than with the rightists,
and at times even with the leftists. In the
first and second Dumas many Old Be-

liever deputies—peasants and workers
from the Volga, northern Russia, the
Urals or Siberia, joined the Labor
Group, while the traditionalist peasantry
was at times Socialist Revolutionary.
The rich Old Believer bourgeoisie was
usually in the "October" group or
among the Cadets, and they embraced
the reforms and constitution of 1905.
For them the parliament was perpetuat-
ing the tradition of the Zemskii Sobor,
the old Muscovite land assembly. On the
eve of the revolution the ancient democratic tradition of the old republics of
Novgorod, Pskov, and Viatka remained
dear to many of them. A few Old Believer millionaires even gave financial
support to the radical revolutionary
movement.

For many years the last emperor,
Nicholas II, believed that the bulk of the
non-Westernized Russian people, the
Great Russian peasantry and merchants,
were supporters of the throne and were
opposed to the radical Westernized intelligentsia. The centuries-long persecution of the Old Faith, however, could
hardly have developed strong sympa-
thies for the régime among these born
traditionalists. The seventeenth-century
schism, religious conflicts, and subsequent Westernization split the possible
supporters of the monarchy into Westernized conservatives and traditionalist
opposition. This split was never overcome, and proved fatal for the monarchy.

Hence, in the decisive years of struggle between the two Westernized opponents—the revolutionary radicals and
the monarchy—the traditionalists were
not on the side of the throne. Whereas
in the seventeenth century the Russian
peasantry and bourgeoisie had sought
to preserve the Muscovite tsardom, their
twentieth-century successors were cool
toward the fate of imperial Petersburg,
and remained a silent and impassive
witness to the Russian drama. The West-

ernized Empire fell without finding support among the most traditional section of the Great Russian people, and the Romanov dynasty was denied even its Vendée.*

* Nowhere in Russia, neither in the Cossack regions of the Don, Kuban, Terek, and the Urals, nor in Siberia and the Maritime provinces, where large groups of the local population participated in the anti-Communist struggle, was the movement monarchist. The Russian counter-revolution, or, better to say, the anti-Communist movement, never became a Russian Vendée or Bretagne.

13

THE LAW CODE OF 1649

EXCERPTS

The code (*Ulozhenie*) of which excerpts appear below was the most comprehensive codification of law undertaken in Russia up to that date. The next codification did not take place until the 1830's. The code consists of 967 articles divided into twenty-five chapters; only the table of contents and chapter xi are presented here. The language of the Russian original has been simplified; footnotes contain further information about the text.

The first six chapters of the Law Code of 1649 are now available in English in Basil Dmytryshyn's *Medieval Russia* (paperback). The Code and the Zemskii Sobor which passed it are discussed in Vasily Kliuchevsky's *History of Russia*, Vol. III. Jerome Blum's *Lord and Peasant in Russia* (paperback) devotes much attention to the peasantry in the seventeenth century. See also George Vernadsky's "Serfdom in Russia," in *Relazioni del X Congresso Internazionale di Scienze Storiche*, III, 248–72. The oppression codified by the law led to the Razin rebellion of 1667–71. For an account of that peasant rising see Sergei Konovalov's "Ludwig Fabritius' Account of the Razin Rebellion," *Oxford Slavonic Papers*, VI, 72–94.

For an anthology of Muscovite law prior to the seventeenth century see *Muscovite Judicial Texts*, 1488–1556, edited by Horace Dewey. The same author has also published a number of articles: "The 1497 Sudebnik," *American Slavic and East European Review*, XV, 325–38; "The White Lake Charter," *Speculum*, XXXII, 74–83; "Judges and Evidence in Muscovite Law," *Slavonic and East European Review*, XXXVI, 189–94; "The 1550 Sudebnik," *Jahrbücher für Geschichte Osteuropas*, X, 161–80; "Trial by Combat in Muscovite Russia," *Oxford Slavonic Papers*, IX, 21–31. See also Oswald Backus', "Muscovite Legal Thought," in Alfred Levin and Alan Ferguson (eds.), *Essays in Russian History*.

THE *ULOZHENIE* OF 1649

Translated and edited by Richard Hellie from the 1737 edition of the *Ulozhenie* (Moscow: Academy of Sciences Press).

154

CHAPTER XI. LEGAL PROCEDURE CONCERNING THE PEASANTS·

1. All peasants[1] who have fled from lands belonging to the Tsar[2] and are now living on lands belonging to church officials,[3] *votchinniki*,[4] and *pomeschiki*[5]

[1] "Peasants" in the context of this chapter include both *krestyane* (peasants who have land and farm it) and *bobyli* (peasants who do not have their own land and who work others' land for hire or engage in non-agricultural pursuits such as trade).

[2] "Lands belonging to the Tsar" include villages which belong to the Tsar as well as agricultural lands belonging to him. The income and produce from these two sources were used to maintain the court and certain governmental functions.

[3] "Church officials" include the patriarch, the metropolitans, the archbishops, the bishops, and the monasteries. Note that they are nowhere specifically permitted to recover their fugitive peasants.

[4] The *votchinniki* were hereditary landowners. The original *votchinniki* dated from the later Kievan and Mongol periods, when each large landowner owed little or no allegiance, duty, or service to anyone. During the process of the consolidation of the Muscovite state many *votchiny* were confiscated by the central power so that by the end of the reign of Ivan IV it appeared as though this form of landownership was destined to disappear in favor of the *pomest'e*. The seventeenth century, however, witnessed the revival and eventual triumph of the *votchina* over the *pomest'e*.

[5] The *pomeshchiki* were service landholders who held their landholdings (*pomest'ya*) only while rendering service to the tsar. When the *pomeshchik* died or otherwise discontinued rendering service, his land (minus a small portion to maintain his widow and minor children) was supposed to revert to the state for reapportionment to others rendering service. This was the basis of the service-class state, whose origins can be traced to the second half of the fifteenth century. Gradually, however, in the seventeenth century the *pomest'ya* became hereditary *votchiny*, and consequently no longer functioned as initially intended: the peasants served the landholder who in turn was to serve the state.

In the original text the following ranks are enumerated; in Chapter XVI each rank was entitled to a specific minimum amount of land in Moscow province, the income from which was intended to maintain the individual in service:

a) Boyare: nobles of the highest rank. They commanded the army and presided over the government chancelleries (the *prikazy*), as well as advised the tsar in the Boyar Council. There were more than 30 boyars in 1649, but only 15 signed the *Ulozhenie* because of a split in their ranks. Each *boyarin* was entitled to at least 200 *chetverti* of land in Moscow province; they usually had 1,000 *chetverti* and more. (A *chetvert'* was about one and one-third acres.)

b) Okolnichie: nobles of the second highest service rank. They worked in the government chancelleries, served as military governors and ambassadors, were members of the tsar's council. They prepared the tsar's journeys and presented foreign ambassadors to the tsar. There were twenty *okolnichie* in the Boyar Council in 1668. They were entitled to 150 *chetverti* of land in the *Ulozhenie*, but usually had more.

c) Dumnye Lyudi: other people, in addition to the *boyare* and *okolnichie*, who advised the tsar in the Boyar Duma and held important positions in the leading chancelleries. They included the *dumnye d'yaki*, non-noble professional government servants in the seventeenth century usually in charge of the most important chancelleries (Foreign Affairs, Military, and Service Land), and the *dumnye dvoryane*, members of the third service rank. During the seventeenth century 42 families held the latter title; two were old families, the rest of uncertain origin. Each was entitled to a minimum of 150 *chetverti* of land. The men who sat in the Boyar Council were the magnates of Muscovy and each had more than an average of 500 peasant households on their estates.

d) Komnatnye Lyudi: persons who served the tsar in his chamber.

e) Stol'niki: members of the fourth court rank. As early as the thirteenth century they waited on the great prince at table (*stol*). Members of the best families served as *stol'niki*. During Aleksei's reign their number reached 500. Some were in military service, others worked in the government chancelleries. In 1664, 114 *stol'niki* served at a dinner given for the English ambassador Charles Howard. In 1638 each *stol'nik* had an

average of 78 peasant households on his lands. According to the *Ulozhenie* each was entitled to 100 *chetverti* of land in Moscow province, in addition to the land he might have elsewhere.

f) Stryapchie: members of the fifth court rank. In the seventeenth century they were found mainly in supply positions and working in the government chancelleries. They were supposed to protect the court peasants from harm, while others waited on the tsar, carried his sword, etc. Still others served the *boyare* and *okolnichie* and some held secondary positions in embassies and on military campaigns. There were 800–900 of them in the mid-seventeenth century. In 1638 the average *stryapchii* "owned" twenty-four households. He also was entitled to 100 *chetverti* of land in Moscow province.

g) Moscow dvoryane: men who often had been promoted to service in Moscow from the provinces and thus became the bottom stratum of the ruling elite of Russia. There were about 1,000 of them in the mid-seventeenth century and they served as ambassadors, military governors, court officials, army commanders, and worked in the government chancelleries. They had an average of 29 peasant households each and were entitled to a minimum of 100 *chetverti* of land in Moscow province.

h) D'yaki: early in Russian history they were personal servants of the prince, often bondmen; they kept the treasury and handled correspondence. Their importance grew as government chancelleries developed in the sixteenth century. In the seventeenth century they usually administered the chancelleries nominally headed by nobles. They often directed local provincial administration and handled all the finances. By the end of the seventeenth century there were about 100 *d'yaki*. Each *d'yak* was entitled to a minimum of 100 *chetverti* of land.

i) Zhil'tsy: Members of a transitional rank between the Moscow and provincial *dvoryane*, usually members of the lesser families of the former and the upper families of the latter. They served as the tsar's bodyguard in his regiment and ran official errands. There were about 2,000 *zhil'tsy* in the seventeenth century and each had an average of 14 peasant households on his lands in 1638. Each was entitled to at least 50 *chetverti* of land.

j) Provincial dvoryane: members of the middle service class who served largely as unit commanders over the *deti boyarskie* in the cavalry. They also played some role in local are to be returned to the Tsar's lands according to the land cadastres of 1627–31[6] regardless of the *urochnye leta*.[7] These peasants are to be returned with their wives, children, and all movable property.

2. The same applies to peasants who have fled from *votchinniki* and *pomeshchiki* to other *votchinniki* and *pomeshchiki*, or to the towns, to the army, or to lands belonging to the Tsar.[8]

3. Fugitive peasants must be returned with their wives, children, and movable property, plus their standing grain and threshed grain.[9] But the possessions which the fugitive peasants owned in the years prior to this code are not to be claimed. If a fugitive peasant gave his daughter, sister, or niece in marriage to a local peasant, do not break up the marriage. Leave the girl with the local peasant. It was not a crime in the

past to receive fugitive peasants—there was only a time limit for recovering them. Therefore the lord of the local peasant should not be deprived of his labor, especially as lands have changed hands frequently so that the present lord may not have been the person who received the fugitives anyway.

4. All *votchinniki, pomeshchiki,* and officials managing the Tsar's lands must have proper documents identifying their peasants in case of dispute. Such documents must be written by public scribes.[10] If there are no public scribes, then they must be written by rural or church clerks. Illiterate landholders must have their documents signed by impartial, trustworthy persons.

5. *Votchinniki* and *pomeshchiki* who did not claim peasants who fled prior to 1627 may not do so now because these landholders did not petition the Tsar

administration, which was, however, under centralized control and direction from Moscow. Each was entitled to a minimum of 70 *chetverti* of land in Moscow province.

k) Deti boyarskie: the bulk of the middle service class, the cavalry which made up the military force of the Muscovite state from the end of the fifteenth century to the mid-1650's. There were about 35,000 members of the middle service class at the time of the *Ulozhenie,* most of them *deti boyarskie.* The term literally means "boyar children," which may mean either that initially they were the sons of boyars, or, more likely, simply the retainers of boyars. By the mid-sixteenth century, at the latest, the term had neither of these meanings, rather signifying simply landholding members of the cavalry. In the sixteenth century *deti boyarskie* were recruited from all social milieus, including cossacks, peasants, and even slaves. This avenue of social mobility was closed at the beginning of the seventeenth century as the rank became hereditary. They were entitled to from 10 to 100 *chetverti* of land in Moscow province and had only an average of 5.6 peasant households each (of those who had any peasants; many did not) for their support. They, as all other servitors

listed above, were usually paid a specified sum annually.

[6] "The land cadastres of 1627–31" (*pistsovye knigi*)—books which recorded the general census taken after the fire of 1626 in Moscow destroyed most of the earlier records. For peasants not included in this census (peasants tried to avoid being included to escape taxation), other sources of legal evidence are listed which may be substituted to prove that a particular peasant belongs on a particular piece of land.

[7] The *urochnye leta*—the fifteen-year limit on seeking out, finding, and returning fugitive peasants. After the repeal of the time limit there was no way a peasant could legally escape serfdom—attachment to a definite piece of land.

[8] The complex formula of Article 1, which applies to peasants who fled from the tsar's lands, is repeated for peasants who have fled from others' lands.

[9] This action could be taken only after appropriate legal measures had been effected.

[10] The money paid to public scribes for writing and certifying documents was one of the major sources of state revenue. The rates are specified in Chapter XVIII.

about their fugitive peasants for so many years.[11]

6. *Votchinniki* and *pomeshchiki* are not to be held responsible for the taxes of fugitive peasants who were registered on their lands in the census of 1646–47 after they have been returned to their rightful lords. Future taxes will be collected from the lords to whom they are returned on the basis of the documents legalizing the return.[12]

7. A *votchinnik* who buys a *votchina* has a right to all the peasants who were inscribed in the land cadastres of 1627–31. If all such peasants are not on the *votchina* as listed in the purchase documents, the purchaser may take from the seller's other *votchiny* replacement peasants with all their movable property, their standing grain, and their threshed grain.[13]

8. All cases concerning fugitive peasants which were settled either by a royal decree or by amicable agreement prior to this code may not be reopened.

9. All peasants who have fled or flee henceforth from the landholder with whom they were registered in the census books of 1646–47 must be returned with

their brothers, nephews, grandsons, wives, movable property, standing grain, and threshed grain without any time limit. Henceforth no one may receive another's peasants and harbor them for himself.

10. Henceforth a person who harbors another's peasants must pay the rightful lord ten rubles per year for each fugitive to compensate the plaintiff for his lost income and the taxes he paid while the peasant was absent and must surrender the fugitive peasants to him.[14]

11. The census records of 1646–47 may be used in disputes over fugitive peasants in cases where the peasants in question or their fathers were not registered in the land cadastres of 1627–31.

12. If a girl flees after the promulgation of this code and marries another landholder's peasant, then her husband and children will be returned with her to her former landholder. The movable property of her husband, however, will not be returned with them.[15]

13. When a widower marries a fugitive peasant girl, any children he had by a previous marriage will not be

[11] This provision was enacted to prevent the extraordinary congestion of the courts which would result if any lord who ever lost a peasant by flight were permitted to petition for his return.

[12] A census was taken in 1646–47. All peasants found living on a piece of land were inscribed as being subject to taxation there. The peasant did not pay his taxes directly, but through the landholder, who was subsequently responsible for the collection of all taxes due from his landholding. This provision freed the landholder from responsibility for the taxes of those fugitive peasants, registered on his lands by the 1646–47 census, who were returned to their proper lords.

[13] This provision protects the purchaser of a *votchina* from fraud and guarantees him that the number of peasants listed in the purchase documents will be there. The number of peasants was as important as the land itself, for

without the former, the land was worthless. Article 3 of Chapter XV states that if a *votchinnik* permits peasants to move from his *votchina*, a subsequent *votchinnik* could not demand the return of the particular peasants who had been permitted to depart.

[14] If one landholder illegally got the benefits of the work of another landholder's peasant, this provision forced the former to compensate the latter for his loss, as well as for the taxes he had to pay for the peasant registered on his estate—regardless of whether the peasant was present and working or not. From this one can gain some idea of the value of labor in the mid-seventeenth century. Other articles indicate the value of animals.

[15] This is intended to penalize the landholder who receives a fugitive by depriving him of one of his workers. The peasant also loses because he would be pauperized by the loss of his property. Note also that an attempt is made to avoid breaking up marriages.

surrendered with him to the lord of his new wife, but will remain with the lord of his first wife.[16]

14. When a plaintiff finds property with the fugitive girl, a court will decide the disposition of the property.[17]

15. If a widowed peasant remarries in flight, then both she and her husband will be returned to the lord of her first husband, provided her first husband was registered with a landholder.

16. If the peasant widow's first husband was not registered with a landholder, then she must live on the premises belonging to the lord of the peasant she married.

17. If a peasant in flight marries off his daughter, then his son-in-law will be returned to the landholder of his wife. And if that son-in-law has children by a first wife, then the children will not be surrendered to the plaintiff.[18]

18. A peasant woman in flight who marries will be returned with her husband[19] to her former landholder.

19. Peasant women who are permitted to marry another landholder's peasant must be given release documents in which they are precisely described.[20]

20. When peasants arrive in a *votchina* or in a *pomest'e* and say that they are free people and wish to live with the landholder as peasants, the landholder must ascertain the truth of their claim. Within a year such people must be brought to Moscow or another large city for certification.[21]

21. The lord who did not check carefully whether such people were free must pay the plaintiff to whom the peasants rightfully belong ten rubles per year per fugitive to compensate the plaintiff for his lost income and the taxes he paid while the peasant was absent.[22]

22. Peasant children who deny their parents must be tortured.[23]

23. Those people of any rank who give loans to another lord's peasants to

[16] Here the marriage is preserved, but the family is broken up.

[17] The court had to decide whether the property belonged to the girl before she fled (in which case the property would be returned with her to her former lord), or whether the property was acquired after the girl fled (in which case the property would probably remain with the lord who harbored her).

[18] Strict consistency is maintained in these legal relationships, but little thought is taken of the children, who are viewed only as future workers. Compare this with Article 3 governing cases originating prior to 1649.

[19] Four categories of peasants are included in this provision:

a) *Kabal'nyi chelovek*: a contract bondman, usually voluntary, who by law had to be freed upon the death of his lord. This institution had been changed and codified in a law of 1597, which served as the basis of Chapter XX of the *Ulozhenie*.

b) *Starinnyi chelovek*: a hereditary bondman who, unlike the *kabal'nyi*, could be sold, given away, and passed to heirs.

c) *Krest'yanin*, and (*d*) *Bobyl'*—see note 1.

[20] The release document (*otpusknaya gramota*) was mandatory so that the landholder who released a woman to marry could not then demand her return with her husband under Article 12. Also, as mentioned in note 10, the writing of these documents was an important source of government income.

[21] All peasants were supposed to be registered in the *Pomestnyi Prikaz*, the governmental chancellery responsible for supervising the *pomest'e* system of government service lands. The main office was in Moscow, others were in Kazan, Novgorod, and Pskov. A free person most likely was one who either had escaped census registration or else had fled the central regions prior to 1627 and therefore was not listed as a peasant in the *Pomestnyi Prikaz*.

[22] A landholder could not escape the penalty of Article 10 by claiming that the fugitive he harbored was a free person.

[23] According to the stipulation of Article 9, children were supposed to live where their progenitors were registered by the 1646–47 census. This article attempts to inhibit denials by a fugitive of his parents to escape being returned to the fugitive's lawful lord.

entice them to their lands will lose the loans when the peasants are returned to their rightful lords.[24]

24. The brothers, children, and relatives of the peasants of some *pomeshchiki* and *votchinniki* were registered in the census books as living in the houses of their fathers and relatives. After the census they separated and began to live by themselves in their own houses. The census of 1646–47 was taken under oath by *stol'niki* and Moscow *dvoryane;* if they did it incorrectly, they were severely punished and others took it a second time. Therefore the census is to be regarded as just and definitive and after September 1, 1648, no one may complain that lords attempted to conceal households by such doubling up to reduce their taxes.[25]

25. In a suit involving peasants and over fifty rubles of peasant movable property or property to which no value is assigned by the plaintiff, if the defendant does not admit that the peasants are on his estate, the case can be decided by taking an oath. If the defendant loses he must pay four rubles apiece for each peasant listed in the suit and five rubles for the property of

each peasant. If a great deal of property is involved, assess the damages in a trial.[26]

26. If the defendant admits that he has the fugitive peasants but denies that the peasants came to him with any property; and if the plaintiff lists the property in his suit and then wins the case by an oath, award him five rubles for the movable property of each peasant and return the peasants to him.

27. If someone denies during a trial that he has someone's peasant and takes an oath on this, and later the peasant turns up on his estate, return the peasant to the plaintiff with all the movable property listed in the suit. Beat the false oath taker with the knout for three days in the market place as an example to others and then jail him for a year.[27] Henceforth do not believe him in any matter and do not grant him a trial against anyone for anything.

28. The children of peasants who are taken from a defendant and surrendered to a plaintiff by a court order must be surrendered even though they were not inscribed in the land cadastres of 1627–31—provided they are living with their parents and not separately.

29. A defendant who denies in legal

---

[24] One way wealthier landholders recruited their labor force was by granting loans to needy peasants. This provision is one of the expressions of the fact that the *Ulozhenie* was written for the benefit of the middle service class, whose members could not afford to grant loans to the peasants.

[25] As mentioned in note 12, the landholders were responsible for the taxes of the peasants. Taxes rarely were assessed on individual peasants, but rather on a whole commune, either on the amount and quality of land under cultivation or on the number and income of the households in the commune. One way to reduce the latter tax was to combine households while a census was being taken. The government encouraged the submission of denunciations of this illegal practice and sometimes would turn over the concealed peasants to the lord who had "discovered" them. Two

years after the census, however, the government decided that all such cases had been discovered and it was willing therefore to rest on the results as revised.

[26] Muscovite legal practice assumed that no one would lie while under oath. But, if he did, see Article 27. Note that a man is valued at less than the movable property the legislators assumed, on the average, he would own. A recent study indicates, however, that in fact the average fugitive peasant actually took about 30 rubles' worth of his own property with him.

[27] A trend noticeable in the *Ulozhenie* is a harshening of the penalties. In early Russian history a fine was levied for almost all crimes; corporal and capital punishment were common features of Russian justice by the mid-seventeenth century.

proceedings that he has another's peasants and property, but then under oath confesses that he has the peasants on his estate, but continues to deny having the property, must pay for the property as well as return the peasants because he lied about the peasants.[28]

30. *Votchinniki* and *pomeshchiki* may not transfer their *pomest'e* peasants to their *votchiny* and thus lay waste their *pomest'ya*.[29]

31. If peasants are transferred from a *pomest'e* to a *votchina* and subsequently *the pomest'e* is granted to another *pomeshchik*, then the new holder of the *pomest'e* may petition the Tsar for the return of the peasants to his *pomest'e* with their movable property, standing grain, and threshed grain.

32. Peasants may voluntarily hire themselves out to work for people of all ranks, but the latter may not hire them on condition of servitude or bondage. When the hirelings finish their work, they must be discharged without any hindrance.[30]

33. Bondmen and peasants who flee abroad and then return to Russia cannot claim that they are free men, but must be returned to their former *votchinniki* and *pomeshchiki*.[31]

34. When fugitive peasants of different landowners marry abroad, and then return to Russia, the landholders will cast lots for the couple. The winning *pomeshchik* gets the couple and must pay five rubles to the landholder who lost because both of the peasants were in flight abroad.

[28] According to the sense of Articles 3 and 12, a landholder who willingly surrendered fugitive peasants probably could keep the property acquired while the fugitive was with him.

[29] Most of the largest landholders had both *pomest'ya* and *votchiny*. A law of 1556 required owners of *votchiny* and holders of *pomest'ya* to render equal military service. Nevertheless transferring peasants from a *pomest'e* to a *votchina* in the eyes of the law removed them from the state's labor force available for assignment to any servitor-*pomeshchik*. Article 30 is another indication that the peasants were legally bound to the land, not to the person of the landholder.

Bound to the land they were serfs, if to the lord's person, they would have been close to slaves.

[30] Chapter XX of the *Ulozhenie* stipulated that a free person who lived with or worked for someone for a period exceeding three months automatically became the latter's bondman, *kabal'nyi chelovek*. A person might do this voluntarily to escape taxation. The purpose of this article was to ensure that the peasant supporting a lord and paying taxes did not fall into bondage.

[31] A bondman (*kholop*) who returned from foreign captivity to Russia was considered a free man. The peasant serf did not enjoy this privilege.

14

MUSCOVITE–WESTERN
COMMERCIAL RELATIONS

Russians of the fifteenth through the seventeenth centuries had contact with only three or four types of Westerners: closely watched diplomats and travelers, technical specialists hired for very high wages, mercenaries retained for specific wars, and merchants. The last, from England, the Netherlands, former Hansa towns, and elsewhere, hoped to obtain items in transit from the Orient and Russian raw materials: hemp, tar, flax, timbers and other ships stores, hides, skins and furs, tallow and fats, potash, caviar, rhubarb, train-oil, linseed, grain, and metals. In exchange the foreigners brought broadcloth and other textiles, munitions, luxury goods, and precious metals. The foreigners were not content to trade with the Russians at the major points and ports of entry, Narva, Pskov, and Arkhangelsk, but established buying and selling networks inside Russia, employing many smaller Russian merchants.

The Russian merchants felt they could not compete with the foreigners. Therefore they began a petition campaign in 1627 to put an end to the practice going on since the time of Ivan IV of foreigners coming into the Muscovite state via the White Sea, and to a lesser extent the Baltic, which was under the control of Sweden. The merchants submitted additional petitions to the government against foreigners in 1635, 1637, 1639, 1642, 1646, 1648–49 (reproduced below), and 1667.

The tsar's court and the aristocracy liked the luxury goods the foreigners brought, and the high officials (such as those of the Foreign Affairs Chancellery) did not want to part with the bribes the foreigners paid, so the government was reluctant to put an end to the privileged position of the foreign merchants. Nevertheless the great merchants capitalized on the feeling against foreigners prevalent in Russia after the Time of Troubles (1598–1618) and coerced the government into expelling the English in 1649 (on the pretext of the regicide) and the other foreigners by decrees of 1654 and 1667. This caused considerable hardship and suffering among the large numbers of lesser merchants who had acted as agents for the foreigners. The government turned a deaf ear to their petitions.

The best economic history of Russia is Peter Lyashchenko's *History of the National Economy of Russia to the 1917 Revolution*. Arne Ohberg in "Russia and the World Market in the Seventeenth Century," *Scandinavian Economic History Review*, Vol. III (1955), No. 2, discusses the products Russia exported. The English involvement in the Muscovy trade is discussed by T. S. Willan in two books, *The Muscovy Merchants of 1555* and *The Early History of the Russia Company, 1553–1603*. An older account is by Mildred Wretts-Smith, "The English in Russia during the Second Half of the Sixteenth Century," *Transactions of the*

Royal Historical Society, 4th series, Vol. IV (1920). The standard work for many years was by Armand J. Gerson, "The Organization and Early History of the Muscovy Company," in his and others' *Studies in the History of English Commerce in the Tudor Period*. See also Nicholas Casimir, "The English in Muscovy during the Sixteenth Century," *Transactions of the Royal Historical Society*, Vol. VII (1878), which contains a number of interesting documents. The theme is continued in an article by I. I. Liubimenko, "The Struggle of the Dutch with the English for the Russian Market in the Seventeenth Century," *Transactions of the Royal Historical Society*, 4th series, Vol. VII (1924). Her article in Vol. I (1918) of the same publication, "The Correspondence of the First Stuarts with the First Romanovs," is also relevant. Walther Kirchner's *Commercial Relations between Russia and Europe, 1400 to 1800: Collected Essays* presents his work of two decades on the subject. A more specialized study is the one by R. H. Fisher, *The Russian Fur Trade, 1550–1700*.

Much information about both Russia and the foreigners themselves can be found in contemporary travel accounts, some of which were written by merchants. An old but still valuable summary can be found in Iosif Kristianovich Gamel' (Hamel), *Early English Voyages to Northern Russia*. Perhaps the most interesting travel accounts (Giles Fletcher, Jerome Horsey, Anthony Jenkinson, and others) were published by the Hakluyt Society; some of these are currently being republished. English translations of the privilege charters the Russians granted the foreigners are presented in some of the travel accounts.

Petition of the *stol'niki, stryapchie, dvoryane*, and *deti boyarskie*, petitioned merchants on forbidding foreign merchants to trade in Russian towns, with the exception of Arkhangelsk.

Written in a report (*doklad*).[1]

In the current year September 1, 1648 —August 31, 1649 the *stol'niki, stryapchie*, Moscow *dvoryane*, provincial *dvoryane*, and *deti boyarskie*, petitioned the Sovereign Tsar and Great Prince Aleksei Mikhailovich of All Rus'. In their petition was written .[their request] that the Sovereign order foreigners not to trade any wares in Moscow, and that the Sovereign order trading with foreigners [be confined] to Arkhangelsk; that the Sovereign order that foreigners not be allowed to leave Arkhangelsk for Moscow and other towns

because the Moscow *gosti*[2] and merchants in sundry markets and enterprises have perished and been completely ruined by the foreigners. Furthermore the same foreigners, being in the Muscovite state, gather much intelligence and write all kinds of things to their own countries.

The *gosti* and the merchants submitted a [separate] petition on this matter to the Sovereign Tsar and Great Prince Aleksei Mikhailovich of All Rus', and wrote in their petition:

It was only recently that many for-

Translated and edited by Richard Hellie from *Sbornik Kniazia Khilkova* (St. Petersburg, 1879), pp. 238–55.

[1] The report is not dated but must have been compiled before the Zemskii Sobor (assembly of the land) which adjourned in late January 1649.

[2] *Gosti*: members of the top merchant guild. There were 20–30 of them in the seventeenth century. In exchange for major trading privileges in Russia and unhampered travel abroad they performed various financial services for the government.

eigners of various states began to come from Arkhangelsk and through Novgorod and Pskov to Moscow and other towns in the Muscovite state to sell their own overseas wares and to buy Russian goods. These foreigners in the Muscovite state have engaged in many trading operations in Moscow and in various towns, are selling their own goods and buying Russian wares for the same customs duties [as before],[3] and are paying very small customs duties to the state by comparison with the Russian merchants. They have driven away the *gosti* and merchants from their foreign goods and enterprises so that [the Russians] have ceased going to Arkhangelsk with their goods and money because of their interference. [The foreigners] outbid them for goods in Moscow and in the towns and do not let them [the Russians] buy. They sell their own overseas goods in Rus' for high prices. The foreigners have begun to import into Rus' poor quality stretched cloth, not the same as they imported earlier. They also have begun to import various other yard goods which are of poor quality by comparison with earlier years and they keep the price high by comparison with former years because they are living in Moscow without paying taxes. In Arkhangelsk and in Moscow a large amount of royal customs duties are not collected from them because they sell many embroidered goods secretly, without paying the duty. The foreigners, English and a few Dutch, went to Moscow from Arkhangelsk on the basis of charters granting them this privilege because they brought to the former sovereigns of blessed memory various embroidered and high quality textiles, sundry high quality goods, drink, and whole spices. For these they charged only their cost, without profit. Those foreigners died long ago. After them, using the same

privilege charters given them [the now deceased], agents of merchants of other countries have come to Moscow. They sell these same privilege charters among themselves abroad and falsely claim to be of the same family. They sell whatever happens to be purchased from them for the Sovereign's use at the highest possible price. They live in Moscow without paying property taxes. If the price is falling on some of their overseas wares in Moscow, they write about this to their partners and employers so that they will not send these wares to Arkhangelsk. When the prices on these overseas wares rise in Moscow, they order them to buy up these wares abroad to keep the price high. Their partners and employers reply to them about the goods and deliberately send people through Pskov and Novgorod to buy up the wares [already on the market] for which there is a great demand and sell their own for a high price. All we Russian merchants of the Muscovite state have suffered great interference in the markets from these foreigners living in Moscow. Many [other] overseas merchants have ceased going to Arkhangelsk for this reason, and it is impossible for others to begin going because these foreigners travel to Moscow and buy up the goods they need in Rus'. They buy up overseas and in Arkhangelsk secretly and without paying any duty the overseas goods which are needed and for which there is a demand and [a good] price in Moscow, causing a great loss to the royal customs. The merchants have perished completely because of them. Other foreigners come to Arkhangelsk but do not send their agents to the upper Volga towns, and these foreigners also suffer great hindrance;

[3] In 1646 the English had been deprived of the right to trade duty free in the Muscovite state.

they do not want to go to Arkhangelsk in the future because of the interference resulting from the fact that their brothers, the overseas foreigners, are living in Moscow and in other towns without paying taxes. Would the Sovereign grant them, the *gosti* and merchants, that the overseas foreigners should be ordered not to be allowed to come from Arkhangelsk and Pskov with their wares to Moscow and to the other towns, not to be allowed to trade in Rus' and not to buy Russian goods in Moscow and in the towns, except in Arkhangelsk and Pskov? And would the Sovereign order them, the *gosti* and merchants, to trade with the foreigners in Arkhangelsk, as it was earlier, so that the overseas foreigners will not multiply in the Muscovite state . . . ?

A memorandum on foreign trade was sent from the Foreign Affairs Chancellery which states: in 1563/64, during the reign of the Sovereign Tsar and Great Prince of blessed memory Ivan Vasil'evich of All Rus', his royal privilege charter was granted to the English merchant Saven'yan Garat[4] and his colleagues.[5] The Great Sovereign granted them freedom to travel in ships to the Muscovite state via the Dvina Land[6] with sundry wares and they were given

the right to come to Moscow and all the towns of the Muscovite state. They could trade duty free.[7]

In 1567/68 his royal privilege charter was given by the Tsar and Great Prince Ivan Vasil'evich of All Rus' to the English merchant Vilim Gart[8] and his colleagues. In the charter it was written that he, the Great Sovereign, had granted the English merchants the right to come in ships to his state, to Kholmogory,[9] to the Dvina Land, and to all his royal patrimony of the North with sundry wares, to Moscow, and to all the towns. They could trade duty free. The Sovereign also granted the English merchants [a monopoly so] that no merchant from any other state could come on any ship, boat, or vessel to any harbor in Kholmogory, on the Ob' river, in Vargav, on the Pechora, on the Kuloi, on the Mezen', on the Pechenga, to Solovetskii Island, in all the estuaries of the Dvina river, and in the whole Dvina district of the North. If they come from any other countries [besides England], confiscate their goods for the Sovereign.[10]

In 1571/72 a third royal privilege charter was granted by the Tsar and Great Prince Ivan Vasil'evich of All Rus' to the English merchant Savel' Garat[11]

---

[4] William Garrard, d. 1571. A wealthy London merchant, Governor of the Russia Co. for several years before his death.

[5] Actually the first charter granted to Western merchants was presented to Richard Chancellor in 1555.

[6] The basin of the Northern Dvina River.

[7] In the sixteenth century foreigners paid an *ad valorem* duty of 1 per cent upon entering Russia, 3.5–5 per cent when selling an item, plus other minor duties and tolls. These charges were higher than those paid by Russians. The Trade Regulations of 1653 raised the rates to 2 per cent at the point of entry, and 6 per cent upon sale. The New Trade Regulations of 1667 charged 4 per cent on goods which were not weighed, 5 per cent on

those which were; for goods to be sold inside Russia 10 per cent *ad valorem* was charged. The Regulations came shortly after a severe debasement of Russian currency, and foreigners were ordered to pay in hard currency which was unobtainable. This would force them to abstain from trade within Russia.

[8] William Garrard mentioned above; foreigners often had more than one name in Russia.

[9] A major trading city upstream from Arkhangelsk.

[10] This was the high point of English privileges which were reduced when the English government did not respond to Ivan's political overtures.

[11] William Garrard.

and his comrades. They were permitted to come in their ships to the Dvina Land, to Moscow, and to all the towns of the Muscovite state and to trade freely.[12] They could go to Kazan' and Astrakhan with the Sovereign's knowledge. They were to pay half of the [usual] customs duties on their wares.

When Tsar and Great Prince Fedor Ivanovich of All Rus' became sovereign of the Muscovite state he wrote to the English Queen Elizabeth that he as sovereign had granted the English merchants [the right] to trade in his state on the basis of the last charter granted during the reign of his father, the Sovereign Tsar and Great Prince Ivan Vasil'evich of All Rus', in 1571/72, signed by Diak Andrei Shchelkalov.

In 1586/87 at the request of the English Queen Elizabeth a royal privilege charter was granted by Tsar and Great Prince Fedor Ivanovich of All Rus' to the English merchants Sir Uland[13] and Tomas Smit[14] and his colleagues. They could trade in Moscow and in all the towns of the Muscovite state and it was decreed that no customs duties were to be collected from them.

In 1588/89 it was written from the Sovereign Tsar and Great Prince Fedor Ivanovich of All Rus' to Queen Elizabeth in care of her ambassador Elizar Fletcher[15] that he, the Great Sovereign, for her, Queen Elizabeth, had ordered granted, according to her request, a

privilege charter to her merchants. He had ordered added to the charter the new favorable articles about which she had written. He permitted them to travel on the road [through Russia] to trade in all states, to Kazan' and to Astrakhan, to all states beyond the Caspian Sea to Persia, to Bukhara, and to all foreign states.

In 1600/01 the English Queen Elizabeth wrote to Tsar Boris in care of her ambassador Prince Rytsar Lee[16] on the free trade of her English merchant subjects and on permitting [them to travel] through the Muscovite state to Persia, Bukhara, and other eastern states. By royal decree the ambassador was told in answer that the Sovereign, for Queen Elizabeth, granted her merchants permission to come into his dominions and ship harbors, to trade freely in all commodities duty free on the basis of the privilege charter granted to the merchant Fryanchik Chirei.[17] At that time permission [to travel] to other states in the east was repealed.

In the past year 1606/07, the English King James wrote to the Sovereign Tsar and Great Prince Vasilii Ivanovich of All Rus' in care of his messenger Ivan Ul'yanov[18] on the free trade of his subjects, the English merchants. By a decree of Tsar Vasilii Ivanovich of All Rus' it was written to King James that he, the Sovereign, had granted his [James's] merchants free trade without payment of duty and ordered them given

---

[12] This means trading without any regulation of prices or commodities to be exchanged as opposed to trading duty free.

[13] Sir Rowland Heyward, d. 1593. Mayor (1570–71) and M.P. for London (1572–81). Governor of the Russia Co. for several years. He received the charter with Jerome Horsey, whose account of a trip to Russia is available in Sir Edward Bond (ed.), *Russia at the Close of the Sixteenth Century.*

[14] Sir Thomas Smith, Governor of the Russia Co. in 1600 and 1611. He represented King James I as Ambassador to Russia in 1604–5,

and published a travel account entitled *Voyage and Entertainment in Russia.*

[15] Giles Fletcher (1548–1611); English Ambasador to Russia in 1588, author of *Of the Ruse Commonwealth*, recently reprinted in two separate editions by Cornell and Harvard University Presses.

[16] Sir Richard Lee, sent as Ambassador to Boris Godunov in 1600–1601.

[17] Sir Francis Cherry, in Russia from the 1850's to the 1610's.

[18] Sir John Merick.

his royal privilege charter. It was not written in these royal privilege charters how many English merchants were permitted to trade in the Muscovite state.

In the past year 1614/15, the English King James wrote to the Great Sovereign Tsar and Great Prince of blessed memory Mikhail Fedorovich of All Rus' in care of his ambassador Prince Ivan Merik, Knight,[19] on the free trade of his subjects, the English merchants. According to his royal decree his royal privilege charter was given to the English merchant Sir Tomas Smit, 16 men and their retinue. He, the Sovereign, granted them permission to come in ships to the Muscovite state, to the Dvina Land, to all the towns of the Muscovite state, to Moscow, to Novgorod, to Pskov, and to all states with any wares and to trade freely without payment of duty.

In the past year 1627/28 the royal privilege charter of Tsar and Great Prince Mikhail Fedorovich of All Rus' and his royal father, the Great Sovereign the Most Holy Patriarch Filaret Nikitich of Moscow and All Rus' was given to the English merchants, Sir John Merick, Knight, and his retinue, 23 men. According to this royal privilege charter they were permitted to come by ship to the port of Arkhangelsk in the Dvina Land as before; from the port they could travel to all the towns of the Muscovite state, to Velikii Ustyug, Vologda, Yaroslavl', Moscow, Novgorod, Pskov, and to all [foreign] states with sundry wares. They could trade freely without paying any duty. If other English merchants came to the Muscovite state in excess [of the number in the] privilege charter, the same customs duty was to be collected from these people on their wares as was collected from other foreigners.

On the basis of these royal privilege charters English merchants and their aides, arriving in the Muscovite state, have traded in sundry wares without paying duty through 1647/48. In the past year 1647/48, by the royal decree of Tsar and Great Prince Aleksei Mikhailovich of All Rus', it was ordered that full customs duty should be collected from the English merchants and their aides on their transactions, as from other foreigners. It is not spelled out specifically for what services these royal privilege charters were granted to the English merchants, but [the following] is noted in the Foreign Affairs Books: as the English Queen Elizabeth wrote in the past year 1600/01 to Tsar Boris in care of her ambassador Prince Rytsar Lee, on the unregulated trade of the English merchants, in that letter of the Queen it is written that in earlier years the trade at the Port of Arkhangelsk was given solely to her English merchants. Besides the English merchants of no other countries came to that port and did not trade in the Muscovite state because the English had discovered the port only with great losses and for that reason the privilege charter was given to them.

After that, in the past year 1614/15, when the English ambassador Ivan Ulyanov[20] was in audience with the Sovereign Tsar and Great Prince of blessed memory Mikhail Fedorovich and was answered by the boyars, Fedor Ivanovich Sheremetev and his colleagues. In the speeches of the boyars and the foreign affairs officials it was written that the Great Sovereign Tsar and Great Prince of blessed memory Ivan Vasilevich of All Rus' had granted and ordered that the English merchants be given his royal charter, that they could trade duty free in the Muscovite state,

[19] Sir John Merick.

[20] Sir John Merick.

and could travel to Persia. Furthermore, no merchants of other states, besides them, could come to Arkhangelsk because, seeking routes to the East Indies, to the Chinese state, they sailed into the Dvina estuary where Arkhangelsk now is and found the harbor. In addition, it was decreed that the Dutch and the Hamburgers could come and trade in the Muscovite state on the basis of royal privilege charters.

In the past year 1613/14 the royal privilege charter of Tsar and Great Prince Mikhail Fedorovich of All Rus' was given to Mark Markov[21] and his three colleagues of the Netherlands to replace an earlier privilege charter given them during the reign of Tsar Vasilii Ivanovich of All Rus'. In it they were permitted to come to the Muscovite state to the ship harbor in Ust' Kola,[22] to the Dvina, to the town of Arkhangelsk, to Moscow, Novgorod, Pskov, and other towns with sundry wares and to trade freely. It was ordered that half customs duty should be collected from them. Royal privilege charters were given to other Dutch and Hamburg merchants, Karp Demulin[23] and his ten colleagues in various years, from 1613/14 through 1637/38, at the request of the Prince of Holland and the Estates General. [Charters were granted] to others, by their petitions, for their service, because they brought into the Muscovite state embroidered goods and sold them to the royal treasury at cost. They made a profit for the royal treasury,[24] they facilitated with aid and com-

fort the Sovereign's affairs in their own lands. According to these royal privilege charters they were permitted to come to the Muscovite state to the ship dock [in Arkhangelsk], to Moscow, and to the towns with sundry wares and they were to trade freely. The full customs duties are to be collected on their wares. Many of these merchants do not come to Moscow, but [other] Dutch and Hamburgers are trading instead of them, claiming to be their relatives and agents, and they come to Moscow on the basis of the earlier privilege charters. Other Dutch merchants, coming to Moscow, traded on the basis of travel documents, and they do not have royal privilege charters. They pay duties on their wares in full. . . .

In the past year 1630/31 the Danish ambassador Maltens[25] was in Moscow and submitted a petition to the Sovereign and asked the boyars that Danish merchants be allowed to travel freely in the Muscovite state, to Novgorod, Pskov, Arkhangelsk, to Moscow, by overland and water routes with sundry wares and to trade freely as previously. [He also asked] that they be permitted to set up houses in these towns.

By the Sovereign's decree the Danish ambassador was told that his Royal Majesty, for brotherly friendship and love of his sovereign King Khrist'-yanus,[26] had ordered 6 or 10 Danish merchants granted the right to come to Moscow, and had permitted them to buy anything and to put up one house

---

[21] Marcus Marcuszoon de Vogelaar, active in the Russia trade until the 1650's. He and his partner, Koenraad van Klinck, had a monopoly on Russian leather and hemp. The Dutch traded in a number of small companies in contrast to the monopolistic English Russia Co. The combined capital of the Dutch was at least three times larger than that of the English.

[22] On the Kola Peninsula, near present-day Murmansk.

[23] Carl de Moulin, a Dutch merchant trading in Russian grain; also manufactured sailcloth and potash in Russia.

[24] The Tsar made a profit of 30–100 per cent on the resale of foreign goods.

[25] Juel Malthe.

[26] Christian IV, King of Denmark and Norway 1588–1648.

each in Novgorod, Pskov, and Arkhangelsk. In Moscow a house was purchased from David Mikolaev, the agent of the Danish King Khrist'yanus who was sent to buy grain. This same David, by a royal order, was permitted to buy another house lot next to his own house for these Danish merchant citizens.

The Sovereign Tsar and Great Prince Aleksei Mikhailovich of All Rus', having heard these extracts, ordered an interrogation of the elected *dvoryane, deti boyarskie, gosti,* merchants, and townsmen: If, according to their petition, the overseas foreigners should be sent out of Moscow and the other towns of the Muscovite state, and henceforth should not be allowed to come to Moscow and the other towns, and if the Russian people should be ordered to trade with them only in Arkhangelsk, would this not result in enmity for the Muscovite state with foreign states? The foreigners have loaned the Russians money; if they will be unable to collect these debts from the Russians right away, then who will pay these debts to the foreigners? The foreigners own houses in Moscow and the towns; if there are no buyers for the foreigners' houses, who will pay the foreigners for these houses?

Thereupon the elected *dvoryane, deti boyarskie, gosti,* and merchants were interrogated according to this royal order. In the interrogation all the elected people said: According to an eternal treaty and confirming charter it was decreed that only the Swedes could trade [by right] in the Muscovite state.[27] There is no eternal treaty of the Sovereign with any other foreign state besides Sweden on trading enterprises, and there was none heretofore. Privilege and travel charters were given to the English, Dutch, and Hamburgers for trading activities depending on the enterprise, and there are no other documents on this. If the Sovereign would order the overseas foreigners sent out of the Muscovite state and order that henceforth Russians must trade with foreigners in Arkhangelsk, this would cause no enmity between foreign states and the Muscovite state because the foreigners themselves are many merchants of various states; [they] will all equally have to trade with the Russian merchants in Arkhangelsk. Much of what the English told the Sovereign is untrue: when in former years, long ago, the *gosti* and merchants traded with foreigners of various states in Arkhangelsk there were at that time sundry overseas goods in the Muscovite state only half as expensive as now, and the wares the foreigners brought were twice as good as they now are. Concerning the fact that the English were given privilege charters by former sovereigns: the English were given these charters on the basis of a false petition that somehow the English had discovered the Arkhangelsk harbor. These foreigners did not find that harbor by any deliberate action: the English were sailing to Ivangorod[28] and they were carried to that harbor by the weather,[29] and they did not find the harbor by a deliberate search. The English who were given the privilege charters for that [discovery] and could trade duty free in all the towns in the Muscovite state

---

[27] There were two "eternal" treaties allowing the Swedes to trade in Russia: the Tiavzino (on the river Narva) Treaty of 1595, and the Stolbovo Treaty of 1617.

[28] On the right bank of the Narva River, opposite the town of Narva, about ten miles from the Gulf of Finland. Built by Ivan III in 1492, it was lost to the Swedes in 1581–90, and again from 1612 to 1704.

[29] A glance at the map will show that this claim is preposterous.

all died before the destruction of Moscow [in the Time of Troubles]. After the destruction of Moscow, [the English,] wishing to monopolize the trade in the Muscovite state, got a charter from the Foreign Affairs Chancellery—it is not known why—permitting `23 English merchants to trade ˙in Arkhangelsk and in the towns of the Muscovite state. Then 60, 70 and more English merchants began to come to the Muscovite state and began to live in the Muscovite state without paying any taxes, as if in their own land, and took away various markets from the Russians. Buying Russian wares, the foreigners began to take them to their own land duty free. The same Englishmen are selling sundry wares to foreigners of various lands. They weigh these goods in their own houses on their own balance scales.[30] They ship [goods] on Dutch, Brabant, and Hamburg ships secretly, [claiming that they are English bottoms,] thereby stealing the royal customs revenue. Here is [yet another] illegal act committed by the merchants of all foreign states: when the ships come to town, the foreigners do not allow the customs officials to inspect their goods. They transfer [the goods] from [their] ships to flat-bottomed sailboats without the customs workers being present, not telling the senior customs officials about it and not showing [presenting for inspection] the overseas goods. When these goods arrive in Moscow and in the towns, they register their wares with the customs for a tenth of their value and less. They take all these undeclared goods to their houses secretly and steal the sovereign's customs revenue.

Here is yet another crime of the English: they were ordered to bring to the

Muscovite state fine cloth, silks, ·satins, taffetas, as they did in the past; to sell embroidered goods to the sovereign's treasury at their cost, without profit; and not to import with them others' goods [concealed] as their own wares. The English merchants Sir John Merik, Knight, and his colleagues, who were permitted to come to the Muscovite state to trade at the request of King Charles never appeared. They sold the royal privilege, the charter, to other foreign merchants. Those merchants brought into the Muscovite state various poor quality goods and stretched cloth.[31] As a result of this foreign trickery people of various ranks of the entire Muscovite state suffered great losses in purchasing [these goods]. They are selling sundry goods to the royal treasury at a great profit. The same Englishmen have begun to commit another crime: violating the royal privilege charters, they have begun to sell wares which are not their own, [including some] spun with gold, and sundry other goods which are not manufactured in their own country, England. For customs purposes they are calling goods of other foreign lands their own wares and bring them to Moscow duty free. In Yaroslavl' they are buying Russian leather for Brabant merchants in their own name duty free, thereby causing great harm to the royal customs. In 1639/40 the customs chief, *gost'* Grigorei Mikitnikov, discovered in the houses of the foreigners many undeclared goods. For their illegal action they were charged double and more customs duty. In 1644/45 the English merchants presented in the customs house 21½ bolts of cloth from Dutch vessels. They said that these were their own English cloths, but an investigation determined that the cloth belonged to

[30] Rather than weighing them in markets on public scales where a fee was charged.

[31] Samuel Collins in his book, *The Present*

State of Russia (1671) claimed that the Dutch supplied Russians with cheap cloth, thus driving out the more expensive English cloth.

Dutchmen, and was not theirs. In 1645/ 46 the customs head Matvei Vasil'ev found on these same foreigners many undeclared wares above those registered. Thus their guilt became clear; they are calling others' goods their own; to escape the duties they are not declaring others' goods in the customs house. Because of their foreign trickery the various merchants of the Muscovite state have perished completely, they have been driven away from their old markets and their age old eternal occupations and become impoverished and burdened with great debts because of a lack of business.

These men of Hamburg, Brabant, and Holland, when a fair began to be held in Arkhangelsk, did not go to Moscow and the other towns of the Muscovite state until the destruction of Moscow because there was an explicit decree in Kholmogory before and even after the destruction of Moscow ordering foreigners of these lands not to be allowed into the Muscovite state with any wares. But the merchants of Hamburg, Brabant, and Holland, on their own volition, in spite of the royal decree, have been coming into the Muscovite state every year with their wares, showing the royal privilege charters they have in the towns, even though these charters were given them by the Foreign Affairs Chancellery on the basis of their false petition. Other foreigners travel about even without royal charters. They have built magnificent buildings for themselves and are selling sundry wares from their own houses separately [not in the markets]; they also sell in the markets without a royal decree. These same foreigners are buying up in Moscow and in the towns sundry Russian goods. In Arkhangelsk they register these goods for shipment overseas, load them on ships, and then trade these

goods among themselves on their ships in port during the fair without paying duty. They also get wares from these overseas foreigners without paying duty and register these goods for transit to Moscow as if these goods had come to them from overseas. As a result of their trickery the royal customs revenue suffers harm and great loss. These same foreigners, living in Moscow and in the towns, go through Novgorod and Pskov to their own lands many times each year with intelligence about what is happening in the Muscovite state and they buy goods on this basis. Whatever goods are selling at a high price in Moscow they agree among themselves to produce. When they come to Arkhangelsk to trade, they buy all the best overseas goods themselves for cash and will only barter for the Russian goods: Having agreed among themselves, they are ordered not to buy goods from Russians. They hold the price high on overseas goods so that the Russians can buy nothing from them and will not come to the fair in the future. Because of their conspiracy many Russians have had to cart their goods back from Arkhangelsk, others were left for the following year in Arkhangelsk. Some Russians, weeping because of this foreign cunning, have had to sell their wares below cost. As a result of their [the foreigners'] deliberate plot Russians have ceased going to Arkhangelsk, and from year to year the royal customs revenues have suffered great losses. When the merchants of Brabant, Hamburg, and Holland did not come to Moscow, prices on Russian goods were high, and various foreign goods were cheaper by half in the Muscovite state than they are now.[32] . . .

[32] The authors of this response were clearly not aware of the world-wide inflation of this period.

Concerning the fact that the for-eigners in the Muscovite state have built themselves houses and magnificent dwellings in Moscow and in the towns: if the Tsar will order their houses and all outbuildings assessed [to determine] what the houses are worth, the *gosti* and merchants collectively will pay the value in cash to the foreigners.

Concerning the debts the merchants of the Muscovite state owe the foreign-ers: the Russian merchants will pay these debts to the foreigners. If there are debtors who are unable to settle immediately, the *gosti* and merchants collectively will pay off the remaining debts to the foreigners. If foreigners claim someone owes them money with-out documentary evidence, the Sover-eign, according to his own royal Law Code (the *Ulozhenie*), should order them to be ignored: if foreigners trusted anyone with a loan which was unsecured, they may, however, sue such people for the debt by taking oaths. The houses which the Swedes have built in Nov-gorod and Pskov according to the terms of the eternal peace treaty shall remain as before.

15

THE MONGOL IMPACT ON RUSSIA

By George Vernadsky

The two centuries of "the Mongol yoke" (13th–15th) unquestionably left imprints on many aspects of Russian life. While this is noted by all historians, very few attempts have been made to analyze the question systematically. Professor Vernadsky, an émigré Russian historian who recently retired from Yale University, devoted one volume of his monumental history of Russia to this period. His analysis of the problem is probably the most extensive available in any language, though it should be noted that is has not been accepted by all historians.

A somewhat outdated treatment on a large scale is Jeremiah Curtin, *The Mongols in Russia*. J. F. L. Fennel's *Ivan the Great of Moscow* deals with the Mongols also. There is an article by Lawrence Krader, "Feudalism and the Tartar Polity of the Middle Ages," *Comparative Studies in Society and History*, I, 76–99. Two Soviet historical novels of this period have been translated into English: Sergei Borodin's *Dmitri Donskoi*, and Valentin Yan's *Batu Kahn: A Tale of the Thirteenth Century*. The latter has an introduction by the noted Soviet historian Bakhrushin. For one aspect of a possible Mongol influence on the Russian court, see Michael Cherniavsky, "Khan or Basileus: An Aspect of Russian Medieval Political Theory," *Journal of the History of Ideas*, XX, 459–76. See also *Essays in Tartar History* by Boris Ischboldin, and Karl Wittfogel, *Oriental Despotism* (paperback). There is a debate between several scholars on "Russia and the East" in *The Development of the USSR* (paperback) edited by Donald Treadgold. George Fedotov's *The Russian Religious Mind*, Vol. II, analyzes the impact of the Mongols on Russian Christianity. For traces of the Mongols in Russian literature see Sergei Zenkovsky (ed.), *Medieval Russia's Epics, Chronicles, and Tales* (paperback), as well as Basil Dmytryshyn's *Medieval Russia* (paperback). A report on the Mongols by the Jesuit traveler John of Plano-Carpini is available in *The Mongol Missions*, edited by Christopher Dawson.

A convenient method of gauging the extent of Mongol influence on Russia is to compare the Russian state and society of the pre-Mongol period with those of the post-Mongol era, and in particular to contrast the spirit and institutions of Muscovite Russia with those of Russia of the Kievan age.

It will be recalled that the political life of the Russian federation of the Kievan period was based on freedom.

The three elements of power, the monarchic, aristocratic, and democratic, counterbalanced each other, and the people had a voice in the government throughout the country. Even in Suzdalia, where the monarchic element was the strongest, both the boyars and the city assembly or *veche* had their say in affairs. The typical prince of the Kievan period, even the grand duke of Suzdal, was merely head of the executive branch of the government and not an autocrat. . . .

The authority of the tsar of Moscow, both ideological and actual, was immensely stronger than that of his Suzdalian forerunners. While the 16th century witnessed the growth of monarchical institutions throughout the European continent, the process nowhere went so far and fast as in East Russia. When the envoy of the Holy Roman Empire, the Austrian Baron Sigismund von Heberstein, arrived in Moscow in 1517, he felt that he entered a different world, politically. He noted that Grand Duke Vasili III surpassed all other monarchs in the extent of his power over his subjects. The Englishman Giles Fletcher who visited Moscow some seventy years after Heberstein's first voyage came to the conclusion that "the state and form of their government is plaine tyrannicall, as applying all to the behoofe of the prince, and that after a most open and barbarous manner."

No less deep was the contrast between pre- and post-Mongol periods in the realm of social relations. The very foundations of Muscovite society were different from those of the Kievan age.

The society of Kievan Russia may be called, with certain reservations, a free society. There were slaves but they were considered a separate group, outside the pale of the nation. The situation was similar to that in ancient Greece: slavery coexisted with the freedom of the bulk of society. The government functioned on the basis of the cooperation of free social classes: the boyars, the city people, and the "men" (*liudi*) in the rural districts. True, there was a group of peasants, the so-called *smerdy*, who were under the prince's special jurisdiction, but even they were freemen. There was also a group of the half-free (the so-called *zakupy*) whose position eventually became similar to slavery, but their enslavement was the result of indebtedness, that is, of the unrestricted interplay of economic forces, not of government action.

In the Tsardom of Moscow of the 16th and 17th centuries we find an entirely new concept of society and its relation to the state. All the classes of the nation, from top to bottom, except the slaves were bound to the service of the state. Ironically enough, the slaves were the only group free from governmental regimentation. This Muscovite system of universal service to the state was aptly called *krepostnoy ustav* (statute of bound service) by Cyril Zaitsev. Both the former apanage princes and the boyars now became permanent servitors of the tsar, as did the lower gentry such as the boyar sons and the *dvoriane* (courtiers). Attempts at resistance to the new régime on the part of the princes and the boyars were crushed by Tsar Ivan IV at the time of the *oprichnina* terror. Through the institution of military fiefs (*pomestia*) the tsars controlled both the gentry's landed estates and the army. The necessity to provide the *pomestia* with labor resulted in the establishment of serfdom, at first only of a temporary nature, on the estates of the gentry (1581). That peasant serfdom was made permanent and sanctioned by the Code of Laws (*Ulozhenie*) of 1649. It was also by provisions of the *Ulozhenie* that the townspeople (*posadskie liudi*) were finally organized into so many closed communes, all of whose members were bound by mutual guarantee to pay taxes and to perform special kinds of services imposed on them. Both the free peasants on state lands and the serfs, as well as the townspeople, were considered the lowest class of the tsar's subjects, free of military or court service but bound to pay heavy taxes and, in some cases, to compulsory labor (*tiaglo,* "burden"). Thus a distinction arose between the *sluzhilye liudi* (men liable to "service" in the technical sense of military and court service) and the *tiaglye liudi* (men liable to *tiaglo*). The "service" (in the above sense) became eventually a characteristic of the nobleman; the "burden" that of a commoner. That distinction became a basic feature of the social régime of the Tsardom of Moscow in the 17th century, and assumed even sharper forms in the St. Petersburg empire of the 18th century. . . .

II

The wholesale looting and destruction of property and life in Russia during the Mongol invasion of 1237–40 was a staggering blow which left the Russian people stunned, and for a time disrupted the normal course of economic and political life. It is hard to estimate the Russian casualties but they must have been tremendous, and if we include the vast throngs of civilians, both men and women, who were enslaved by the Mongols they can hardly have been less than 10 per cent of the total population.

The cities suffered most in the debacle. Such old centers of Russian civilization as Kiev, Chernigov, Pereiaslav, Riazan, Suzdal, and the somewhat younger Vladimir-in-Suzdalia, as well as a number of other towns, were thoroughly destroyed, and the first three named above lost their former importance for several centuries. Only a few major cities in West and North Russia such as Smolensk, Novgorod, Pskov, and Galich (Halicz) escaped devastation at that time. The Mongol policy of conscripting master craftsmen and skilled artisans for the khan's service added a new burden even for those cities which had been spared physical destruction during the first period of the conquest. A quota of the best Russian jewelers and craftsmen was sent to the great khan. As we have seen, Friar John of Plano Carpini met one of them, the goldsmith Kuzma, in Guyuk's camp. Many others were requisitioned by the khan of the Golden Horde for his personal service as well as to build and embellish his capital, Saray. Artisans of various kinds—smiths, armorers, saddlers, and so on—were also assigned to the ordus of the members of the house of Juchi as well as to those of the major commanders of the Mongol armies in South Russia. . . .

Another serious casualty of the Mongol conquest was the art of stone cutting and fretwork. The last masterpiece of that sort was the stone reliefs in the Cathedral of St. George in Iuriev-Polsky in Suzdalia, which were completed just a few years before the Mongol onslaught. The building crafts in general suffered a serious setback in East Russia. Fewer stone buildings were erected in the 1st century of Mongol domination than in the century before, and the quality of the work deteriorated markedly.

Russian industrial production in general was also seriously disrupted by the Mongol invasion and Mongol policies toward craftsmen. Even Novgorod was affected at first, but it recovered early; its industrial depression lasted about half a century. In most of East Russia the depression persisted a full century. Only in the mid-14th century, when

Mongol control over Russia eased considerably, did the revival of certain branches of industry, especially the metallurgical, become noticeable. Throughout the 15th century most of the city crafts made a rapid progress. Not only Tver and Moscow but some of the smaller towns like Zvenigorod became lively industrial centers. . . .

III

Agriculture was less affected by the Mongol invason than were the industrial crafts. In those parts of southern Russia which were subject to their direct control the Mongols themselves encouraged raising crops, such as millet and wheat, for the needs of their army and administration. In other parts of Russia it was the agricultural population which paid the bulk of the tribute collected by or for the Mongols, and so the Mongols had no motive for disrupting the productivity of agriculture. The same was true of hunting and fishing. The mining of iron and the production of salt (by evaporation) also continued unabated, especially as most of the deposits of near-surface iron ore (which alone was mined in Russia in the Mongol period) and most of the saltworks were located in the Novgorod territory; those in the northern part of the Grand Duchy of Vladimir also were beyond the immediate reach of the Mongols.

The steady growth of agriculture in East Russia in the Mongol period resulted in making it the leading branch of the national economy. Its expansion in the central and northern parts of the country was an aspect of the movement of the population, in the first period of Mongol domination, to the areas which seemed safest from encroachment, such as the regions around Moscow and Tver. The northeastern sections of the Grand Duchy of Vladimir beyond the Volga, chiefly the regions of Kostroma and

Galich, were also rapidly colonized. With the increase of population, more and more forests were cleared to make tilling possible. . . .

Let us now glance at the development of commerce in Russia during the Mongol period. As we know, control of the commercial routes was an important aspect of Mongol policy, and international trade constituted one of the foundations of the Mongol Empire, as well as of the Golden Horde. The khans of the Golden Horde, and especially Mangu-Temir, did much to promote the trade both of Novgorod and of the Italian colonies in the Crimea and the Azov area. The Mongol regional governors also patronized commerce, as the story of Baskak Ahmad shows.

Hence it might have been expected that Mongol domination would be favorable to the expansion of Russian trade. On the whole it was, but not throughout the period. In the first century of Mongol dominance Russian internal commerce suffered a serious setback because of the disruption of city crafts and the resulting inability of the cities to satisfy the demands of the villagers. As for foreign trade, in the reign of Berke it was all but monopolized by the powerful corporations of Moslem merchants of Central Asian origin. Only in the reign of Mangu-Temir were Russian merchants given their chance—but they knew how to use it. As has been mentioned, in Uzbeg's reign (1314–41) there was a large Russian colony in Saray, and merchants must have constituted the core of it. From the story of the execution of Grand Duke Michael of Tver in Uzbeg's camp in the north Caucasus (1319), it is known that a number of Russian merchants lived there at that time. According to the story, they wanted to place Michael's body in a nearby church but were forbidden by the Mongols to do it. As we know from the account of Tokhtamysh's campaign (1382), by that time the Russians controlled the Volga shipping. The Russian chronicles of the period display a good knowledge of the geography of the Golden Horde and on various occasions mention not only Saray but other commercial centers like Urgenj and Astrakhan. Information about them must have been supplied by the merchants. . . .

Owing to the free trade policies of Mangu-Temir and his successors, Russian trade with the West also expanded during the Mongol period. Novgorod entertained a lively and profitable commerce with the Hanseatic League. Moscow and Tver traded with Novgorod and Pskov as well as with Lithuania and Poland, and through them with Bohemia and Germany. Since woolen cloth was an outstanding item of import to Russia from the West, the Moscow merchants dealing with the West were known as "the clothiers" (*sukonniki*). In the earlier period, as we know, Novgorod received cloth of fine quality from Ypres. In the 14th and 15th centuries clothing industries developed in Central Europe, especially in Saxony, Bohemia, and Moravia. It was from Bohemia and Moravia that most of Moscow's imported cloth came in the 16th century, but there is no evidence of similar large-scale exports from those countries to Russia in the 15th century. Locks manufactured in Tver were exported from East Russia to Bohemia in the 14th and 15th centuries.

IV

Juridically speaking, Russia had no independent government in the Mongol period. The great khan of Mongolia and China was considered suzerain of all Russian lands, and as we know, at times actually interfered with Russian affairs. For practical purposes, however, the khan of the Golden Horde was the supreme ruler of Russia—its "tsar" as the Russian annals called him. No Russian prince was entitled to rule over his land without the required patent of authority from the khan. . . .

From the political angle, the destruction of most of the major cities of East Russia during the Mongol invasion was a crushing blow to the urban democratic institutions which had flourished in the Kievan period all over Russia (and continued to flourish in Novgorod and Pskov during the Mongol period). Moreover, it was from the population of those cities which escaped the destruction or were restored that the only determined opposition to Mongol rule we know of came during the first century. While the princes and boyars succeeded in adapting themselves to the conquerors' requirements and establishing a *modus vivendi* with them, the townspeople, especially the artisans, who lived under the constant threat of conscription, seethed with indignation at every fresh oppressive measure introduced by the new rulers. Because of this, the Mongols on their part were determined to crush the opposition of the cities and to eliminate the *veche* as a political institution. For this task, as has been seen, they engaged the cooperation of the Russian princes, who were themselves afraid of the revolutionary tendencies of the *veche* in Rostov as well as in a number of other cities.

The cooperation of the Mongols and the princes prevented the general spread of city rebellions in the second half of the 13th century and quelled the sporadic and isolated revolts which flared up from time to time in Rostov and elsewhere. The authority of the *veche* was thus drastically curbed, and by the mid-14th century it had ceased to function normally in most East Russian cities and could be discounted as an element of government. When in the 1370's the East Russian princes began to resist the Mongols, at least one cause of friction with the *veche* was eliminated. As in the case of the arrest of Mamay's envoys in Nizhni Novgorod in 1374, the anti-Mongol activities of the *veche* of that city were approved by the local prince. On the whole, however, both princes and boyars continued to be suspicious of the riotous spirit of the *veche*. While they asked the townspeople to cooperate with them against the Mongols, they intended to keep the leadership in their own hands. Consequently the *veche* was all but eliminated as a permanent branch of the government. As we have seen, the princes even succeeded in doing away with the representation of the interests of commoners in their administration by the *tysiatsky*; in 1375 that office was abolished. It was not so easy to eradicate the *veche*, however. While not allowed to function in normal times, it rose again as soon as the princes and boyars failed in their leadership. The temporary seizure of power by the commoners of Moscow at the time of Tokhtamysh's invasion is a typical example of the revival of the *veche* in time of crises even if that revival did not last long in each case. . . .

In spite of all their influence on the course of state affairs and in spite of the growth of their landed estates, the Muscovite boyars did not succeed, during the Mongol period, in clearly defining their political rights. What factors prevented their building up firm, constitutional guarantees for the functioning of their council? The existence of the supreme Mongol power was certainly a leading one. As the authority of the Russian princes, including the grand duke of Moscow, derived from the khan's patent, the prince could always ask the khan for protection against any internal opposition. The power of the *veche* was

curbed by the combined efforts of khan and princes. The boyars must have known very well that in case of any violent conflict with them the prince could be expected to appeal to the khan. When the Golden Horde was strong the khan's patent was not a mere scrap of paper; it was a mandate. Another check on the potential political aspirations of the East Russian boyars in the Mongol period was the attitude of the city people, especially the lower classes. In spite of the decline of the *veche* as an institution, the townspeople could not be discounted altogether as an element in Russian politics. And they could be expected to object violently to the establishment of any kind of aristocratic constitution. While repeatedly frustrated by the grand duke in their attempts to revolt prematurely against the Mongols, the commoners did not oppose the princely power in principle, since the grand duke as head of the armed forces was the only leader they could look to to head a successful national revolution against the Mongols in the future. In contrast, the commoners were suspicious of the boyars as a group and did not trust them. The antiboyar riots in Moscow in 1357 are an example of this. In any case, from the point of view of the commoners the prince was a lesser evil than the boyars, and the boyars realized that in any conflict between them and the prince the latter would be supported not only by the khan but by the townspeople as well. . . .

Future events were to bring bitter disappointment to the East Russian boyars in their reliance on their traditional freedom. What they thought was solid. rock beneath their feet had turned to sand by the close of the 15th century. That freedom of service which was an aspect of the federative constitution of Kievan Russia proved incompatible with the interests of the growing Moscow monarchy. With the change in political atmosphere, violations by the grand duke of the principle of freedom of service became almost unavoidable. Some violations of this sort occurred in the Mongol period. The first notable instance was the case of Ivan Veliaminov. When he left Moscow and went over to the prince of Tver, in 1374, his estates were confiscated, and later on, when he was caught by the Muscovites, he was executed. It may be argued that this was a moment of sharp political conflict and of national emergency, but still the violation of principle cannot be denied. Another similar episode occurred in 1433 when the Moscow boyar Ivan Vsevolozhsky went over to Grand Duke Vasili II's rival, Iuri of Galich. His estates too were confiscated. This was again a period of sharp conflict, of a civil war in which both sides disregarded not only treaties but moral precepts as well. Yet as a result of such repeated actions a tendency developed at the court of Moscow to deny the right of boyars to leave at will and under all circumstances. Those boyars who tried to use their freedom in a time of crisis were now considered deserters or traitors. The new notion gained ground rapidly, and by the early 16th century— when Moscow absorbed all the regional principalities—the Moscow boyars found themselves bound to the grand duke's service. Besides, at the time of the *oprichnina,* many of them lost their patrimonial estates and were granted fiefs (*pomestia*) instead. . . .

V

The unification of East Russia was a protracted process which continued, with ups and downs, throughout the Mongol period and was completed only in the early 16th century during the reign of Vasili III. It has often been asserted in the historical literature that the khan himself contributed to the uni-

fication by making the grand duke of Moscow his chief tax collector. On the basis of the actual story of Mongol-Russian relations told in the two preceding chapters we know that this view is erroneous or at least exaggerated. The khans understood well the dangerous implications of giving too much power to a single Russian prince. Consequently, in the first half of the 14th century the khan sanctioned the division of East Russia into four grand duchies and commissioned each of the four grand dukes to collect taxes within his realm. It was only in 1392 that Khan Tokhtamysh, being in a desperate situation and needing the assistance of Vasili I of Moscow, authorized him to annex the Grand Duchy of Nizhni Novgorod. The two other grand duchies, Tver and Riazan, remained intact at that time. In addition to keeping Russia politically divided, the Tatars, whenever they were afraid of the growing power of some Russian prince, tried to sow seeds of discord between him and his potential allies. If a conflict followed, they were in a position either to offer their mediation, and thus reassert their authority, or to punish the prince of whom they were suspicious. The Russian princes were well aware of this crafty device, and in several of the interprincely treaties of this period we find a clause by which the signatories bound themselves not to listen if the Tatars attempted to set one of them against the other. But the Russians did not always have the good sense to carry out their good intentions. . . .

Let us now examine the rise of the grand ducal power in the Grand Duchy of Vladimir and Moscow, the one which succeeded in absorbing all the others. From the point of view of Mongol law, the authority of the grand duke of Moscow, as well as that of the other Russian grand dukes and princes, was based primarily on the khan's patent. As we know, in the Kievan period only princes of the house of Riurik were entitled to occupy the Russian princely thrones. The Mongols accepted the principle of the exclusive rights of the Riurikovichi (descendants of Riurik)—in those Russian lands which were not put under the direct authority of the khan. Since the Mongols themselves were ruled by the Golden Kin, the Russian principle of a single ruling house was close to their own concepts. It may be mentioned in this connection that when, in the 14th century, the new dynasty of Gedymin was recognized in West Russia the Mongols agreed to deal with some of the Gedyminovichi as well. In this case, however, the khan's new vassals emancipated themselves quickly from the Mongol power, and the "submission" of Iagailo to Mamay's puppet khan and then to Tokhtamysh was in essence an alliance rather than vassalage.

The recognition by the Mongols of the rights of the Riurik dynasty was a wise step which saved them from much trouble. It also made it easier for the Russians to accept Mongol suzerainty. The Riurikovichi continued to rule Russia—to the extent that they were allowed to—but they now ruled on the basis of both their genealogical rights and the khan's investiture. The old principle of assigning thrones by genealogical seniority, which had already declined in the late Kievan period, now became even less valid, both because the khans often disregarded it in assigning the princely patents and because conditions in Russia changed considerably. The patrimonial principle of the transfer of power from father to son in each principality now came to the fore; nowhere did it prove as vital as in the principality of Moscow and, after the virtual merger of Moscow with Vladimir, in the Grand Duchy of Vladimir and Moscow. The patrimonial principle, then, may be considered the psychological basis of the power of the house of Daniel (the Danilovichi) of Moscow. While they first applied it to the principality of Moscow, they soon extended it to the Grand Duchy of Vladimir as a whole.

As has been mentioned, from the practical point of view the grand duke's domains constituted one of the important foundations of his power. The intermingling of the grand duke's manorial rights with his authority as a ruler has led many historians and jurists, like Boris Chicherin, for example, to speak of the complete victory of private law over public and the disappearance of all notions of statehood in Muscovy of this period. To prove his theory Chicherin refers to the testaments of the Moscow princes. The theory may seem convincing at first glance but is indeed an example of oversimplification of historical reality. One has to be cautious in applying abstract legal patterns to the interpretation of medieval notions and terminology. Actually the prince's authority was not entirely submerged in the sphere of his private interests. A clear expression of the gradual growth of the idea of the state may be found in the preference given by each Moscow ruler to his eldest son. Then as later there was no rule of primogeniture in the provisions on intestate inheritance in the Russian codes, and so the idea of *majorat* did not influence the institutions of the Russian private law. The landed estates, whether princely or boyar, were divided equally between all the sons, with special provisions made for the maintenance of mother, widow, or daughters.

This rule even in regard to state domains prevailed in most East Russian principalities of the Mongol period, but not in Moscow. Even in Moscow, to be sure, each prince was bound by family traditions to grant an apanage to each of his sons, but, in contrast to the other principalities, he usually made the share of the eldest son, the heir to the throne, larger than those of the others. At first the material advantage of the eldest son was not very conspicuous. As a matter of principle, however, the disposition was of great importance, as any succeeding prince could easily raise the ratio in favor of his eldest son. According to the will of Dmitri Donskoy, who left five sons, the share of the eldest in the payment of each 1,000 rubles of Mongol tribute (which is an indication of the revenue each received from his share of lands) was 342 rubles (instead of the 200 rubles it would have been if the shares had been equal). Dmitri's grandson, Vasili II, assigned 14 cities to his eldest son, Ivan III, as against 12 which were divided among the four other sons. Ivan III carried the same principle even further, leaving his eldest son 66 cities and to the four others together only 30. The motive of these dispositions was to secure the dominance of each succeeding ruler among his kin, if not yet complete unity of princely government. As the arrangements were contrary to the spirit of Russian private law, we may see in them elements of the state law.

When the Golden Horde weakened, the grand duke of Moscow felt himself secure enough not only to bequeath shares of his dominions to his sons but also to appoint the successor to the grand ducal throne itself. Dmitri Donskoy was the first to "bless" his eldest son Vasili I with the Grand Duchy of Vladimir. But Vasili did not ascend the throne without receiving the khan's patent. When Vasili I made his will he did not dare to dispose of the grand duchy. As we know, his son Vasili II gained the throne with great difficulty, against the opposition of his uncle Iuri. After that he twice lost and twice recovered it. To secure the rights of his eldest son, Ivan III, Vasili II proclaimed him grand

duke and co-ruler late in 1448 or early in 1449. Because of this and of the increase of his power in the second half of his reign, Vasili II had no hesitation in "blessing" Ivan III with his "patrimony," the grand duchy. The latter ascended the throne on the basis of that blessing, not bothering about confirmation from the khan.

VI

In the Kievan period the main branches of princely administration were the judiciary, the military, and the financial. The prince was the chief justice and commander of the army, and his agents collected the taxes and court fees. After the Mongol invasion the supreme direction of all administrative functions was assumed by the tsar, the Mongol khan. The authority of the Russian princes shrank considerably. The princes now had to obey the khan's orders, and their administrative competence in their own realms was strictly limited; they could exercise it only within the narrow sphere of affairs left to their discretion by the Mongols.

As regards the judiciary, all the Russian princes were now under the authority of the khan and of the Supreme Court of the Mongols, and as we know a number of them were executed by order of the khan for real or alleged state crimes. The khan also settled most major litigation among the Russian princes. Russians drafted into the Mongol army were subject to Mongol military law.

Moreover, all litigation between Russians and Mongols was subject to trial in the Mongol court. There was for example the case of the descendants of Prince Boris of Rostov versus the descendants of Tsarevich Peter of the Horde. Peter, as we know, became a Greek Orthodox, and so were his descendants. From the khan's point of view, however, they remained Mongols and of the royal blood at that. So when

182   *The Mongol Impact on Russia*

Boris's descendants tried to seize the lands belonging to the monastery founded by Peter, the latter's grandson appealed to the khan. The Mongol court upheld the rights of Peter's descendants in this case, which, it may be added, was a just settlement of the controversy. Although in this affair the interests of a monastery were involved, it was tried as a civil suit. As a general rule, however, the church was protected by the khan's yarlyk against any infringements upon its rights and privileges. The violators, if they were Mongols, were subject to the Mongol courts. If they happened to be Russians, the Russian princes were probably bound to punish them. If the prince failed to act, the church undoubtedly could appeal to the khan.

With his juridical prerogatives firmly established at the higher level, the khan did not interfere with litigation among the Russian boyars and commoners, allowing the prince in each given locality to continue his judicial functions. Because of such policies, of all the branches of princely administration the judiciary was the one least affected by Mongol rule. And yet, as the Russians became familiar with Mongol criminal law and the Mongol courts, they proved ready to accept some of the patterns of Mongol jurisprudence. Even Vladimir-sky-Budanov, who, on the whole, tends to minimize Mongol influence on Russia, admits that both capital punishment (unknown to the *Pravda Russkaia*—Russian Law code—of the Kievan period) and corporal punishment (applied only to slaves in the Kievan period) entered Muscovite law under Mongol influence. According to the provisions of the Dvina Land Charter of 1397 issued by Grand Duke Vasili I of Moscow, each thief was to be branded; for the third theft the penalty was death by hanging. The death penalty by beheading was also established for traitors, as may be seen from the Veliami-

nov case. In Ivan III's *Sudebnik* (Code of Laws) of 1497 capital punishment was ordered for the following categories of crimes: sedition; theft of church property; homicide; *podmet,* that is, leaving things at another's house in order subsequently to accuse him of theft; and arson. An inveterate murderer and brigand known to society as such (*vedomyi likhoi chelovek*) could also be executed if implicated in any serious crime.

It should be mentioned in this connection that in the same period capital punishment was introduced in the city of Pskov. In this case, however, it was not Mongol but Western law which served as a pattern. Owing to their geographical position and lively trade with the German cities, both Novgorod and Pskov were much more open to Western influences than Moscow. As a matter of fact, the penal law of England, France, and Germany in the late Middle Ages and early modern period was as harsh or even harsher than Mongol criminal law. Both capital and corporal punishment were prescribed for a variety of crimes. In Germany decapitation and hanging were the usual forms of execution of a criminal; and many other methods of inflicting death were in use, such as burning at the stake, burying alive, drowning, the wheel, quartering, and piercing with a pole. In Pskov capital punishment was ordered for four kinds of crimes that were considered most offensive: theft in the precincts of the Pskov Kremlin, horse stealing, spying, and arson. The form of execution was not mentioned in the Pskov charter; it was probably either decapitation or hanging, depending on the nature of the crime. In Novgorod in the same period drowning criminals in the Volkhov River seems to have been the preferred form of execution.

It was also during the Mongol period and presumably under Tatar influence that torture became a regular part of

Muscovite criminal procedure. The *Sudebnik* of 1497 prescribes that the suspect be tortured without either prejudice or connivance; the main object of the torture apparently was to obtain both confession and information about accomplices. The official in charge was instructed, however, not to let the victim make any slanderous accusations against innocent persons. It would not be amiss to note that torture was widely used in the West in this period. In the 14th century it was recommended by the Roman Catholic Church in the trials of heretics. In the 15th century it was habitual both in France and Germany to use torture at the interrogation of criminals. In France both the secrecy of criminal procedure and the use of torture were legalized by the ordinances of 1498 and 1539. In Germany Emperor Charles V tried to limit the use of torture in his Ordinance on Criminal Law (*Halsgerichtsordnung*) (1532) but failed to stop the abuses. The Pskovians did not follow the new pattern in this respect; torture was not sanctioned by Pskovian law.

While some influence of Mongol penal and trial law on Muscovite law can hardly be denied, there is no positive evidence of the Russians' borrowing from the Mongols any outstanding feature of court organization. We might note though that a minor official of the local courts in northern Russia in the 16th and 17th centuries was known as *yaryga*, which is obviously derived from the Mongol *jargu* (*dzargu, yargu*), "judge."

VII

In matters of taxation and army conscription the khan exercised full and direct power in Russia for more than half a century. The post-horse service (*yam*) established by the Mongols they used for their own needs. The khan also reserved for himself the right of coin-

age. Under this system, which lasted intact down to the early 1300's, the Russian grand dukes and princes retained only fragments of their former authority in matters of military and financial administration. Each prince was allowed to keep a small contingent of troops—his retinue—and to collect some minor local taxes as well as the manorial taxes. One hardly can speak of independent princely administration for this period. The situation changed when the grand dukes were commissioned to collect the Mongol tribute, as well as the *tamga*, within the confines of their principalities, on their own responsibility, though at first under the supervision of a Mongol commissar. Presumably the grand dukes also supervised the conscription of soldiers for the khan's army, and the post-horse service. The basic system of military and financial districts, the *t'my*, was left intact, but now the grand duke's tax agents (*danshchiki*) collected the tribute instead of the Mongol *baskaks*. The conscription of craftsmen seems to have been discontinued. The grand dukes encountered no difficulties in collecting taxes since during the sixty-odd years of immediate Mongol control the people were cowed into obedience and well trained in the performance of their duties to the state.

While the princes were merely the khan's commissioners and were constantly under the control of Mongol officials, the abandonment of the old system yet had significant results. The princes were again allowed to perform their administrative functions, even if they had to follow the Mongol pattern of administration which they had no authority to change. In fact they soon discovered that the new system could be financially profitable to them, since after paying the quota of tribute required for each *t'ma* they could turn whatever surplus there was into their own treasuries. As the number of *t'my* of the Grand Duchy of Vladimir was greater than that of any other grand duchy, the Moscow rulers profited most from the situation.

With the revolt of Dmitri Donskoy against Mamay, and even more after the fall of Tokhtamysh, a new phase opened in Mongol-Russian relations: one of considerable autonomy of the Russian lands. The grand dukes and princes continued to acknowledge themselves the khan's vassals and paid him tribute—not always regularly—but they took over the internal administration of their principalities almost without interference from the khan. The princes now began to coin their own money, with the khan's name on it, to be sure, in addition to their own. The foundations of the Mongol administrative system were not changed, however, since the grand dukes found them convenient and efficient. So it was on the basis of the Mongol patterns that the grand ducal system of taxation and army organization was developed in the late 14th to 16th centuries. . . .

All the moneys collected were kept in the grand duke's treasury (*kazna*) and managed by the treasurer (*kaznachei*). The fact that both these Russian terms are borrowed from the Turkish is a clear indication that the institution itself was created after the Mongol pattern. . . .

Let us now consider the changes which occurred in the Russian army organization during the Mongol period. There can be no doubt that the Russians —who first met the Mongols as enemies and then became, for a long period, their subjects—acquired a thorough knowledge of the Mongol army system and could not but be impressed with its efficiency. It will be recalled that a number of Russian princes with their retinues had to participate in various campaigns undertaken by Mongol khans.

Suffice it to refer here to the role of the Rostov princes in Mangu-Temir's expedition against the Alan mountaineers in 1277–78 and the participation of the Moscow and Suzdal princes in Tokhtamysh's expedition against Timur a century later. Besides, scores of thousands of Russians were drafted into the Mongol army at regular intervals if not yearly. Hardly any of those who were taken to China and settled there ever had a chance to return to Russia, but some of those used by the khans of the Golden Horde in South Russia, as for example by Tokhta against Nogay in 1298–99, might be expected to make their way back home after the close of the campaign and to tell the Russian authorities about their experiences. . . .

The Russians familiarized themselves with the Mongol tactic of enveloping the enemy on both flanks (the Vozha River battle of 1378 is a good example of this). Furthermore, they introduced some Mongol armor and weapons into their own army. It will be recalled that as early as 1246 Daniel of Galicia's troops were equipped after the Mongol fashion. In their war against Riazan, in 1361, the Muscovites used the lasso quite successfully. The equipment of the Muscovite troops of the 16th century also shows definite Mongol influence.

The Russian army of the Kievan period consisted of two main parts: the prince's retinue (*druzhina*) and the city militia under the authority of the chiliarch (*tysiatsky*). The rural population was not subject to mobilization and as a rule did not take any part in the campaigns. The Mongol invasion changed the whole picture. First of all, for the needs of their own armed forces, the Mongols established a rigid system of universal conscription, including in it the entire rural population. Second, by destroying or depopulating the Russian cities and curbing the authority of the veche, they shattered the foundations of the city militia system; the *tysiatsky* now had little to do as an army chief, and as we know the office itself was eventually abolished. . . .

After the decline of the Golden Horde the grand dukes of Moscow became able to use, whenever necessary, the system of universal conscription established by the Mongols. It was on the basis of the Mongol system that Dmitri Donskoy succeeded in mobilizing the army with which he defeated Mamay at Kulikovo Pole. His son Vasili I used general conscription once more when he prepared to meet Tamerlane's invasion. In the 16th century conscription was used on several occasions. At that time it became known as the *posokha*, since the required quota of recruits was assessed per *sokha*. . . .

VIII

The changes which occurred in East Russia during the Mongol period in the position of the social classes were not as drastic as those in government and administration, but no less significant. It may be said that throughout the Mongol period the foundations of the old social order—the free society—were gradually and persistently chipped away without at first affecting the façade. At the time when Ivan III announced Russia's emancipation from the Mongol power and conquered Novgorod, the framework of the new structure was all but ready, and the new order, that of a service-bound society, became clearly noticeable. This is especially true of the position of the old upper class of Russian society, the boyars; paradoxical as it may seem, the process of their subordination to the monarch was completed sooner than the regimentation and enserfment of the lower classes.

Moscow boyardom consisted of varied and heterogeneous elements. Some of the boyars of the 14th and 15th centuries belonged to the old boyar clans of the Grand Duchy of Vladimir. Among them were the Buturlins, the Cheliadnins, the Kutuzovs (all three of these families claiming originally to be of German descent), the Morozovs, the Veliaminovs (these were of Varangian ancestry), and the Vorontsovs. Quite a number of the Moscow boyar families were of West Russian origin. To this group belonged the Pleshcheevs and the Kvashnins. Besides the West Russians, a number of Lithuanians and, later on, Poles entered the service of the grand dukes of Moscow. It must be borne in mind that when our sources refer to families of "Polish and Lithuanian origin," they mean that they hailed from Poland and Lithuania, but their exact ethnic origin is not always clear. Some of the boyars were Polonized West Russians. Others claimed to be of "Prussian" origin. As by the end of the 13th century Prussia, originally a Baltic (Lithuanian) country, had been thoroughly Germanized, "Prussian" origin must in this case have meant German. To this group the Khvostovs, the Romanovs (originally known as the Koshkins and then as the Zakharins), and the Sheremetevs belonged. The Golovins and the Khovrins were of Greek descent. Last, but not least, some of the best boyar families of Moscow were of "Tatar" (Mongol or Turkish) origin. Prominent among them were the Veliaminov-Zernovs (not to be confused with the original Veliaminovs). The Saburovs and the Godunovs were branches of this family. The Arsenievs and Bakhmetevs established themselves in Russia in the late 14th and mid-15th centuries respectively.

By 1450 the position of the boyars as a class was seriously undermined by the appearance of a new aristocratic group, that of the servitor princes (*sluzhilye kniazia*), as well as by the steady growth of the lower gentry (the *dvoriane*) which centered around the grand duke's *dvor*.

The formation of the class of the servitor princes was a protracted historical process, and the class itself was as heterogeneous as that of the boyars. In the course of the 14th and 15th centuries a number of East Russian princes, all descendants of Riurik, found it convenient or necessary to cede or sell their sovereign rights to the grand duke of Moscow. Among them were some of the princes of the house of Rostov, as well as those of Nizhni Novgorod and Suzdal. In addition, a number of the Riurikovichi whose principalities were situated in the land of Severia (mostly in the upper Oka River basin) found themselves in the no man's land between Muscovy and Lithuania and threatened by both these powers. Some of them pledged their allegiance to the grand duke of Lithuania, but others, like the nia, also went to Moscow. Among them were the Patrikeev princes (descendants of Gedymin's son Narimunt). Lastly, as we know, some of the Juchid princes entered Russian service during the reign of Vasili II; these were known as the tsarevichi or even as the tsars, if they happened to have reigned in their own name in Kazan or Siberia before com- Obolenskys, for example, chose to enter the service of the grand duke of Moscow. A number of Lithuanian princes, descendants of Gedymin (the Gedyminovichi), being for various reasons dissatisfied with the state of affairs in Lithuaing to Moscow. In the 1500's they ranked highest among the princes serving the tsar of Moscow. In the course of the 16th and 17th centuries lesser Tatar nobility, such as the Kudashev and Engalychev princes, following in the wake of the Juchids, found their way to Moscow; so did some members of the Circassian and Georgian nobility, like the Cherkassky and the Imeretinsky princes. . . .

It would not be amiss now to glance at the ethnic origins and composition of the Russian nobility as a whole (including boyars and princes) as it consolidated itself in the 17th century. According to N. P. Zagoskin's computation, 229 Russian noble families were of "West European" (including German) origin; 223 of Polish and Lithuanian origin; 156 of "Tatar" and other Oriental origin. Against those families of alien ancestry, 168 families belonged to the house of Riurik; 42 were of unspecified "Russian" origin; and 97 families of uncertain ancestry. Some of the families of so-called Polish-Lithuanian ancestry must have been West Russian. Still, the families of Russian origin were obviously a minority. Zagoskin's figures refer to the later period. It must be borne in mind that the influx of "Tatar" families into the Russian nobility greatly increased after the reign of Vasili II. The majority of Russian noble families of West European and Polish origin settled in Russia only in the 17th century and some of them even later. Therefore the proportion of families of Russian origin in the composition of Moscow boyardom must have been higher in the Mongol period than later. . . .

IX

In the Kievan period the citizens of the large towns were free from taxes; and they formed their own militia (*tysiacha*, "thousand") in which they served as free citizens, not as conscript soldiers. Conscription and taxation introduced by the Mongols, coupled with the curbing of the veche, basically changed the status of the urban class in East Russia. (Novgorod and Pskov, it will be recalled, succeeded in maintaining their autonomy, and their citizens kept their full political and individual rights throughout the Mongol period.) When East Russia emancipated herself from the Mongols, the grand duke of Moscow did not revoke the Mongol system of taxation and conscription but used it for the needs of his own government. That system was now further expanded: in 1478 Novgorod was annexed to Moscow, and in 1510 Pskov. The old free institutions of the two cities were then abolished.

With the disintegration of the political freedom of the East Russian cities, the economic differentiation between wealthy and poor citizens assumed new significance. The top layer of the Muscovite merchants, the *gosti* and *sukonniki*, became a privileged minority high above the bulk of the townspeople. In the course of the 16th century that top layer was divided into three groups: (1) the *gosti*, the richest wholesale merchants; (2) the *gosti* hundred (*gostinnaia sotnia*), a corporation of the less rich *gosti;* (3) and the *sukonniki* hundred (*sukonnaia sotnia*), the corporation of the *sukonniki.* All of them were exempt from direct taxes as well as from any compulsory labor services. For the privileges they enjoyed the merchants of these three groups had to assist the tsar in the financial administration of the tsardom and the collection of the indirect taxes.

Deprived in this way of their most valuable element, the *tiaglo*-bound mass of the burghers was organized in two groups: the "middle" burghers (*serednie*), such as retail merchants and master artisans; and the "junior" burghers (*molodshie*), also known as the "black" people (*chernye liudi*), that is, the petty artisans and the half-skilled and unskilled workers. They formed the so-called "black hundred" (*chernaia sotnia*). Most of the middle and junior burghers lived outside the city proper, in the *posad* (town settlement). By 1550

they were known as the *posadskie liudi* ("townspeople" in the specific sense of the *tiaglo*-bound middle and lower classes of the urban population). The scale of compensation for offenses against the honor of the people of various classes established in Ivan IV's *Sudebnik* gives an adequate notion of the difference in social and economic position of different urban groups. The fine for offending against the honor of a *gost'* was 50 rubles; against the honor of a middle-class burgher, 5 rubles; for offending the honor of a lower-class *posadski* 1 ruble was sufficient.

In the 17th century, following the crisis of the Time of Troubles, the Moscow government took steps to bind the townspeople to their communes. In 1613 it ordered the *posadskie* who had fled from the capital during the troubles forcibly returned to Moscow; in 1619 a general ordinance was issued that all the *posadskie* who had migrated earlier should return to their respective towns all over Russia. By the provisions of the Code of Laws (*Ulozhenie*) of 1649 the commune was finally consolidated as a closed group to which all its members were permanently bound. Any member who left the commune without the government's permission was to be punished by deportation to Siberia. In 1658 the death penalty was established for moving from one *posad* to another. . . .

X

In medieval Russia, as in the medieval West, the Christian church played a leading role in the nation's spiritual life. Therefore, especially after the victory of Islam in the Golden Horde, there was little occasion for direct Mongol influence on Russia in the religious sphere. Indirectly, however, the Mongol conquest affected the course of development of the Russian church and the spiritual culture in various ways. The first shock of the Mongol invasion was as painful to the church as to the other aspects of Russian life and culture. Many outstanding clergymen, including the metropolitan himself, perished in the destroyed cities; many cathedrals, monasteries, and churches were burned or looted; hosts of parishioners were killed or enslaved. The city of Kiev, the metropolis of the Russian church, was so devastated that for many years it was unfit to serve as the center of the church administration. Of the eparchies, Pereiaslav suffered most and the bishopric was closed.

It was only after the issuance of Mangu-Temir's immunity charter to the Russian clergy that the church found itself on firm ground once more and could gradually reorganize; as years went by, it became even stronger in some respects than before the Mongol onslaught. Indeed, ruled by Greek metropolitans or by Russian metropolitans ordained in Byzantium, and protected by the khan's charter, the church in Russia was in this period less dependent on the princely power than in any other period of Russian history. In fact the metropolitan on more than one occasion served as arbiter in interprincely disputes. This was also a period in which the Russian church was able to build up a strong material basis for its activities. As the church lands were immune from interference by state authorities, either Mongol or Russian, they attracted an increasing number of peasant settlers, and the ratio of their production to the total agricultural ouput rose steadily. This was especially true of the monastery estates. A degree of prosperity achieved by the church toward the end of the first century of Mongol domination greatly helped in the performance of its spiritual activities.

Among the tasks the church faced in the Mongol period, the first was that of giving spiritual advice and moral support to the embittered and exasperated people, from princes to commoners. Connected with this was a more general mission—to complete the Christianization of the Russian people. In the Kievan period Christianity became firmly established among the upper classes and the townspeople. Most of the monasteries founded in that period were located in the cities. In the rural districts the Christian layer was rather thin, and the remnants of paganism were still unconquered. Only in the Mongol period did the rural population of East Russia become more thoroughly Christianized. This was achieved both by strenuous efforts of the clergy and by the growth of religious feeling among the spiritual elite of the people themselves. Most of the metropolitans of this period spent much time traveling throughout Russia trying to correct deficiencies in church administration and to direct the activities of the bishops and priests. Several new eparchies were organized, four of them in East Russia, two in West Russia, and one in Saray. The number of churches and monasteries grew steadily, especially after 1350, both in the cities and the rural districts. According to Kliuchevsky, about thirty monasteries were founded in the first century of the Mongol period and five times as many more in the second century. A characteristic trait of the new monastic movement was the initiative shown by individuals, young men of ardent religious spirit who took monastic orders in order to go to "the wilderness"—deep into the woods—for hard work in primitive conditions as well as for prayer and meditation. The disasters of the Mongol invasion and of the interprincely strife as well as harsh conditions of life in general were conducive to the development of this mentality. . . .

In literature the spirit of the church found expression first of all in the bishops' sermons and in the lives of saints, as well as in the biographies of certain Russian princes who, it was felt, deserved to be canonized, so that their biographies were written in the style of the lives of saints. The underlying idea of most of these works was that the Mongol yoke was a visitation of God for the sins of the Russian people and that only true Christianization could lead the Russians out of their plight. The sermons of Bishop Serapion of Vladimir (1274–75) are typical of this attitude. He blamed for Russia's sufferings primarily the princes who had sapped the nation's strength by their constant quarrels. But he did not stop at that. He reproved the common people for clinging to remnants of paganism as well as for their superstitions, and urged every Russian to repent and become Christian in spirit and not in name only. Among the princes of the first century of Mongol rule the lives of Grand Duke Iaroslav and his son Alexander Nevsky are of special interest. Iaroslav's biography has been preserved only in fragments. It was conceived as a national tragedy in the first act of which Iaroslav happened to be a leading actor. In the introduction the happy past of the Russian land was admiringly described. Probably it was to be followed by a description of the catastrophe which befell Russia, but that part has been lost. The introduction has been preserved under a separate title, the "Lay of Russia's Ruin" (*Slovo o pogibeli zemli russkoi*). It is perhaps the highest achievement of Russian literature of the early Mongol period. In the life of Alexander Nevsky the emphasis is on the military valor he displayed in the defense of Greek Orthodoxy against the Roman Catholic crusade.

As in the Kievan period, the clergy of the Mongol age played an important role in the compilation of the Russian chronicles. The work all but stopped after the Mongol invasion. The only chronicle written between 1240 and 1260, known to us in part, was that of Rostov. Its editor was Bishop Cyril of that city. As D. S. Likhachev has convincingly shown, Cyril was helped by Princess Maria, daughter of Michael of Chernigov and widow of Vasilko of Rostov. Both her father and her husband were killed by the Mongols, and she devoted herself to charities and literary work. In 1305 a chronicle was compiled in Tver. This was partly copied in 1377 by the Suzdal monk Laurentius (the writer of the so-called Laurentian Codex). In the 15th century there appeared in Moscow historical works of a wider scope, like the Trinity Chronicle (started under the direction of Metropolitan Cyprian and completed in 1409) and the even more ambitious digest of annals compiled under the editorship of Metropolitan Photius around 1418. The latter served as a basis for further work which resulted in the great digests of the 16th century—the Voskresensk and the Nikon chronicles. Novgorod, throughout the 14th century and down to her fall, was a center for the writing of her own historical annals. It should be noted that many of the Russian chroniclers, and especially the editors of the Nikon Chronicle, showed excellent knowledge not only of Russian events but of Tatar affairs as well.

XI

In the Russian lay literature of the Mongol age, both written and oral, a twofold attitude toward the Tatars can be noticed. On the one hand there was a feeling of repulsion, of opposition to the nation's oppressors, on the other a psychological undercurrent of attraction to the poetry of steppe life. Recalling the longing of a number of 19th-century Russian writers such as Pushkin, Lermontov, and Leo Tolstoy for the Caucasus and the picturesque life of the Caucasian mountaineers is helpful in understanding this mentality.

Owing to the tendency to repulsion, the *byliny* of the pre-Mongol age were revised to fit the new situation, and the name of the new enemy—the Tatars—was substituted for that of the old (the Cumans). Simultaneously new *byliny* and historical legends and songs were created dealing with the Mongol phase of Russia's struggle against the steppe peoples. Batu's destruction of Kiev and Nogay's raids on Russia served as topics for contemporary Russian folklore. The Tatar oppression of Tver and the revolt of the Tverians in 1327 not only were recorded in the chronicles but apparently constituted the basis of a special historical tale. And of course, as has been mentioned, the battle of Kulikovo Pole became the subject of a variety of patriotic stories, parts of which were used by the chroniclers and which later were recorded in full in writing. Here we have a case of merging of the oral and written forms of the old Russian literature. The "*Zadonshchina*," whose topic belongs to the same cycle, is obviously a piece of written literature.

As to the element of attraction, the poetry of steppe life and warfare was already felt by the creators of *byliny* in the pre-Mongol age. This same psychological process continued now. Even in the patriotic tales of Kulikovo Pole the chivalry of the Tatar knight whose challenge was accepted by the monk Peresvet was noted with obvious admiration. In the pre-Mongol Russian *byliny* there were undeniable close parallels to the Iranian and early Turkish heroic songs. In the Mongol age Russian folklore also was influenced by "Tatar" (Mongol and Turkish) poetic patterns and themes. Presumably Russian soldiers drafted into the Mongol armies were the means of acquainting the Russians with Tatar heroic poetry. Tatars settled in Russia must also have brought Tatar motifs into Russian folklore.

The enrichment of the Russian language with words and terms borrowed from Mongol and Turkish or from Persian and Arabic through Turkish was still another aspect of the same process of cultural osmosis. By 1450 the Tatar (Turkish) language had become fashionable at the court of Grand Duke Vasili II of Moscow, which was strongly resented by many of his opponents. Vasili II was accused of excessive love of the Tatars "and their speech" (*i rech ikh*). It was typical of the period that a number of Russian noblemen in the 15th, 16th, and 17th centuries assumed Tatar surnames. Thus a member of the Veliaminov family became known as Aksak (which means "lame" in Turkish) and his descendants as the Aksakovs. Similarly, one of the Shchepin-Rostovsky princes was called Bakhteiar (*bakhtyar* in Persian means "fortunate," "rich"). He was the forefather of the Bakhteiarov princes, a line which became extinct in the 18th century.

A number of Turkish words entered the Russian language before the Mongol invasion, but the real influx started in the Mongol age and continued in the 16th and 17th centuries. Among the terms borrowed from Mongol and Turkish (or through Turkish from Arabic and Persian) in the sphere of administration and finance, such words as *dengi* (money), *kazna* (treasury), *tamozhnia* (customshouse) may be mentioned here. Another group of borrowings is connected with trade and merchandise: *bazar* (bazaar), *balagan* (booth), *bakaleia* (groceries of certain kinds), *barysh* (profit), *kumach* (red cloth), and others. Among the borrowings for clothing, headgear, and footwear are the following: *armiak* (peasant overcoat), *bashlyk* (a kind of hood), *bashmak* (shoe). Naturally enough, an important group of borrowings is that connected with horses, their color, and their breeding; for instance *argamak* (thoroughbred steed), *bulanyi* (dun), *tabun* (drove of horses). Many other Russian words denoting household objects, food and drink, as well as fruit and vegetables, metals, and precious stones also were borrowed from Turkish or from other Oriental languages through Turkish.

A factor in Russian intellectual and spiritual development whose importance is hard to evaluate is the role of the Tatars who settled in Russia and were converted to Christianity, and of their descendants. The case of Tsarevich Peter of the Horde, founder of a monastery in Rostov, has been already mentioned. There were other similar instances. A prominent 15th-century Russian religious leader who also founded a monastery, St. Pafnuti of Borovsk, was grandson of a *baskak*. In the 16th century a boyar son of Tatar extraction, Bulgak by name, was ordained priest and after that there was always a priest in the family, down to Father Sergius Bulgakov, a well-known Russian theologian of the 20th century. And there were other outstanding Russian intellectual leaders of Tatar extraction like the historian N. M. Karamzin and the philosopher Peter Chaadaev. Judging from his name, Chaadaev must have been of Mongol ancestry, for Chaaday is a contraction of the Mongol name Jagatay (Chagatay). Presumably Peter Chaadaev was a descendant of Chingis-Khan's son Jagatay. It is both paradoxical and typical of the melting pot of Russian civilization with its heterogeneous ethnic elements that the "Westernizer" Chaadaev was of Mongol extraction and the "Slavophile" Aksakov family was of Varangian ancestry (a branch of the Veliaminovs). . . .

XII

It is hard to tell whether the Muscovites themselves seriously believed in the stories of the crownings of Vladimir the Saint and Vladimir Monomach. In any case they did not put all their eggs in the Byzantine basket, being well aware of the historical connection between the Tsardom of Moscow and the Golden Horde. And indeed it was but natural for the Muscovite ruler to take the title of his former suzerain. Moreover, when the Russian counterattack started and the Russians conquered the khanates of Kazan and Astrakhan (in 1552 and 1556 respectively), the Russian tsar could claim to have become heir to at least two of the Golden Horde succession states. The implications of the conquest were emphasized by the Moscow government in its effort to obtain for its ruler recognition of the title of tsar from the king of Poland. A Russian note handed to the Polish and Lithuanian ambassadors in 1556 stated in addition to the Byzantine argument, along the lines of the two stories above, that besides the Russian land God gave Ivan IV the tsardoms of Kazan and Astrakhan, "and the throne of Kazan and Astrakhan has been a tsar's see from the origins." It may be added that a 17th-century Muscovite writer, Gregory Kotoshikhin, who was thoroughly familiar with his country's institutions and traditions, also considered the conquest of Kazan and Astrakhan the historical foundation of the Tsardom of Moscow.

An important aspect of the continuity of Mongol traditions in the Muscovite monarchy was the Mongol influence of the etiquette of diplomatic negotiations. Many a Western envoy to Muscovy complained of the stiff and ridiculous formalities of the diplomatic ritual. As a matter of fact, when we look back now on those mutual offenses and claims and counterclaims about etiquette by the Russian and Western diplomats of the 16th and 17th centuries, some of the notions of the Western envoys seem to us as absurd as the Muscovite. At the root of the misunderstandings lay the fact that Westerners and Russians followed different bodies of rules, and that the Russian ceremonial reflected the Mongol pattern in many respects.

The basic Muscovite concept of the duties of a government toward foreign ambassadors and of the rights of ambassadors with respect to the government in the country of their destination differed markedly from the Western concept. From the Mongol point of view—shared by the Muscovites—an ambassador was a guest of the ruler to whom he was accredited. That ruler had to provide him, and his suite, with free transportation, lodgings, food and drink, and to guard his safety. While the Westerners did not object to free lodgings and food, they protested on many occasions that Moscow's care for their safety amounted to keeping them constantly under guard. On the other hand, the Russian ambassadors who had to travel in the West were indignant when they had to pay—and sometimes exorbitantly—for their transportation and maintenance. In both Mongol and Muscovite diplomatic ceremonial much attention was paid to mutual gifts. Not only did the rulers exchange presents but ambassadors were expected to offer appropriate gifts to the ruler they visited. A Muscovite rule, patterned on Mongol etiquette, forbade any foreign envoy to be armed when received in audience by the tsar. Many a Western ambassador resented being required to part with his sword before entering the audience hall, but all had to comply with the rule. When the foreign envoy entered Russia he was met at the frontier by a special official (*pristav*). Muscovite (as well as Tatar) etiquette required that envoy and *pristav* dismount simultaneously to greet each other in the name of their respective sovereigns. Then the *pristav* rode at the right of the ambassador. For reasons hard to understand, the Westerners objected violently to these two rules and tried every possible device to circumvent them. Most, however, had to accept the inevitable.

The familiarity of the Muscovites with Mongol ways of diplomacy helped them greatly in their dealings with Oriental powers, especially with the succession states of the Golden Horde. In a sense Russia herself was such a succession state, and after the breakup of the Golden Horde the ruler of Russia seemed to be entitled to present his claims for leadership in the Mongol-Tatar sphere. Since as we have seen the so-called Golden Horde was actually known as the White Horde, the tsar of Moscow, as successor of the khans of this horde, was now called the "white tsar." As late as the 18th and 19th centuries the Russian emperor was still the white khan (*tsagan khan*) to the Kalmyks and the Buriats. The feeling among many Turkish and Mongol tribes that the Russian tsar was the successor of the Mongol khans created a favorable situation psychologically for the extension of the tsar's rule over those tribes. Moscow diplomats consciously or subconsciously took advantage of the situation. In this sense it may be said, as Prince Nicholas Trubetskoy did, that the Russians inherited their empire from Chingis-Khan.

XIII

The emancipation of East Russia from Mongol rule was the result of a combined effort of the Moscow grand dukes, the church, the boyars, the gentry, and the commoners—in fact of the whole nation. The new monarchy which was created in the tortuous process of emancipation was based on principles alien to the Russians of the Kievan period. All classes of East Russian society were now subordinated to the state. It might have been expected that once the goal of emancipation was achieved the Muscovite regime would relax and at least some of the old liberties would be restored. Actually, as we know, the opposite happened. Regimentation of the social classes progressed unchecked and reached its peak about 1650, two centuries after the end of the Mongol rule.

Why this seeming historical paradox? The answer is obvious: the precarious position of the Moscow monarchy on the international scene and the constant danger of war. In the southeast and south Muscovy was still threatened by the Tatars; in the west the struggle for power between Moscow and Lithuania (after 1569, between Moscow and Poland) continued to flare up at almost regular intervals; in the northwest, after having annexed Novgorod, the Moscow government had to take over the task previously performed by the Novgorodians, that of containing the pressure of the Livonian Knights and of Sweden in the area of the Gulf of Finland and Karelia. When Moscow defied the authority of the khan of the Golden Horde, there still remained several Tatar succession states, and the Tatars continued to raid the southern and eastern provinces of Muscovy almost yearly, looting and seizing thousands of captives. Thus the drain on Russian resources increased rather than decreased after the emancipation of the grand duke of Moscow from Mongol rule. There were no natural boundaries in the steppes between Muscovy and the Tatars, and the Moscow government had to keep the whole frontier constantly guarded. Both the Kasimov Tatars and the frontiersmen and Cossacks proved useful, but regular army troops had to be mobilized every year as well. An elaborate system of fortified defense lines was built up,

but on many occasions the Tatars would pierce them and pour into the country between and behind them. Under the circumstances, the only way to solve the problem seemed to be to establish firm Russian control of the steppes, by either conquest or diplomacy. From the geopolitical point of view, Ivan IV's dash down the Volga to Astrakhan was an important move since it cut the steppe zone into two sectors, each of which could now be taken care of separately. But that was only the beginning of Russia's bid for sovereignty over the peoples of the steppes. The process continued throughout the 17th and the 18th centuries, ending, in the south, with the annexation of the Crimea in 1783.

The struggle in the west, while not continual and not as exasperating as the process of containing the Tatars, was on the whole no less costly since it required, in the periods of acute crises, stronger and better-equipped armies and more expenditure for armament plants. The situation was certainly not propitious for any relaxation of governmental controls. On the contrary, new taxes were required and the taxation system was to be tightened rather than liberalized. The creation of the new army based on the *pomestie* system raised the problem of supplying agricultural labor to the *pomestia,* and this, as we have seen, led to serfdom. As a result of all this, the regimentation of the social classes which started during the Mongol period and was originally based on the Mongol principles of administration, was carried further and completed by the Muscovite government. Autocracy and serfdom were the price the Russian people had to pay for national survival.

16

THE FRONTIER   EXCERPTS

By B. H. Sumner

The late B. H. Sumner, once Warden of All Souls College at Oxford, agrees with Russia's greatest historian, Kliuchevsky, that colonization was perhaps the leading factor in the Russian historical experience. While he stresses the physical factors of Russian existence, he combines them skilfully with political and economic elements. There are some interesting comparisons with the frontier in America; for more information on this subject, see the article by Roger Dow, "Prostor: A Geopolitical Study of Russia and the United States," *Russian Review*, I, 3–17, and Donald Treadgold, "Russian Expansion in the Light of Turner's Study of the American Frontier," *Agricultural History*, XXVI, 147–52. For an interpretation of the military frontier see Valentine Bill, "The Circular Frontier of Muscovy," *Russian Review*, IX, 45–56. Robert Kerner's *The Urge to the Sea* describes Russian movements along the river routes. For the expansion eastward see Clifford Foust, "Russia's Expansion to the East through the 18th Century," *Journal of Economic History*, December 1961; George Lantzeff, "Russia's Eastward Expansion before the Mongol Conquest," *American Slavic and East European Review*, VI, 1–10; and George Lensen (ed.), *Russia's Eastward Expansion* (paperback). For a general treatment of the role of geography see Vasily Kliuchevsky, *A History of Russia*, Vol. I; Philip Moseley, "Aspects of Russian Expansion," *American Slavic and East European Review*, VII, 197–213; George Vernadsky, "The Expansion of Russia," *Transactions of the Connecticut Academy of Sciences*, XXXI, 391–425; and John Morrison, "Geographic Factors and Fancies in Russian and Soviet Expansion," in George Hoffman (ed.), *Recent Soviet Trends*. There are three historical atlases, all in paperback: George Goodall, *The Soviet Union in Maps*; Arthur Adams, *et al, An Atlas of Russian and East European History*; and Allen Chew, *An Atlas of Russian History*.

1. TYPES OF FRONTIER

The Soviet Union—four times the size of Europe, but with less than half its population; as large both in extent and numbers as the whole of the North American continent—is the outcome of revolution on an immense scale and in all spheres of life. Despite the break with the past and just because of the very extent of its success, the Soviet Union has inherited from the Russian empire two of its most pervasive features: it continues to be a land of many peoples and to be a land of colonization. Throughout Russian history one dominating theme has been the frontier; the theme of the struggle for the mastering of the natural resources of an untamed country, expanded into a continent by the ever-shifting movement of the Russian people and their conquest of and intermingling with other peoples. . . .

The lands that are included in the Russian S.F.S.R. are made up of the core of Muscovy, stretching from the Oka to the northern Dvina, welded into a state by about 1500, and of the Muscovite empire, the far-flung conquests made roughly between 1550 and 1650. (There are important later additions, such as St. Petersburg [1703], the North Caucasus steppes and the Caucasus Mountains [1760–1860], the Amur region and Vladivostok in the Far East [1860], but they are relatively small.) Muscovy in the century following 1550 had expanded gigantically to the east and south-east before the great advance westwards at the expense of Poland and Sweden, most of which was the work of Peter the Great and his successors. The Muscovite empire, the heir of Tatar khanates, was, to a large extent, an Asiatic state before its transformation into the Russian empire, turned towards the West. Thus, Smolensk, only two hundred miles west of Moscow, and Kiev were not finally won until 1667, by which time Kazan and Astrakhan had been Muscovite for over a century, and for some twenty years there had been a Muscovite post four thousand miles away on the Pacific. . . .

Consider first the linguistic or national frontiers, which have now been crystallized in the Soviet administrative boundaries marking off the different constituent republics and autonomous national areas, and which show only too clearly the Soviet inheritance of the multi-national Russian and Muscovite empires. In summary outline, it is the fringes that are compactly non-Russian: the Central Asian republics (except Kazakhstan, now half-Russian), the Transcaucasian republics (except the oil centre of Baku), and the new Baltic and Moldavian republics. White Russia, which is and always has been overwhelmingly White Russian, and the Ukraine, which is in majority Ukrainian, are different in that the two peoples are very closely allied to the Great Russians, with whom they form the eastern branch of the Slavs. Elsewhere, the numerous non-Russian peoples, mostly of Finnish or Tatar origins, in the course of the centuries have become absorbed or increasingly outnumbered, as the unresting sea of Russians has seeped in and around or flooded over them.

The linguistic map of the Russian S.F.S.R., outside its central core of the old Muscovy, is a mosaic, but one colour, the Russian, vastly predominates. The non-Russians, where they are compact, form islands or, for the most part, islets, and it is only in the Caucasus mountain regions and in the mixed forest and wooded steppe lands of the middle Volga–Kama–Urals that they are both numerous and contiguous to each other. Hence it took the Russians the first sixty years of the nineteenth century to reduce the Caucasian mountaineers—the equivalent of the North-West Frontier in India; and the great stretches of the middle Volga–Kama–Urals were the scene of two to three centuries of intermittent struggle between the Russian conquerors and colonists and Finnish-Tatar peoples, that was not closed until the last of the large-scale Bashkir risings in the revolt of Pugachov (1773–75). . . .

As with American so with Russian expansion, in the greater part of the north and Siberia the outer edge of the advancing wave was 'the meeting point of savagery and civilization,'[1] though this does not hold true to the same extent of the advance to the south. Russian like American development exhibits 'not merely an advance along a single line, but a return to primitive conditions on a continually advancing frontier . . . social development has been continually beginning over again on the frontier.' In both, the advance of the settlers' frontier was uneven, with tongues of settlement pushed forward and indentations in the wilderness, due to varieties of soil and forest, the course and character of rivers and lakes, the lie of portages and routes and very latterly railways, the presence of salt or minerals, the location of army posts or defence lines, and the varying powers of resistance of non-Russians or Indians. Above all, both the Russian and the American advance has been that of the agriculturist against the forest nomad and the plains nomad; the conquest of the grasslands for the first time by the plough, in North America during the last century at a ruinously rapid rate of soil exploitation, with erosion now a national problem of the first order, in Russia at a serious but less ruinous rate owing to the much slower tempo of her development and the comparatively small use of machinery on the land until the last dozen years.

Far away back, before the Russian agriculturist came the Russian hunter-fisherman-beeman. Fur, game, fish, honey, and wax provided essentials for clothing, food, and light, as well as the wherewithal for tax payments, rarities for the rich and the staples of early Russian exports. Hunter and trader were apt to be one and the same, and often

enough merged into river pirates or mounted buccaneers. Of necessity the hunting grounds of the little companies of trappers were fluctuating and indeterminate, in a vast land with so few inhabitants, in dependence on wild-life migrations and tales of what lay untapped farther afield. The hard struggle to make a living, cupidity, adventure, pride in skill with trap, net, and bow, with canoe and axe, later the organized plans of Novgorod merchant-adventurers and Volga princelings—combined to push the frontier ever onward to the east and north. To the south it was different. There the Tatar peoples of the steppes were strong, and the Russian frontiersman, as we shall see, was for long thrown back onto the defensive; but there eventually, in the sixteenth century, the most famous type of Russian hunter-frontiersman was thrown up, the Cossack.

The lumberman, specialized as such on any scale only within the last three centuries, fashioned a pioneer frontier of his own type. The miners' frontier is still more recent, hardly dating on a telling scale from before 1700, when Peter the Great created a largely new iron and copper industry, mainly in the Urals, and thrust out in more determined search for gold and silver in Siberia. The lure of gold produced its own variety of mining frontier with its own special history, but gold, even though Soviet development has made the Union the second largest producer in the world after South Africa, has played a less important role than the non-precious metals. From Peter onwards the state, directly or indirectly, planted mining colonies of serfs or deportees, who made Russia in the eighteenth century the largest European producer of iron ore, and who at one and the same time tamed the forest both to charcoal and to agriculture and drove another wedge into the life of the Bashkirs and Siberian tribes.

---

[1] This and the following quotation are from F. J. Turner, *The Frontier in American History.* Subsequent quotations, unless otherwise stated, are from sources contemporaneous with that to which they refer.

Iron in conjunction with coal produced an even greater colonizing effect when in the later nineteenth century the large-scale working of the Donets coal basin and the Krivoi Rog iron-ore region caused the influx of Ukrainian and Great Russian peasants into new mining villages and new industrial centres, the uprush of the great South Russian coal and heavy industry which has been so immensely extended during the last twenty years. Similarly elsewhere during the last seventy years workers of coal, iron, copper, lead, oil, and under the Soviet régime of much else, have repeated under new forms mining frontier conditions and have transformed the colonization map. The unrelenting pace of Soviet industrialization, above all in the Far North, the Urals, Kazakhstan, and the Kuznetsk basin of central Siberia, has revolutionized the miners' frontier, which together with its dependent industrial giants has become the great melting-pot of the Soviet peoples.[2]

2. FOREST AND STEPPE

Much the greater part of Russian history has been played out in five great zones, stretching from the south-west to the north-east, similar in their prevailing low elevation and, in certain respects, in climate, but differing widely in humidity, soil, and geological structure. Usually the zones overlap and shade into each other without clearly marked limits. Except for the first, they are not European and Asiatic zones, but both together; hence the recent term Eurasia as a geographical expression for the unity of the bulk of the Russian

empire or the Soviet Union, a conception harnessed and adapted by some contemporary historians.

(i) The zone of mixed forests, deciduous and conifer, spruce and Scots fir, larch, birch and aspen, oak and lime, ash and elm, but (in Russia proper) no beech or yew or holly; for the most part composed of the so-called podzol soils, grey sands and clays with a very low humus content, with much bog and lake; a zone roughly forming a great triangle, Lake Ladoga–Kazan–south of the Pripet marshes. This became the core of Muscovy.

(ii) The zone of conifer forests stretching to the north of (i) to the tundra, the Arctic version of the steppes, and to the east hundred mile after hundred mile more than one-third the way round the globe to the Pacific Ocean.

(iii) The wooded steppe or meadow-grass steppe zone, to the south of (i) and (ii), to the south of the line of the spruce; the debatable, savannah-like stretches between forest and true steppe, mostly with a variety of rich black-earth soils; until the eighteenth century far more wooded than now; the favourite setting of Turgenev's novels.[3]

(iv) The feather-grass steppe zone, waving ostrich-grey-plumed grasslands before the coming of the plough a hundred years ago; to the south of Kiev–Kharkov–Kuibyshev (Samara) the Trans-Siberian; again composed of black-earth soils; treeless save in the valleys or deep-cut ravines; the land of the tall 'embrace . . . of a green-yellow ocean, besprinkled with millions of spring flowers' (Gogol, *Taras Bulba*, 1834); like 'the green, ocean-like expanse of prairie, stretching swell beyond swell to the horizon' (Parkman, *The Oregon Trail*, 1846–47).

[2] Admirable illustrations of the Soviet mining frontier are provided by J. D. Littlepage and D. Bess, *In Search of Soviet Gold* (1939), the unvarnished account of the ten years' experience of an American mining engineer in Soviet Asia; and of the Soviet industrial frontier by John Scott, *Behind the Urals* (1943), an excellent firsthand account of the early years of Magnitogorsk.

[3] For instance his unmatched *Sketches of a Sportsman* (1852)—the title varies with each translation—one of the classic pictures of the Russian land and the Russian peasant.

(v) The wormwood steppe zone, narrow along the Black Sea, shading off eastwards into saline steppe and eventually sand or stone desert in Central Asia; the arid ranches and pampas of the chestnut and yellow-grey soils, which are still in the main what they have always been, the preserves of the pastoral nomad. . . .

(i) THE ZONE OF MIXED FORESTS

. . . Between 1000 and the Mongol conquest in the thirteenth century the most vital event in the history of the Russians, apart from their conversion to Christianity, was their settling of the lands between the Oka and the Volga, later to become the centre of Muscovy. This was achieved at the expense of Finnish tribes in occupation of them, who were gradually conquered and assimilated or driven farther afield, leaving the map still thickly studded with their river and other place names. It was accompanied also by continued struggle on the east with the Finnish Mordva and with the strongly organized Moslem Bulgars, centred around the junction of the Volga and the Kama. The southern advance into the steppe, as will be shown later, failed to be maintained against the nomad peoples, and the Mongol invasion of 1237–40 set the seal on the victory of the steppe. For the next two centuries the Russians, broadly speaking, were confined to the forest. . . .

In the ninth century, while the Norsemen were raiding and conquering in western Europe and the British Isles, their Swedish Viking kinsmen, the Varangians, penetrated the Baltic–Black Sea river routes and set themselves at the head of Kiev Russia, a loose bundle of the Russian districts, whose tribal organization was by then much decayed. Commerce, which grew and flourished until about 1200, contributed much to the rapid cultural and political rise of Kiev Russia. Apart from the long-distance transit trade, the Russians supplied furs and wax and honey, hides and tallow, and slaves; they received luxury goods and weapons, affecting directly only the top layer of society. The external contacts of Kiev Russia, particularly with the Byzantine empire, bringing Christianity, writing, and the arts, ultimately had the greatest consequences, but the flourishing trade and the brilliance of a few centres like Kiev did not alter the main basis of the great bulk of the population, agriculture and forest life.

The prevailing method of cultivation had been temporary cropping on the ash of burnt-over forest or scrub or on the more open spaces of wild grassland. The clearings, after a few years of continuous cropping, were either abandoned to revert to waste or kept as rough pasture until their productivity might be restored. Gradually the socketed axe replaced its less effective forebears. Gradually the plough-stick was superseded by the horsedrawn wooden 'hook' plough, which by about 1000 had become usual. It was eventually developed, by the sixteenth century, into the light wheelless wooden plough, with coulter, mould-board, and iron share, which with various modifications remained until this century the prevailing type of plough used by the peasantry throughout Russia outside the black-earth zone.

By the sixteenth century the scattered plots and rudimentary technique had given way on the estates of the big landowners to relatively more intensive cultivation on a two- or three-field basis, with some dunging and with nucleated villages; and after the Time of Troubles (1604–13) development was rapid into the open, three-field communal system, with scattered individual strips, typical of medieval western Europe and henceforward of Russia right down to the Revolution. Rye was the staple crop;

barley, oats, and some wheat were grown; but the grain supply of the mixed forest zone was uncertain. The north-west was always dependent on imports and, as the population grew, the whole of this zone, together with the northern pine forests, has been classed as the 'consuming provinces' for the last two hundred years.

Around Novgorod and in the upper Volga region flax and hemp were grown from very early times and became, together with the handicrafts based on them, increasingly important. From the eighteenth century they formed one of the chief items of Russian exports and developed into a large-scale modern industry. Stock-raising, for draught animals, hides, and tallow, was originally of more importance than in the recent centuries when Muscovy could draw on the steppes to the south. . . .

(ii) The Zone of Conifer Forests

Into the zone of the solid conifer forests, much sparser in any open land, poorer in soil, and yet more rigorous in climate, Russian colonization, ever since the eleventh century, thanks to the wealth of waterways thrust out long tentacles, developing from trading-tribute forays and reaching out to the White Sea, the northern Dvina, and even the Urals. The thinly settled Finnish and Lapp tribes offered what resistance they could, and in some cases it was stubborn, but, just as to the south, there was much assimilation, and it was only between the Volga and the upper Kama that some of these peoples lived on unrussified, in dwindling numbers. There was no marked dividing line between the northern forests and lakes and the more southerly region, but climatic and other natural conditions made agriculture entirely subsidiary, save along the upper courses of the Dvina River. The lure that beckoned the adventurer

groups and then the Novgorod bands, organized by rich merchant-landowners and led by tough, experienced boatmen-pioneers, was above all fur—sable, marten, fox; better and more numerous the farther north and east the 'companies' pressed; beaver, squirrel, otter, of much less worth, but invaluable for ordinary use (beaver still common right down to the seventeenth century all over Russia, north of the true steppes). Fishing, sealing, and whaling in 'the blue sea-ocean' drew men to stud the coast with little settlements, sending back to faraway Novgorod walrus ivory, blubber oil, and seal skins (admirable for the strongest ropes and thongs). These and, above all, fur, tar, pitch, and potash formed the staples of Novgorod's exports through the Hanse merchants to the western lands.

Along the White Sea shores and elsewhere salt made a new frontier. From the fifteenth century the industry expanded greatly, and there was a large export to the south. Thanks largely to salt two famous rival monasteries, Solovetsky (founded 1436) and Byelozero (founded 1397), developed into semi-governmental centres of industry and of defence against the Swedes, while in the north-east towards the Urals the Stroganov family emerged as the chief salt monopolists two generations and more before their 'conquest of Siberia' (1581). . . .

For the next two hundred years the North, from the Volga and Lake Ladoga to the White Sea, grew greatly in prosperity and importance and developed differently from the rest of Muscovy. The English discovery of the White Sea route to Muscovy, dating from Richard Chancellor's voyage in 1553, and the failure of Ivan the Terrible in the next twenty-five years to batter his way to the Baltic in the face of the Poles and the Swedes transformed the northern Dvina into the gateway of Muscovy.[4] English and Dutch merchants vied for the Muscovy and Persian trade, and the great route up the Dvina from Arkhangel (founded 1585) to Vologda and thence to Moscow became a main artery.

The customs books of the seventeenth century and the efflorescence of architecture in the northern towns bear vivid witness to their prosperity. For instance, the wealthy burghers of Yaroslavl, where the route to Moscow crossed the Volga, raised the most remarkable group of churches of the century in the Russian style; unique in their size, their elaborate brick and coloured-tile decoration, and the copiousness of their frescoes, which owed much to Dutch illustrations of the Bible and other Western influences.[5] It was not until Peter the Great succeeded where Ivan the Terrible had failed that the North declined: then St. Petersburg and Riga promptly killed Arkhangel and the North sank into neglect. . . .

When the Western nations were thrusting afield in the Americas and the Indies, the Russians spanned the continent of Asia with a rapidity—some fifty years—to rival even the Spaniards a century earlier; ever pressing on, 'to the east of the sun, to the passage of the great Tsar Alexander, to the most high mountain Karkaraur, where dwell the one-footed, one-armed folk.' The conquest of Siberia was the continuation of the Russian penetration of the unending northern forests east of the Urals, which

are no dividing barrier; and until the eighteenth century the Russians remained almost confined to the forest and tundra zones, except in the extreme west of Siberia where the black-earth wooded steppe thrusts up its most northerly wedge. . . .

In any case it was the forest not the steppe that the Russians wanted. Fur still was the magnet: the sable led them on and on, by the great river routes closely linked by portages—to Mangazeya (the Siberian variant of Potosi of 1600), to the Yenisei (1607), to the Lena (1632), to the extreme north-east and the Pacific itself (about 1640), where the reindeer and dog tribes as yet knew not the use of bronze or iron. The Russians met strong resistance only around Lake Baikal from the Buddhist Mongolian Buryats, and a definitive counterstop only in the Amur basin. There for the first time they came up against the organized solidity of civilized power, the Chinese empire under the new Manchu Ch'ing dynasty, and for the first time encountered rival firearms. In the Amur region there were twenty-five years of intrepid exploration and colonization by runaways and of intermittent ferocity and battling with Chinese forces. Then in 1689 the first treaty between Russia and China was concluded. The Amur was kept by China and the savagely inhospitable Stanovoi mountains remained the frontier for a hundred and seventy years. The boundary posts that were set up were to be inscribed in five languages—Chinese, Russian, Manchu, Mongol, and Latin: with the Chinese negotiators there had been a Jesuit Father. China not only halted Russia; she also gave her what is now a national drink: fifty years earlier (1638) the first tea via Siberia had reached Russia.

This astonishingly rapid conquest of the Asiatic forest lands was due to six main reasons:

---

[4] The English discovery of Russia (not only of the North) and relations with her are vividly portrayed in the accounts of mariners and agents of the Muscovy Company, printed in the Everyman edition of Hakluyt's *Voyages*, vols. 1 and 2 (especially Willoughby, Chancellor, Burrough, Jenkinson, Horsey, and Fletcher).

[5] There are excellent photographs of the mid- and late-seventeenth century churches of Yaroslavl and other northern centres in D. R. Buxton, *Russian Medieval Architecture* (1934).

(1) The Russians did not have to adapt themselves to any considerable extent to new physical or climatic conditions. Their own Russian North was substantially similar, and for centuries they had been adept at using water routes. (2) Their expeditions were only a few hundred strong, but they had greatly superior weapons and implements, particularly firearms, clumsy though they were. Various types of Cossacks, however unruly they often were, furnished an admirable spearhead of frontiersmen. (3) The peoples of northern Asia were few in numbers, for the most part dispersed in primitive, mutually hostile hunting tribes, and prepared to some extent to serve with the Russians against each other. (4) The inexhaustible demand for furs in Muscovy and in Europe put a premium on rapid expansion farther and farther eastwards in search of better skins and more plentiful supplies. (5) The Russian equivalents of the *coureurs des bois* of French Canada were possessed of indomitable hardihood, energy, and courage: love of gain was mated with spirit of adventure, endurance and resource with rapacity and cruelty. (6) Behind, and frequently at odds with, the independent frontier pioneers the Muscovite government plodded laboriously. Expansion east of the Yenisei was mainly a result of local initiative, but there followed eventually the armed support of the faraway central authority, the methodical securing of stockaded posts on the river routes, the planting down of an administration. . . .

To an even greater extent than in French Canada the fur trade dominated Siberia in the seventeenth century. Fur was an indispensable source of revenue and export for the Muscovite government. Hence its policy aimed at controlling tightly the trade through the fur tribute imposed upon non-Russians and through strict limitation of private trade.

The regulations were intricate and constantly varying. Evasion of them was equally constant. The natives hunted mainly with bows and arrows, the Russians with traps and nets. The effect of the Russian impact on the backward northern tribes was in general as disastrous as the American impact on Red Indian life. On the one hand Moscow was prolific in instructions 'not to drive them out of the Tsar's favour'; on the other hand there was a flood of other instructions, the gist of which was 'to take the fur tribute, according to the number of the people and their occupations, as much as possible.' There could be no shadow of doubt which profited most the authorities on the spot. One particular effect of the fur tribute system was that, since converts did not pay it, missionary activities by the Orthodox church were for long discountenanced in Siberia. The Orthodox Church was for the Russians.[6]

Much the greater part of the state fur revenue came from the annual tribute in furs from the natives, the *yasak*, a combination of Russian and previous Siberian practice. In addition the state levied a tax of a tenth on all furs acquired by Russian hunters or traders, and it also exercised rights of pre-emption. There was no state monopoly of the fur trade, as there was for instance of silk and caviare, until about 1700 attempts were made to make fur exports to China and other Asiatic countries a state monopoly. In the middle of the seventeenth century, when the fur trade was at its height, the private trade was nearly three times as large as the state fur revenue. This private trade in Siberia was wholly in the hands of Russians; for-

[6] The conditions of Russian missionary work in north-east Siberia in the nineteenth century are inimitably described in Leskov's deeply imaginative story *On the Edge of the World* (1876), translated (1922) in *The Sentry and Other Stories.*

eigners were rigidly debarred. Nevertheless, the regulations governing the *yasak*, the tax of a tenth, and pre-emption were all designed to secure the state first pick of the best furs, especially sables, and despite much corruption and smuggling the contribution of furs to the Muscovite revenue was very important, in the best years perhaps over ten per cent of the total revenue. This fur revenue, apart from other revenues from Siberia, seems from the scanty figures available to have brought in a large profit over and above the expense of administration. Probably about four-fifths of the Siberian furs were exported (in Europe mainly to Holland and the German lands from Arkhangel and Novgorod).

Already by 1700 both the absolute and the relative value of the fur trade had much declined, and the principal state fur interest became concentrated on the Chinese market. In Europe the competition of North American furs was telling heavily, and the heyday of Siberia as a fur El Dorado was past. Thus in the eighteenth century the fur trade lost its dominant position. West of the Yenisei the fur frontier had by then yielded place to that of the peasant settler and the miner. In 1700 there were probably considerably over 330,000 Russians in Siberia (compared with 250,000–300,000 Americans in the thirteen colonies). Half a century earlier an official estimate (1662), for what it is worth, had put them at 70,000. From the time of Peter the Great the state concentrated more on mining development, and organized exploration and exploitation of gold and silver were pushed ahead, though the Siberian gold rushes did not occur until the nineteenth century.

In 1767 private trade with the non-Russians was allowed without restrictions. Thereafter for the first time trading companies developed on western models, which concentrated on a new Pacific expansion of the fur and sealing frontier. Under a group of remarkable merchant-adventurers and sea-captains, the Russian-American Company, somewhat similar to the East India Company, spread a new brand of Russian imperialism across the Bering Strait into Alaska and down the North American coast. By 1820, with a Russian outpost almost as far south as San Francisco and with the Russians active in the Hawaii islands, it seemed almost possible that the North Pacific might become a Russian lake and North America be divided between the United States, Great Britain, and Russia. In the face of American and British pressure, however, the Russian government withdrew to Alaska, found this too costly, and eventually succeeded in selling it to the United States in 1867.

The Russians were too few on their icebound Pacific, and too far from it. Their true line of expansion lay in the rich and varied Amur basin, where they had been halted ever since 1689. Thanks to a masterful pro-consul, Muravyov-Amursky, and to the weakness of the Chinese government during 'the Taiping Rebellion,' Russia acquired in 1860 all the northern bank of the Amur and the coastline down to Vladivostok, a vast new frontier for the Cossack and peasant pioneer, the miner and the lumberman. Meanwhile Siberia proper had changed character. Her life no longer centred in the great northern forests, but was intertwined with the black-earth steppe lands to the south.

(iii) The Steppes

. . . The Russian challenge to the steppes, radiating out from Kiev, itself on the frontier of the mixed forest and the wooded steppe, was epitomized in the grand-prince Svyatoslav (died 972), 'stepping like a pard,' warring from the Danube and Constantinople to the Caspian and the middle Volga, scheming a

Slav variant of a Dnieper–Black Sea–Danube steppe dominion. For another century Russian expeditions sallied out from Kiev, usually with success, to clear the river route to Byzantium or eastward into the steppe. Thereafter they proved less and less successful against the latest Turkish newcomers in the Black Sea steppes, the Polovtsy.

Sustained conquest was never achieved by the Russians and settled colonization, with a few exceptions, fluctuated within a hundred and fifty miles or so east and south of Kiev. Relations with the Polovtsy and other nomads were frequently peaceable as well as hostile: there was some intermarriage, the taking in of broken nomad tribes as frontier guards, and much trade: as the Russians pushed on in the steppe, similar conditions bred something of a similar way of life. In the end, in face of the Mongol peril Russians and Polovtsy attempted combined resistance.

After 1125 the Russians were continually on the defensive: the great trade-route to Byzantium had become very dangerous and the result of the first crusade (1095–99) was to divert Byzantine commercial interest from the North. There were too few Russians on the steppe frontier; those to the north combined less and less with the exposed southern outposts. It is possible that at any rate the steppes west of the Dnieper might have been permanently mastered by the Russians but for the internal dissensions of the Russian principalities. The sacking of Kiev in 1169 by Andrew Bogolyubsky, prince of Vladimir, far to the north-east in the Oka-Volga Mesopotamia, in a sense symbolized the declining interest of the northern Slavs in the southern steppes. There was a grim nemesis seventy years later when Batu's war host reduced the Mesopotamia no less savagely than Kiev, and in fact three years earlier (1237–38).

The Mongol conquest meant that the Russians were forced into subjection and back into the zone of the mixed forests. For two centuries frontier settlement did not edge farther south than the hazardous fringes of the woodland steppe between the Oka and the headwaters of the Don. . . .

By about 1450, when the Ottomans were capturing Constantinople, the Horde had split up into the three rival khanates of Astrakhan, Kazan, and the Crimea, and a little later the Nogai horde, paramount in the open steppes east of the Volga, and the khanate of the Siberian Tatars to the east of the Urals. The accompanying dissensions enabled Ivan the Great to rid himself of tribute and any formality of dependency (1480). The stage was being set for the great Muscovite advance from the forest against the steppe, but the breakdown of the Golden Horde marked no diminution, on the contrary an increase, in the frequency of Tatar raids, especially from the side of Kazan.

The advance began down the Volga, not the Don, against the Kazan Tatars, who were relatively near and at the time a greater danger than the Crimean Tatars, far away to the south and difficult to strike at. Kazan itself was not finally captured until 1552 by Ivan the Terrible, when the khanate was annexed, after nearly a century of Muscovite efforts to reduce it, in part by war in part by establishing Tatar adherents as khans. The same inter-mixture of Russian and Tatar is exemplified in the policy begun in the mid-fifteenth century of granting lands to renegade Tatar princes and taking them into frontier service, a policy of assimilation which continued to be a main feature of Russian relations with Tatars and other eastern peoples.

The conquest of Kazan had been a long and costly undertaking, but it was followed by a rapid sweep right down the Volga to its mouth and the easy seizure of Astrakhan (1556). Henceforward the rich ribbon of the Volga trade-route was in Muscovite hands, a winding waterway through the steppes, but not in itself the master-key of the steppes. A challenge from the Ottoman empire, with its vassals the Crimean Tatars, for a moment (1569) endangered the new-won conquest and opened the vista of the Volga as another Danube. The challenge was not pressed; the Tatars and the Ottomans were at odds; Lepanto followed (1571), and the Crimean Tatars, though they raided and burnt Moscow in that same year, disputed the Don steppes rather than the Volga lands.

Muscovy set about holding the great trade-route by fortified frontier posts on its banks between Nizhni-Novgorod (Gorki) and Astrakhan, such as Samara (Kuibyshev), Saratov, and Tsaritsyn (Stalingrad). The Volga never bred an organized Cossack 'host' like that of the Don, but it remained until as late as 1800 a happy hunting ground and refuge for Cossack bands, river pirates, and a medley of vagrants from up river, combustible material that broke into raging flames in the revolts of Stenka Razin and Pugachov. Settled colonization was still more retarded by the habitual raids of the Nogai Tatars (a very loosely organized horde), of the much more tightly organized Buddhist Mongolian Kalmuks (nomad incomers of the early seventeenth century), and of the Moslem nomad Bashkirs of the middle Urals, who struggled against Russian subjection right down to the end of the eighteenth century. The lands of the khanate of the Kazan Tatars, the heirs of the Volga Bulgars, were equally composite, including various Tatar-Finnish peoples in the mixed forest and border steppes of the middle Volga. They also took long to subject fully or to assimilate, and their main river valleys were not solidly occupied by Russian colonists until about 1650.

Even a hundred and fifty years after the conquest the Russian stockaded defence lines that marked the limits of secure colonization had not pushed much farther south than about the latitude of Samara (Kuibyshev), and not so far south to the east of the Volga; roughly the southern limits of the wooded steppe. Beyond still lay 'the wild grounds.' Then from the second quarter of the eighteenth century there was adopted a sustained policy of reducing to 'hereditary fear' the Bashkirs (themselves by now in part succumbing to settled life) and of developing new mines and metal works in the Urals and new defence lines which separated the Bashkirs from the Kazakhs and the Central Asian steppes. The disaster of the revolt of Pugachov (1773–75), which set alight the Urals and all the Volga below Nizhni-Novgorod (Gorki), proved only temporary. From the end of the century the rich black-earth steppes between the Volga and the Urals became opened for good to the agriculturist, in the shape of the serf-owning landowner.[7]

Farther to the south, below Saratov, in the arid chestnut-soil steppe merging into the saline and semi-desert stretches of the lower Volga, agricultural colonization could make little headway without developed dry farming or irrigation. The most successful settlers here were German peasants, first tempted with special privileges by Catherine the Great; a solid block of over 400,000 at their maximum in 1914, who remained distinctively German though with few connexions (at any rate until the last twenty years) either with Germany or with the leading German group in Russia, the Baltic German landowners. The First World War threatened them with whole-

[7] A vivid picture of colonization in this region is given in Sergei Aksakov's *The Family Chronicle* (paperback), one of the classics of Russian prose.

sale expulsion to the East. The Second World War has seen the threat actually put into operation and the end of the Soviet autonomous republic of the Volga Germans a year before the great battle for Stalingrad close by.

To the west of the Volga, in the Don and lower Dnieper basins, there was the same dominant feature, the struggle against the way of life of the nomads, in this case primarily the Crimean Tatars. But here, in contrast, Muscovy was in competition with a Western organized state, Poland, and with the power of the Ottoman empire, of which the Crimea was from 1475 a tributary dependency. Here again in contrast there was no rich trade-route like the Volga to be seized at a leap by the Muscovite government. Leap there was, but it was due to the free Cossacks speeding down the Don and establishing their centre about 1600 along its lower reaches in semi-independence of Moscow. At the same time social conditions in Poland fomented a similar outflow of Ukrainian hunting pioneers into 'the wild grounds,' who formed themselves into the Zaporozhian ('beyond the cataracts') Cossack 'host' on the lower Dnieper, very similar to that of the Don Cossacks, and an even pricklier thorn in the flesh of all who came in their path.

The Crimean khanate was a well-organized state of pastoral Tatars, based on the very mixed Crimea, where there was agriculture and handicrafts and much commerce. Their numbers have been much exaggerated, and it is improbable that in the seventeenth century at any rate the khan could put into the field more than 30,000 horsemen at the utmost, a number that was later much reduced. The Tatars made up for their lack of numbers by their mobility and tactics, in which they were at a great advantage in that they aimed not at the defeat of the enemy (they evaded battle if they could), but at the capture of booty—slaves and stock.

Four times within seventy years (1521–91), riding up their three main trails crouched 'like monkeys on greyhounds,' they raided north of the Oka into the heart of Muscovy and in 1571 they burnt Moscow itself. After 1591 they never succeeded in crossing the Oka, and gradually their raids penetrated less and less far northwards. The big musters headed by the khan in person became rare. The habitual danger was the swoop of small bands a few hundred strong, 'running about the list of the border as wild geese flie, invading and retiring where they see advantage.' As late as 1676–79 the constable of Orel received one hundred and seven messages as to such 'short and sudden rodes.' Still, under Peter the Great, there were raids into the Kharkov region almost every year between 1710 and 1718, one of which years was reported to yield the Tatars over 14,000 prisoners, a suspiciously high figure.

The reasons why the Crimean Tatars for some three centuries proved such difficult foes for Russians and Poles alike were their military specialization, distance, the fact that behind them lay the power of the Turks, and the fact that they acted now in conjunction with the Russians, now with the Poles, now with the Zaporozhian Cossacks against the other. The Russian military equipment only became superior to that of the Tatars as their firearms increased in quantity and improved in quality, and even so this superiority was usually of avail only in the timbered country or in holding forts and redoubts, not in the open treeless steppe; just as the American cattle-ranchers in the Great Plains had little advantage over the horse Indians until the coming of the six-shooter.

The Crimea itself was six hundred and fifty miles direct from the Oka, and far more in actual riding miles. The last three hundred were across the feather-grass and wormwood steppes, in which water and provisioning were acute difficulties. The Poles never attempted to strike at the heart. The Russians in the mid-sixteenth century were inclined to follow up their capture of Kazan and Astrakhan by a mortal blow at the Crimea, but Ivan the Terrible decided that the distances were too great and turned to the Baltic.

The Russians did not pass from the defensive to the offensive until the frontier was far down on the edge of the wooded steppe. Even then (1687, 1689) they signally failed to cope with the supply problem in the great stretches of open steppe between the Donets and the Crimea. Fifty years later (1736–38) they were successful in reaching the stronghold of the Tatars, who could put up little resistance beyond 'scorched earth' tactics and suffered fatal damage, even though the Russian commander lost half his army through sickness. The successes in Catherine the Great's first Turkish war (1768–74) sealed the fate of the khanate. It was a prey to internal dissension and in 1783 the Crimea yielded itself to Russian rule.

The advance to the Black Sea, unlike that to the Caspian, had been slow, but it was sure, for it was based on a continual process of settled colonization at the expense of the seasonal rhythm of pastoral nomadism. From about 1500 the northern fringes of the wooded steppe belt were a debatable ground between Tatar bands and Russian frontiersmen pushing southwards, followed slowly by the plough, into the virgin black-earth lands that were acting as a magnet to the peasants of central Muscovy, more and more hard pressed by landowners and the state. But, unless they went Cossack, they could not escape from the state and they needed its protection.

In the course of the sixteenth century the Muscovite government built up an elaborate, fourfold defence system, initially intended to prevent the Tatars crossing the Oka, but additionally providing security for colonization. The system included the founding of fortified garrison centres settled by the government with military colonists, and in the last twenty years of the century there was rapid progress in consolidating the frontier. The advance of settlements was along the tributaries of the Don or Oka, then navigable for small boats, in the wooded valleys which provided the essential timber and better means of defence than the swelling open country. During the next twenty years (1600–1620), owing to the Time of Troubles, the frontier 'went Cossack' and there was chaos. It was only after 1633 that the defence system was thoroughly reorganized and the planned advance resumed, marked by the founding of more garrison centres and the construction of the Byelgorod defence line roughly along the northern limits of the present Ukraine and thence north-eastwards to Voronezh, Tambov, and the Volga at Simbirsk. . . .

Into the Muscovite frontier a new element swelled to a great scale after 1650 when the Ukrainians rose against the Poles and turned to Moscow. The bulk of the original Ukrainian immigrants formed five regiments, which took up land in the middle Donets region, founded and garrisoned Kharkov and other towns with a new defence line in advance. They enjoyed special privileges, including the much-prized right of free brewing and distilling, and until far into the eighteenth century were allowed comparative autonomy in their Slobodskaya Ukraine, free Ukraine, joining on to the west with their compatriots in the Little Russian provinces, the so-called Left-bank Ukraine (i.e., on the left bank of the Dnieper), which the Poles were forced to admit as part of Muscovy in 1667. Behind the soldier-settlers came other non-military farmers, traders, and artisans, mostly families of some means. Ukrainian colonization was much less dependent on the state than Great Russian. To the northward of Kharkov, Ukrainians and Great Russians for long kept apart, but from the late eighteenth century they merged together. To the south it was different; the solid Ukrainian colonization maintained itself and spread over the open steppe; Great Russian penetration on a large scale took place only with the industrial and mining development of the last sixty years.

The Ukrainian line of the seventeen-thirties, from the Donets to the Dnieper on the borderland of the wooded and the feather-grass steppes, was the last of the big fortified lines. By then Slobodskaya Ukraine had not far short of 400,000 inhabitants: its military character as a frontier region was all-pervading. To the north frontier conditions were largely a relic of the past; the lesser 'men of service' had become state peasants and were being swamped by the gentry moving south with their serfs and the three-course open fields in strips. Forty years later (1774) the Russians were down to the Black Sea and controlled the mouths of the Dnieper, the Don, and the Kuban. The Zaporozhian Cossacks were broken up and transplanted (1775), the Crimea passed into Russian hands (1783), and the Turks for the third time within fifty years were soundly beaten (1787–92) and yielded the coastal steppes between the Dnieper and the Dniester.

The frontier was now the open Black Sea steppes, New Russia. Behind, the fertile zone of the black-earth wooded steppe, with its woods by then much depleted, developed into the land *par excellence* of serfdom and grain cultivation, where Great Russian landowners acquired vast estates, Ukrainian officers followed their example and transformed themselves into serf-owning gentry, and Polish landlords retained their position and their serfs when the Right-bank Ukraine (i.e., on the right bank of the Dnieper) came under Russia by the second partition of Poland (1793). . . .

By the middle of the nineteenth century New Russia had grown to 2,250,000, by 1900 to well over 6,000,000 (if Bessarabia and the Don are included, the numbers would be nearly doubled). Wheat-growing had largely replaced stock-raising, based on a variegated extensive system of cultivation, not on the three-field system. The density of the rural population was still sparse, two to three times less than the crowded black-earth lands of the old Ukraine, but already in 1900 it was fifty per cent greater than the density of the whole of Iowa, cities included, in 1920; and Iowa is comparable in many respects in climate and soil conditions. By 1900 half the land was held in individual ownership, mostly by the gentry in great estates, and only forty per cent in communes. By then, too, the coal of the Donets basin and the iron ore of Krivoi Rog had begun industrialization, and wheat was somewhat less dominant. Thus New Russia, the land of the open steppes, differed considerably from the wooded steppe zone to the north, almost solely given over to agriculture, serfdom, and the commune, solidly Great Russian or Ukrainian.

3. TYPES OF COLONIZATION

During the past ten centuries of Russian expansion there has been a constant tug or struggle between the compulsory and the voluntary elements, between the authorities—at times damming back, at times forcing forward—and the individual and the family—at times determinedly on the move, at times reluctantly conscripted. For long a certain degree of mobility, as has been noticed earlier, was encouraged or ne-

cessitated by the nature of forest economy and by the prevailing agricultural
technique. In the early centuries the evidence is insufficient to decide whether
compulsion by the princes and their chief
retainers and by merchant-adventurers
or the voluntary cooperation of freemen
played the bigger role in colonization;
but it is undoubted that the special advantages, economic and military, that
the former offered were essential factors
in the settling of what became the core
of Muscovy.

For the two centuries after 1350 the
monasteries played an important part
as centres of new settlement, especially
to the north of the Volga, but thereafter they were not, except in the middle
Volga, conspicuous. Missionary activity
in advance of occupation or conquest
was a rare exception, and later there
was nothing corresponding to the colonizing work of the churches, for instance in New Zealand. . . .

The most striking type of free colonization, dependent on a combination
of individual initiative and group spirit,
was the Cossacks, whose history, in
particular that of the Don Cossacks, supplies an admirable sample of the Russian conquest of the steppe and of the
gradual extension of state power at the
expense of local autonomy in accordance with the transformation of the
structure of frontier society.

The original Cossack was a 'vagrant'
whether from Muscovy or the Polish
Ukraine, a steppe frontiersman; bee
hunter, beaver hunter, game hunter,
fisherman, pastoralist; half-going Tatar; pushing farther and farther afield
in the sixteenth century. He might develop into a rancher; he might take
service as scout and light horseman
(the original meaning of the Tatar word
kazak); he might turn bandit-freeboot-
er: usually he combined by turns all
these occupations. The Cossacks were a
liberty-loving and equalitarian but un-

ruly and marauding element, and they
played an anarchic and destructive role
in the Time of Troubles (1604–13). In
1600, in complete contrast with 1900,
they represented to some extent the
challenge of social revolution by the
underdog and the untamed.

On the frontier, however, as free-
booter rivals to the nomads they might
be a great asset, as Muscovy, though not
Poland, found. By 1600 the boldest
spirits had gone down river far away
south into the feather-grass steppe and
had organized themselves in three separate Cossack 'hosts,' on the middle and
lower Don, the middle Ural River, and
the lower Dnieper where the Zaporozhian ('beyond the cataracts') Cossacks
played a somewhat similar role for the
Ukrainians under Poland as the other
Cossacks did for the Great Russians under Muscovy.[8] All three 'hosts' were
stoutly Orthodox, a fact of special importance in the struggle of the Ukrainian Cossacks against Poland.

Apart from these three spontaneous,
independent 'hosts,' Cossacks were used
by the government for courier and other
military services, and in the eighteenth
century the state formed, more or less
on the model of the original 'hosts,'
Cossack defence forces to guard and
settle the frontier, in the North Caucasus, the southern Urals, Siberia, and
latest of all in the Far East. They enjoyed special privileges, but unlike the
Don, Ural, and. Zaporozhian Cossacks
they were founded and always controlled by the ministry of war.

The Don Cossacks, recruited mainly
from Great Russians, maintained themselves for a hundred years, until 1671,
in semi-independence of Moscow as a

---

[8] Gogol's prose epic *Taras Bulba* (1834;
translated in various editions) on the Zaporozhian Cossacks in the seventeenth century,
for all its romantic idealization, gives the feel
of the steppe and the fighting spirit of the Cossacks with compelling power.

'host,' organized on a military basis, but democratically governed by an assembly and elected officers, with full control of admission into their ranks. For this first hundred years they were very nominal subjects of 'the White Tsar.' They paid no taxes and had free trading rights. 'We fight,' they declared, 'for the House of the Immaculate Virgin and the Miracle Workers of Moscow and for thee . . . Sovereign Tsar and Grand Prince of Great and Little and White Russia, Autocrat and Sovereign and Possessor of many Hordes.' In fact, like any other of his hordes they fought, pillaged, and negotiated when and as they pleased, particularly with the Crimean Tatars and the Turks holding the Don delta with their stone fortress of Azov. They then mustered probably about 10,000 fighting Cossacks; equally formidable as river or sea corsairs and as land buccaneers. For long they despised the plough as the badge of bondage. Boasting 'we serve for grass and water, not for land and estates,' they lived by fishing, stock-breeding, trading, and hunting, above all for slaves and booty, raiding far afield in 'the wild grounds,' along the paynim shores of the Black Sea, or, as they sang, 'like young falcons . . . on Mother Volga . . . on the blue sea, the blue sea, on the Caspian.'

But they depended as well on the annual grant made by Moscow, flour, munitions, and cloth. This was their Achilles' heel. The distribution of the grant was made by the Cossacks themselves, but the amount was fixed by Moscow, and it paid the 'host' to keep itself small. Yet they were too few to oust the Turks from Azov, save for a brief spell, and they needed the succour of Muscovy. A democratic oligarchy began to harden; then an inner ring of the senior officers grew well-off; outside, the floating, unprivileged semi-Cossack

fringe increased as more and more runaways from the North trekked down; for the Don clung to its tradition of being an asylum for all and sundry.

The divorce between the richer, old established Cossack families of the lower Don and the needy newcomers showed itself to be acute when the former stood against the two leaders of revolt, Stenka Razin and Bulavin (1670–71 and 1707–8). Moscow suppressed the risings with some assistance from the Cossack oligarchy. Henceforward (1671) the Don Cossacks were bound to the tsar by oath of allegiance. The right of asylum was more and more effectively challenged by the government. The southward surge of colonization from Muscovy made it possible to deprive the 'host' of its middle Don lands (1708), and Peter the Great went a long step further in state control by abolishing the free election of the commander (ataman) of the 'host' and directly appointing him himself (1723).

Henceforward the atamans, holding office for long periods but failing to become hereditary, worked in closer and closer accord with St. Petersburg, and so did the senior officers, themselves after 1754 no longer elected but appointed by the war ministry. Together they formed a governing oligarchy and the old assembly of the 'host' counted for little. The privileges and more especially the duties of the Cossacks became more closely defined: they figured regularly in the Russian campaigns of the eighteenth century and began to be used as an internal police force. Agriculture had spread now that there was a plentiful supply of non-Cossack labour. By the end of the century the officer class had become large landowners and they succeeded in securing admission into the 'estate' of the gentry, with the consequent legal right to own serfs. The frontier by now had moved south to the

Kuban and the North Caucasus steppes.[9]

For the next hundred years the Don Territory formed 'a province governed by special institutions,' but in law and administration more and more assimilated to the rest of Russia. It grew greatly in population and wealth. By 1914 the Don Cossacks supplied nearly 150,-000 cavalrymen, but as a whole they formed by then well under half the total population of about 4,000,000, though they owned three-fifths of the land. Divided amongst themselves, they stood over against the great mass of incomers, ex-serfs, independent farmers, labourers, and coal-miners. Rostov, founded in 1761, which was non-Cossack, had grown to be a city of over a hundred thousand and the greatest centre of the south-east.

Thus two centuries of colonization had transformed the frontier and radically changed the structure of Cossack society. The Cossacks had always differentiated sharply between themselves and Russians: while continuing to cherish the forms of their traditional customs and privileges, they developed a new tradition of loyalty to the tsar, not only as against his enemies abroad, but as well against his enemies at home. The watchwords of one of their songs in the 1905 Revolution summed up the attitude of the Cossack right wing: 'We don't need a constitution. We don't want a republic. We won't betray Russia. We will defend the Tsar's throne.' And so they did. But many of the poorer Cossacks and the non-Cossack people on the Don swung to the left. Divisions were deep, and in 1918 when it came to civil war the Don did not prove a reliable

bastion for the White armies.[10] Death, emigration, and deportation thinned the Cossack ranks; the victory of the Bolsheviks, and later collectivization, spelt disaster for many of them. Then in 1936 the Kremlin altered course, formed special Cossack contingents in the Red Army, and harnessed the old fighting traditions of the Cossacks to the new Soviet patriotism, with results that the German army has only too bloody reason to know.

There remains to consider one last sample of colonization and of the interplay of the compulsory and the voluntary, of the state and the individual or independent group, as seen in ' the modern development of Siberia. . . .

Peter the Great, in search of minerals and trade-routes to Central Asia, had pushed out the frontier and established new chains of Cossack posts to check nomad pillaging. His successors continued his work, particularly in the extreme west of Siberia, well-watered and with good black-earth soils, but settlement was for long slow and sparse, a mixture of serfs ascribed to mines, Cossacks, 'men of service' settled by the state, particularly for transport duties, and independent peasants and runaways, many of them sectarians fleeing from religious persecution. Siberia never knew the gentry and bonded serfdom to any extent, but the commune, passing from cooperative clearing of the land through various stages of development, was general. Legally the land was in the first place state or imperial land: in fact most of the settlers simply worked as much land as they needed with nothing but first occupancy as their title, until with increasing pressure on the natural resources the commune

[9] Life on this frontier a generation later is brilliantly illustrated in parts of Lermontov's classic *A Hero of Our Times* (1840) and graphically described in Tolstoy's equally autobiographical novel of the Terek line *The Cossacks* (1862) (various translations of both).

[10] Sholokhov in his well-known novel *Quiet Flows the Don* (1929) has painted on an immense canvas the Don during the 1914 war and the first years of the Revolution.

gradually evolved various types of periodical redistribution and other forms of economic control over the freedom of action of individual families. Right down to the end of the nineteenth century surveyed land grants remained the exception.

Almost throughout that century the official policy was to discourage or prevent movement into Siberia, except for one period of enlightened state-aided migration of state peasants. Ascription to the mines continued to be a regular feature, and a series of gold rushes, very nominally controlled by the government, brought new developments. For the first time now deportation bulked large in Siberia. Between 1823 and 1881 nearly 700,000 persons were exiled or deported across the Urals, to hard labour mostly in mines or on construction work, to prison camps, disciplinary battalions, or mere police supervision.[11] Apart from the criminal element, the very numerous political exiles, such as the Decembrists and the Poles, contributed innovations in agriculture and industry, as well as to science and education. The share of the deportees in the making of Siberia has, however, usually been exaggerated. It was considerable only east of the Yenisei, and on the whole the importance of deportation was probably less than in the early history of Australia. A very large number returned to Russia after serving their time, and those that stayed were generally looked askance at by the born Siberians.

What really made modern Siberia was the unappeasable land hunger of the Russian peasantry and the coming of the railway. The flow of settlers, largely

in defiance of government regulations, at times dwindled to a trickle, but in the eighteen-eighties it swelled mightily and the old methods of attempted governmental restriction were palpably breaking down. The great famine of 1891 and the building of the Trans-Siberian, begun in that same year, caused a gigantic outpouring. The railway, like the Canadian Pacific built a decade earlier, turned a stream into a torrent. Despite ebbs and flows, despite the Russo-Japanese war, the population of Siberia and the Far East doubled within twenty years. In 1800 there had been rather over a million people; the 1897 census gave five and three-quarter millions; by 1914 there were over ten millions, nearly half as many again as in Canada, and Siberian cooperatives were competing successfully on the English butter market. This very rapid expansion was mainly confined to Siberia proper, i.e., between Lake Baikal and the Urals. Eastwards of Lake Baikal the stream of colonists—whether by land or by sea half round the globe from the Black Sea ports—ran much lower, despite the inducements of the government. Meanwhile, here in the Far East, Chinese migration on a scale even larger than that into Siberia was transforming Manchuria, the battle ground of Russian and Japanese imperialism.

The Trans-Siberian and the mass movement east forced the government to change its policy. A special colonization department was set up (1896) which attempted to organize migration and settlement. Regulations were poured forth on surveying, cheap transport rates, tax and other exemptions, grants in money and kind, and loans. Nevertheless, perhaps half of the incomers came on their own, weary or suspicious of the delays and complexities of bureaucracy. They came mostly from the overcrowded northern and central black-

[11] Dostoevsky has written unforgettable descriptions of his Siberian prison life in *The House of the Dead* (1857). *The Letters of Lenin* (translated and edited by E. Hill and D. Mudi, 1937) give a good picture of what in fact exile to a village in eastern Siberia (not imprisonment) meant.

earth lands; usually in large groups, not too badly off; preceded by 'locators' to discover suitable sites. Some settled in the old Siberian villages; most in new. By 1914 the best and most accessible land was taken up, and the Russian peasant-farmer was already pressing ominously on the grazing grounds of the Kazakhs, since transformed by their 1916 rebellion and the effects of the Soviet Revolution. . . .

Soviet Siberia, unlike the new Siberia of 1890–1917, has grown above all through the new or vastly expanded mining and industrial frontiers born of the five-year plans. The uprush of towns on an ultra-American scale has been the dominant feature, both in Siberia proper and in the Far East. Magnitogorsk, Novosibirsk, Stalinsk, Komsomolsk, previously non-existent or diminutive, are known now the world over. Agricultural development has been far less striking, save recently in the open steppe. Even more than before 1914 Siberia is mixed in composition, though as before predominantly Russian. Deportations on a very large scale and the insatiable demand for hands have dragged and drawn men and women from all parts of the Union. Soviet Siberia—still sprawling, wasteful and erratic, brutal and unsparing—has attracted as never before the energies and imagination of Soviet youth.

17

THE PROBLEM OF OLD RUSSIAN CULTURE

By Georges Florovsky; Nikolay Andreyev; James Billington

The three contributions which follow are a sample of the debate on the chief cultural problems of the pre-Petrine period we have been examining in this volume. Professor Florovsky taught Eastern Church history at the Harvard Divinity School and is now at Princeton University. Mr. Andreyev is lecturer in Slavonic studies at Cambridge University. Mr. Billington is professor of Russian history at Princeton.

A Soviet comment on the pieces below is Dmitry Likhachev, "Further Remarks on the Problem of Old Russian Culture," *Slavic Review*, March, 1963. Large-scale interpretations of early Russian culture are available in Wladimir Weidle, *Russia Absent and Present* (paperback); Arthur Voyce, *Moscow and the Roots of Russian Culture*; James Billington, *The Icon and the Axe*; as well as George Fedotov, "The Religious Background of Russian Culture," *Church History*, Vol. XII. On the large subject of Byzantium and Russia see Dimitry Obolensky, "Russia's Byzantine Heritage," *Oxford Slavonic Papers*, Vol. I. The church relationship is discussed in *Moscow and East Rome* by William Medlin. See also Francis Dvornik, "Byzantine Influence in Russia," in *The Root of Europe*, edited by M. Huxley. The Soviet point of view on the subject is analyzed in a chapter on "Byzantine Cultural Influences," in Cyril Black's *Rewriting Russian History* (paperback).

As for the individual topics mentioned below several studies might be suggested. An analysis of the Russian pagan heritage will be found in George Vernadsky's *Origins of Russia*, pp. 108–73. For folklore see Yuri Sokolov's *Russian Folklore*. Kievan Russia's urban tradition is described in the Soviet work *The Towns of Ancient Rus* by Mikhail Tikhomirov. There is a comprehensive study of *The Art and Architecture of Russia* by George Hamilton. Victor Lasareff, a prominent Soviet art historian, writes on *Russian Icons from the Twelfth to the Fifteenth Century* (paperback). Anatole Mazour, "Curtains in the Past," *Journal of Modern History*, Vol. XX, is a study of Muscovite self-isolation in the seventeenth century.

Old Russia stood in a very definite cultural succession. She was in no sense isolated in the cultural world. She entered the commonwealth of civilized nations when she was christened by the Byzantines. She received then, together with the Christian faith, an impressive cultural dowry—a complex of cultural

Abridged from the *Slavic Review*, XX, 1–42, by permission of the editor. Footnotes have been omitted.

values, habits, and concerns. The Byzantine inheritance of ancient Kiev was conspicuous. The city itself was an important cultural center, a rival of Constantinople, an adornment of the empire. It was not the only center: Novgorod in any case must be mentioned. The literary production of the Kievan period was intense and diverse. Russian art was also taking shape. Behind the documents of the time we cannot fail to discern cultural activity, cultural forces. We discern groups and individuals eagerly committed to various cultural tasks. The movement of ideas has already begun.

The Kievan achievement must be regarded in a wider perspective. It was an integral part of the incipient Slavic culture. V. Jagić once suggested that in the tenth century there was a chance that Slavic civilization might have developed as a third cultural power, competing with the Latin and the Greek. The Bulgarian literature of the Simeonic age was already so rich and comprehensive as to stand comparison with the Byzantine. Indeed, it was the same Byzantine literature, but already indigenized. This cultural promise was curtailed and frustrated. The great cultural impetus was checked. Yet the promise was real, and the actual achievement was by no means negligible. Of course, this incipient Slavic civilization was deeply rooted in the Byzantine tradition, just as Western culture was rooted in the traditions of the classical world. But it was more than a repetition or an imitation. It was an indigenous response to the cultural challenge. And it was mainly from Bulgaria that a rich supply of literary monuments was transferred to Kiev and other centers. Cultural taste and skill were formed. Cultural interests were aroused. Kievan Russia was not isolated from the rest of the Slavic world, as it was not separated from

Byzantium and the West, or from the East. Kievan Russia was able to respond conscientiously to the cultural challenge. The ground was already prepared.

At this point certain doubts may be reasonably raised. First of all, the promise was actually frustrated, even if the measure of this frustration and lack of success should not be exaggerated. Was this due only to adverse conditions—the Germano-Latin pressure on the Western Slavs, the defeat of Bulgaria by the Greeks, the Mongolian conquest of Russia? Or was there an inherent weakness, a constitutional disease, that arrested the development both in Old Russia and in the Balkans? The adversity of external conditions was bound to have at least a psychological impact on the whole cultural situation, but further questions may be asked, and indeed have been asked, by modern scholars. Was the Byzantine inheritance a healthy one? Was the task undertaken by the Slavs sound and reasonable? Was their attempt to create a new national culture a sound enterprise? Or was it doomed to failure by its inner inconsistency? The questions were sharply put, and answers were often negative.

It was inevitable that in the beginning the cultural elite should have been small, and the outreach of its activity rather limited. It was development at a normal pace. But was the Byzantine civilization really "received" in Old Russia? Golubinsky, for one, bluntly denied the fact. St. Vladimir wanted to transplant culture to his land, but his effort failed completely. Culture was brought in and offered but not taken, and, as Golubinsky added, "almost immediately after its introduction it disappeared without leaving any trace." Until Peter's time there was no civilization in Russia. There was no more than plain literacy, that is, the skill to read and to copy texts. Literacy, not literature, was the upper limit of Old Russia, according to Golubinsky. "Literacy, not culture—in these words is summarized all our history for the vast period from Vladimir to Peter the Great." Before Peter, Russians were, on the whole, quite indifferent to culture and enlightenment—*prosveshchenie* was Golubinsky's own term. Those few contradictory instances which he had to acknowledge, Golubinsky would hastily dismiss as incomprehensible riddles. No contemporary historian would dare to endorse these sweeping generalizations of Golubinsky. But under some other guise they are still repeated. It must be noted that Golubinsky in no sense held the Greeks responsible for the Slavic failure. He never contested the value of Byzantine civilization. He only felt that probably the Byzantine offered too much at once, and also expected too much from the newly baptized nations. The fault was with the Russians themselves. Some others, however, would shift the blame to Byzantium. According to Jagić, the greatest misfortune of the Slavs was that they had to be reared in the school of senility: a young and vigorous nation was to be brought up on the decrepit culture of a moribund world that had already lost its vitality and creative power. Jagić was quite enthusiastic about the work of the Slavic Apostles. He had only praise for their endeavor to stimulate indigenous culture among the Slavs. But he had no appreciation for Byzantine civilization. This attitude was typical of his generation, and also of the next. The failure was then inevitable: one cannot build on a rotten foundation. There was no genuine vitality in the Old Slavic civilization, because there no longer was living water in the Byzantine springs. Seemingly there was a promise, but actually there was no hope.

The charge has been repeated recently in a new form. Quite recently the late Professor George Fedotov suggested that the cause of Old Russian backwardness, and indeed the tragedy of Russian culture at large, was precisely the attempt at indigenization. He had serious doubts about the benefits of the use of the Slavic vernacular. Having received the Bible and a vast amount of various religious writings in their own language, the Slavs had no incentive to learn Greek, for translations once made were sufficient for immediate practical needs. They were enclosed, therefore, within the narrow limits of an exclusively religious literature. They were never initiated into the great classical tradition of Hellenic antiquity. If only our ancestors had learned Greek, speculated Professor Fedotov, they could have read Homer, could have philosophized with Plato, could have reached finally the very springs of Greek inspiration. They would have possessed a golden key to classical treasures. But this never happened. Instead they received but *one* Book. While in Paris, a poor and dirty city as it was in the twelfth century, the Schoolmen were already discussing high matters, in the golden and beautiful Kiev there were but monks engaged in writing chronicles and lives of saints. In other words, the weakness and backwardness of Old Russia depended upon that narrow foundation, exclusively religious, on which its culture had been built. The charge is by no means new. The lack of classical tradition was often emphasized as one of the peculiar and distinctive features of Old Russian culture. Fedotov's imaginary picture is pathetic, but is his argument fair and sound? The West seems to have had the golden key of Latin. How many in the West, however, were using that key for the purpose of which Fedotov speaks? And was the Latin known at that time sufficient for the task? Classical values were transmitted rather indirectly through Christian literature.

Platonism was accessible through Augustine, Pseudo-Dionysius, Origen, and Gregory of Nyssa. It could be no less readily discovered in Byzantine ecclesiastical sources. The Christian Hellenism of Byzantium neither impresses nor attracts Fedotov. He has a twisted picture of Byzantium: Byzantine Christianity appears to him to be a "religion of fear," of *phobos*; human values were suppressed in it. Anyhow, Fedotov contended that Kievan Russia never accepted this grim version of Christianity and developed its own conception: humanitarian and kenotic. And, in fact, that picture of Kievan Russia which Professor Fedotov himself has given us in his impressive book, *The Russian Religious Mind,* is bright and moving. Kievan Christianity, in his appraisal, has perennial value: "that of a standard, a golden measure, a royal way," in his own phrase. Indeed, we are given to understand that its attainments were so high because the Russians did not follow either the Byzantines or the Bulgarians, because they created their own Christian vision and way. In any case, it appears that Kievan Russia was vigorous and creative—at least in one field. What is more significant, basic human values were firmly established, high ethical standards acknowledged, and personal initiative disclosed and encouraged. There was strong human impetus in the Kievan culture. One has to assume, as was indeed Fedotov's own contention, that cultural growth and advance were impeded at a later stage. The absence of the classical tradition probably was not so tragic and fatal.

There is an increasing tendency in modern historiography to idealize the Russian beginnings. The Kievan period is depicted as a kind of golden age, a golden legend of Russia. Dark times came later—after the Mongolian conquest. There was a visible decline in literary production, and there were no outstanding personalities in this field. A closer scrutiny of extant sources, however, corrects this first impression. Writers of that time, from the twelfth century to the fifteenth, are aware of problems with which they are wrestling —the problems of the artistic craft: problems of style and representation, problems of psychological analysis. There were in Russia at that time not only scribes and *nachetchiks,*[1] but true writers. There were not only skillful craftsmen but real masters in art. The recent studies of D. S. Likhachev are very suggestive, especially his analysis of the problem of man in the literature and art of Old Russia. Behind the stylistic devices used by the artists one can detect their spiritual vision, and this vision was the fruit of reasoning and contemplation. The new wave of the "South Slavic" impact did not mean just a transfer of new literary documents, mainly translations, of spiritual and hagiographical content. It was a wave of inspiration, a deep spiritual movement, stemming from the great Hesychast tradition, revived at that time both in Byzantium and in the restored Bulgarian kingdom. Both writers, chroniclers and hagiographers, and painters, including the iconographers, were fully aware of the problem that they had to wrestle with—the presentation of human personality. It may be true that their concept of personality and character was different from the modern view, and probably at this point their insight was deeper. They did not depict fixed characters; they saw men in process obsessed and confronted with problems, in the state of decision and indecision. One may speak almost of their "existentialist" approach to the problem of man. One may contend that psychology based on the concept of temptation,

[1] I.e., dogmatic interpreters of the Bible.

inner struggle with the passions, conversion and decision, was a deeper psychology than that which would deal with the fixed character. In any case, it is more dynamic and less in danger of falling into schematism of characteristic types. In the great Russian art of the fourteenth and fifteenth centuries one discovers not only a high level of artistic mastery but also deep insights into the mystery of man. And this art was not only produced at that time but appreciated. Obviously, there was both a demand for this high art and an understanding of it, in circles which could not have been very narrow. It would not be an exaggeration to assume that the aesthetic culture of that time was refined and profound. It was still a religious culture, but artistic methods were adequate to the problem of revealing and interpreting the ultimate mysteries of human existence in all its unruly and flexible complexity. The challenge probably came from outside—from Byzantium once more—but the response was spontaneous and creative. There was more than dependence or imitation. There was real response.

One may be tempted to regard precisely this "dark" period, the period of intensive political and internecine strife, as the climax of Old Russian culture. Indeed, Russian art definitely declined in the fifteenth and especially in the sixteenth century and lost its originality and daring. The literary culture, however, was preserved on a high level till the Time of Troubles, and even later. The ideological content of literature became more comprehensive in the sixteenth century. There was an enormous synthetic effort in various fields of culture at that time. Strangely enough, it seems that precisely that synthetic effort, powerful and dynamic as it was, was the most conspicuous sign and symptom of decline, or at least of an internal crisis. The cultural inheritance

of Moscow was rich and comprehensive enough to suggest the idea of systematization. The great national state, aware and conscious of its vocation or destiny, needed a culture of great style. But this culture had to be built up as a system. It was an ambitious and attractive task. The plan "to gather together all books available in Russia," which was undertaken under Metropolitan Macary in the middle of the sixteenth century, was probably a naive and simplistic expression of a deeper conception. The plan itself was deeply rooted in the awakened consciousness of national greatness. But the vision was intrinsically static, and there was in it more than just a reflection of political ambition. There was a deeper urge for "establishment." The overarching idea was that of order. The danger to culture implied therein was probably felt in certain quarters. It has been usual to emphasize the importance of the conflict between the "possessors" and "nonpossessors" in the late decades of the fifteenth and the early decades of the sixteenth century. At one time the sympathy of the historian was rather on the side of St. Nilus of Sora and the Trans-Volga Elders. It seems that now the sympathy has been shifted to the other side. In any case, St. Joseph has won. And the idea of an established order was his greatest commitment. Indeed, he himself never speculated on the themes of culture. Nor, probably, did St. Nilus. But there is undoubtedly deep truth in the suggestion that it was in the tradition of St. Nilus that the only promise of cultural advance was available. Cultures are never built as systems, by orders or on purpose. They are born out of the spirit of creative initiative, out of intimate vision, out of spiritual commitment, and are only maintained in freedom. It may be contended that Moscow missed its opportunity for cultural progress when it yielded to the temptation of building its culture on the social order of the day—*po sotsial'nomu zakazu*, as it were. . . .

The most disquieting question in the history of Old Russian culture is this: What was the reason for what can be described as its intellectual silence? There was a great art, and there was also an intensive creative activity in the political and social field, including ideological speculation. But surely nothing original and outstanding has been produced in the realm of ideas, theological or secular. It was easier to answer this question when it was assumed that Old Russia was simply primitive, slumbering and stagnant. But now we know that in many other respects Old Russia was able to attain a high level. Still one may be tempted by easy answers. It may be suggested, and actually has been suggested more than once, that the "Russian soul" was, by its inner constitution, rather speculative or intuitive than inquisitive, and that therefore the language of art was the only congenial idiom of self-expression. It may be suggested, on the other hand, that the "Russian soul" approached the mystery of Christian faith by way of charity and compassion and was therefore indifferent to the subtleties of theological speculation. It does not help very much if we try to collect scattered data indicating that a certain amount of philosophical information was available to people of Old Russia. A solid amount of patristic writings was indeed in circulation, but there is no proof that theological interest had been awakened. All easy formulas are but evasions. And the riddle remains. Moreover, all speculations that operate with the precarious concept of the "Russian soul" are utterly unsafe. Even if "national souls" do exist, they are made, shaped, and formed in history. For that reason they cannot serve as a principle of interpreta-

tion. Again, the character of the "Russian soul" has been so diversely described and defined as to require a thorough re-examination. It has been usual to emphasize the irrational aspect of Russian mentality and its constant lack of form. There is enough evidence to the contrary. With adequate reason it has been contended that the "Russian soul" had always a strong feeling and understanding for order and form, and this specific insight was the root of its great aesthetic achievements. In its extreme expression it led to ritualism, to the worship of external forms. Kliuchevsky had much to say about the thrill of rite and habit when he attempted to explain the genesis of the great Russian Schism. And the same striving after orderliness has created in Russia what we call *byt*.[2] Of course, it may be claimed that underneath the *byt* there was always chaos. Finally, we are left with an antinomy, with an unresolved paradox.

In the total perspective of Russian historical development the paradox is even more spectacular. In the later period, after the Reform, Russians have appeared to be probably one of the most intellectual nations in Europe, inwardly troubled by all "damned problems" of religion and metaphysics. Exercise in philosophy, of various shapes and shades, and commitment to theory and speculation were the distinctive mark of the Russian mind in the last two centuries. This striking phenomenon was usually explained by Western influence, direct and indirect. It was suggested that dormant curiosity had been awakened by the challenge of Western thought. One should ask at this point why this intellectual curiosity was not awakened by the challenge of Byzantine civilization, which was renowned and notorious for its unquenchable commit-

[2] I.e., mode of life.

ment to speculation, in a measure offensive for the sober taste and mind of the West. Byzantium was not only dogmatic, but ever searching and rather unquiet in its heart. Indeed, Byzantium knew the mystery of harmony and cosmic order. But it also knew the thrill of search and the "clouds of unknowing." But Byzantine challenge did not awaken the alleged Russian soul.

The tragedy of Old Russia, which led to its inner split and impasse, was not a tragedy of primitivism or ignorance, as has been contended more than once. It was a tragedy of cultural aberration. The charge of Golubinsky and of Fedotov is valid to some extent, but they were unable to phrase it properly. One may suggest that Byzantium had offered too much at once—an enormous richness of cultural material, which simply could not be absorbed at once. The charm of perfection was tempting: should not the whole harmony be transplanted? The heritage was too heavy, and too perfect, and it was thrilling in its harmony, in its accomplishment. Art also requires training, but in this case training is probably more formal—the acquisition of technical skill. In the realm of the mind, training is indissolubly bound with the essence of the task. In this realm questions are no less important than answers, and unresolved problems, the "perennial questions," are the real stimulus and token of mental advance. Old Russia seems to have been charmed by the perfection, completeness, and harmony of Byzantine civilization, and paralyzed by this charm. Once more it must be stressed that Russian Byzantium was not just a servile repetition but a new and peculiar version of Byzantine culture, in which one can discern a true creative power. Some years ago I inscribed the chapter of my book, *The Ways of Russian Theology*, dealing with Old Russia: "The Crisis of Russian Byzantinism," and have re-

phrased it in the text: "The crisis of Byzantine culture in the Russian spirit." The phrase was misunderstood by the critics and reviewers, or rather was not understood at all. I am willing to assume full responsibility for the vagueness: I should have explained my thought in a more explicit way. What I wanted to say then I am bound to repeat now. The crisis consisted in that the Byzantine achievement had been accepted, but Byzantine inquisitiveness had not. For that reason the achievement itself could not be kept alive.

The crisis became conspicuous in Moscow in the seventeenth century, in that great age of changes, shifts, and troubles in the Russian state and society. It was an age of great cultural confusion. Certain elements of Byzantine achievement were strongly challenged, including the traditional "symphony" of state and church. Moscow was moving hesitantly toward an increasing secularization of its political order. The impact of Western mentality was growing, first in the form of the new Kievan learning, which itself was an unfortunate hybrid of Polish and quasi-Byzantine factors. The spread of this pseudomorphic culture was felt at Moscow more as a shock or offense than as a challenge, and provoked only resistance along with blind imitation. There was a search, but it was a search for ready solutions. Probably it was a blind alley. And then came the Reform.

The ultimate tragedy was that the Reform itself was promoted in the same old manner. There was again the thrill of accomplishment or achievement. The spirit of the Reform was intrinsically utilitarian. There was again a charm— a charm of Western achievement, of Western habits and forms. Curiosity was aroused, but was it a sound and sober intellectual curiosity? The new civilization was accepted in its ready form, into which the life of the nation could not be fitted. There was an effect of astonishment, but no real awakening. The new culture was much less organic than the old one, and therefore even less spontaneous and creative. It is instructive that it was possible to present the whole history of Russian literature, including its ideological content, as a story of Western influence, as a story of consecutive waves of imported ideas and forms. Was the cultural initiative really awakened? One may have very grave doubts. It is not surprising that a paradoxical resistance to culture as such has been one of the vigorous trends in the new culture; though it was to some extent provoked also by the thought of a Westerner, Rousseau, it was deeply rooted in the psychology of "reformed" Russians. Was not the way of simplicity higher than the way of culture? Technical culture has indeed been transplanted. But did Reform promote any disinterested concern for higher culture? Was it a real advance in comparison with the culture of Old Russia? During the whole modern period complaints were loudly voiced on this theme: there was no genuine *will for culture*, although admiration and even respect for culture were rather widespread. The root of the trouble was still the same: Culture was still regarded as an order, as an achievement, as a system. For that reason one could propagate the acceptance of foreign forms; they were finished and ready to hand. Indeed, there was sometimes much vigor and also much obstinacy in this endeavor of adaptation, and it could instill vitality into the products. The thrill of the modern Russian culture is in its scattered explosions—the deeds of individuals. But there was no general culture. . . .

ANDREYEV: PAGAN AND CHRISTIAN ELEMENTS IN OLD RUSSIA

THE HERITAGE OF PRE-CHRISTIAN RUSSIA

. . . It is noteworthy that this pre-Christian Slavic Russia was known to the Scandinavians as the "land of towns" and that the anonymous Bavarian Geographer (866–90) also referred to the large number of "towns." Some information about the characteristics of this civilization is provided by the Russian Chronicles. Traces of pagan influence are to be found in decorative folk art; in some cases motifs and patterns of the most ancient origin have persisted into the twentieth century. Today, archaeological research has given us a picture of the tastes of the early Slavs, examples of their handicrafts and of the kind and quantity of their material possessions. Unfortunately, the wooden architecture of the time has not been preserved; the tragedy of all Old Russian architecture was its vulnerability to that scourge of medieval Russia—frequent and destructive fires. It may be assumed, however, that the architecture of that period with its decorative carving, its *gornitsy* or upper rooms, its porches, and the variety of form shown in the roofing of buildings often attained real aesthetic merit.

The text of the treaties signed with Byzantium by Oleg (911) and Igor (944) bears witness to the existence of a distinctive social system, and it has been suggested that they indicate certain aspects of the Slavs' "customary law." As early as the seventh century Byzantine authors noted, not without surprise, that the Slavs and Antes "are not governed by one man but from ancient times have lived in democracy: they discuss together what is good or harmful for them." Byzantines, accustomed to autocratic government, considered this "disorder and anarchy." There can be no doubt that the *veche* was already an important institution in the social structure of pre-Christian Russia and had its roots in the distant past of the Slav peoples.

The most striking witness to the existence of civilization among the Russian Slavs is found in their religious beliefs, which were inspired by nature: they had a faith in magic powers that was closely connected with the cult of "Moist Mother Earth." Reflected most vividly in Russian folklore, these beliefs proved exceptionally tenacious and vigorous. *The Lay of the Host of Igor,* in which the writer refers to the Russian people collectively as the "grandson of Dazhbog," is rich in references to heathen deities and is inspired throughout by an essentially pantheistic conception of the world, of nature, and of poetry. Since this poem is perhaps the most brilliant expression of the persistence of the old pagan tradition, it is scarcely surprising that the ecclesiastical copyists were not particularly concerned with preserving it.

Thanks to the pertinacity of pagan beliefs among the masses of the people, there arose the phenomenon of *dvoeverie* (ditheism), whose existence is confirmed by historians of all schools; this belief is still alive in some places today.[3] Kievan and Muscovite history is rich in examples of the perpetual struggle waged by the Church to put down pagan survivals. It also seems probable that, to a certain extent, ecclesiastical suppression of the popular Russian theater (the *skomorokhi*) was inspired by the same fear of the non-Christian moods induced by these singers of "diabolic songs," these demonstrators of "unhallowed" customs and "satanic" rites. A recently discovered wall painting in Melyotovo dating from 1465 shows a remarkable image on the west wall of the church representing Antichrist in the guise of a wandering player: a unique apotheosis of the Church's condemnation of that "devil's brood,"

the *skomorokhi*. Obviously, too, as in Western countries, certain attributes of the pagan deities were passed on to Christian saints.

All these examples (which could be multiplied many times) are presented here only as reminders of the very considerable vigor and longevity of Russia's pagan heritage. Christianity in Russia was not transplanted into an uncultured soil, into a wild desert, but into a powerful community which, though scattered and illiterate, had its own customs, art, and religion and which, in some sectors, had long maintained contacts with other civilizations. Although certain influential groups and even, perhaps, whole centers such as Tmutorokan had previously accepted Christianity, its subsequent introduction as the official religion of the state was conditioned by the predominantly political motives of St. Vladimir.

The new official religion, if the Kherson version of the conversion is to be believed, was brought into Russia much like any other trophy of a successful campaign. Paganism had a considerable hold on the population; a few years before the conversion, Vladimir had attempted to erect a pagan Pantheon in Kiev to strengthen the ideological unity of the state. Not surprisingly, there was considerable resistance to the new faith —in some districts right up to the twelfth century (the rising of the *volkhvy* [pagan priests] and other incidents). Naturally, the ·Grand Dukes and the Chris-

[3] During the author's archaeological and archaeographic expeditions to Petserimaa in Estonia in 1937 and 1938 on behalf of the Kondakov Institute in Prague, he witnessed striking examples of the persistence of this *dvoeverie* in the Pskov-Petseri Monastery itself: devout local women would bring "offerings" of country produce (butter, eggs, and cream) to lay before a wooden statue of St. Nicholas the Miracle-Worker—gifts which were subsequently collected by the monks for the use of the abbot.

tianized upper stratum of the society of that time were anxious to transform "the Greek faith" into a national religion as quickly as possible. Certain events of the reign of Yaroslav the Wise —the appointment of a Russian as Metropolitan of Kiev; the cult of Vladimir, who was pronounced "the equal of the apostles," the true teacher of the newly-converted country, and a saint (Constantinople opposed his canonization for a long time)—prove that the Russians did not wish to be "led" by the Greeks but claimed the right to choose what suited them from the "Byzantine heritage." Such traces of cultural indocility are even apparent in the hagiography of the period. Thus the first Russian saints, Boris and Gleb, died not for the sake of Christ but in the name of obedience to their elder brother, laying the foundations, as it were, for the essentially Russian idea of nonresistance to evil. Their canonization also called forth opposition on the part of the Greeks, who generally were not inclined to encourage religious nationalism among newly converted peoples. It may be that it was in this early period of Russia's struggles for some autonomy in her ecclesiastical existence that there first sprouted the seeds of Grecophobia, which was to become traditional in Old Russia and was to combine curiously with an ill-defined nostalgia for the old pagan world. This inherent resistance to Byzantium was to manifest itself more than once—though later, after the people had fully assimilated Christianity, it was to take the form of the defense of the purity of Orthodox faith: in the vexing question of the appointment of the metropolitans at Vladimir-on-the-Klyazma; in the attitude Russia assumed towards the Florentine Union; in her reaction to the fall of Constantinople; and in the formulation of the famous theory of the Third Rome. This

tendency reached its culmination in the seventeenth century when the Old Believers, in a kind of reprise of the themes of the first expositor of Russian Grecophobia, Hilarion of Berestov, did not grudge even their lives in the struggle against the enunciation of principle of the Patriarch Nikon: "I am Russian, but my faith is Greek." In many ways the violence of their opposition to this principle was not so irrational as is usually believed.

Indisputably, Byzantine influence after the introduction of Christianity gave both form and content to Russian culture, but the pagan foundation acted as a counterbalance which prevented the full and unquestioning absorption of the Byzantine heritage.

MEDIEVAL CULTURE AND ITS DECLINE

Christianity was at first largely confined to the towns; it was not by chance that during the first centuries most monasteries were founded either in or near towns. The spread of enlightenment was carried out intensively throughout the first hundred years after the conversion, but it was directed chiefly at serving the aims and purposes of the dynasty and the Church itself. The process took a long time. It needed the Mongol invasion, which laid waste to all the large towns (the centers of the new learning) except Novgorod and Galich, and the almost simultaneous encroachments of the Teutonic knights on the Western borders, which marked the beginning of the *Drang nach Osten*, before Christianity (albeit still tinged with survivals of paganism) became thoroughly assimilated by the masses of the people. The Church became the focus of all hope, not only celestial but also terrestrial, and came to be identified with the spirit of Russia itself. The alien world revealed to the Russians at the time of the conversion—

a monotheistic, hierarchic world of contradictory values and the consciousness of sin—at last took on a specifically national form and was accepted by the people as their own. St. Sergius of Radonezh, equally sensitive to all aspects of his complex heritage, embodies the supremely harmonious national ideal of this period. He is at once monk and nature lover, gentle with his spiritual children and a lover of toil; he is a hermit but is able to direct a monastic community; he is the teacher and the inspiration of a whole pleiad of Russian ecclesiastical figures of the fourteenth and fifteenth centuries; but he is also the servant of the rising realm of Muscovy and takes his stand above the pettiness of local interests. He is simple and wise, a man of action and a mystic. He is a bright light for the Church, for the state, and for the illiterate peasant. He is very close in spirit to another great luminary of medieval Russia, the incomparable genius of religious art, Andrei Rublev. Both are distinguished by a harmonious combination of the purest Christian outlook and a remarkably loving regard for man—who is in fact the object of the Christian message in general and of the Orthodox interpretation of Christianity in particular. These two men stand out as supreme representatives of the cultural achievement of Old Russia and are not unworthy to take their place among the best exemplars of medieval Christendom. The over-all quickening of cultural activity in the fourteenth and fifteenth centuries, without which these two figures could not have flourished, appears to many historians as the highest point achieved by the civilization of pre-Petrine Russia; certainly in the field of painting, the art of Andrei Rublev and of his school is recognized both by his contemporaries and by modern historians of art as the culmination of this achievement. . . .

Humanism, the first stirrings of a scientific approach to the surrounding world, and thoughtful criticism of established ideas and practices were appearing in the West, but they had no place in the beleaguered Russia of that time. Nevertheless, the first stirrings of a similar impulse are to be found in the religious heresies of the fifteenth and sixteenth centuries and in the various utterances of individual freethinkers; these tendencies were of course rigorously suppressed by the "Church Militant," which had entered into a marriage of convenience with the lay authorities as represented by the Grand Dukes and later Tsars. As Professor Florovsky rightly points out, the very extensive work on the propagation of knowledge undertaken by Metropolitan Macary in the sixteenth century was really an attempt to canalize and organize learning rather than a genuine work of creation: it was, in fact, purely "educational," and was devoted to the collecting and codifying of information rather than to original thought.

This period, however, was not one of complete stagnation in the world of ideas. Strangely enough, the innovations of the time found expression within the Church itself and, under the protection of militant orthodoxy, in the spheres of church architecture and of religious painting. The Muscovite period is marked by many completely new developments in architecture. It is significant that even when foreign architects were called in (as, for example, during the building of the Moscow Kremlin in the fifteenth century), they did not reproduce Western models but apparently worked under definite directions from their Muscovite patrons and in styles that corresponded to Russian aesthetic canons. Buildings constructed between the fifteenth and seventeenth centuries—stone cathedrals, palaces, the great houses of individual magnates, fortifications, the walls and gateways of monasteries and wooden churches—are all distinguished by innovations in style and by excellent technical workmanship. In the Muscovite, as in the Kievan period, architecture remained one of the highest creative achievements of Russian civilization.

The impact of new ideas was expressed in the sphere of icon painting by innovations in composition in the so-called mystico-didactic style, the introduction of which was in part the direct result of Western (Roman Catholic) influence. Previously, religious art had been almost exclusively confined to simple subjects: "portraits" of Christ, the Blessed Virgin, the apostles and saints, or scenes from the Gospels. But in the fifteenth century artists began to launch into "theological philosophizing"; some compositions were so complex that they required an explanatory commentary and caused considerable intellectual fermentation. Artists developed liturgical themes and created entirely original cycles of frescoes, new in content, in color distribution, and in the actual technique of painting. In reply to a question about one of these icons the leading authority of the period, Maxim the Greek, replied that such icons "are not painted anywhere but in Russia." Now he has been proved right: at the end of the fifteenth century and during the sixteenth century, Russian icon painting was indeed uniquely innovatory in content and made interesting and important advances in the technique necessary to deal with more complex and more detailed, frequently multifigured, compositions. This is a new chapter not only in the history of Russian religious art but also in the history of thought in Muscovite Russia, in which a new and more speculative frame of mind struggles for expression in the new compositions and techniques. These lead away from the clarity and harmonious insight of Rublev, but they create a new

"language," at once more complex and more esoteric, adapted to the treatment of mystical and didactic themes.

The first signs of disintegration in the sphere of icon painting do not appear until the seventeenth century, after the Time of Troubles, when features of poorly understood naturalism begin to penetrate the work of the craftsmen who painted icons, in part as a result of the influence of West European pictures. The famous objections of Patriarch Nikon and of Protopop Avvakum were directed against this wave of naturalism. Nevertheless, even the lofty icon painting of Simeon Ushakov and other real masters of the seventeenth century is subject to the new tendencies towards the secularization of Russian culture. This process of secularization continued throughout the seventeenth century, gaining particular impetus from the beginning of the schism which foreshadowed the end of that unity of outlook conditioned by the Orthodox Christian interpretation of the world, which for seven centuries had been so carefully nurtured by church and state. Secularization penetrated literature, education, and methods of recording history; the reforms of Peter the Great were already ripening within a Russia that was growing out of its medieval ideals. The trenchancy of Nikon and, later, of Peter caused profound schisms where there might have been evolution. As in Vladimir's time, "revolutionary methods" were preferred to "evolution." It is interesting that the common people, in the seventeenth as in the tenth century, remained either passively submissive or actively hostile to the "reformers." This second cultural schism was still unhealed at the time of the 1917 Revolution.

BILLINGTON: IMAGES OF MUSCOVY

In his essay Professor Florovsky brings a rare combination of sympathetic understanding and restless questioning to the study of Russian culture. Cutting through a century of scholarly clichés about "Old Russia," he finds inadequate not only the cultural provincialism of erudite liberals like A. Pypin and S. Soloviëv, whose real interests lay in post-Petrine Russia, but also the simplified explanations of Old Russian cultural development presented by church historians like Golubinsky and sympathetic students like Buslaev and Fedotov. As in his penetrating *Ways of Russian Theology*, he quietly draws attention away from easy answers to difficult but important questions. It would be presumptuous for anyone—let alone a non-Slav far inferior in age and wisdom to Father Florovsky—to pretend to answer them, but one can at least gain valuable guidance for a fresh appraisal of Old Russia by facing up to four major tasks that his discussion sets before us: (1) distinguishing different periods and regions within pre-Petrine Russian culture, (2) accounting for its "intellectual silence," (3) analyzing its inner structure, and (4) appraising separately its historical fate and its intrinsic worth.

(1) Any consideration of Old Russian culture invites one major division —which is both chronological and regional—between Kiev and Muscovy. There is, to be sure, a bridge between them through Vladimir-Suzdal; but the cosmopolitan, urban culture of the former centered on the Dnepr and and the southwestern steppe is clearly distinct from the more monolithic and monastic culture of the latter centered on the Volga and the northeastern forests. The culture of Kievan Russia has been, as Professor Florovsky points out, exhaustively studied and somewhat idealized in recent years; but the impression has been created of a kind of cultural vacuum between the fall of Kiev and the rise of Petersburg. . . .

The distinctiveness of Moscow from Kievan Russia is illustrated by the fact that the city is not even mentioned in the chronicles until the middle of the twelfth century, did not have its own permanent prince until the early fourteenth, and possessed none of the great monuments of Byzantine architecture to be found in nearby Vladimir or Suzdal. The political accomplishments of its grand princes were aided by their special links with the Mongols, but its material and spiritual culture was almost entirely the product of the monastic revival that began with the founding of the monastery of the Holy Trinity in 1337 in the woods northeast of Moscow. In one of the most remarkable missionary movements in Christian history, faith and culture were soon taken 750 miles due east to the foothills of the Urals by Sergius' disciple, Stephen of Perm. By 1397, the year after Stephen's death, the movement had penetrated three hundred miles due north when another disciple, St. Cyril, founded his famous monastery on the White Lake; and forty years later it carried yet another three hundred miles north with the founding of the great Solovetsk Monastery on a bleak archipelago in the White Sea. In northeast Russia alone some eighty monasteries were founded in the fourteenth century (nearly as many as had existed up to that time in all of Russia); and some seventy more were added in the first half of the fifteenth. These cloisters remained the center of the culture that developed and spread on to the Pacific in a second wave of eastward expansion in the late sixteenth and early seventeenth century.

The monasteries were often military and economic as well as religious centers, and the culture that developed in them reflected both the harsh material conditions and the fundamentalist faith of a frontier people. Religion was essentially practical. Even in Kievan times theology had been historical rather than rational; and for Muscovy religion meant victory in battle, deliverance from the plague. Men were—for practical reasons—more literate than is often thought, but they were less literary than many writers about "Old Russian literature" would have one believe. They worshiped with sounds, images, and incense rather than words and ideas. Thanks to God was expressed in such communal rites as the building of *obydennye tserkvi,* wooden temples that were fashioned out of the virgin forest between sundown of one day and sundown of the next, while the women sang hymns of praise and burned candles before icons. Indeed this culture expressed itself best in practical construction—of wooden churches and buildings, which have almost totally disappeared, and of great stone churches and monasteries, which still exist in various stages of neglect throughout the USSR. The latter are no less remarkable than the transplanted Byzantine splendors of early Kiev and Novgorod and reflect the fruitful addition of wooden construction forms and of foreign techniques: Italian in the rebuilt Kremlin of the late fifteenth century, oriental in the sixteenth-century St. Basil's Cathedral in Red Square, Persian and Dutch in the great seventeenth-century cathedrals of Yaroslavl. Some idea of the richness and variety of Muscovite architecture can be gained by looking at two of its last and greatest monuments: the massive, yet simple and beautifully balanced ensemble of the Kremlin in Great Rostov; and the soaring and exotic lonely wooden church of the Transfiguration at Kizhi, with its twenty-two ascending barrel vaults (*bochki*) and superimposed, onion-shaped cupolas.

(2) Part of the answer to the "intellectual silence" of Old Russia lies in the harsh frontier conditions of Muscovy. Part also lies in the decisiveness and brutality of the Muscovite subjugation of a third distinct cultural entity within "Old" Russia: the politically sophisticated culture of westward-looking Novgorod and Pskov (the golden age of which lies in the period between the decline of Kiev and the full victory of Moscow). But why the continued silence of the great monasteries and prosperous trading centers even in the later period, when Novgorod and Pskov had been absorbed and contacts with the West were manifold? Why the Muscovite preference for rhetoric rather than reason, the "golden-tongued" Chrysostom rather than the "cursed logic" of the early Greeks? Why was the ordering of knowledge seen as the "swaggering" of heretical "almanach mongers," and theological disputation as irreverent "comedies and masquerades before the portals of our Lord"? . . .

Perhaps the most important explanation for the intellectual silence lies in the nature of the Byzantine impact on Russia; for Byzantium was no more a monolith than Old Russia, and its influence on the latter was concentrated in two very distinct periods, and exercised in each case largely through the intermediacy of Balkan Slavs. The first wave of South Slav influence (which brought Christianity and the main features of Byzantine culture to Kievan Russia) occurred at a time when the great doctrinal controversies of the Eastern Church had been settled and its energies newly engaged in the artistic creativity that followed the defeat of the iconoclasts. Thus, the almost fundamentalist attachment to inherited forms and formulas and the bias toward an aesthetic rather than a philosophic culture—already noticeable in Kievan times—merely reflect the exultation of new converts over the general Byzantine "victory of Orthodoxy" and the return of the icons. The second wave of South Slav influence brought a more specifically antirationalist bias, bearing the decisive imprint of the antischolastic Hesychast mysticism of fourteenth-century Byzantium. The Hesychast belief that ascetic discipline, inner calm (*hesychia*), and unceasing prayers of the spirit would prepare man for divine illumination was the major spiritual force behind the proliferation of monasteries and smaller spiritual communities (*skity*) in fourteenth- and fifteenth-century Muscovy. Hesychasm helped impart to the quickening spiritual life of Muscovy its suspicion of "Latin" definitions and sacramentalism; and the South Slav chroniclers' inclination towards apocalypticism—in the face of the Turkish conquest of Serbia, Bulgaria, and then Constantinople itself in the late fourteenth and mid-fifteenth century—was echoed in the north in the early sixteenth century at the time of the fall of Pskov, and magnified in the seventeenth when the latinized Poles overran Muscovy itself. The nervous religiosity and prophetic intensity of Muscovy provided the raw energy and sense of destiny that enabled Russia to become a great power in the course of the struggle with Poland in the seventeenth century; but these qualities also left a fateful legacy of irrational, anarchistic, and even masochistic impulses.

(3) There was a structure to the civilization of Muscovy; but it is to be sought not in the words of a *Codex Justinianus* or a *Summa Theologica* but in the forms of the iconostasis, the wall of holy pictures that separated the altar sanctuary from the rest of a Muscovite church. In Byzantium and Kievan Russia icons had often adorned the central or "royal" doors leading through this partition, even the low screen or arcaded barrier itself. But it is in Muscovy that one first finds the ordered, many-tiered screen of icons often extending up to the ceiling: a pictorial encyclopedia of the Christian faith and a graphic expression of a hierarchical and ritualized religious society. Already in the earliest surviving iconostasis (the three-tiered screen painted in the late fourteenth century for the Archangel Cathedral in the Moscow Kremlin by several monastic artists including Rublev) one sees a richness of color and grace of composition equal to anything in Christian art; and one sees how functions once borne by mosaic and fresco art were being taken over by the icon in the wooden world of Muscovy. . . .

As an ensemble, the iconostasis provided (like the elaborate chronicles and genealogies of the Muscovite period) a continuing record of sacred history, moving from the Old Testament patriarchs and prophets in the highest row to the local saints in the lowest. The central panels moved down to man—as had God himself—through the Virgin to Christ, who stood at the center of the main row of panels and immediately over the royal doors. Modeled on the *pantokrator* that had stared down in lonely splendor from the central dome of earlier, Byzantine cathedrals, the figure of "Christ enthroned" acquired on the iconostasis a less severe expression and an entourage of holy figures deployed on either side and inclined towards him in adoration. He now had a gospel in his hand opened to the text: "Come unto me, all ye that travail and are heavy laden, and I will refresh you. . . ."

(4) Far from diminishing the importance of Old Russian culture (as Professor Florovsky's article might be taken to imply), consideration of its historical fate apart from its inner structure makes it seem even more deserving of serious study. For this "old" culture—its ritualized Orthodox worship, its animistic popular cosmology, and its heroic

oral epics—remained the dominant one for most Russians down to at least the mid-nineteenth century. The ordinary muzhik continued to view as something alien to him both the Swedo-Prussian rule of the Petersburg bureaucracy and the patina of Polish and then French culture adopted by the ruling aristocracy. The continuing hold of Old Russian culture is demonstrated in three concrete and far-reaching developments in post-Petrine Russia: (*a*) the virtual secession from participation in the political and cultural life of the empire by the Old Believers (who regulated most of the internal commerce and much of the manufacturing of early modern Russia); (*b*) the violent and recurring peasant rebellions with their idealization of the past and belief in the return of a "true Tsar"; and (*c*) the revival and expansion of the Hesychast tradition of monastic elders and inner piety in the late eighteenth and early nineteenth century. . . .

FLOROVSKY: REPLY

I am most grateful to my commentators for their candid remarks and suggestions. Indeed, the main purpose of my original essay was precisely to provoke discussion. It was a query, not a summary and not a digest. Problems must be first sharply focused and carefully identified before they can be taken up profitably and eventually solved. On many points raised in my paper I have no solution to offer. I am only asking questions. Yet it is important to ask proper questions.

Now, in reply, I have to stress once more the basic plurality in the historical approach itself. "Societies" and "cultures" cannot be unconditionally identified, although cultures have *historical* significance only in so far as they are embodied in certain particular societies, which serve as their bearers,

and are cultivated and propagated in these societies. Yet, on the other hand, different societies may share the same culture, and the continuous existence and growth of a culture may be effected in a sequence or succession of different societies. Professor Billington seems to ignore this crucial distinction. He tends to dissociate Moscow and Kiev. He goes so far as to suggest that "Russian history in many ways really begins with the rise of Moscow." The Kievan period then becomes a kind of isolated episode, unrelated to the later formation of Russia, an archaic phenomenon. Indeed, the ancient Kievan state and Muscovy are two different "societies," of different social structures and in quite different situations, with different territorial bases and different international settings. And yet there was still an obvious and unbroken "succession" and unity: Kievan inheritance was an integral part of the Muscovite cultural tradition, though it was, of course, reinterpreted and reassessed.

In spite of all regional shifts and changes, "Russian culture" was one and continuous from the archaic Kievan times to the most modern times of the new Russian Empire. One cannot subtract *historically* the "Kievan inheritance" from the general economy of that complex and comprehensive bloc that we call "Russian culture." And this continuity is not just an artifact of modern historiographical interpretation. This continuity was reflected in the very process of cultural formation and can be traced on several levels. Probably the most conspicuous instance is in the history of Russian epics. The merry Prince Vladimir is the key figure in the Russian *byliny,* which assumed their final shape in the creative memory of the Russian North. Ancient Kiev, as unhistorically (that is, in the perspective of another development) as it may be pictured in the *byliny*, is an integral and pivotal part of the Russian total epic memory and tradition. Kiev was never forgotten in the North. The other instance is the complex history of old Russian *letopisanie*.[4] All later chronicles and chronographs compiled in various centers of the North—Vladimir, Novgorod, Tver, or Moscow itself—usually included the old Kievan material and were permeated with a strong feeling and conviction of uninterrupted cultural succession. . . .

The whole problem of historic continuity between Kiev and Moscow must be investigated cautiously and judiciously. It is an intricate and delicate problem. Actually, it is the crucial problem of pattern and scope of Russian history. Is Moscow a true and legitimate successor of ancient Kiev, or is it a new beginning altogether and a separate formation? Or did ancient Kiev find its organic continuation rather in the Galician kingdom of Daniel, and later in the Lithuanian state? This is a commonplace of Polish and Ukrainian historiography, and for that reason it requires a cautious re-examination. Now, apart from all political considerations, one is able to discern a cultural unity of "all Russia" grounded in common faith and in common national memories. Once more we have to emphasize the basic difference between "culture" and "society." Of course, Moscow society was a distinctive formation, very different from that of ancient Kiev, and the Moscow culture of the fourteenth and later centuries was, in many respects, a new development. In a wider perspective, however, Kiev and Moscow did belong together, as also did Moscow and St. Petersburg. . . .

Let us turn now to the problem of Russian beginnings. Dr. Andreyev's reminder of the pre-Christian heritage of Russia is certainly relevant and wel-

come. Indeed, the very reception of the Byzantine Christian heritage was possible only because the ground had been already well prepared. For that reason the reception of the Byzantine heritage was more than imitation or just repetition; it was rather a creative response or recreation of imported cultural values and ideas. The fact remains, however, that the only Russian culture we know, that is, the culture that was embodied and reflected in literature and art, was built on a Byzantine foundation and was a direct continuation of the Byzantine cultural endeavor and effort. Even *The Lay of the Host of Igor* reflected the patterns of Byzantine rhetoric. Of course, foreign traditions were superbly indigenized, and it is easy to detect manifold national motives. But the bases, and probably the driving power also, were mainly Byzantine. D. S. Likhachev, in his recent general survey of *The Culture of the Russian People from the Tenth to the Seventeenth Century*, rightly stresses this point. Christianity was a religion with a highly developed literature, which Russian paganism lacked. Accordingly, Russian literature stemmed from the Christian Byzantine spring. Dr. Andreyev identifies many national motives as "pagan," and as such they had to remain alien to the total structure of the cultural whole. More important was, of course, the national tension between the Greeks and the Slavs. I would prefer complete caution at this point. We should not read too much of later Grecophobia into the texts of the pre-Mongolian times. At that time, it seems, the spirit of political and canonical independence did not yet control the inner life of culture. Metropolitan Hilarion himself was deeply Byzantine in his style and ethos, as were Cyril of Turov and Clement of Smolensk. In-

---

[4] I.e., chronicle writing.

deed, Tsar Simeon of Bulgaria was as king and politician a staunch enemy of Byzantium, and yet culturally he was profoundly Greek—an accomplished Byzantine literate. The Slavs at that time were sensible enough to recognize the universal value of that Christian culture which had been offered to them in Greek garb and shape and in the context of Byzantine political expansion. Indeed, this universality was implied in the initiative of SS. Cyril and Methodius themselves. The *cultural* Grecophobia in Russia was a much later development, and its growth—in Muscovite times—has hardly strengthened Russian culture. Culture, in its deepest sense, can never simply emerge out of "national spirit." It is always initiated by "reception," by inheriting accumulated traditions, by assessing the universal stock of higher values. In this sense true culture is itself universal and supranational. And even the formal strength of any particular culture is first expressed in the scope and span of its synthetic power. True culture is always catholic, in the Socratic sense of the word. . . .

The major riddle of Old Russian culture was, of course, its "intellectual silence," or rather, dumbness. Professor Billington tends to explain it by external factors, such as "the harsh frontier conditions of Muscovy." I would not claim to have a satisfactory answer to the riddle, but I would look for it in the inner structure of the Muscovite spiritual world. The "harsh frontier conditions" did not prevent or impede the flowering of art, that is, the awakening and maturing of the aesthetic insight. Why should they, by themselves, impede the intellectual awakening? In fact, there was enough intellectual curiosity in Moscow society, but there was no genuine intellectual drive. The lack was especially conspicuous in the seventeenth century. What was the reason? Once more, I do

not pretend to have an adequate answer to this crucial question. But I do still feel that my provisional hypothesis of a "charm of accomplishment" deserves further exploration, especially because it applies both to the Muscovite culture and to the westernizing endeavors of the eighteenth century, and even, probably, to the various utilitarian and moralistic trends of the nineteenth century. I do not suggest, as has been done more than once, that anti-intellectualism, or indifference to abstract problems and speculation, is an essential characteristic of the "Russian soul," the alleged *âme russe*. I do not believe in the existence of any such "collective soul." National characters, if such do exist, are being made in history, and change. Yet, there. is still some continuity of basic attitudes, although radical anti-intellectualism developed in Russia under foreign influence and at a comparatively late date. In any case, the structure of the "Russian soul," as can be observed in its cultural expressions, is rather antinomical and cannot be reduced to any simple formula. The "thrill of accomplishment" has a utopian tenor; it implies the expectation that the ideal may be adequately and definitively realized or incarnated. The dynamism of search is subdued to the static pattern of accomplishment.

Professor Billington invokes also another external factor: the brutal subjugation of the westward-looking Novgorod and Pskov. The annexation of these two republics was rather harsh and brutal—so much must be conceded. But it is hardly historically fair to idealize the constitution and policy of these two republics. Historically speaking, one may contend that this annexation was a progressive endeavor and was justified by the general logic of national development and integration. What is much more important, from the cultural point of view, is that all basic achievements of Novgorod and Pskov were actually included in the Moscow "gathering of culture" in the sixteenth century, so that this Moscow synthesis was almost entirely composed of Novgorod material. Whatever may be said about the political aspect of the annexation, little if anything has been lost of the Novgorod cultural heritage. And it is still uncertain whether the westward orientation of the two northern republics was a real asset and a token of advance and not an entanglement in antiquated social and economic policies of the Hanseatic League.

Indeed, Professor Billington mentions a number of other factors: the lack of classical heritage, the laxity of diocesan structure in the Church, the lack of a commonly accepted body of canon law and of any clear distinction between law and morality. All these topics must be discussed and examined in detail. Only, it seems, they are rather symptoms than factors. Did I play down the impact of the lack of classical heritage? In fact, it must be shown in what manner this lack actually impeded intellectual growth in Russia. I dare only to contend that there was enough stimulating challenge in that theological inheritance which was received from Byzantium and appropriated in Russian culture. But the challenge was not responded to in the sphere of intellect as it was responded to creatively in the realm of art. This is what I have labeled "intellectual silence." Was the reason for this phenomenon already given in the very nature of the Byzantine impact on Russia—that is, in the nature of the Byzantine inheritance itself—or was it rooted in the manner and character of the response? This is the crucial question. Where was rooted the bias toward an aesthetic rather than a philosophical culture? In the Byzantine heritage itself, or in the attitude of the Russians? In Byzantium, in any case, the period of iconoclasm and the one immediately after was characterized not only by an activity in the realm of art but also by a strong philosophical revival. Nor is it fair to overstress the anti-intellectual bias of the Hesychast movement, which stood rather in the mainstream of the Greek intellectual tradition. The Byzantine defense of holy icons was not primarily a vindication of art or ritual but basically a dogmatic endeavor—the defense of the crucial and ultimate reality of Incarnation. This theological, that is, "intellectual," aspect was gradually lost in the disproportionate growth of ritual, as splendid as its artistic achievement and as moving as its emotional appeal might have been. Now, St. Sergius himself did not care at all for splendid temples or for gorgeous rites and robes, and it was just in the spirit and the temper of St. John Chrysostom. But the thrill of splendor finally prevailed. It was not St. Sergius' legacy or tradition. And, in fact, "splendor" itself rapidly degenerated into decoration and ornamentation, on the Russian soil, and not without a Novgorod impact. To sum up, it is difficult to explain *historically* both the general "unsuccess" of Old Russian culture and, in particular, its "intellectual silence," simply by certain external circumstances and conditions, or by the deficiencies of the Byzantine inheritance. There were also some deeper internal causes. In spite of its strength and richness, the Muscovite culture failed to accomplish its purpose and collapsed.

CHRONOLOGY

860–1240	PERIOD OF KIEV RUSSIA
862	Traditional date of summoning Rurik the Varangian to rule in Novgorod
911	Treaty of Oleg with Byzantine Empire
941	Expedition of Igor against Constantinople
957	Visit of Olga to Constantinople, where she is baptized
988	Baptism of Vladimir and conversion of Russia Kherson taken
1030	Iaroslav starts first school in Novgorod, with 300 sons of notables and priests
1037	Santa Sofia, Kiev, begun
1045–57	Building of Santa Sofia, Novgorod
1054	Split between eastern and western churches
1054–73	*Russkaia Pravda*, law code, composed
1067	First serious raids of Polovtsy
1071	Pagan magicians provoke risings in Kiev and Novgorod, want to kill bishop
1095	First election of prince in Novgorod
11th century	Birch-bark documents first appear Novgorod streets paved with lumber (first Paris pavement, 1184) Wooden water pipes laid in Novgorod
1116	Primary Chronicle composed
1125–1200	Second version of *Russkaia Pravda*
1126	First election of *posadnik* in Novgorod
1147	First written mention of Moscow
1156	First elected bishop of Novgorod
1167	Sadko builds a church in Novgorod
1169	Sack of Kiev by Andrei Bogoliubsky, prince of Vladimir-Suzdal His seige of Novgorod fails Legend of the intervention of the icon of the Virgin

1185	Prince Igor Sviatoslavovich of Seversk marches against Polovtsians
1195	First Novgorod treaty with German towns and Gotland
1196	Princely agreement grants Novgorod right to select prince
1204	Capture of Constantinople by Fourth Crusade: Latin Empire until 1261
1215–36	Thirteen changes of prince in Novgorod
1223	First Mongol invasion: Russians defeated on the Kalka
1227	Death of Genghis Khan
1237–42	Mongol conquest of Russia

MONGOL PERIOD
1240–1480

1240	Victory of Alexander Nevsky over Swedes on Neva
1242	Battle on the Ice: Nevsky's victory over the German Order
1248	Pope Innocent IV sends two cardinals to Alexander Nevsky in Novgorod to persuade him to adopt the Catholic faith
1253	Founding of first Sarai as capital of the Golden Horde
1259	Uprising against Tartar taxes in Novgorod
1270	Novgorod treaty with Hansa
1275	Population of Russia about ten million
1294	First Russian icon which is dated and signed (Novgorod)
1300	Metropolitan of Kiev settles at Vladimir
1326	Final establishment of Metropolitan in Moscow
1337	Foundation of Trinity Monastery by St. Sergius
1348	Pskov secures independence of Novgorod
	Swedish King Magnus marches against Novgorod
1362	Kiev taken by Grand Duke of Lithuania, Olgerd
1367–68	First stone fortifications of Moscow Kremlin
1371–75	Heresy of Strigol'niks (Shearers) in Novgorod
1378	Feofan the Greek paints first frescoes in Novgorod
1380	Victory of Dmitri Donskoi over the Tartars at Kulikovo
1382	Moscow burnt by Tokhtamysh
1390–1430	Active life of icon painter Andrei Rublev
1395	Defeat of the Golden Horde by Timur the Lame (Tamerlane)
1430–66	Disintegration of Golden Horde
	Formation of Khanates of Crimean Tartars, Kazan, and Astrakhan
1436	Foundation of Solovetsky Monastery
1439	Council of Florence
	Reunion of eastern and western churches
1441	Metropolitan Isidore deposed for accepting Council of Florence

1553	Opening of the White Sea route by Chancellor
1555	Granting of charter to Russia Company (England)
1556	Capture of Astrakhan
1558	Stroganovs granted land on Kama River
1558–83	Livonian war, against Poland and Sweden, for possession of Baltic
1560's	Edition of Domostroi (House-Orderer), a book of principles of family life
1564	First book printed in Moscow
	Kurbsky flees to Lithuania
1565–72	Ivan the Terrible's reign of terror: the *oprichnina*
1566	First *Zemskii Sobor* (Consultative Land Assembly)
1570	Ivan the Terrible's pogrom in Novgorod: January 2 to February 13
1571	Crimean Tartars burn Moscow
1571–1600	Fortification of southern frontier
	Beginning of Don, Zaporozhian, and Ural Cossacks
1580's	Boris Godunov sends eighteen Russians to study abroad —none return
1581	Yermak and the beginning of the conquest of Siberia
	Privilege of St. George's Day (Iur' ev Den'), November 26, abolished
1585	Foundation of Archangel
1587–98	Boris Godunov as "Lord Protector"
1588	Giles Fletcher in Moscow
1589	CREATION OF MOSCOW PATRIARCHATE
1590's	Rostov becomes seat of Metropolitan
1601–3	Famine
	Erection of Ivan Velikii tower
1604–13	Time of Troubles
1606–7	Revolt of Bolotnikov
1610–12	Poles occupy Moscow
1611–17	Swedes occupy Novgorod
1613	Election of Michael Romanov as tsar by *Zemskii Sobor*
1618	Peace with Sweden
	Loss of any outlet to Baltic
1634–38	Two visits of Adam Olearius to Moscow
1636	Patriarch orders all musical instruments burned
1648–49	Risings in Moscow and other towns
	Zemskii Sobor
	Code of Tsar Alexis
1649	Abolition of English trading privileges
1650's	Moscow population about 200,000
1650	Patriarch forbids use of conical towers in church architecture and standardizes sacred "five-domed church" on a square plan

1652	Foreigners in Moscow required to live in *Nemetskaia Sloboda* (a suburb) and forbidden to mix with the population
1653	Last full meeting of *Zemskii Sobor*
1654	Church Council adopts Nikon's reforms
1654	BEGINNING OF THE SCHISM
	Union of Ukraine with Muscovy
	Baroque influences on Moscow
1660's	Moscow linked with Amsterdam and Berlin by regular postal service
1664	Grigorii Kotoshikhin flees to Sweden
1666	Church Council deposes Patriarch Nikon
1667	Cession to Muscovy of Kiev, Little Russia, and Smolensk
1670–71	Revolt of Stenka Razin
1671	Avvakum writes his *Life* in prison
1672	Russian embassies sent to all major European states
	Plays begin to be given at Moscow court
1674	*Synopsis*—first textbook of Russian history—appears
1684	Sophia's decree institutes formal persecution of Old Believers
1689	Peter the Great takes over the government
	Treaty of Nerchinsk with China

CORRELATION *of* READINGS IN RUSSIAN CIVILIZATION

Vols. I, II, and III with Representative Texts

CLARKSON, JESSE D., *A History of Russia*, Random House, 1964

Chapter Nos.	Related Selections in READINGS IN RUSSIAN CIVILIZATION	Chapter Nos.	Related Selections in READINGS IN RUSSIAN CIVILIZATION
1	I: 16	19	II: 36, 37
2	I: 1	20	II: 35
3	I: 2	21	II: 39–41
4	I: 3–5	22	II: 38
5	I: 6, 10, 15	23	II: 42, 43
6		24	III: 44
7	I: 7–9	25	III: 45
8		26	III: 46
9	I: 11–13	27	
10	I: 14, 17	28	III: 47
11		29	III: 48
12	II: 18	30	III: 49–51
13	II: 19	31	III: 55, 56
14	II: 20–22	32	III: 52–54
15	II: 23–27	33	
16		34	III: 57, 58
17	II: 28, 30	35	III: 59–62
18	II: 29, 31–34	36	III: 63–69
		37	III: 70–72

DMYTRYSHYN, BASIL, *USSR: A Concise History*, Scribners, 1965

Chapter Nos.	Related Selections in READINGS IN RUSSIAN CIVILIZATION	Chapter Nos.	Related Selections in READINGS IN RUSSIAN CIVILIZATION
1		5	III: 47, 48
2	III: 44, 45	6	III: 49–56
3	III: 46	7	III: 57–62
4		8	
		9	III: 63–72

ELLISON, HERBERT J., *History of Russia*, Holt, Rinehart, and Winston, 1964

Chapter Nos.	Related Selections in READINGS IN RUSSIAN CIVILIZATION	Chapter Nos.	Related Selections in READINGS IN RUSSIAN CIVILIZATION
1	I: 16	13	III: 44–45
2	I: 1–5	14	III: 46
3	I: 6–10, 15	15	III: 47
4	I: 11–14, 17	16	III: 48
5	II: 18	17	
6	II: 19–22	18	III: 49–56
7	II: 23	19	
8	II: 24–27	20	III: 57, 58
9	II: 28–31	21	III: 59–62
10	II: 32–37	22	
11	II: 38–41	23	III: 63-70
12	II: 42–43	24	III: 71, 72

FLORINSKY, MICHAEL T., *Russia: A History and an Interpretation*, 2 vols., Macmillan, 1953

Chapter Nos.	Related Selections in READINGS IN RUSSIAN CIVILIZATION	Chapter Nos.	Related Selections in READINGS IN RUSSIAN CIVILIZATION
1	I: 1, 2	25	
2		26	
3	I: 15	27	II: 23
4	I: 6	28	II: 24
5	I: 3, 4	29	
6	I: 5, 10	30	
7		31	II: 25–27
8	I: 7–9	32	
9		33	
10	I: 13	34	
11	I: 11, 12, 14, 16, 17	35	
12		36	II: 33
13	II: 18	37	II: 28–32
14		38	II: 34, 36, 37
15		39	II: 35
16		40	II: 38–41
17		41	II: 43
18	II: 19	42	II: 42
19		43	
20		44	
21	II: 20, 21	45	III: 44
22		46	III: 45
23	II: 22	47	
24		48	III: 46

FLORINSKY, MICHAEL T., *Russia: A Short History*, Macmillan, 1964

Chapter Nos.	Related Selections in READINGS IN RUSSIAN CIVILIZATION	Chapter Nos.	Related Selections in READINGS IN RUSSIAN CIVILIZATION
1	I: 1, 2, 16	15	II: 28–33
2	I: 3–5	16	II: 34–42
3	I: 15	17	
4	I: 10	18	II: 43
5	I: 6	19	III: 44, 45
6	I: 7–9	20	III: 46–48
7		21	III: 52–56
8	I: 13	22	III: 49–51
9	I: 11, 12, 14, 17	23	
10	II: 18	24	III: 57, 58
11	II: 19	25	III: 59–62
12	II: 20–22	26	III: 63–72
13	II: 23, 24	27	
14	II: 25–27		

HARCAVE, SIDNEY, *Russia: A History*, 6th ed., Lippincott, 1968

Chapter Nos.	Related Selections in READINGS IN RUSSIAN CIVILIZATION	Chapter Nos.	Related Selections in READINGS IN RUSSIAN CIVILIZATION
1	I: 16	17	II: 36, 37
2	I: 1–5, 15	18	II: 33
3	I: 6–10	19	II: 31
4	I: 11–14, 17	20	II: 39–41
5	II: 18	21	II: 42
6	II: 19	22	II: 43
7	II: 20–21	23	III: 44, 45
8		24	III: 46
9	II: 22	25	III: 47

HARCAVE, SIDNEY, *Russia: A History*, 6th ed., Lippincott, 1968

Chapter Nos.	Related Selections in READINGS IN RUSSIAN CIVILIZATION	Chapter Nos.	Related Selections in READINGS IN RUSSIAN CIVILIZATION
10		26	III: 48
11	II: 23	27	III: 49–51
12	II: 24	28	III: 52–56
13	II: 25–27	29	III: 57, 58
14		30	III: 59–62
15	II: 28–30	31	III: 63–72
16	II: 34, 38		

MAZOUR, ANATOLE G., *Russia: Tsarist and Communist*, Van Nostrand, 1962

Chapter Nos.	Related Selections in READINGS IN RUSSIAN CIVILIZATION	Chapter Nos.	Related Selections in READINGS IN RUSSIAN CIVILIZATION
1	I: 16	19	II: 37
2	I: 1, 2	20	II: 35, 38
3	I: 15	21	II: 39–41
4	I: 3–5, 10	22	
5	I: 7–9	23	II: 25–28
6	I: 6	24	
7		25	
8	I: 11–14, 17	26	
9	II: 18	27	II: 42–43
10		28	III: 44, 45
11		29	III: 46
12	II: 19	30	III: 47, 48
13	II: 20–22	31	
14		32	III: 49–51
15	II: 23	33	III: 52–56
16	II: 24	34	
17	II: 29–31	35	III: 57
18	II: 32–34, 36	36	III: 58
		37	III: 59–62
		38	III: 63–72

PARES, BERNARD, *A History of Russia*, Vintage Books, 1965

Chapter Nos.	Related Selections in READINGS IN RUSSIAN CIVILIZATION	Chapter Nos.	Related Selections in READINGS IN RUSSIAN CIVILIZATION
1	I: 16	15	II: 22
2	I: 1, 2	16	II: 23
3	I: 15	17	II: 24
4	I: 3, 4	18	II: 25–27
5	I: 5, 10	19	II: 28
6	I: 7–9	20	II: 29–33
7	I: 6	21	II: 34–37
8		22	II: 38
9	I: 11–13	23	II: 39–41
10	I: 14, 17	24	II: 42, 43
11		25	III: 44–48
12	II: 18	26	III: 49–56
13	II: 19	27	III: 57–72
14	II: 20, 21		

PUSHKAREV, SERGEI, *The Emergence of Modern Russia, 1801–1917*, Holt, Rinehart, and Winston, 1963

Chapter Nos.	Related Selections in READINGS IN RUSSIAN CIVILIZATION	Chapter Nos.	Related Selections in READINGS IN RUSSIAN CIVILIZATION
1	II: 23	7	II: 36, 37
2		8	II: 35, 39–41
3	II: 24–27	9	
4		10	II: 38, 42
5	II: 28	11	II: 43
6	II: 29–34		

RAUCH, GEORG VON, *A History of Soviet Russia*, 5th rev. ed., Praeger, 1967

Chapter Nos.	Related Selections in READINGS IN RUSSIAN CIVILIZATION	Chapter Nos.	Related Selections in READINGS IN RUSSIAN CIVILIZATION
1	III: 44–46	6	III: 52–56
2		7	
3		8	III: 57, 58
4	III: 47–51	9	III: 59–62
5		10	III: 63–72

RIASANOVSKY, NICHOLAS V., *A History of Russia*, Oxford University Press, 1963

Chapter Nos.	Related Selections in READINGS IN RUSSIAN CIVILIZATION	Chapter Nos.	Related Selections in READINGS IN RUSSIAN CIVILIZATION
1	I: 16	22	II: 20, 21
2		23	
3	I: 1	24	II: 22
4		25	II: 23
5	I: 2	26	II: 24
6		27	
7		28	II: 25–27
8	I: 15	29	II: 29, 31
9	I: 3, 4	30	II: 34
10		31	II: 35, 39–42
11		32	II: 30, 36–38
12		33	II: 28, 32, 33, 43
13	I: 5, 10	34	III: 44, 45
14		35	
15	I: 7–9	36	III: 46–48
16		37	III: 49–56
17		38	III: 57–58
18	I: 6, 13, 14	39	III: 59–62
19	I: 11, 12, 17	40	III: 63–66
20	II: 18	41	III: 67–71
21	II: 19	42	III: 72

SETON-WATSON, HUGH, *The Russian Empire, 1801–1917*, Oxford, 1967

Chapter Nos.	Related Selections in READINGS IN RUSSIAN CIVILIZATION	Chapter Nos.	Related Selections in READINGS IN RUSSIAN CIVILIZATION
1	II: 18–22	11	II: 29–31
2		12	
3	II: 23	13	II: 32–34
4		14	II: 36, 37
5	II: 24	15	II: 35
6		16	
7		17	II: 39–41
8	II: 25–27	18	II: 38
9		19	II: 42
10	II: 28	20	II: 43

TREADGOLD, DONALD W., *Twentieth Century Russia*, 2d ed., Rand McNally, 1964

Chapter Nos.	Related Selections in READINGS IN RUSSIAN CIVILIZATION	Chapter Nos.	Related Selections in READINGS IN RUSSIAN CIVILIZATION
1		16	
2	II: 22–29, 31–33	17	III: 49–51
3		18	III: 52–56
4	II: 35	19	
5	II: 34, 39–41	20	
6		21	
7	II: 30, 36, 37	22	
8	II: 38, 42, 43	23	III: 57
9	III: 44, 45	24	III: 58
10	III: 46	25	
11		26	
12		27	III: 59–62
13	III: 47, 48	28	III: 63–66
14		29	III: 67–72
15			

VERNADSKY, GEORGE, *A History of Russia*, 5th ed., Yale University Press, 1961

Chapter Nos.	Related Selections in READINGS IN RUSSIAN CIVILIZATION	Chapter Nos.	Related Selections in READINGS IN RUSSIAN CIVILIZATION
1	I: 1, 16	10	II: 28–34
2	I: 2	11	II: 36–38
3	I: 3–5, 15	12	II: 35, 39–41
4	I: 7–9	13	II, III: 42–46
5	I: 6, 10–14, 17	14	III: 47–51
6	II: 18–21	15	III: 52–56
7	II: 22, 23	16	III: 59–62
8	II: 25–27	17	III: 57, 58
9	II: 24	18	III: 63–72

WREN, MELVIN C., *The Course of Russian History*, 3d ed., Macmillan, 1968

Chapter Nos.	Related Selections in READINGS IN RUSSIAN CIVILIZATION	Chapter Nos.	Related Selections in READINGS IN RUSSIAN CIVILIZATION
1	I: 16	12	II: 28–33
2	I: 1	13	II: 34–38
3	I: 2, 5	14	II: 39–43
4	I: 3, 4	15	III: 44–46
5	I: 6, 10	16	III: 47, 48, 52–56
6	I: 7–9	17	III: 49–51, 64, 66, 67, 70
7	I: 11–17	18	III: 59–62
8	II: 18	19	
9	II: 19–22	20	III: 57, 58, 65, 71
10	II: 23	21	III: 63, 68, 69, 72
11	II: 24–27		

WALSH, WARREN B., *Russia and the Soviet Union*, University of Michigan Press, 1958

Chapter Nos.	Related Selections in READINGS IN RUSSIAN CIVILIZATION	Chapter Nos.	Related Selections in READINGS IN RUSSIAN CIVILIZATION
1	I: 16	16	II: 32–34, 36–37
2	I: 1, 3, 4	17	II: 35
3	I: 2, 5	18	II: 39–41
4	I: 15	19	II: 38, 42, 43
5	I: 7, 8, 9	20	III: 44–45
6	I: 6, 10–14, 17	21	III: 46
7	II: 18	22	
8	II: 19	23	III: 47, 48
9	II: 20, 21, 22	24	III: 49–56
10	II: 23	25	
11	II: 24	26	III: 57, 58
12		27	III: 59–62
13	II: 25, 26, 27	28	
14	II: 28–31	29	III: 63–72
15			

INDEX VOLUME I